DAILY DOSE OF PSΨCHOLOGY

365 LESSONS

on Cognitive Biases from Headlines to History

FABIAN GLESS

Copyright © 2024 by Fabian Gless (BHAB Ventures UG)

All rights reserved. No part of this publication may be reproduced, distributed, or transmitted in any form or by any means, including photocopying, recording, or other electronic or mechanical methods, without the prior written permission of the publisher, except in the case of brief quotations embodied in critical reviews and certain other noncommercial uses permitted by copyright law.

For permissions requests, write to the publisher
at the address below:

Psychologie Fachverlag Berlin
℅ BHAB Ventures UG
Krossener Straße 18
10245 Berlin
Germany

hello@daily-dose-psychology.com
www.daily-dose-psychology.com

ISBN: 978-3-911346-00-9

Cover design by Dragan Bilic
Interior layout by Dragan Bilic

First Edition: 05, 2024

10 9 8 7 6 5 4 3 2 1

Contents

Daily Dose of Psychology 5

January 11

February 43

March 73

April 105

May 137

June 169

July 201

August 233

September 265

October 297

November 329

December 361

Bibliography 393

About the author 425

DAILY DOSE OF PSYCHOLOGY

Thinking behind the book

This book is designed to get you thinking about the way you think.

In a world of endless choices and information overload, our minds have developed fascinating ways to cope. Sometimes these mental patterns serve us well, like when they help us learn from past experiences or stick to proven solutions. Other times, they lead us astray—making us overconfident about predicting the future, reluctant to embrace change, or too quick to find evidence that we were right all along. Understanding these patterns of thought isn't just an intellectual exercise—it's a key to understanding ourselves and the countless small decisions that shape our lives.

In navigating the complexities of life, we all depend on mental shortcuts known as heuristics. A heuristic is essentially a rule-of-thumb enabling us to make decisions with limited information. Think of heuristics as your brain's efficiency tools—they help you navigate life's countless decisions without getting overwhelmed.

For example, consider choosing between two brands at a store. You often opt for the brand you recognize over an unfamiliar one, even with no prior knowledge of its quality. This "familiarity heuristic" simplifies decision-making by relying on recognition instead of detailed comparison.

Or consider how emotions influence our perception of risks and benefits. For instance, if someone enjoys smoking, they might downplay the health risks associated with it, influenced by the "affect heuristic." This heuristic shows how our feelings towards an activity can overshadow statistical evidence, guiding our judgments and decisions based on emotion rather than rational analysis.

One last example, consider you see a guy with glasses, reading a science book about psychology. You might instantly assume he must be intelligent or perhaps a scientist. The "representativeness heuristic" involves making judgments about someone or something based on how closely they match our stereotypes of a particular category, frequently leading to oversimplified and inaccurate conclusions.

While heuristics are invaluable shortcuts that simplify complex tasks, they can sometimes lead us astray. This is where cognitive biases come in. A cognitive bias is essentially what happens when a heuristic misfires—it's a systematic error in thinking that occurs when our mental shortcuts don't quite fit the situation at hand. Think of heuristics as tools in your mental toolkit: they're incredibly useful most of the time, but like any tool, they can be misapplied. When a heuristic leads you to a predictably irrational conclusion or judgment, that's a cognitive bias at work.

For instance, while the familiarity heuristic often serves us well (choosing familiar brands can be a decent strategy), it can transform into the "mere exposure effect"—a cognitive bias where we prefer things simply because we've seen them before, even when better alternatives exist. Similarly, while using stereotypes can help us quickly process information about our environment, this same heuristic can lead to harmful prejudices and discrimination when applied uncritically.

The concept of cognitive bias has captivated psychologists and behavioral economists since pioneers Amos Tversky and Daniel Kahneman revolutionized our understanding of human decision-making in the early 1970s. My personal fascination with cognitive biases began in my early twenties, through books, TED talks, and YouTube videos on the subject.

Understanding the flaws in our rational thinking profoundly changed my worldview and self-perception. Realizing that imperfection is inherent to the human condition made me more stoic and relaxed about life.

Despite reading numerous insightful books on cognitive biases, I often found it challenging to apply this knowledge in daily life. While recognizing my own tendencies in the examples provided, integrating these insights into my thinking proved difficult.

Moreover, I realized that the scientific nature of most literature on this topic poses a significant barrier to general enjoyment. For instance, I recommended Daniel Kahneman's masterpiece "Thinking,

Fast and Slow" to many, believing it essential for everyone. Yet, none of the recipients completed it. These observations—the lack of practical application and the high entry barrier—inspired me to write this book.

Thinking behind the book layout

In this book you will learn about 61 carefully selected cognitive biases—ones I find most important, interesting, or entertaining. What makes this book unique is how it revisits the most crucial biases throughout the year, each time revealing a new facet through fresh stories and new angles. By exploring these thinking patterns across different domains—from business decisions to personal relationships, historical events to everyday choices—you'll discover how deeply these biases are woven into every aspect of our lives.

Each bias is presented with a consistent layout: a catchy title poses an intriguing question that relates to the topic, followed by the date and the formal name of the cognitive bias being discussed. The main text begins with a clear definition and explanation of the concept, followed by engaging real-world examples and research findings that illustrate how this pattern of thinking manifests in our daily lives. Throughout the book, you'll find QR codes on select pages that link to fascinating videos, articles, and other content that deepen your understanding of the topic in entertaining ways.

Inspired by "The Daily Stoic," I believe in the power of integrating learning into our daily rituals. Just as we might start our mornings with coffee, taking a few minutes to understand how our minds work can become a meaningful part of our day. This format serves two purposes: it makes complex psychological concepts more digestible, and it prevents the information overload that often stops us from finishing—or truly benefiting from—traditional books about the topic. Each day's reading is designed to be both brief enough to fit into your busy schedule and substantial enough to give you something to reflect on throughout your day.

How my own perspective changed while writing this book

Initially, my goal was to combat cognitive biases by identifying and labeling these mental shortcuts, hoping to mitigate their impact on my decision-making and thinking. This book was envisioned as a tool for recognizing and remembering biases, to clarify our rational thought processes.

However, my perspective evolved as I explored the subject more deeply. I realized that many cognitive biases, once considered mere errors or quirks, serve essential survival functions, rooted in our evolutionary history. These biases enable quicker, more efficient judgments—often a necessity in environments where speed is crucial.

I also discovered the critical role these biases play in social interaction and mental well-being. Far from being mere flaws, they are fundamental to human cooperation, social dynamics, and maintaining a positive outlook amidst life's uncertainties. Labeling these cognitive processes as "errors" simplifies their complex, often beneficial nature.

This journey has transformed my understanding of cognitive biases from a battle to an appreciation of their complexity and utility. I hope this book enlightens you about the nuanced and beneficial aspects of these biases.

Dedication

This might be my first and only chance to write a dedication in a book, so let's make it count!

To Theresa, the love of my life, my cheerleader, and the unwavering pillar of support behind my book project. Your belief in this book's greatness, voiced in countless encouragements, transformed my doubts into determination.

To my parents, Angelika and Heinz-Peter, who instilled in me the kind of motivation that made this book possible. I am grateful for every push, nudge, and outright shove in the right direction.

And to my grandfather, Christian, who has fundamentally shaped my curiosity and the path that led here. He might not be here to read my work, but I feel he would have liked the book.

A heartfelt acknowledgment to the people helped me to make this book happen: Teodora, Kervin, Dragan, Ljubomir, Stanislava, Sam, Eduard, Romeo, Johannes, Philipp, Tobi, Josi and Angela. Your hands-on help, from drafting to the final touches, has been the backbone of this endeavor. Thank you for your unwavering commitment and labor that brought these pages to life.

∞
JANUARY

Are You Insuring Against Reality or Disaster Hype?

January 1st

AVAILABILITY BIAS

The availability bias is our tendency to make decisions based on information that comes to mind quickly and easily. It's a mental shortcut that gives more weight to information that was learned recently or that is easy to remember, for example, because it is an emotionally loaded memory. Our brain wants to save mental energy. So, we often go with the first information that comes to mind instead of putting in more mental effort to dig deeper.

A prime illustration of the availability bias at work is the aftermath of Hurricane Katrina's devastation in New Orleans in 2005. Between 2001 and 2006, the annual growth rate in flood insurance policy sales averaged only 0% to 4%. However, following Hurricane Katrina, this growth rate surged to 14.3%, representing a more than threefold increase. Interestingly, even in areas with a very low likelihood of experiencing a flood, the pervasive coverage of Hurricane Katrina across national media influenced people's decisions to purchase insurance.

Individuals residing in relatively safe areas were driven to purchase flood insurance by their perceived risk, rather than the actual threat. Their decision hinged on the prominence of the Hurricane Katrina incident in their minds. The event's recency, its ability to evoke strong emotional responses (such as fear and panic), and the fundamental threat to safety led many to safeguard themselves against a similar potential catastrophe, even though the statistical probability of it occurring in certain regions was quite low.

This pattern of increased flood insurance purchases following major incidents is consistent worldwide. Decisions influenced by the availability bias often overlook the full range of information. Our brain tends to prioritize the most recent, frequent, vivid, extreme, and negative information, prompting us to act on it. Despite having access to concrete facts and data, we unconsciously emphasize more salient details when rationalizing our choices.

Happy New Year by the way!

Astro-Not: Are Horoscopes Really Written in the Stars?

January 2nd

FORER EFFECT OR BARNUM EFFECT

The Forer effect, also known as the Barnum effect, describes the observation that people will give high accuracy ratings to personality descriptions that are supposedly tailored specifically for them. However, in reality, these descriptions are vague and general enough to apply to many people. This effect can help explain why some beliefs and practices, like astrology, palm reading, graphology, and some types of personality tests, are so popular.

"This is so 'me'!" is a common reaction when reading our horoscope in a lifestyle magazine. Yet, to our disappointment, this sense of identification stems from the Barnum effect, which leads us to accept general and vague descriptions that could fit many people as personally accurate.

Our zodiac sign is often consulted for self-knowledge or self-awareness. Many of us take quizzes and tests, consult "expert" zodiac readers, and browse the Internet for ample descriptions of our signs and ascendants, hoping that somehow we will make the right decisions or discover what events are waiting for us in the future.

While some of the information we find in horoscopes will greatly resonate with us, we should not ignore that it was made specifically to fit as many people as possible. Due to the Barnum effect, there's a high chance we would relate to most zodiac signs' descriptions. We are complex human beings who experience a wide spectrum of emotions. If your zodiac sign claims that "Aries are sociable people, but only with a select group of friends," you are very likely to remember past or present experiences in which this exact trait was manifested. During your life, you have experienced a lot, and our brain will very likely find events that match the description.

We have to accept that there's no personality test or zodiac reading that will ever formulate an accurate description of who we are. These can only present general, utterly vague assumptions that will get us enthusiastic to keep reading.

Why Can't Top Execs Admit Their Mistakes?

January 3rd

SELF-SERVING BIAS

The self-serving bias is our tendency to take credit for good things that happen to us and blame other things or people for bad things that happen. We do that because we have the desire to feel good about ourselves. Being responsible for good things happening boosts our confidence and gives us a sense of control in our lives. When we blame external factors for bad things that happen to us, it can help us feel better about ourselves by protecting our ego.

The best expression of poor leadership by a CEO is to avoid taking responsibility when things go wrong. Of course, many failures are too complex to blame on a single person.

One effect that could explain this behavior is the self-serving bias, which means that when things go well, we are more likely to take credit for them. In contrast, if the outcome is negative, we either dismiss our role in the failure or point the blame to someone else.

This seemed to be the general attitude of former HP CEO Carly Fiorina, who led the company between 1999 and 2005. Even if she had good managerial abilities, she was often criticized for lacking long-term vision. Under her leadership, HP had lost half its value and thousands of employees. She also made some poor decisions, such as merging with PC company Compaq, which ended up being a financial disaster for both parties.

Carly Fiorina, on the other hand, never acknowledged her inability to lead HP. Instead, she blamed the company's losses on external factors. For example, she said that the uncertain economy, employees, or investors were to blame for the company's struggle, which are clear signs for self-serving bias. Instead, she boasted about "doubling revenue" during her time at HP, yet many critics didn't find any numbers to back up her claims. HP's revenue did double during Fiorina's tenure, largely due to mergers with Compaq and other companies. However, the company underperformed by a number of other metrics, including net income and stock price.

Beauty and the Bias: Do Attractive People Win in Court?

January 4th

HALO EFFECT

The halo effect is a type of cognitive bias in which our overall opinion of a person or brand affects how we feel about the specific qualities of that person or brand. If we have a good feeling about something as a whole, we are more likely to think that its individual parts are good as well. We do that because it saves cognitive effort to use our overall impressions as a shortcut to make judgments rather than evaluating each aspect of something separately.

It's hard to believe that something as serious as sexual harassment could be judged inaccurately based on something as superficial as physical appearance. Yet, this was the conclusion of a research study.

In this experiment, it was found that participants in the experiment were more likely to believe the testimonies of good-looking individuals. All participants read extensive trial summaries that contained photos of the people being accused, the defendant, and the person that made the accusation, the plaintiff. For instance, when an attractive defendant was accused by a less attractive plaintiff, the highest percentage of guilty verdicts was observed. On the other hand, the combination of a good-looking defendant and a less attractive plaintiff resulted in the lowest number of guilty verdicts. The judges believed attractive women who accused an unattractive men of harrassment but judges were reluctant to belive an unattractive women that accused a handsome men.

This phenomenon can be attributed to the halo effect, a cognitive bias that leads us to assess people's personalities or qualities based on a single positive or negative attribute. For example, attractive individuals are often seen as kind, friendly, smart, or morally upright. In the sexual harassment cases studied, the judges were swayed by the "beauty equals goodness" thinking. As a result, they were more likely to find less attractive defendants guilty and put more trust in the claims of attractive plaintiffs.

Watch this video about the superpower of beautiful people

Surcharge or Discount?

January 5th

FRAMING EFFECT

The framing effect occurs when we draw different conclusions from identical information based solely on how that information is presented. This can happen when something is framed either positively or negatively, or as a gain versus a loss - we naturally tend to avoid losses in such situations. Our judgment can also shift depending on which features of the information are highlighted, even though the underlying facts remain exactly the same.

Since 1976, credit card surcharges have been illegal in the United States. Before that, business owners charged extra if customers paid with a credit card to offset the payment fees they had to pay to Visa or Mastercard. The credit card industry worked very hard to make that happen. After lobbying Congress for two years, the credit card industry finally got Congress to put its preferred speech code into place. After that, businesses were not allowed to charge extra if a customer paid with a credit card. However, if a customer paid in cash, they could still get a discount.

This isn't just a change in words. The credit card industry was very aware of the powerful framing effect and its consequences. The way we look at $1 changes depending on whether it's a discount or a surcharge. People will think of a surcharge as a loss and a discount as a gain. As you know, we dislike losses more than we like gains. Therefore, the new law resulted in more people paying with credit cards and fewer paying with cash.

In 2017, a New York hair salon called Expressions Hair Design took the state to the US Supreme Court over the state's ban on credit card surcharges. The salon argued that it has a constitutional right to charge extra fees. The salon cited a 2000 Dutch scientific study that found that most cardholders (74%) saw surcharges as a loss. The Supreme Court ruled in favor of the hair salon because it concluded the law was an unwanted regulation on speech and recognized the influence of the framing effect on consumer behavior in this case.

Can We Really Predict a Crisis or Are We Just Blinded by Hindsight?

January 6th
HINDSIGHT BIAS

The hindsight bias is also called the "I-knew-it-all-along" effect. It describes the retrospective overestimation of predictability. In the present, it's hard to tell how something will turn out in the future, but is easy to understand how or why an event happened in retrospect. This bias happens because we mistakenly assume that we had the same understanding of an event before it happened as we do after it happened.

We all know that it is easier to construct a plausible explanation for an event once we know its outcome. Sense-making works best in retrospect. This happened with many financial crises before, and it will most likely happen again. For investors, the regret of not acting on key moments in the stock market can lead to the idea that they (in retrospect) saw all of this coming. This is precisely the hindsight bias at work.

Many financial bubbles are perfect examples of hindsight bias. After the dot-com bubble in the late 1990s and the Great Recession of 2008, many analysts were ready to pinpoint trivial events predicting financial troubles. However, before these problems took concrete shape, barely anyone could talk about a potential incoming crisis. Yet many self-proclaimed experts and future predictors claimed that all the data was there and showed that financial concerns were indeed real. However, if they were right—and if most of these events were foreseeable—perhaps the economic troubles should have been avoided altogether?

Daniel Kahneman, the founding father of behavioral economics and Nobel Prize winner, puts it very well: "The illusion that we understand the past fosters our overconfidence in our ability to predict the future." Investors suffer from hindsight bias when they "saw it all coming." This leads them to believe they understand the past, which results in overconfidence in their ability to predict the future—a truly vicious circle.

What Is Your Favorite Animal From a Disney Movie?

January 7th

ANTHROPOMORPHISM

Anthropomorphism is our natural tendency to attribute human traits, emotions, and intentions to non-humans, for example, animals, gods, natural forces, and the like. We do this because we naturally know more about human traits than non-human ones. Therefore, these come easier to mind, and that saves mental energy.

Anthropomorphism has been a staple of storytelling for centuries. From ancient mythologies to modern-day animated films, creators have long employed this cognitive bias to make their content more engaging, relatable, and inspiring.

Disney's animated films have featured anthropomorphic animal characters since the 1940s, starting with Bambi. Disney and Pixar have released 79 animated movies until 2016, with 27 of them featuring anthropomorphic animal characters as protagonists, antagonists, or supporting characters. In these movies alone, there are 317 anthropomorphic characters. In the famous Pixar movie "WALL-E," the main character, a robot named Wall-E, shows a range of human emotions, such as loneliness, love, and curiosity. Similarly, in Disney's "The Lion King," the animals exhibit human emotions, relationships, and social structures. The main character of the story, Simba, goes through feelings of guilt and love.

The success of Disney movies demonstrates the power of anthropomorphism in capturing the hearts and minds of audiences. By giving human traits and emotions to animals, creators can make their stories more relatable, encouraging viewers to connect with the characters on a deeper level. This connection, in turn, can lead to greater emotional investment in the story. Disney, Pixar, and other animation studios have known for a long time that making animals or things behave like people is a great way to tell a story. By leveraging anthropomorphism, they create masterpieces that resonate with viewers of all ages.

Did You See "Wild Wild Country" On Netflix?

January 8th

GROUPTHINK

Groupthink is when our desire for harmony and conformity within a group leads to dysfunctional decision-making. Group members prioritize agreement over critical evaluation, resulting in a loss of individual creativity and thinking. This can lead to an inflated sense of confidence in the group's abilities, an undervaluation of opponents, group pressure, and potentially harmful actions towards outsiders.

The Rajneesh movement, led by Guru Bhagwan Shree Rajneesh and his followers known as Sannyasins, offers a striking example of groupthink in action.

The Rajneesh movement, founded in the 1970s, attracted thousands of followers worldwide. The Sannyasins held an unwavering belief in their guru and his vision. Everyone in the commune wore shades of red, which signified strong unity.

The group constructed a commune in Oregon to create a utopian society based on their spiritual beliefs. The new city for the Sannyasins was called Rajneeshpura. Having built their own city resulted in a collective sense of invincibility and a dismissal of potential threats or criticisms from locals or the government. The Rajneesh movement consistently underestimated and looked down on their opponents. In the commune, traditional relationships were discouraged in favor of free love, which can be seen as a way to break down individual attachments and focus loyalty towards the group. Leaving the group was made difficult, both emotionally and logistically, reinforcing the need for conformity and discouraging dissent.

The culmination of the groupthink phenomenon within the Rajneesh movement was the 1984 bioterror attack in the town The Dalles, Oregon. In an attempt to influence local elections and gain control of the county, members of the movement deliberately contaminated local salad bars with salmonella, leading to the poisoning of over 750 people. This bioterror attack is a clear example of groupthink driving dangerous and criminal action towards outsiders.

Watch the trailer for the Netflix series on the Rajneesh movement

Frozen in FOMO?

January 9th

BANDWAGON EFFECT

The bandwagon effect refers to the phenomenon in which a belief or behavior becomes more popular as more people adopt it. This can lead to a self-reinforcing cycle, as the increased popularity of the belief or behavior encourages more people to adopt it. The effect is caused by our desire to conform to social norms and our belief that the majority must be correct. It can also be caused by peer pressure and the fear of being left out or made fun of if we don't fit in.

The Ice Bucket Challenge, which swept across the globe in 2014, perfectly illustrates the bandwagon effect in action. This viral campaign was designed to raise awareness and funding for Amyotrophic Lateral Sclerosis (ALS) research. Millions of participants worldwide embraced the challenge of drenching themselves with ice-cold water and challenging others to follow suit.

The campaign's impact demonstrates the remarkable power of the bandwagon effect, raising an astounding $220 million worldwide and generating 2.4 million tagged videos on Facebook alone. The Ice Bucket Challenge succeeded because it masterfully leveraged social attention and pressure. As social media feeds became saturated with videos of friends, family members, and celebrities participating, people felt an increasing urge to join simply because everyone else was doing it. This created a powerful cascade effect, with each new participant adding to the campaign's unstoppable momentum.

The bandwagon effect is fundamentally rooted in our innate desire to conform to social norms and our belief that majority actions indicate correct behavior. Peer pressure and the fear of rejection or ridicule serve as powerful motivators driving this phenomenon. The Ice Bucket Challenge thus stands as a perfect example of how the bandwagon effect can mobilize massive numbers of people behind a single cause, while also demonstrating the remarkable potential of social influence to drive collective action and achieve significant impact.

Watch famous people take the Ice Bucket Challenge

Can Superstition and Finger Snaps Sway the Odds?

January 10th

ILLUSION OF CONTROL

The illusion of control occurs when we believe we have more control over external events than we do. We frequently believe we have (or had) some control over events that are actually random. Researchers have found that people who feel in control will engage in healthier behaviors, feel less stress, and have better overall mental health. Therefore, this illusion makes us feel better about ourselves and the world around us, but it can also seduce us into relying on superstitions.

The illusion of control frequently manifests in casino-style games, where players engage in irrational rituals, hoping to sway the outcome in their favor. One such game is craps, where participants wager on the results of a pair of dice. Anyone familiar with probability calculations understands that dice rolls follow a uniform distribution—meaning that rolling any number has the same mathematical likelihood as rolling any other number.

A particularly insightful study observed the behavior of craps players and revealed clear evidence of the illusion of control. For instance, players believed that the force of their dice throw influenced the outcome, with a hard throw supposedly resulting in a high number and a soft throw yielding a low number.

Another method players used to exert control over the dice involved snapping their fingers after the dice were thrown and rebounded off the backboard. This ritual, rooted in the belief that finger-snapping would guide the dice to the desired number, was so ingrained in some players that they never rolled the dice without accompanying the action with a loud snap. They even developed a ritual to counteract the perceived negative effects of accidentally dropping the dice, which involved rubbing both dice on the ground.

These seemingly irrational strategies align with the players' belief systems, which center on the notion that performing specific rituals grants them more control over the game's outcome. This serves as a prime example of the illusion of control, where individuals mistakenly believe they can influence events beyond their control, despite clear mathematical evidence to the contrary.

Watch this video on how to play craps

How to Make a Rolls Royce Look Like a Bargain?

January 11th

ANCHORING BIAS

Anchoring bias occurs when a specific reference point, or "anchor", influences our decision-making process. This anchor could be a number or any other kind of cue, even if it is completely unrelated to the decision at hand. Despite this, we often use the anchor as a starting point and adjust our decisions or judgments from there, without realizing it. As a result, our final estimates, decisions, or judgments can be significantly different from what they might have been without the influence of the anchor.

Is a $300,000 Rolls-Royce an expensive car? The answer to this question largely hinges on who you're asking and the context of the comparison. High-end car brands such as Rolls-Royce and Maserati have notably ceased their participation in traditional car shows due to the perception that their products are too expensive relative to other car brands.

Interestingly, these brands have adopted a new strategy: showcasing their automobiles at yacht and aircraft shows instead. Anchoring explains this strategic shift. In the context of purchases, a certain product serves as an anchor, and all subsequently viewed products are compared against this initial benchmark.

The marketing strategy that Rolls-Royce and Maserati use is fundamentally based on this idea of anchoring. By positioning their cars amidst million-dollar yachts and aircraft, their cars seem less expensive by comparison. As Rory Sutherland, Vice Chairman of advertising company Ogilvy & Mather, humorously observed at a GDS summit, "If you've been looking at Lear jets all afternoon, a $300,000 Rolls-Royce is just an impulse buy."

This statement demonstrates the effectiveness of strategic anchoring: after considering high-cost items like jets, a Rolls-Royce priced at $300,000 may seem like a relatively minor expenditure.

Is Karma a Bitch?

January 12th

JUST WORLD HYPOTHESIS

The Just World Hypothesis is the belief that the world is just and fair, and that people get what they deserve. This means that if someone is experiencing bad things, it is because they have done something to deserve it and are punished. On the other hand, if someone is successful or happy, it is because they made good choices and are rewarded. This idea can be comforting because it gives us a sense of control over our lives and the belief that we can influence our own outcomes.

You have probably used the word "karma" before, even if you didn't attach any religious meaning to it. You most likely did it to make sense of random patterns in your existence, such as a terrible misfortune. The concept of karma and the bias of the "just world hypothesis" are both related to the idea of moral causation.

Karma is a concept in Eastern religions and philosophies that refers to the idea that actions have consequences and that individuals are responsible for their destiny based on their actions in previous lives or in the present. According to karma, good actions lead to positive consequences, while bad actions lead to negative consequences.

The main difference between the two, though, is that karma is based on the idea of reincarnation and the notion that actions from past lives can have an effect on the present. The just world hypothesis, on the other hand, is a cognitive bias that operates on a more immediate and observable level in the here and now.

Despite this difference, both concepts can be used to explain why people may attribute the outcomes of events to an individual's moral character rather than considering external factors that may be at play. Both karma and the just world hypothesis can lead people to overlook the role of chance, circumstance, and systemic inequalities in shaping people's lives, which can ultimately result in victim-blaming and a lack of empathy for those who are struggling.

Why Did Some 9/11 Survivors Hit Ctrl+Alt+Del Before Escaping?

January 13th

OSTRICH EFFECT OR NORMALCY BIAS

Normalcy bias, also known as "ostrich effect," makes us downplay warnings about dangers or ignore negative situations completely. We underestimate how likely it is that a disaster will happen and how it might affect us. We do that because we want to avoid an unpleasant emotional impact in the short term. The name comes from the popular (but false) belief that ostriches bury their heads in the sand when in danger.

You would imagine that the first reaction of anyone trapped in the World Trade Center buildings on 9/11 was to leave everything behind and get away. Yet, stories from people who were involved in the event show that human behavior is not that predictable.

Elia Zedeno was one of many people who were inside the World Trade Center. In a Time magazine article, she described how she took her time to get out of the building. Like many others, she was in disbelief at what was going on and hoped that the situation was not as bad as it seemed. She recalled, "What I really wanted was for someone to scream back, 'Everything is OK! Don't worry. It's in your head!'"

Yet she wasn't alone in her hesitation. According to the National Institute of Standards and Technology (NIST), approximately 1,000 people took the time to shut down their computers, which took approximately 6 minutes on average, before heading downstairs. Consider their situation: they were stuck in a building that had just been the target of a terrorist attack.

Psychology suggests that there are several reasons that stop people from reacting to dangerous situations. One of them is the ostrich effect, which makes people minimize warning signs to avoid confronting a terrible incident. The brain doesn't immediately respond to a catastrophe to avoid an overly negative emotional impact. People who were trapped in the two skyscrapers on 9/11 knew there was something wrong, but a part of them didn't want to accept the terrible reality.

What seems unthinkable from the outside - taking time for ordinary tasks during an extraordinary crisis - is actually a deeply human response that any of us might have displayed in the same situation.

Is Emily in Paris' Ignorance a Classic Case of Dunning-Kruger?

January 14th

DUNNING–KRUGER EFFECT

The Dunning–Kruger effect describes our tendency to overestimate our own abilities in areas that we are unskilled in or lack knowledge in. This happens when we know just enough to think we are great but not enough to tell the difference between good and bad. We just don't know yet what we could do better. The effect also applies to society as a whole. The most uninformed citizens are often also the most confident ones.

In "Emily in Paris," the main character, Emily Cooper, is an American in her late 20s from Chicago. She receives an unexpected job offer in Paris and moves there. She is responsible for providing an American point of view and social media presence to a well-known French marketing firm. As she adjusts to the challenges of living in Paris and balances her career, new friendships, and busy love life, clashes between different cultures arise.

French critics have criticized the show for portraying the inhabitants of the French capital as caricatures of stereotypes and for depicting the French as mean, lazy, philandering, sexist, and unfaithful. A French YouTuber, who happens to be from Paris, has nothing good to say about the show: "It is a brutally ignorant show, but it is so confident in its ignorance that it also ends up coming across as arrogant!"

The producers and directors of the show have repeatedly stated that "Emily in Paris" is a love letter to French culture. However, the Dunning-Kruger effect may be at work here. This is where one may believe they understand a subject, but in reality, they lack the knowledge to distinguish between admiration and ridicule.

Throughout the show, also Emily's confidence shines through as she takes charge of her life in Paris. Emily's confidence in navigating both cultural and professional environments in Paris, despite her apparent lack of language skills and cultural awareness, shows the Dunning-Kruger effect. She assumes she understands the subtleties of French culture, mistaking superficial experiences for genuine insight.

Watch this video discussing how 'Emily in Paris' romanticizes ignorance

How to Win the Lottery

January 15th

ILLUSION OF CONTROL

The illusion of control occurs when we believe we have more control over external events than we do. We frequently believe we have (or had) some control over events that are actually random. Researchers have found that people who feel in control will engage in healthier behaviors, feel less stress, and have better overall mental health. Therefore, this illusion makes us feel better about ourselves and the world around us, but it can also seduce us into relying on superstitions.

The "illusion of control" was first identified in a pioneering study by psychologist Ellen Langer in 1975.

Imagine participating in a lottery at your workplace. You're given the choice to select your own lottery ticket or be assigned one at random. This was the setting of Langer's experiment. Surprisingly, those who chose their tickets believed they held a higher value, even though, logically, all tickets had an equal chance of winning. This illustrates how the mere act of choosing can instill a false sense of control over a completely random outcome.

In another experiment, Langer explored how familiarity with the symbols on a lottery ticket affects this illusion. Participants were given tickets with either familiar letters of the alphabet or unfamiliar symbols. When given the chance to trade their ticket for one in a different lottery with a higher chance of winning, those with familiar letters were less likely to trade. This reluctance demonstrates how familiarity can bolster our confidence in controlling chance events, even when it's clearly random.

These experiments were revolutionary in demonstrating the illusion of control. They highlight a fundamental aspect of human psychology: our tendency to overestimate our influence in situations where chance, not skill, is the primary factor.

When Should You Really Quit a Dull Movie?

January 16th

SUNK COST FALLACY

The sunk cost fallacy is when we make a decision based on how much we have already invested in something rather than on whether it is the best choice for us right now. When we feel like we have already invested a lot in something, we feel like we would be losing something if we were to let it go. Another reason that the sunk cost fallacy occurs is because we tend to focus on the past rather than the present when we make decisions.

For many of us, time is precious. It is certainly not a coincidence that we think of it in similar ways we think about wealth: "time is money," "saving time," "spare time." With these associations, it makes sense to approach our actions, tasks, and personal relationships as "time investments." However, there's a downside to being aware of the time we invest: spending time on something makes us more likely to continue it, even if it no longer brings us tangible benefits or personal satisfaction.

This is recognized as the sunk cost fallacy, where we continue an endeavor if we have already invested monetary or time resources into it. One example that might already be familiar to many is watching movies and TV series.

Perhaps you heard some recommendations about a particular entertainment show or movie, so you decided to watch it. Unfortunately, halfway through, you realize that the plot is not really to your taste. But are you really going to waste those 30-40 minutes you put into watching it? "Of course not," would eagerly admit many of us who are under the influence of the sunk cost fallacy. So you carry on investing even more time simply because the idea of wasting 30 minutes of your life makes you psychologically uncomfortable.

A noteworthy study found that younger people are more susceptible to the sunk cost fallacy. The older we get, the more we realize that continuing to invest in worthless experiences only to make our resources worthwhile isn't a very productive thing to do.

DIY: A Billion-Dollar Question of Self-Worth and Identity?

January 17th

IKEA EFFECT

The IKEA effect refers to our tendency to place a disproportionately high value on objects that we helped create, such as IKEA furniture. We do that regardless of the quality of the end product. This bias helps us to feel better about ourselves in two ways. First, we want to feel that our effort was well invested and that we did not waste our time but instead created something of value. Secondly, creating things makes us feel more competent.

The do-it-yourself industry received an unprecedented boost during the pandemic in 2020. The market for DIY retail goods was estimated to be worth $848.20 billion globally in 2021 and is expected to increase to $1,278.00 billion by 2030. This amount is comparable to Spain's GDP. So, what's the deal with DIY?

One of the reasons for our increasing preference for DIY items is the so-called "IKEA effect." But the IKEA effect has a deeper explanation. One study proposed that handmade and self-designed objects touch on our sense of competence and personal identity.

Feeling good about ourselves is a core psychological need that we can fulfill by creating something that can be admired by others. When we are co-creators of goods rather than passive recipients, we get the chance to express our ideas and creativity. As a result, we will perceive the final product as more valuable since it has a personal touch and reflects a part of ourselves. In one experiment in the study, for example, participants were willing to pay a higher price for an IKEA box they built themselves than for an identical one built by someone else.

The study found that the IKEA effect happens with both practical and enjoyable products and that people think their self-made items are as good as those made by experts. The IKEA effect occurs only if people complete the assembly of the items; if they disassemble them or do not finish assembling, their perceived value does not increase.

Therefore, the next time you'd rather do it yourself than buy it elsewhere, you'll know why.

Do You Feel Like a Forensic Expert After Watching Csi?

January 18th

AVAILABILITY BIAS

The availability bias is our tendency to make decisions based on information that comes to mind quickly and easily. It's a mental shortcut that gives more weight to information that was learned recently or that is easy to remember, for example, because it is an emotionally loaded memory. Our brain wants to save mental energy. So, we often go with the first information that comes to mind instead of putting in more mental effort to dig deeper.

The so-called "CSI effect," which has arisen from the popularity of TV shows like CSI, offers a compelling example of the availability bias in action. The widespread viewership and dramatic portrayals of forensic science in crime dramas have made forensic evidence highly available in the minds of viewers.

The impact of the "CSI effect" is widely believed to influence jurors' decisions in criminal trials. According to a 2008 survey, 80% of all American legal professionals thought that forensic television programs had influenced their decisions.

Crime dramas like "CSI" often depict forensic science as a decisive factor in solving cases, with forensic experts using cutting-edge technology to unveil evidence. These portrayals give the impression that forensic evidence is always available, reliable, and definitive, which contributes to the unrealistic expectations of jurors in real-life trials. The availability bias manifests in two main ways: first, jurors may expect more forensic evidence than is available or necessary, resulting in a higher rate of acquittal when such evidence is absent. When there is no forensic evidence, it is difficult for jurors to believe that a case can be resolved without it. Second, jurors may have greater confidence in forensic evidence than is warranted, resulting in a higher rate of conviction when such evidence is present.

The "CSI effect" demonstrates the potency of the availability bias by altering jurors' expectations for forensic evidence, thus skewing acquittal and conviction rates.

Are We Trading Lifelong Bliss for a Quick Fix of Happiness?

January 19th

HYPERBOLIC DISCOUNTING

Hyperbolic discounting is our tendency to favor more immediate payoffs in comparison to later payoffs. We do prefer the immediate reward, even when it is objectively less valuable. We all make decisions today that we would have preferred not to have made in the future due to hyperbolic discounting. Our brains are hardwired to do so because immediate reward meant a better chance of survival in evolutionary terms.

Neglecting the future and living for today is irrational, yet many of us do it—even if we have to pay for the consequences at some point. This is what hyperbolic discounting is all about: missing out on the bigger picture and focusing on things that feel good, right here and right now.

It seems that not even serious wake-up calls, like chronic illness or severe health issues, reduce our hyperbolic discounting. Instead of inspiring caution, our brain responds to impending danger or uncertainty by reducing the importance of the future in our decision-making process. This is the case for those who resort to urgent measures, such as coronary artery bypass surgery, to prevent life-threatening heart conditions. Yet, only 10% of those who have the surgery make the necessary lifestyle changes to prevent future medical interventions, chest pains, and premature death. The rest of the patients decide to choose comfort and indulge in the short-term pleasures of unhealthy food and a couch potato lifestyle.

Even when the risks are as high as death, many of us cannot fight hyperbolic discounting. We fail to consider the health and well-being of our future selves when the present is so full of opportunities for instant pleasure. Because of this, we enjoy the moment and suffer in the future. We develop physical conditions, incur financial debt, and drown in addictions that are hard to conquer. When choosing immediate gratification over long-term payoffs, it is worth asking ourselves—what would our future selves want us to do now?

Watch this genius TED Talk of Tim Urban about the mind of a master procrastinator

How Can Repetition Breed Belief?

January 20th

ILLUSORY TRUTH EFFECT

The illusory truth effect causes us to believe information is true if we hear it repeatedly, even when it's not. This happens because repeatedly hearing the same information makes it familiar, and our brain processes familiar things more easily. This ease is due to the activation of well-established neural pathways, which require less effort to process than new or unfamiliar information. When our brains process information with less effort, we tend to interpret this ease as a sign of truth. Thus, if something is easier to understand, we are more likely to believe it's true.

"If you tell a lie big enough and keep repeating it, people will eventually come to believe it." This quote is attributed to Nazi propaganda chief Joseph Goebbels. This strategy of repetition continues to resonate in the age of social media, where repeated exposure can validate false narratives. The illusory truth effect encapsulates this idea: when information is repeated sufficiently, people start to accept it as true.

This vulnerability in human cognition underscores why the role of content moderators is critical. Facebook has many regular content moderators that maintain a semblance of order on the platform. They spend most of their days cleaning up the social network's most toxic content. Some of this content is related to hate-mongering conspiracy theories and misinformation. These moderators described an intriguing phenomenon when speaking with The Verge. The moderators The Verge spoke with said that they and their coworkers often found themselves believing strange, often hateful conspiracy theories that they would have laughed off under normal circumstances. Others said they had paranoid thoughts and many worries about their safety. One even started to bring a gun to work due to the constant exposure to threatening and extremist content, which heightened his sense of personal threat.

The relentless exposure to the same information gradually seeped into the minds of the moderators, demonstrating the insidious power of the illusory truth effect.

Read about the lives of Facebook moderators in America

Outsmarting Yourself: Does Expertise Make You More Susceptible to Scams?

January 21st

OVERCONFIDENCE EFFECT

We speak of the overconfidence effect when our subjective confidence in our judgments is higher than their objective accuracy. We can overestimate a variety of things, including our own performance or likelihood of success, our abilities in comparison to others, and the certainty of our answers or judgments.

Overconfidence can be a double-edged sword. While it's essential to have faith in our abilities, excessive and unfounded confidence can lead to the overconfidence effect. A study conducted by the University of Exeter on investment scam victims provides a clear illustration of the overconfidence effect.

The research conducted interviews with scam victims and uncovered that these individuals often have considerable knowledge about the subject matter of the scam. Paradoxically, this increased understanding can actually heighten their susceptibility to becoming victims. For example, if someone knows a lot about stocks and investing, they might be more likely to fall for an investment scam. Believing that their expertise makes them immune to scams, these individuals become overconfident in their ability to detect and avoid fraud. Because of their perceived immunity to fraud and their level of expertise, victims believed that scams were highly improbable and unbelievable.

Another intriguing finding revealed that scam victims reported investing more cognitive effort in evaluating scam content than non-victims. This contradicts the intuitive suggestion that people fall victim to scams because they invest too little cognitive energy in investigating the content and thus overlook potential information (for example, in the small print) that might reveal the scam. The researchers suggest that this increased cognitive effort reflects the victims being "drawn in" by the scam, whereas non-victims often discard scams without giving them much consideration.

Discrimi-nation: Is Our In-Group Bias Fueling Unfair Judgment?

January 22nd
INGROUP BIAS

Ingroup bias is when we like and support people who are part of our own group more than people who are not part of our group. These groups can be divided based on seemingly trivial observable traits. This is rooted in the intrinsic human need for a group identity, which provides a sense of belonging and purpose. Additionally, we all have a desire to feel good about ourselves, and one way to achieve that is to see our own group as being superior to others.

We grow up favoring people from our groups: our friends or those who support the same sports teams. These preferences have been strongly embedded in our minds since we were young. This so called ingroup bias appears as a preference for individuals who are members of our groups over those who do not have the same attributes. One consequence of ingroup bias is being more lenient with the mistakes made by those who belong to our group. Studies demonstrate that white people were quick to excuse a European American's bad behavior. In contrast, they were prepared to hold an African American accountable for the same error more harshly.

The most common consequence of ingroup bias is discrimination and racism. In the U.S., for example, the conflict between the police and African Americans has a long history. There are many stories of people complaining about police officers being more likely to detect crimes committed by people of color than by white citizens. In fact, the death of 46-year-old black man George Floyd by a police officer in 2020 was one such incident that sparked widespread outrage. He was arrested for using a counterfeit $20 bill. Many people argued that a white person would have been better handled in a similar situation. However, as Floyd was perceived as an outsider by the white police officers, he was subjected to merciless and ultimately fatal treatment.

Ingroup bias is one reason for differential treatment and discrimination against those who are different in some way.

Why Are We Still Waiting for Hose-Cleaning Homes?

January 23rd

ILLUSION OF VALIDITY

The illusion of validity is a cognitive bias where we overestimate our ability to understand and predict an outcome based on the information we have. When analyzing new information, we rely on things we already know, for example, stereotypes and prior beliefs. When we assume that what we know is valid enough to predict what will happen in different contexts, we make confident predictions that can turn out to be utterly inaccurate.

It's easy to make bold predictions based on mind-blowing information. For example, people who just discovered waterproof fabric a few decades ago thought this would revolutionize the entire cleaning industry.

In 1950, Waldemar Kaempffert, the science editor of the New York Times, wrote an intriguing article titled "Miracles You'll See In The Next Fifty Years." One of the predicted miracles was related to housekeeping. He describes how a regular housewife will use a hose to clean everything in the house in just a few minutes. Because everything is made of synthetic fabric and waterproof plastic, she doesn't need to wash rugs, draperies, tablecloths, and napkins separately in the washing machine. She just needs to turn on the water, which will run down a drain in the middle of the floor, and then dry everything out with a blast of hot air.

Looking at it from our current perspective, these predictions may sound naive. But you can be sure that some people in the past were certain this idea would come true at some point. That's because we fall victim to thinking errors such as the illusion of validity, which leads us to predict outcomes based on a limited piece of information we have. In that 1950s article, the author thought that a small advancement in cleaning practices or household fabrics could allow him to foresee what the future of cleaning would look like. We can confirm he was wrong, at least for now.

Read the article
"Miracles You'll See In
The Next Fifty Years"
from 1950

Can We Escape the Web of Our Own Opinions?

January 24th

CONFIRMATION BIAS

Confirmation bias is our tendency to look for, acknowledge, favor, and remember information in a way that supports what we already think or believe. This bias occurs when we ignore information that contradicts our ideas or interpret ambiguous facts as evidence supporting our existing beliefs. Situations that involve emotionally charged topics, strongly held beliefs, or things we really want to happen are most susceptible to this bias.

Critics have argued that search engine algorithms create "filter bubbles of information." Eli Pariser, author of the book "Filter Bubbles," explains that the Internet gives us "what we want to see." Filter bubbles of information maintain our current views, interests, and opinions and prevent us from being exposed to different perspectives. Let's take search engines as one concrete example and examine the mechanics.

Search engines for example use the time spent on a website or the time it takes you to click back to the search result page from a webpage as a signal for the quality of their search results. If you spend little time on the website or click back to the search result page quickly, this might indicate that you didn't like the suggested page. Search engines collect this data to give you "better" search results. This helps them make more money because if you like the results, you're more likely to use their service more often.

Due to confirmation bias, we tend to believe and engage with information that is congruent with our existing beliefs and discard information that is not. Our behavior trains the search engine to show us more of what is congruent with our beliefs and less of what is not.

That is just one example of how confirmation bias can create filter bubbles online. The fact that someone with opposing viewpoints is exposed to vastly different information when searching or browsing online is not really on our minds. Unfortunately, many of us do not know that filter bubbles of information exist and are a real danger. As a result, we might think that what we perceive as our version of reality is everyone's reality.

Learn more about how news feed algorithms supercharge confirmation bias

Ending on a High Note: Are We Biased by Our Last Impressions?

January 25th

PEAK–END RULE

The peak-end rule states that we tend to judge an experience based on the most intense moment as well as how the experience ended. The overall memory of the experience will be based on the average of the peak moment and the end. This bias happens because we remember events in snapshots rather than in their entirety. Furthermore, we remember things better when they are emotionally intense (the peak) or more recent (the end).

The phenomenon known as the "peak-end rule" posits that the final moment or peak intensity of an experience holds greater influence over our memory of the event than the cumulative effect of all its moments. This cognitive bias shapes how we remember experiences. For instance, an average holiday with an extraordinary final day can prompt us to recall the trip as a thoroughly enjoyable experience.

One iconic experiment that validates the peak-end rule involved individuals immersing their hands in cold water. The experiment was divided into three rounds: In the first round, participants submerged their hands in 14 degrees Celsius (57 degrees Fahrenheit) water for 60 seconds. The second round replicated the conditions of the first but added an extra 30 seconds at a slightly less cold temperature of 15 degrees Celsius (59 degrees Fahrenheit). In the final round, participants were given the choice between repeating either Round 1 or Round 2.

On the face of it, it would seem more logical to opt for Round 1, which entails 60 seconds of discomfort as opposed to the 90 seconds in Round 2. Yet, intriguingly, 80% of participants expressed a preference for repeating Round 2. This counterintuitive choice can be attributed to the final 30 seconds of Round 2, during which the water temperature, though still uncomfortable, became slightly less chilly, thereby ending the experience on a more tolerable note. As such, participants remembered Round 2 as being more pleasant, underscoring the potent influence of the end of an experience on our memory.

Is Your Willpower Checked Out at the Checkout Line?

January 26th

DECISION FATIGUE

Decision fatigue is the mental exhaustion that comes from having to make a lot of complex decisions in a short amount of time. It is similar to using a muscle that becomes more fatigued the more we use it in a short period. This happens because our brain has a limited amount of mental energy and willpower to use for making decisions. This phenomenon can be caused by external factors such as stress and lack of sleep and can lead to difficulty concentrating, irritability, and impulsive behavior.

Why do all supermarkets display snacks next to the checkout tills? You have probably guessed that this isn't a random placement since most supermarkets have it. In fact, it is a simple technique that encourages impulse buying. By the time we get to the checkout line, our willpower is already depleted. We've already used all our cognitive energy to resist making expensive, unhealthy, or unnecessary purchases throughout our shopping trip, so now's the best time to market that small chocolate bar.

This sales strategy is so effective because of decision fatigue, which occurs after making a series of complex decisions within a short timeframe. Our mental energy isn't unlimited, and likewise, decision-making is quite a cognitively costly process. If we make a series of decisions for a while, we'll find out that their quality will begin to decrease. This is why supermarkets will try to upsell small purchases like candy, snacks, and chewing gum when people are most fatigued. Little fun fact: the Germans have a very specific word for those supermarket checkout snacks — "Quengelware," which translates to "whining goods."

Some of these whining goods are strategically placed in the checkout area, targeting children who grow impatient towards the end of their parents' shopping trip. Additionally, parents are more likely to concede at the checkout, worn out from denying their children's unreasonable demands throughout the shopping trip. Decision fatigue is real; just observe it as you find yourself reaching for that chocolate bar at the end of your next grocery shopping session—whether for yourself or after giving in to your kids.

50 Shades of Grey Matter: Can Nuanced Thinking Bridge Divides?

January 27th

BINARY BIAS

Binary bias is our tendency to categorize things or people into two distinct categories, often based on their perceived characteristics or attributes. This can lead to oversimplification, stereotyping, and discrimination. We do that because it helps us make sense of the world around us quickly. From an evolutionary perspective, we need to quickly distinguish between potential allies and threats, categorizing people as friends or foes.

Psychologist Peter T. Coleman has been aiming for over two decades to bring together polarizing views on complex issues and help people reduce their binary bias. In one of his experiments, he had people read articles that covered both sides of a complex topic, like abortion or gun control. He presented two people, respectively, with two versions of articles. Both versions carried the same information but expressed it differently. One of the articles described black-and-white perspectives on the problem, while the other article was framed differently to encompass multiple, more nuanced viewpoints on the issue. The two people reading that article had to generate a common statement and sign it.

Which pair do you think had a higher likelihood of generating a common statement they both wanted to sign? The pair that read the black-and-white article or the pair that read the nuanced article? 100% of the pairs that read the nuanced articles generated a joint statement about abortion laws, and just 46% of the other pairs found common ground. The study shows that providing a nuanced perspective on controversial issues helps overcome binary bias.

Unfortunately, the media—and talk shows in particular—generate attention by capitalizing on binary bias. They try to present us with polarized views (which exacerbates the collective binary bias) because two people shouting at each other is far more entertaining than considering different angles and nuances of the same story.

Watch a TED Talk about the attraction of a polarized America

Monte Carlo Missteps: Can Losing Big Teach Us a Winning Lesson?

January 28th

GAMBLER'S FALLACY

The gambler's fallacy arises from the mistaken belief that past events can affect the probability of future outcomes that are actually independent of the past. It is often manifested in the belief that a certain outcome is more or less likely to occur due to its frequency in the past, despite the fact that the probability remains the same. This fallacy is often driven by a desire for pattern-finding and prediction, as well as a dislike of uncertainty.

The gambler's fallacy, also known as the Monte Carlo fallacy. This is because a classic example of this fallacy occurred on the night of August 18, 1913, at the Monte Carlo Casino.

On this fateful night, patrons noticed that the roulette wheel had landed on black 10 times in a row. As the streak continued, more and more people in the casino became intrigued. Convinced that the roulette wheel was overdue for a red outcome, they began to place their bets on red. Their flawed reasoning was that the more the wheel had landed on black in the past, the higher the chances it would land on red in subsequent spins.

However, the roulette wheel did not land on red until the 27th spin. While those who placed their bets on red for the 27th spin did win, the majority of the bettors suffered significant losses. This unfortunate outcome occurred because they believed that a prolonged streak of black outcomes would increase the likelihood of a future red streak, even though these events were entirely random and independent of one another.

The Monte Carlo event remains one of the most famous examples of how the gambler's fallacy can lead to significant financial losses due to erroneous thinking patterns. It highlights the importance of understanding that probabilities for independent events remain constant, regardless of past outcomes.

It Is Never Your Fault, Is It?

January 29th

SELF-SERVING BIAS

The self-serving bias is our tendency to take credit for good things that happen to us and blame other things or people for bad things that happen. We do that because we have the desire to feel good about ourselves. Being responsible for good things happening boosts our confidence and gives us a sense of control in our lives. When we blame external factors for bad things that happen to us, it can help us feel better about ourselves by protecting our ego.

The Ford-Firestone scandal of 1999 provides a prime example of self-serving bias in corporate behavior. Both companies were implicated in the crisis involving faulty tires on Ford Explorer vehicles that led to numerous accidents and fatalities. Their initial response focused on deflecting responsibility, with Firestone suggesting that tire abuse and underinflation by consumers were contributing factors.

In 1996, as later revealed by a company employee, Ford first suspected problems with Firestone tires following reports of accidents, including several fatal ones. When Ford requested data from Firestone, the tire manufacturer insisted there were no issues with their products. The situation reached a critical point in August 2000, when Firestone finally recalled 6.5 million tires after the federal government linked them to at least 203 deaths and more than 700 injuries. Most of these tires had been installed on Ford Explorer vehicles.

Throughout the crisis, both companies exhibited classic self-serving bias in their responses. Firestone acknowledged producing some faulty tires but argued that the design of Ford vehicles also contributed to the accidents. Ford, conversely, maintained that the issue was exclusively related to the tires. The controversy escalated until May 2001, when Ford launched a $3 billion program to replace an additional 13 million Firestone tires. Even then, Firestone continued to defend their tires' safety while insisting that Ford vehicles were partially responsible for the accidents. This scandal clearly demonstrates how self-serving bias can influence corporate behavior, as both companies persistently attributed negative outcomes to external factors while minimizing their own role in the crisis.

Was It Really Predictable?

January 30th

HINDSIGHT BIAS

The hindsight bias is also called the "I-knew-it-all-along" effect. It describes the retrospective overestimation of predictability. In the present, it's hard to tell how something will turn out in the future, but is easy to understand how or why an event happened in retrospect. This bias happens because we mistakenly assume that we had the same understanding of an event before it happened as we do after it happened.

Victim-blaming involves attributing abuse to the actions of the victim, a concept that might seem counterintuitive to many. Yet, for others, it is a common practice. Studies suggest that this tendency is further intensified by hindsight bias, particularly in cases of rape.

In a study, subjects read detailed descriptions of an interaction between a man (the boss) and a woman (the employee) that ended in three possible ways: negative (the man raped the woman), positive (the woman gets promoted), and neutral (the man takes the woman home). In the rape story, for example, the woman hugged her boss, drank alcohol, and went to his house before he raped her. Half of the students in these three scenarios were asked to explain an alternative outcome for all three scenarios.

Interestingly, the other half of the students, who were not asked to imagine a different outcome, said that the way the three scenarios ended was very likely. Even worse, the victim's blame was greatest in the rape outcome. In other words, many participants saw the rape incident as a natural consequence of the victim's actions. The subjects wondered why the victim did not do something to prevent the rape or act differently so that she did not "trigger" it.

This study shows that hindsight bias increases victim blaming. Our brain starts to build causal links between certain events (for example, a hug) and the outcome (rape) and judge them as predictable. This is the very fallacy of the bias: we think the outcome was predictable. However, it is actually not predictable when the events are still in progress.

Can We Balance Compassion and Self-Preservation?

January 31st

COGNITIVE DISSONANCE

Cognitive dissonance describes the mental discomfort we experience when there is a conflict between our beliefs, actions, or perceptions. This discomfort often arises when our actions contradict our beliefs or when we hold two opposing beliefs simultaneously. To alleviate this discomfort, we may adjust our beliefs, perceptions, or actions to create a more consistent internal state. Achieving this internal consistency is crucial, as it helps maintain our sense of identity and coherence.

Most of us like to think, "I am a good person." Therefore, one of our values is kindness. However, when confronted with a volunteer for a humanitarian cause on the street, we may choose to ignore them. This discrepancy between our value of kindness and our actual behavior generates mental discomfort known as cognitive dissonance.

Let's explore how we may attempt to resolve this cognitive dissonance. One option is to act in accordance with our values by signing a petition or making a donation. Alternatively, we might seek validation from others who share our lack of action, such as those who argue that petitions are ineffective and humanitarian campaigns are not as they seem. Finally, we can modify our beliefs about the cause of the campaign, making it appear unworthy of support. The psychological mechanism of adjusting beliefs influences both daily interactions and responses to global issues, as recent research shows.

A 2019 research study on the refugee crisis in Europa demonstrates that when people feel their own needs are not met, they are more likely to seek out and endorse negative information about refugees. This behavior can be explained as an attempt to reduce cognitive dissonance. By finding and accepting negative information about refugees, individuals can justify their lack of empathy and still view themselves as good people since they now perceive the refugees as the "bad guys." This process leads to increased discrimination and fear, particularly when media coverage emphasizes negative aspects of the refugee movement. In this way, the search for unfavorable information about refugees helps people cope with cognitive dissonance and maintain a positive self-image.

∞
FEBRUARY

Are Vitamins Really Helping?

February 1st

ILLUSIONS OF CAUSALITY

The illusion of causality occurs when we erroneously perceive a cause-and-effect relationship between two events. Assessing evidence requires cognitive effort, so our brain seeks mental shortcuts to expedite the process. This cognitive bias leads us to hastily infer a causal connection, even if there is none. This stems from our evolutionary need to comprehend the causes of events quickly in our surroundings for the sake of survival.

Many people consume vitamins with the belief that these supplements will enhance their health. Indeed, the global market for vitamins and supplements was valued at a staggering $129.60 billion in 2021. However, a growing body of research and advice from medical professionals suggests that for most healthy individuals, vitamins may not provide benefits beyond those of a placebo and, in some cases, could even be harmful.

One of the key factors driving the consumption of vitamins is a cognitive bias known as the "illusion of causality." This bias leads individuals to mistakenly attribute their recovery from ailments, such as a cold, to the consumption of vitamins. For instance, if a person starts taking vitamin C after experiencing cold symptoms and subsequently recovers, they may erroneously credit the vitamins for their recovery. In reality, their recovery might have occurred naturally over time, irrespective of their vitamin intake.

The efficacy of vitamins in pill form is generally overstated, with most healthy adults not needing them to maintain their health. According to Dr. Cohen from Harvard Medical School, the consumption of a well-balanced diet rich in fruits and vegetables provides all the necessary vitamins. The belief that supplements could somehow shield against diseases or enhance overall health lacks robust scientific support. In fact, excessive intake of certain supplements, like vitamin A and calcium, can lead to adverse health effects, including an increased risk of prostate cancer. Special consideration is warranted for vitamins D, B12, and B6. Strict vegans often require a vitamin B12 supplement and few foods naturally contain significant levels of vitamin D and adequate sunlight exposure can be difficult to achieve, even during summer months.

Why Exactly Did I Get That Tattoo?

February 2nd

END-OF-HISTORY ILLUSION

The end-of-history illusion refers to our tendency to underestimate the extent of personal changes that will occur in the future. While we acknowledge that our personalities, values, and tastes have evolved over time, we often believe that they will remain relatively stable going forward. This misconception persists regardless of age. The illusion arises because we find it hard to imagine personal changes and thus assume that such changes are unlikely to occur.

Did you ever get a permanent tattoo, only to regret your decision a few years later? Perhaps you never anticipated that your tastes and preferences would change so much in the future. If you had strong feelings about a tattoo idea that meant a lot to you, you might have assumed that you would always feel that way, except that you didn't. Don't worry; you are not alone. The global tattoo removal market was worth $4.34 billion in 2021. It is estimated to reach $12.15 billion by 2030, which is roughly the GDP of Namibia.

The reason you assumed that a temporary preference could be a permanent decision is that you were under the end-of-history illusion. According to this bias, we underestimate how much we are going to change in the future and erroneously believe that our major changes are already behind us. While it was natural to undergo a lot of change in your teenage and early adulthood years, your personality is now more stable and will remain so for the rest of your life. This is how the end-of-history illusion lies to you. In reality, you're always changing. While some changes may not feel as dramatic and intense as previous ones, you're not staying the same either. Your environment, the world changing, and the natural passing of time are all leaving their mark on who you are.

Now that you know that, perhaps you can better understand where those tattoo regrets come from. Perhaps you'll also be more cautious about permanent decisions. Nothing ever stays the same, even if it feels like it does.

What's the Real Struggle with Stuttering?

February 3rd

HALO EFFECT

The halo effect is a type of cognitive bias in which our overall opinion of a person or brand affects how we feel about the specific qualities of that person or brand. If we have a good feeling about something as a whole, we are more likely to think that its individual parts are good as well. We do that because it saves cognitive effort to use our overall impressions as a shortcut to make judgments rather than evaluating each aspect of something separately.

Stuttering is a speech disorder that affects one's fluency and flow of speech. However, communication is not the most severely affected aspect of someone who stutters. People with this speech disorder often struggle with bad self-image, low self-confidence, and social anxiety. These issues are often caused by the feedback they receive from others. For instance, children with stuttering are frequently bullied in school or perceived to be less capable and intelligent than others.

One reason for this attitude towards stuttering is the halo effect. According to this bias, we tend to perceive people as a whole based on some distinct aspects of their personalities, such as looks, intelligence, or morality. If someone is outstandingly smart, the halo effect will improve our overall impression of them, even if they're not the most ethical or best-looking person. The opposite happens to people who struggle with stuttering: they are likely to be perceived as inferior because of their speech problems. Research studies point to the fact that people who stutter are stereotyped as more hesitant, tense, insecure, and self-conscious than non-stutterers.

One famous person who struggled with this issue was Joe Biden. President Biden said in an interview that "stuttering is the only handicap that people still laugh about" and empowered young people to overcome the low self-esteem that occurs as a result of this problem. Perhaps they need to overcome their negative halo effect and not let a speech difficulty affect their self-image.

Watch Joe Biden share a story on how he overcame stuttering

Is Your GPS a Roadmap to Disaster or Trusty Co-Pilot?

February 4th

AUTOMATION BIAS

Automation bias means that we are likely to follow the advice of automated systems, like those in airplane cockpits or on your phone (think autocorrect, Google Maps). We tend to ignore contradictory information made without automation, even if it is correct. In decision-making, we like to take the path of least cognitive effort. We are happy to accept the answers that automated systems give us because it is often easier than having to think for ourselves.

Maybe you've been there before. You follow Google or Apple Maps without thinking because you are driving in an area you have never been before. The next thing you know, your car is sitting in the middle of a crowded farmer's market. You're bewildered and apologetic while people yell at you to move your vehicle. If you feel bad about this, know that there are worse cases out there.

For example, some people trusted their GPS so much that they drove straight into the Pacific Ocean. It happened to a group of Japanese tourists visiting Moreton Bay in Australia who were patiently following their navigation system's instructions to get to North Stradbroke Island. The three tourists noticed they had entered the bay, but since the GPS told them to drive ahead, they carried on. About 50 yards into the bay, they realized they weren't able to drive any further. They attempted to turn around, but the incoming tide forced them to leave the vehicle behind. By 3 p.m., the car was stuck in 2 meters of water.

As funny as this story sounds, it also shows the dangers of our overreliance on automated systems. Unfortunately, these systems are also subject to errors, even if we think they aren't. So even if we use automation in our lives, it doesn't hurt to run through our minds. Unless you really like to find yourself in unusual places, such as the Pacific Ocean.

Read about another case of overreliance on navigation systems

Survival of the Fittest Frame:
How Does Perspective Impact Decisions?

February 5th

FRAMING EFFECT

The framing effect occurs when we draw different conclusions from identical information based solely on how that information is presented. This can happen when something is framed either positively or negatively, or as a gain versus a loss - we naturally tend to avoid losses in such situations. Our judgment can also shift depending on which features of the information are highlighted, even though the underlying facts remain exactly the same.

In an intriguing study examining the framing effect, researchers presented identical treatment options to both cancer patients and healthy volunteers, but with different framing approaches. Participants were divided into three groups. The first group received positively framed information, such as "With this treatment, there is a 70% chance of survival." The second group encountered a negative frame: "This treatment carries a 30% probability of dying." The third group received both probabilities. Despite the treatments being identical, the framing led to markedly different choices.

When survival was emphasized, participants – both cancer patients and healthy volunteers – demonstrated a stronger preference for the more effective, albeit toxic, treatment. The term 'survival' appeared to instill hope, encouraging patients to consider a potent treatment despite its potential side effects.

Interestingly, the pattern shifted when survival chances fell below 50%. The preference for the toxic treatment declined significantly, with an even steeper decrease when the dying probability was highlighted. This switch suggested that a higher perceived risk of mortality shifted participants' focus from quantity to quality of life.

The study underscores the power of communication in influencing decision-making, offering a vital lesson for healthcare providers. They must remain mindful of the framing effect when discussing treatment options, as the manner of presenting information can significantly influence a patient's treatment preferences.

Workplace Favoritism Is Annoying and Irrational

February 6th

AVAILABILITY BIAS

The availability bias is our tendency to make decisions based on information that comes to mind quickly and easily. It's a mental shortcut that gives more weight to information that was learned recently or that is easy to remember, for example, because it is an emotionally loaded memory. Our brain wants to save mental energy. So, we often go with the first information that comes to mind instead of putting in more mental effort to dig deeper.

It's no secret that workplace decisions aren't always fair. You may have witnessed colleagues with less experience getting promoted or receiving benefits before you. Similarly, it can be frustrating when your boss doesn't seem to recall your hard work and expertise when discussing a raise.

Nonetheless, not all workplace decisions are made with ill intent. Some simply result from human error, particularly due to the availability bias. This cognitive bias causes us to give more weight to events that personally affected us or had an emotional impact on our own experience. Here's a specific example:

Two employees with comparable leadership abilities are being considered for a promotion. The first employee makes a small error on a project they are working on, but this mistake has no immediate consequences for the hiring manager. On the other hand, the second employee makes a mistake of equal gravity, but this error has an immediate impact on the manager. Consequently, the manager's schedule is disrupted, causing them emotional distress. While the first employee's mistake was just as significant, it didn't affect the manager or create any additional problems.

Which employee is less likely to be promoted—the first or the second? Since people tend to remember emotionally charged memories more vividly, the hiring manager is more likely to recall the second employee's error because it had a direct influence on their emotions. This demonstrates how the availability bias can unconsciously influence workplace decisions, even when decision-makers intend to be fair.

To Sell Or Not To Sell?

February 7th

ENDOWMENT EFFECT

The endowment is the idea that when we own an object, we tend to value it more than we would if it were someone else's. The mere feeling of ownership makes us value it more. One reason for this effect is that we are loss-averse. We really dislike losing things. Ownership therefore influences how we value an object and how much we are willing to accept in exchange for it.

Imagine that you bid in an eBay auction for an iPad. You are the highest bidder, and you already imagine how nice it will be to relax with the iPad and coffee on your couch on Sunday, reading news articles. Two minutes before the end of the auction, someone dares to bid higher. You are likely to surpass your initial budget to acquire the iPad you already imagined owning.

In the same way, wine connoisseurs who purchase a case of fine wine may be reluctant to sell it, even if that wine has increased in value enormously. They may even prefer to drink the wine themselves rather than sell it to someone else. As research has consistently demonstrated, people typically demand far more to sell something they own than they would be willing to spend to buy it in the first place. Both examples illustrate the endowment effect in action.

The endowment effect manifests in many ways, typically because of the psychological attachment we develop to things we own. This is what makes "try before you buy" such a compelling marketing tool. It allows buyers to form attachments to things before making a purchase.

Even primatologists researching chimpanzees and orangutans have found evidence of the endowment effect. Such findings suggest that it may be part of our evolutionary history to attach more value to something we possess than what we would pay to acquire the same thing if we didn't already own it. For this reason, the endowment effect is closely related to loss aversion, since we are more reluctant to lose something we have than to gain something of equivalent value.

What Would It Take For a Philosopher to Skip Their Bubble Bath?

February 8th

OSTRICH EFFECT OR NORMALCY BIAS

Normalcy bias, also known as "ostrich effect," makes us downplay warnings about dangers or ignore negative situations completely. We underestimate how likely it is that a disaster will happen and how it might affect us. We do that because we want to avoid an unpleasant emotional impact in the short term. The name comes from the popular (but false) belief that ostriches bury their heads in the sand when in danger.

We all avoid confronting painful realities from time to time, such as checking our loan account or hopping on the scale after an indulgent holiday. If you feel bad about your lack of bravery, it might comfort you to know that there are some people who could take their bath while the world around them was literally burning.

This thinking error, our inability to confront difficult situations, earned its name "the ostrich effect" because we all tend to stick our heads in the sand when we're not in the mood to deal with bad news. The Roman philosopher Gaius Plinius Secundus, known as Pliny the Elder, demonstrated this effect in perhaps the most unusual situation imaginable. According to letters preserved by his nephew, Pliny the Elder liked to take his time, even when the famous volcano Vesuvius was about to erupt right next to him.

The letter described: "[Pliny the Elder] ordered a bath to be got ready, and then, after having bathed, sat down to supper with great cheerfulness. Meanwhile, broad flames shone out in several places from Mount Vesuvius. But my uncle, in order to soothe the apprehensions of his friend, assured him it was only the burning of the villages, which the country people had abandoned to the flames."

Why look around you to see the world on fire when you can deny it and just take a bath? Coincidentally or not, Pliny died in Pompeii, the Roman city that was destroyed due to the volcanic eruption of Mount Vesuvius.

Are Police Officers Snoozing on Equality?

February 9th

STEREOTYPING

Stereotypes exist when we think that a category of people always has certain characteristics or behaviors. The brain has a natural tendency to put things into groups. By grouping into categories, we can process our environments more efficiently. It is a mental shortcut that saves time and mental energy. Because of that, we might assume that certain stereotypes apply to a certain member of a group even though we know nothing about that individual.

Can social stereotypes explain the ongoing conflict between police officers and African Americans? Why would those responsible for upholding justice display discriminatory behavior? While there are numerous complex factors at play - including historical inequalities, systemic issues, training methods, and institutional policies - one recent study offers an intriguing glimpse into just one small piece of this complicated puzzle.

A study examining the effect of implicit biases (or unconscious stereotypes) on the perception of African Americans revealed an unexpected connection. Researchers tested eighty police officers using the Implicit Association Test (IAT), a scientific tool that measures unconscious attitudes, to determine whether their responses toward African Americans were influenced by factors such as sleep deprivation. The results showed that police officers demonstrated a stronger tendency to associate people of color with weapons on days when they had insufficient sleep. While this finding about sleep deprivation represents just one small factor in a much broader issue, it suggests that mental fatigue may amplify existing unconscious biases.

Even though this particular bias wasn't consistently present, its emergence during periods of sleep deprivation hints at deeper underlying issues in our society. Unfortunately, this raises broader questions about the objectivity of trusted institutions such as the police. No matter how committed we are to justice and equality, some stereotypes run deeper than our conscious desire to remain unbiased. These prejudices are so deeply embedded that it requires significant mental effort to recognize and overcome them.

Can You Drop Out and Win Like Steve Jobs and Bill Gates?

February 10th

SURVIVORSHIP BIAS

Survivorship bias is the mental short-cut we take when we focus on a certain subgroup that made it through a selection process—the survivors—and ignore the ones that didn't—the failures. Because we don't pay equal attention to both survivors and failures, we might mistakenly assume that a shared trait of the survivors caused their survival. This seduces us to mistake correlation for causation.

Have you ever read the story of a successful college dropout who left a strong mark on the world? Such stories can powerfully shape our thinking about our own educational choices.

People who cite famous college dropouts like Steve Jobs, Bill Gates, and Mark Zuckerberg to justify their decisions to quit formal education fall prey to survivorship bias. Their reasoning goes: "If these successful people didn't need a degree to make it so far in life, neither do I!"

The main problem with this type of reasoning—and survivorship bias in general—is that it blinds us to the thousands of people who also quit college but didn't achieve prosperity. Instead, we focus only on those who "made it," because their stories are the most visible ones. For every college dropout who became successful, there are hundreds of people who weren't as fortunate.

In fact, research shows that 94% of the United States' most successful business leaders graduated from college. This reinforces the strong correlation between education and life achievement. Yet, the stories of Bill Gates, Steve Jobs, and other famous entrepreneurs remain particularly inspiring, precisely because of survivorship bias. They represent the exception, not the rule.

Therefore, it's crucial to remember that we might be subject to survivorship bias when we're tempted to use exceptional examples to guide our decision-making.

Read this article about 10 successful billionaire college dropouts

Mirror, Mirror on the Wall: Are We Building Robots Too Human After All?

February 11th

ANTHROPOMORPHISM

Anthropomorphism is our natural tendency to attribute human traits, emotions, and intentions to non-humans, for example, animals, gods, natural forces, and the like. We do this because we naturally know more about human traits than non-human ones. Therefore, these come easier to mind, and that saves mental energy.

Perhaps one of the clearest examples of our ever-present tendency to anthropomorphize is seen in humanoid robots. These machines are not only designed to have physical features that resemble those of a real person, but they are also programmed to behave like human beings. One notable example is a robot named Ameca, currently in development at a company called Engineered Arts. Ameca is being trained to recognize faces and assess who is paying attention during conversations. As Ameca's creator told The Economist, "Currently, it's the worst-ever party guest. It butts in on every conversation and never shuts up." However, this behavior is expected to change soon.

Society's growing inclination to humanize robots has sparked widespread concerns about an "AI invasion," where machines could potentially overtake our society. This fear stems from our persistent effort to create entities that mirror ourselves in both appearance and behavior – a direct result of our anthropomorphic thinking. As these robots grow increasingly sophisticated, they will undoubtedly assume more of our traditional roles and responsibilities. While transferring certain tasks to machines might seem beneficial in theory, we face a crucial challenge: we are not yet prepared to support those who will find their roles taken over by machines, nor are we prepared to help these individuals find new purpose in a world where human contribution is increasingly diminished.

The more we anthropomorphize objects and invest them with behavior, cognition, and intelligence, the more chances they have to compete with us. If not kept under control, this could become a danger as it conflicts with our desire to control the world around us.

Watch a video of Ameca expressions with GPT-4

Do You Know How Disastrous the Bay of Pigs Invasion Was?

February 12th

GROUPTHINK

Groupthink is when our desire for harmony and conformity within a group leads to dysfunctional decision-making. Group members prioritize agreement over critical evaluation, resulting in a loss of individual creativity and thinking. This can lead to an inflated sense of confidence in the group's abilities, an undervaluation of opponents, group pressure, and potentially harmful actions towards outsiders.

The Bay of Pigs invasion was a botched attempt by anti-Castro Cuban exiles and the CIA to overthrow Fidel Castro's regime in 1961. The initial plan called for a group of approximately 1,400 CIA-trained Cuban exiles to launch an invasion at the Bay of Pigs, with the expectation that their arrival would trigger a widespread popular uprising against Castro's government. The operation was designed to appear as an independent Cuban rebellion, concealing U.S. involvement to maintain plausible deniability. It serves as a striking example of groupthink because it displays high degrees of overconfidence within a group, disregard for other opinions, and, as a result, poor communication and planning.

The U.S. government's overconfidence led them to dismiss crucial concerns raised by military advisors, particularly Colonel Jack Hawkins, who questioned the invasion's feasibility. The group's emphasis on maintaining secrecy overshadowed operational success, while their disregard for external perspectives proved costly. They relied on flawed intelligence that underestimated Castro's forces and ignored Soviet warnings about the invasion plans being compromised.

Compounding the debacle, poor communication and coordination played a significant role. For example, airplanes were painted with Cuban colors and markings in an attempt to pass them off as Castro's aircraft. However, CIA planners gave little thought to the fact that their planes had a solid nose, quite unlike the transparent nose on Castro's planes. Additionally, backup planes arrived an hour late, likely due to confusion over the time zone difference between Nicaragua, where they started, and Cuba.

The Bay of Pigs invasion continues to serve as a prime example of how groupthink can lead to catastrophic failure in decision-making.

A One-Way Ticket with the Bandwagon to Bubble Trouble?

February 13th

BANDWAGON EFFECT

The bandwagon effect refers to the phenomenon in which a belief or behavior becomes more popular as more people adopt it. This can lead to a self-reinforcing cycle, as the increased popularity of the belief or behavior encourages more people to adopt it. The effect is caused by our desire to conform to social norms and our belief that the majority must be correct. It can also be caused by peer pressure and the fear of being left out or made fun of if we don't fit in.

In the world of investing, it's particularly difficult not to fall prey to trends and opportunities that promise to get you rich quick. When everyone around you chooses a certain investment opportunity, your natural tendency will be to jump "on the bandwagon."

A bandwagon trend typically starts with one or several success stories, which lead people to apply the same strategy or follow the same path in hopes of achieving similar results. One notable example is the "dot-com bubble." During the bull market of the late 1990s, massive investments in Internet-based businesses like Qualcomm, MicroStrategy, and Pets.com fueled this well-known speculative bubble.

Because investors were eager to invest billions in the next big Internet sensation, dozens of tech startups emerged. The fundamental issue was that many did not yet have a real product, revenue, or business case. In many instances, these startups possessed nothing more than a domain name. Several of these brand-new Internet firms went public, generating success stories of investors and employees who made fortunes by selling their shares. Despite lacking viable business models, many companies attracted millions of dollars in investment from both private and professional investors. The fear of missing out (FOMO) was a key driver of the bandwagon effect.

Investors felt pressure to join the trend to avoid missing potential gains, leading them to make impulsive decisions without proper research. Unfortunately, the dot-com bubble burst in 2001, causing numerous Internet companies to collapse. In total, the burst of the bubble wiped out $1.7 trillion in value.

Watch this video about the Dot-Com bubble

Was Phaethon the First Dunning-Kruger Poster Boy?

February 14th

DUNNING–KRUGER EFFECT

The Dunning–Kruger effect describes our tendency to overestimate our own abilities in areas that we are unskilled in or lack knowledge in. This happens when we know just enough to think we are great but not enough to tell the difference between good and bad. We just don't know yet what we could do better. The effect also applies to society as a whole. The most uninformed citizens are often also the most confident ones.

The concept of the Dunning-Kruger effect may be modern, but this behavioral pattern has been present throughout human culture and appears in various myths and legends. A striking example is the Greek myth of Phaethon.

In ancient Greek mythology, Phaethon was the mortal son of Helios, the god of the sun. Each day, Helios drove his chariot across the sky, pulling the sun behind him to provide light and warmth to the earth. Desperate to prove his divine heritage, Phaethon insisted on driving his father's sun chariot for a day. Despite Helios's warnings that he was inexperienced and unprepared for such a task, Phaethon remained undeterred, convinced of his ability to control the powerful steeds that pulled the chariot.

As the tale goes, Phaethon quickly lost control of the sun chariot. The consequences were disastrous: scorching the earth, creating deserts, and freezing the outer reaches of the world. In an attempt to restore balance and save the planet, Zeus was forced to strike down Phaethon with a thunderbolt.

Phaethon's overconfidence led him to insist on undertaking a task he was ill-prepared for, ultimately resulting in catastrophic consequences. Despite his complete lack of experience with the chariot, Phaethon believed he could manage it perfectly. This overestimation of his competence perfectly exemplifies the Dunning-Kruger effect: his lack of experience and understanding of the task's complexity blinded him to both the potential risks and his own inadequacy.

Coincidence or Conspiracy?
Why Do We Suddenly See Things Everywhere?

February 15th

FREQUENCY ILLUSION OR BAADER–MEINHOF PHENOMENON

The frequency illusion is when you notice something, you start to notice it every time it happens. This makes you think it happens a lot, even though it doesn't. This bias is also known as the Baader–Meinhof phenomenon. It happens when heightened awareness of something creates the impression that it is happening more frequently than it actually is.

We all have experienced times when we felt that once we heard news about something, it was suddenly everywhere. For example, that book your friend randomly mentioned suddenly seems to be all around you: in commercials, magazines, and conversations between strangers on the subway. What you're experiencing is a common case of the frequency illusion, also known as the Baader-Meinhof phenomenon. It describes the feeling that a concept or thing you just found out about suddenly seems to crop up everywhere.

The effect derives its name from the Baader-Meinhof Group, also referred to as the Red Army Faction (RAF). This was an ultra-left-wing German terrorist group that was predominantly active during the late 1960s. In 1986, a man named Terry Mullen heard for the first time about the group. Subsequently, he started seeing the term in various sources. It seemed as if everyone was talking about it, even though the group hadn't been active since the 1970s. Mullen shared his experience in a letter to a local Minnesota newspaper. Soon, his story created a domino effect among other newspaper readers, who all seemed to experience similar stories with the term. Once they learned about this term, they realized it was everywhere, yet they were profoundly under the influence of the frequency illusion. This led psychologists to call it Baader-Meinhof phenomenon, after the term that made it popular.

Did you get all the details of this story? Your attention processes are now programmed to ensure that you'll notice the Baader-Meinhof effect whenever you encounter it next.

Watch a trailer for the movie "Baader Meinhof Complex"

Can Confirmation Bias Skew Our Views on Vaccines?

February 16th

CONFIRMATION BIAS

Confirmation bias is our tendency to look for, acknowledge, favor, and remember information in a way that supports what we already think or believe. This bias occurs when we ignore information that contradicts our ideas or interpret ambiguous facts as evidence supporting our existing beliefs. Situations that involve emotionally charged topics, strongly held beliefs, or things we really want to happen are most susceptible to this bias.

One of the most notorious examples of confirmation bias in medical history occurred when a researcher's pre-existing beliefs led to a damaging vaccine controversy.

In 1998, a British medical journal, "The Lancet," published a study claiming a definite link between the measles-mumps-rubella (MMR) vaccine and autism in 12 children. The study was conducted by Andrew Wakefield, a former physician and later disgraced academic who would be barred from practicing medicine in 2010. This research became one of the most controversial pieces in the scientific community.

The reason? Later investigations debunked the study's conclusions by revealing that the striking claims were, in fact, nothing but the result of the researcher's biases and manipulation attempts. Wakefield proposed a theory that the MMR vaccine damaged the intestinal lining (causing enterocolitis - inflammation of intestine and colon), which he claimed allowed certain proteins to enter the bloodstream and reach the brain, supposedly leading to autism. He manipulated and altered the data from interviews with parents and children to fit these pre-existing ideas about the dangers of vaccines.

Subsequent discussions about the ethical concerns of the study proposed that one key factor leading to these results was the researcher's confirmation bias. In this case, the confirmation bias manifested in Wakefield's unwavering belief that vaccines caused autism while rejecting any information that might contradict his perspective.

Read an article about how Andrew Wakefield fueled autism-vaccine fears

Are We Biased Towards Zero-Risk, Even When It's Not the Best Option?

February 17th

ZERO RISK BIAS

The Zero Risk Bias is a mental shortcut that makes us prefer a risk-free option, even if this choice is not the most rational or beneficial one. In uncertain situations, the mere possibility of something happening is emotionally more important than how likely it is to happen. So, we'd rather get rid of the possibility all together.

Biased thinking fuels irrational judgments. This is more likely to happen in situations that involve a degree of risk to our health and lives. Getting rid of one relatively small risk entirely is often given more importance than being efficient and making sound decisions. This is what the zero-risk bias means.

The following study is an excellent example. Participants were asked to rate a made-up scenario about cleaning up the polluted landfills of two cities. Let's call these cities Metropolis and Gotham. The landfill in Metropolis could cause eight cases of cancer annually, while the landfill in Gotham could lead to four cases annually. How would you rank the following three alternative approaches?

Option one would reduce the number of cancer cases from eight to four for Metropolis and from four to two for Gotham. Option two would reduce the number of cancer cases from eight to six and from four to zero. The third option would reduce cancer cases from eight to three and from four to three.

Even though option two is the worst option for reducing cancer cases, 42% of those who responded thought it was better than at least one of the other options. Zero-risk bias led people to prefer the reduction of cases to zero for one site, even if the total number of lives saved with this strategy is lower than the number that would be saved if the same resources had been expended toward partially cleaning up two different waste sites. We humans have a strong preference for total risk removal over partial risk reduction.

Is the Fear of Loss Ruining Your Investments?

February 18th

LOSS AVERSION

Loss aversion means that the perceived loss of value from losing an object is greater than the perceived value of getting it. The pain of losing is twice as strong as the pleasure of gaining. The factors that influence this bias have been extensively researched. Among others are cultural factors (collectivist cultures have less loss aversion than individualist cultures) and socio-economic factors (powerful and wealthy people are less loss-averse).

Reflecting on your past investing mistakes may provide some solace when you consider this phenomenon. In 1985, research scientists Shefrin and Statman investigated how the fear of loss can lead even seasoned investors to make poor financial choices. The discomfort associated with losing often prompts investors to hold on to stocks that have decreased in value (relative to their purchase price) while selling those that have risen in value since the time of purchase. This behavior is characterized by the tendency to sell winners too early and ride losers too long.

It's important to differentiate between unrealized and realized gains and losses in this context. When a stock's value fluctuates, it represents a "paper gain or loss," which only becomes realized when the stock is sold. Selling a stock that has increased in value creates a realized gain, while selling one that has decreased results in a realized loss.

Research has shown that stocks performing well in the last six months are more likely to continue performing well in the next six months, while those performing poorly tend to maintain that trend. The logical approach would be to retain stocks that have recently appreciated in value and sell those that have declined. However, many investors exhibit a tendency to do the opposite.

This phenomenon occurs because people generally fear losses more than they appreciate gains. In the long run, it's often better to accept a loss and move on to a new investment opportunity rather than cling to the hope that a losing investment will eventually turn in our favor.

Can We Outsmart Lady Luck?

February 19th

ILLUSION OF CONTROL

The illusion of control occurs when we believe we have more control over external events than we do. We frequently believe we have (or had) some control over events that are actually random. Researchers have found that people who feel in control will engage in healthier behaviors, feel less stress, and have better overall mental health. Therefore, this illusion makes us feel better about ourselves and the world around us, but it can also seduce us into relying on superstitions.

People often think they are in control, even when they are not. For instance, a compelling study of over 130 gambling addicts shows how gamblers believe they possess special skills, knowledge, or other advantages that make them successful at gambling. While gambling is fundamentally a game of chance, they rationalize previous instances when they "did well" to justify their continued gambling and further losses, believing in an inevitable big win.

The illusion of control is not just wishful thinking that somehow things will turn out our way; it's about genuinely believing that we have the ability to change things in our favor. The illusion stems from past situations where we seemingly influenced the odds. This gives us reason to believe that we can use these perceived skills in the future as well.

While it's easy to recognize this illusion when gambling is involved, it manifests in many other aspects of life. Consider your personal relationships: sometimes you might feel that you didn't do enough to make someone like you, but in reality, you're forgetting that there's another person involved in the relationship and that not everything is within your control.

Believing that we are always in control of everything can lead to unnecessary regret, making us think we didn't do all that we could when it was never in our power to determine the outcome.

Feeling Center Stage in the World?

February 20th

SPOTLIGHT EFFECT

The spotlight effect is our tendency to think that other people are paying more attention to us than they really are. It makes us feel like we are always "in the spotlight." This happens because our brains are wired to pay more attention to ourselves than to others. Additionally, we are more aware of changes concerning ourselves compared to others. The effect occurs in both positive (like a personal success) and negative situations (like something we are embarrassed of).

Do you know the movie "The Truman Show"? If not, watch it. In this fantastic film, Jim Carrey portrays Truman Burbank. Unbeknownst to him, Truman has been the protagonist of a popular TV series since infancy. Producer Christof created a fictional world where Truman is constantly watched by more than 5,000 cameras. Later in the film, Truman says, "Maybe I'm losing my mind. But it feels like the whole world revolves around me somehow." In Truman's case, it is actually true. We all experience this feeling occasionally, although probably to a lesser degree. There is a name for that phenomenon: the spotlight effect.

The spotlight effect is a bias that makes us believe there's a spotlight on us at times and that all eyes are scanning every move and gesture we make. Many people have reported feeling very guilty about sneezing or coughing in public during the 2020 pandemic, and that was not only because health behaviors were a huge concern for us but also because we're all likely to be affected by the spotlight effect.

The assumption that people around us closely notice our behavior comes from being overly self-conscious and not realizing that other people's perspectives are different from our own. In reality, most people are too busy thinking about themselves to pay attention to the actions of others. A more accurate way of thinking is to realize that we don't have enough cognitive energy to notice everyone all the time. Besides, we're all too busy thinking about what others think of us. Now that you know this, you're free to leave all that anxiety at home whenever you go out.

Watch the trailer for 'The Truman Show' from 1998

Can Believers Bounce Back from Galactic Ghosting?

February 21st

COGNITIVE DISSONANCE

Cognitive dissonance describes the mental discomfort we experience when there is a conflict between our beliefs, actions, or perceptions. This discomfort often arises when our actions contradict our beliefs or when we hold two opposing beliefs simultaneously. To alleviate this discomfort, we may adjust our beliefs, perceptions, or actions to create a more consistent internal state. Achieving this internal consistency is crucial, as it helps maintain our sense of identity and coherence.

In the 1950s, Leon Festinger undertook a study that would become a hallmark of understanding cognitive dissonance, and it revolved around a UFO cult he infiltrated, known as The Seekers. This group, under Dorothy Martin's leadership, fervently believed that the world would end on December 21, 1954. Dorothy claimed to channel messages from extraterrestrial beings from a distant planet named Clarion.

On December 17th, Dorothy announced that at precisely 4:00 PM, a spaceship would land in her very backyard to take her away. The group prepared for this otherworldly meeting. But as the clock ticked away, no spaceship appeared. As the time passed without a spaceship's arrival, the cult members experienced profound cognitive dissonance, struggling to reconcile their belief in the prophecy with the clear evidence that their anticipated rescue had not occurred. Yet, instead of questioning their beliefs, they came up with an explanation: this was merely a "practice session" for the real event. On December 20th, they eagerly awaited an alien visitor at midnight, expecting to be escorted to a spacecraft. To justify the no-show, the group pointed out a time difference between two room clocks. But when both clocks chimed midnight and no visitor appeared, cognitive dissonance intensified as the group struggled to align the harsh reality with their unwavering belief.

At 4:45 AM on December 21, Dorothy proclaimed a new message from the aliens: Earth's God had chosen to spare the planet, all thanks to the group's unwavering faith. This convenient revelation allowed them to sidestep the crushing weight of cognitive dissonance. They clung to their beliefs, now even more emboldened, thinking they had played a pivotal role in Earth's salvation.

Is Love Really Blind, or Just Stressed Out?

February 22nd

MISATTRIBUTION OF AROUSAL

Misattribution of arousal occurs when we experience physical symptoms of arousal, such as a fast heartbeat or sweaty palms, and incorrectly attribute these symptoms to the wrong cause. This phenomenon arises because various triggers—like fear or romantic excitement—can produce similar physical responses. Our brains, trying to find patterns and make sense of these signals, may link the arousal to an incorrect source.

You might know the Netflix show "Love is Blind." In this famous TV series, 15 men and women go on blind dates to find love. They talk without seeing each other, and they only meet face-to-face after they propose marriage. After that, they have four weeks to live together, meet each other's families, and discover their hobbies. At the end of these 4 weeks, the wedding ceremony takes place, and they decide whether to get married.

When watching the show, you may wonder if it's possible to make a marriage decision in just a few weeks. Could something else be influencing their strong emotions? The misattribution of arousal explains that people can sometimes mistake the cause of their physical symptoms. Feelings like love, fear, or stress cause similar physical signs, such as a faster heartbeat, difficulty breathing, and sweaty hands.

When these symptoms appear, your brain tries to find a reason. It might think, "You're feeling excited; it must be the person you're with!" This theory implies that the love the couples in "Love is Blind" feel could be in some cases due to stress being confused with love. The unfamiliar environment on the set and the immense pressure of making life-changing decisions can create a great deal of stress for the participants in the show. Additionally, being on a Netflix show with millions of viewers can create stress for anyone, right?

In case you wondered: Out of 31 couples who got engaged on the show, nine from six seasons have remained married after saying yes at the altar. Despite potential misattributions in some cases, the show has fostered some lasting marriages.

Watch this "Love Is Blind" trailer

Banking on the Wrong Numbers?

February 23rd

ANCHORING BIAS

Anchoring bias occurs when a specific reference point, or "anchor", influences our decision-making process. This anchor could be a number or any other kind of cue, even if it is completely unrelated to the decision at hand. Despite this, we often use the anchor as a starting point and adjust our decisions or judgments from there, without realizing it. As a result, our final estimates, decisions, or judgments can be significantly different from what they might have been without the influence of the anchor.

The anchoring effect is one of the most commonly used heuristics in human judgment and decision-making. One fascinating eye-tracking study showed that people rely on simple initial details that greatly influence their financial decision-making.

In the eye-tracking experiment, people visually scanned a fee information document for a potential new account in a bank and only paid attention to certain, very present information, such as the annual fee, while disregarding other overall costs or benefits. When asked to compare the first document to another one, they compared the two offers just in regards to the information they were anchored on first and made decisions based that.

If the charge associated with the annual fee in one offer was higher than in the other, people got anchored on this information only. They failed to integrate other annual fees displayed in the document, such as debit cards, prepaid cards, and home banking. As a result, they missed important big-picture details that could help them recognize the most advantageous products. For example, if the annual fee charge was high, subjects completely overlooked other features that compensated for this cost and made the offer more advantageous.

This visual search strategy, influenced by the anchoring bias, distorts our financial behavior, especially for individuals who are not highly financially literate. To ensure that we do not get too stuck on certain details that make an offer seem better, we have to actually read the small print.

Why Are Gifted Children Often Bullied?

February 24rd

CRAB-BUCKET EFFECT

The Crab-bucket effect is a metaphor used to describe a situation where someone is trying to climb up and achieve something, but they are constantly being pulled down by others who are not supportive or who try to hinder their progress. The idea behind the metaphor comes from how crabs actually act when they are stuck in a bucket. If one crab tries to climb out of the bucket, the other crabs will grab onto it and pull it back down.

Crab fishermen do not need to buy lids for their crab buckets. It might sound like a very random statement, but it can teach us a lot. If one crab tries to get out of the bucket, the others will stop it. The fisherman may leave the bucket without a cover because he knows that every time one crab attempts to escape, the others will make an extra effort to bring it back into the bucket.

Sometimes, it's difficult for us humans to feel happy about other people's achievements. It might have to do with the fact that we perceive their success as a threat or that if others succeed while we fail, we feel inferior. These attitudes can be so intense that we might even unknowingly sabotage the success of those around us. We might withhold our support, discourage them, or—worst of all—bully and mock them.

Perhaps this explains why kids don't always like the kids who stand out in a good way at school. Even worse, they are often the target of bullying and exclusion from social groups. Crowds and groups do not feel happy when one of their members gets further ahead or surpasses the norm. So, to prevent it from getting out of the social bucket, they sabotage the outlier's efforts in order to keep them in the same place. In a sense, crab behavior attempts to maintain the status quo and ensure that all group members remain equal.

What's More Deadly: Fireworks or Asthma?

February 25th

AVAILABILITY BIAS

The availability bias is our tendency to make decisions based on information that comes to mind quickly and easily. It's a mental shortcut that gives more weight to information that was learned recently or that is easy to remember, for example, because it is an emotionally loaded memory. Our brain wants to save mental energy. So, we often go with the first information that comes to mind instead of putting in more mental effort to dig deeper.

What is the correct order for the following causes of death, from common to rare: tornadoes, asthma, fireworks, and drowning?

You probably ended up with a similar order: tornadoes, fireworks, asthma, and drowning. But don't worry if, like many other people, you got this wrong. Our propensity is to vastly overestimate the likelihood of deaths from tornadoes and fireworks while drastically underestimating those from asthma and drowning. In fact, to be more precise, each year in the U.S., about 8 to 10 people die from fireworks, about 80 die due to tornadoes, about 3,500 die from asthma, and close to 4,000 drown. The reason you probably made incorrect guesses about these numbers is that you're exposed to news about each type of death in entirely different amounts. If you open a newspaper, chances are you'll see news about someone dying because of fireworks rather than asthma. Why? Some deaths, like drowning and asthma, are so common that they don't make attention-grabbing news. Because of this, such incidents rarely make the headlines.

What we see in the media has major implications for how we construct our worldview. If we expose ourselves to news of big tragedies, we're more likely to use that available information when drawing conclusions about the state of the world. We do this because of the availability bias, which prioritizes information that comes to our minds quickly and easily. This explains why we were wrong about the death causes above – their media availability makes them seem more frequent than they actually are.

Is Your Partner Really Slacking, or Are You Just Biased?

February 26th

SELF-SERVING BIAS

The self-serving bias is our tendency to take credit for good things that happen to us and blame other things or people for bad things that happen. We do that because we have the desire to feel good about ourselves. Being responsible for good things happening boosts our confidence and gives us a sense of control in our lives. When we blame external factors for bad things that happen to us, it can help us feel better about ourselves by protecting our ego.

One common source of conflict among couples is dissatisfaction with the perceived effort each partner puts into the relationship. For instance, you and your partner recently moved in together and are working to make your house feel welcoming. You sense that your partner is not nearly as eager to engage as you are. However, before jumping to conclusions, you should question whether your perception of your efforts versus your partner's efforts is accurate.

There is a good chance that self-serving bias is interfering with your judgment. This cognitive bias makes it easy for us to notice our own efforts and attribute successful outcomes to ourselves, while leaving us with a diminished ability to recognize other people's contributions. When it comes to failures and shortcomings, the pattern reverses: we often find a scapegoat to put the blame on and remain oblivious to the part we played in it.

Behavioral scientist Dan Ariely illustrated self-serving bias perfectly in one of his "Talks with Google." He suggested asking any couple how much of the household chores each person individually contributes. Their answers will invariably add up to more than 100%. This occurs because it is easy for us to see our own contributions. "I do all the cooking. It takes so much time. My partner pays the bills. Easy stuff."

Due to our inability to perceive all the contributions of others, we frequently underestimate the efforts of the people around us.

Are We Seeing Predictions or Just Connecting Dots?

February 27th

HINDSIGHT BIAS

The hindsight bias is also called the "I-knew-it-all-along" effect. It describes the retrospective overestimation of predictability. In the present, it's hard to tell how something will turn out in the future, but is easy to understand how or why an event happened in retrospect. This bias happens because we mistakenly assume that we had the same understanding of an event before it happened as we do after it happened.

Indeed, it's significantly easier to draw connections between a statement and an event after the event has occurred. Consider, for example, the belief that Nostradamus foretold the terrorist attack on the World Trade Center in New York. This interpretation becomes plausible when reading the following lines:

"Earthshaking fire from the centre of the earth will cause tremors around the New City. Two great rocks will war for a long time, then Arethusa will redden a new river."

With the World Trade Center event in our historical context, we might interpret the two great rocks as the towers, the new city as New York, and the center of the earth, metaphorically, as the World Trade Center. Further, the mention of Arethusa and a new river could metaphorically refer to the 9/11 Memorial's waterfalls within the footprints of the towers. Arethusa, in classical mythology, is a nymph who transformed into a fountain, an image that aligns with the transformation of the towers' sites into reflective pools. However, this association largely stems from hindsight bias. After an event occurs, it's easy to link Nostradamus's ambiguous phrases to it, but these interpretations are always made after the fact; they only appear predictive when viewed through the lens of hindsight.

Similarly, some argue that Nostradamus predicted Queen Elizabeth II's death. "Because they disapproved of his divorce. A man who later they considered unworthy. The People will force out the King of the islands. A Man will replace who never expected to be king." In light of Queen Elizabeth II's passing and King Charles's ascension, these words seem like an accurate prediction. But without the actual events, the prophecy's meaning remains vague and ambiguous.

Can Familiarity Breed Liking for Words We Do Not Understand?

February 28th

MERE EXPOSURE EFFECT

The mere exposure effect says the more we are exposed to something, the more we like it. Familiarity breeds liking. When asked to make a choice, we tend to prefer what is familiar, even if this is not the optimal choice. One reason for this behavior is that evolution has taught us to be careful around new things. Everything unfamiliar could be potentially dangerous. When we see something over and over again without any bad results, we assume it is safe.

In cognitive science, it is no longer a secret that our preference for something increases the more we become familiar with it. This is why we may develop feelings for work colleagues we see daily or enjoy the food we eat regularly. Very often, it is the feeling of familiarity that makes us fonder of people, environments, and foods. But does this acquired liking also increase for words we don't even know the meaning of?

A field experiment tested the idea that simply being exposed to a stimulus (e.g., a word) multiple times increases one's preference for it. Advertisements in a newspaper used by two universities exposed their readers to five different Turkish-sounding words. These words were displayed at various frequencies in the newspaper, meaning that some of them were read very often while others were displayed more rarely.

In the second part of the experiment, the readers of the newspaper, who had the chance of being exposed to these words, were given some questionnaires that asked them to rate how good or bad the Turkish words sounded. The results of the study mirrored the assumption of the mere exposure effect; more specifically, the respondents gave the highest rating to the words they read most often. In contrast, the words they were least exposed to received the lowest ratings. The words exposed at intermediate frequencies were given moderate ratings.

Interestingly, despite the readers being unaware of the meanings of these words—which, in fact, held no meaning in any language—the most frequently encountered words were still rated as having a better sound.

How Does Gender Affect How We Judge Leaders' Mistakes?

February 29th

GENDER BIAS

Gender bias refers to a widely held set of implicit biases that discriminate against one gender. These biases include stereotypes like men being more logical and women more emotional. When there are no gender indicators, people often default to assuming subjects are male. Gender bias also manifests in double standards used to judge behavior - for instance, when men are praised for their sexual activities while women are derogated.

Not all mistakes are equal. Research shows that gender significantly influences how corporate leaders are judged for different types of mistakes. This disparity reveals how deeply gender bias affects leadership evaluation, with each gender facing harsher criticism in different areas.

In a revealing study, participants read news articles about an auto manufacturer's leader. The articles varied in two key aspects: the leader's gender and the type of mistake made (ethical or competence-related). After reading, participants indicated their likelihood of purchasing a vehicle from the company.

The results revealed a clear pattern of gender-based double standards. When women leaders made ethical mistakes, such as misleading stakeholders or making morally questionable decisions, people reported significantly lower purchase intentions compared to when men made similar mistakes. However, when men demonstrated competence-related errors, such as poor strategic decisions or management failures, they faced notably harsher judgment than women making the same mistakes.

These findings reflect deeply ingrained gender expectations in our society. Women are typically viewed as more attuned to others' needs and expected to maintain high ethical standards, leading to harsher criticism when they fail in this domain. Men are traditionally expected to demonstrate strong competencies and leadership skills, resulting in more severe judgment when they show professional incompetence. This differential treatment shows how gender stereotypes create unfair evaluation standards for both male and female leaders.

∞
MARCH

Can You Judge the Quality of a Decision Separately from the Outcome?

March 1st

OUTCOME BIAS

We are subject to outcome bias when we judge a decision by its outcome. This is biased because we should rather base our judgment on the quality of the decision at the time it was made, given what was known at that time. We never have all the information we need, and every result has random and unpredictable parts. Bad outcomes are not always a sign of bad decision-making.

Let us take a look at a very interesting experiment, where a group of researchers wanted to see how people evaluate someone's competence and decision-making skills based on different outcomes.

In this experiment, participants were asked to evaluate a medical decision on a scale from 3 (clearly correct) to −3 (incorrect and inexcusable). They were presented with a medical scenario, consisting of a case, a decision, and an outcome. The researchers reminded the participants to "evaluate the decision itself and the quality of thinking that went into it." The first scenario involved a 55-year-old man with a heart condition who received advice from his doctor to have a bypass operation. The surgery had an 8% chance of death. In this scenario, the operation succeeded. Since the outcome was favorable, most participants agreed that the decision-maker was competent and the doctor's thinking process was sound.

The second scenario had a different outcome: this time, a negative one in which the patient died. The doctor had access to the same exact information as in the first scenario. In this case, participants rated the doctor's decision-making more negatively, attributing the poor outcome to erroneous thinking. It is obvious how the outcome (positive versus negative) changed participants' perception of the doctor's decision.

This is the result of outcome bias, which makes us evaluate the quality of a decision solely through the lenses of its outcome.

Are Celebrities Truly as Perfect as They Seem?

March 2nd

HALO EFFECT

The halo effect is a type of cognitive bias in which our overall opinion of a person or brand affects how we feel about the specific qualities of that person or brand. If we have a good feeling about something as a whole, we are more likely to think that its individual parts are good as well. We do that because it saves cognitive effort to use our overall impressions as a shortcut to make judgments rather than evaluating each aspect of something separately.

Can you imagine a celebrity who's classy, attractive, and wealthy making awkward mistakes, using bad words, or being racist? If you find this exercise a little difficult, your judgment might be affected by the halo effect. According to this bias, we generalize someone's strong traits across their entire personality. What results is a shallow perception of people based on a single aspect or trait they have.

The halo effect might also be the reason we idolize celebrities as "perfect." If someone is famous, talented, rich, and attractive, it's difficult to imagine that they, too, make mistakes. Consider this story about the actress Reese Witherspoon. During one driving incident, she was extremely rude to a police officer who pulled her over, which led to her arrest for disorderly conduct. She ignored the police officer's instruction to stay in the car, resisted arrest, and even arrogantly asked him if he knew who she was.

If you are a Reese Witherspoon fan, this story might shock you a bit. You may remember her as someone nice, talented, and an overall good person. Your perception of Reese Witherspoon was constructed around largely positive attributes, and you never thought that her behavior could be so outrageous that she would get arrested. Of course, in theory, you know that someone can make terrible mistakes, regardless of how kind, well-intentioned, or talented they are. Yet these negative aspects of someone's personality are not the first ones that come to mind when you think of a celebrity you deeply admire.

Read this article with photos of Reese Witherspoon being arrested for disorderly conduct

How Did the Normalcy Bias Contribute to the Catastrophe of Katrina?

March 3rd

OSTRICH EFFECT OR NORMALCY BIAS

Normalcy bias, also known as "ostrich effect," makes us downplay warnings about dangers or ignore negative situations completely. We underestimate how likely it is that a disaster will happen and how it might affect us. We do that because we want to avoid an unpleasant emotional impact in the short term. The name comes from the popular (but false) belief that ostriches bury their heads in the sand when in danger.

In 2005, during Hurricane Katrina, one of the deadliest hurricanes in U.S. history, New Orleans authorities issued an emergency evacuation order. Despite the warnings, some residents chose to stay, a decision that may seem baffling to many. The reasoning behind this decision was complex. While financial constraints played a role for some residents, another significant psychological factor was at work: the normalcy bias.

New Orleans residents had long been accustomed to storms, given the city's geographical location. Many had grown up witnessing the power of these storms, and over time, they had developed a sense of complacency or even invulnerability. When Hurricane Katrina, a storm of unprecedented magnitude, approached, some residents chose to stay, believing it would be just another storm they could weather, as they had done before. They waited for the storm to pass, not fully grasping its severity, even as authorities warned of the impending danger.

Unfortunately, the storm they had normalized was far from normal. The National Hurricane Center reported that the event was directly or indirectly responsible for 1,833 fatalities, making it a stark reminder of the power of nature. Katrina also caused an estimated $161 billion in damage, making it the costliest hurricane in U.S. history at that time. The storm destroyed or damaged more than 850,000 homes. The conditions some people had normalized far exceeded their definition of normal, leading to devastating losses of life and property.

Too Many Pills to Swallow:
Do More Choices Lead to Worse Decisions?

March 4th

DEFAULT EFFECT

When offered a choice that has a pre-selected default option, we tend to choose this default option. This is called the default effect. Defaults are the options that take effect if we do nothing. Our brains try to save as much mental energy as possible. Accepting the default option saves energy because we don't have to think about the pros and cons of each choice.

Imagine you are undergoing treatment with your trusted doctor for persistent hip issues. You've tried multiple medications and therapies, but unfortunately, none have alleviated your symptoms. Your doctor ultimately suggests surgery to get our hip replaced. However, upon reviewing your medical records, your doctor realizes there is still one untried medication. If this medication is effective, surgery may not be necessary.

A study presented this scenario to a large group of experienced doctors, but with a variation. For some physicians, the number of untried medications was two instead of one. This seemingly minor difference shouldn't affect the doctors' recommendations, right?

Interestingly, the physicians' recommendations did vary depending on the number of potential medications. When there were two untested drugs, the challenge of choosing between them led most doctors to forgo recommending either treatment, opting instead to proceed with surgery, the current default option. Conversely, when there was only one untried medication, physicians found it easier to recommend the new treatment and delay surgery.

The study revealed that when faced with the complexity of deciding between two different medications, many physicians simply adhered to the default option of surgery. No reasonable physician would favor hip replacement surgery over two unexplored medications upon consultation; however, when surgery is established as the default option, the influence of the default effect determines the course of action.

Watch Dan Ariely's TED Talk

Can Your Voting Booth Location Influence Your Vote?

March 5th

PRIMING EFFECT

The priming effect occurs when something we see or hear influences our thoughts or actions without us being aware of it. This can happen with words, pictures, or sounds we encounter. When our brain is primed, it becomes easier for us to think about, remember, and act on related information because the things we read, see, or hear activate connected information in the brain.

Voting is rarely an objective choice. There are many factors that influence the political parties, social initiatives, or projects we support. Take, for instance, the location of the voting station—something you might not expect to have an impact. It turns out that environmental visual cues, such as the location of the polling station, can influence voting behavior.

These cues can "prime" our brain to perceive a situation in a new way. Yet we're not always aware of this subtle influence. According to the priming effect, exposure to a cue (such as the surroundings in which we vote) can inadvertently influence our actions (voting behavior). While this may seem surprising, it was the conclusion of a research study. In 2000, people in Arizona were asked to express their votes for a local decision to increase funding for school facilities. Naturally, the polling stations were spread out in different locations, which allowed researchers to compare how voting environments influence campaign outcomes.

When analyzing the number of final votes, researchers found that there were significantly more votes in favor of school funding from those who voted in a school precincts than those who voted in random locations. Despite voters' personal political beliefs, demographics, or the specific characteristics of their neighborhood, those who cast their ballots in a school were more inclined to support school funding initiatives.

The explanation for this? Researchers claimed that it has to do with the priming effect - the school environment acted as a "primer" for voters' decisions, reminding them of the importance of education.

What Price Do We Pay for Free Games?

March 6th

SUNK COST FALLACY

The sunk cost fallacy is when we make a decision based on how much we have already invested in something rather than on whether it is the best choice for us right now. When we feel like we have already invested a lot in something, we feel like we would be losing something if we were to let it go. Another reason that the sunk cost fallacy occurs is because we tend to focus on the past rather than the present when we make decisions.

This psychological principle is particularly evident in the gaming industry. One easy way to hook people into an internet game is to let them play for free. Game developers have something precious to gain from this strategy: people's commitment. Once someone is hooked, they will not want to let their invested time go to waste, so they'll keep playing. Many mobile games feature large in-game shops and persistent banners that urge players to buy items to progress faster. Players who are unwilling to spend money are instead forced through grinding and repetitive tasks to obtain the resources they need to advance in the game.

A prime example of this is the mobile game Diablo Immortal, an action role-playing game that received very poor ratings from players due to its perceived heavy focus on monetization tactics. One reviewer describes the issue many players see: "This is not a game; it is psychological warfare. It starts out fair on lower levels to hook you in, then they start pulling every trick in the book to convince you to spend money for nothing in return. One would assume that there were more psychologists working on the game than there were gameplay programmers and designers." If that were the case, these psychologists' main tool was the sunk cost fallacy.

Previous investments of money, time, and effort in a game are a powerful motivator for continued play. And this strategy works: Diablo Immortal was an unbelievably huge financial success for the company behind the game. The game grossed more than $300 million globally, just five months after its initial release, proving how effectively the sunk cost fallacy can be exploited in game design.

Read some user review of Diablo Immortal

Won't Somebody Please Think of the Children?

March 7th

FRAMING EFFECT

The framing effect occurs when we draw different conclusions from identical information based solely on how that information is presented. This can happen when something is framed either positively or negatively, or as a gain versus a loss - we naturally tend to avoid losses in such situations. Our judgment can also shift depending on which features of the information are highlighted, even though the underlying facts remain exactly the same.

The surge in children diagnosed with gender dysphoria seeking gender-affirming care has ignited a divisive debate in the US. The framing effect significantly influences the narratives on both sides.

Progressives frame the rise in children seeking gender care as a sign of social progress and freedom, arguing that access to gender-affirming care, including puberty blockers, hormone therapies, and surgeries, is crucial for transgender children's well-being.

Conversely, conservatives view the same information as evidence of a harmful practice causing irreversible damage to minors. They argue that these medical interventions, labeled "mutilation," pose risks to minors' physical and mental health and should be restricted or banned. Florida's recent rule prohibiting puberty blockers, hormone therapies, or surgeries for gender dysphoria in minors exemplifies the conservative stance. Republican lawmakers are advancing a bill that would criminalize providing gender-affirming care to minors and ban state funds for covering such care for adults. Governor DeSantis defended the rule, stating it is not "sinful" to prohibit the "mutilation" of minors.

While both perspectives aim to protect the well-being of children, the framing effect highlights the challenges of finding common ground for constructive dialogue.

Are We Assembling Our Own Overwork Nightmare?

March 8th

IKEA EFFECT

The IKEA effect refers to our tendency to place a disproportionately high value on objects that we helped create, such as IKEA furniture. We do that regardless of the quality of the end product. This bias helps us to feel better about ourselves in two ways. First, we want to feel that our effort was well invested and that we did not waste our time but instead created something of value. Secondly, creating things makes us feel more competent.

Despite having access to advanced technology that can ease our workload, many of us still prefer to burden ourselves with endless tasks, both in our personal lives and the workplace. Some seem to wear tiredness as a badge of honor. We feel valuable when we decline events because we are busy. And even when we have a day off, we find a way to fill it with things to do. Why do we feel greater satisfaction when we put more effort than necessary into our lives? If you don't, you probably know someone who fits the description.

According to the IKEA effect, people see things as more valuable when they have been partially involved in assembling them. When we work harder for something instead of obtaining it on a silver platter, we feel better about the outcome. Can the IKEA effect explain why some of us are "addicted" to an intense workload?

A research paper that discussed the cognitive biases behind our tendencies to exacerbate our workload suggests that the IKEA effect is indeed at play here. This cognitive bias leads us to prolong our work hours because we place greater value on the work we do ourselves than the work done by others. As a result, we are reluctant to delegate work to others since we feel the outcome will not be as valuable. This can result in a higher workload that affects our physical and mental health.

To overcome the IKEA effect, we have to question whether working harder for something makes the outcome truly more valuable or if this is purely something we delude ourselves with.

Overpaying for Underperformance?

March 9th

ILLUSION OF VALIDITY

The illusion of validity is a cognitive bias where we overestimate our ability to understand and predict an outcome based on the information we have. When analyzing new information, we rely on things we already know, for example, stereotypes and prior beliefs. When we assume that what we know is valid enough to predict what will happen in different contexts, we make confident predictions that can turn out to be utterly inaccurate.

Even in business, our decisions are rarely rational. Important decisions, such as whom to hire and how much to pay them, can be significantly influenced by cognitive biases.

A study titled "Paying More to Get Less," conducted by Matthew Bidwell at the Wharton School of Business, reveals an intriguing trend. Companies tend to pay external hires 18% more than their internal employees, despite no guarantee of superior performance. This approach seems illogical, considering the higher cost, increased risk, and lower probability of success associated with hiring externally. External hires often lack essential company-specific knowledge and established relationships within the organization.

The research pinpoints a critical issue: external hires may appear more qualified due to observable factors such as educational background and documented experience. However, these factors don't necessarily translate into actual job performance. Conversely, internal candidates have proven track records within the organization, providing a more accurate reflection of their capabilities. Yet, this familiarity can be a double-edged sword. Hiring managers are acutely aware of internal candidates' shortcomings, which might unfairly overshadow their strengths. Meanwhile, the deficiencies of external candidates remain unknown, leading to an overestimation of their potential.

This phenomenon clearly reflects an illusion of validity, where companies overestimate their ability to predict the performance of external hires based on the content of a polished resume. Consequently, they undervalue their internal candidates, leading to potentially costly hiring mistakes.

Read more about this study

Who Decides What You See On Instagram or Facebook?

March 10th

CONFIRMATION BIAS

Confirmation bias is our tendency to look for, acknowledge, favor, and remember information in a way that supports what we already think or believe. This bias occurs when we ignore information that contradicts our ideas or interpret ambiguous facts as evidence supporting our existing beliefs. Situations that involve emotionally charged topics, strongly held beliefs, or things we really want to happen are most susceptible to this bias.

Have you ever found yourself curious about why certain posts appear on your social media feed while others don't? It is the work of complex algorithms that analyze vast amounts of data regarding your online activities. These algorithms are designed to predict and present content that you're likely to interact withThese social media algorithms capitalize on our innate confirmation bias. Let's say, for instance, that you support abortion rights; the algorithm identifies this preference from your past interactions and then predominantly shows you content that reinforces these views. This makes sense because we're naturally inclined to engage with information that aligns with our beliefs. However, this interplay between algorithmic functions designed to maximize engagement and our own innate confirmation biases leads to the formation of "filter bubbles." Within these bubbles, we're insulated from differing perspectives and predominantly exposed to information that validates our preexisting beliefs. Due to confirmation bias, we are likely to remain in the same ideological echo chambers on social media.

Interestingly, many people remain unaware of the forces at play behind the content they see on social media. A 2015 study involving Facebook users revealed that 62.5% of participants did not know that the content they see is tailored by algorithms. Another study from 2023, using a different methodology, still found a comparable lack of awareness, with 47.3% of participants unaware of the extent to which algorithms influence the content they consume.

Watch Eli Pariser's TED Talk about filter bubbles

False Balance: When Does Encouraging Debate Go Too Far?

March 11th

BINARY BIAS

Binary bias is our tendency to categorize things or people into two distinct categories, often based on their perceived characteristics or attributes. This can lead to oversimplification, stereotyping, and discrimination. We do that because it helps us make sense of the world around us quickly. From an evolutionary perspective, we need to quickly distinguish between potential allies and threats, categorizing people as friends or foes.

We should all strive to remain open to alternative perspectives, especially when faced with complex issues that defy simple classification. Our tendency towards binary bias—simplifying issues into two opposing categories—can sometimes obscure the truth rather than clarify it. This becomes particularly problematic in cases where the evidence strongly supports one viewpoint over another. By insisting on a balanced treatment of both sides, even when one lacks substantial evidence, we risk distorting the reality of the issue.

Let's take one concrete example. Climate change is an environmental issue that has received a lot of attention from scientific research. Numerous pieces of evidence now indicate that global warming is increasing, and it does so because of our collective actions. However, there are still many who deny this fact. This wouldn't be such a major issue in theory since everyone is entitled to an opinion. The issue arises when the media insists on presenting both sides of the argument ("climate change is real" versus "it is not") as if they were equally valid and open to discussion. The media's endeavor to present all sides of an argument fairly, even when one side has no substance at all, is known as "bothsidesism." The results frequently include spreading false information and validating bad actors by giving them the same attention and airtime as legitimate experts in talk shows or articles.

While the media's intentions are well-founded, they can do more harm than good. Insisting on having two radically different perspectives on an issue is a great example of binary bias in action.

Read this article about 'bothsidesism'

Riding the Rails to Recruitment:
Get the German Army Back on Track?

March 12th

MERE EXPOSURE EFFECT

The mere exposure effect says the more we are exposed to something, the more we like it. Familiarity breeds liking. When asked to make a choice, we tend to prefer what is familiar, even if this is not the optimal choice. One reason for this behavior is that evolution has taught us to be careful around new things. Everything unfamiliar could be potentially dangerous. When we see something over and over again without any bad results, we assume it is safe.

The German armed forces (the Bundeswehr) were facing the issue of people's lack of interest in a military career, as well as a lack of goodwill among German citizens. Since the compulsory civil service was scrapped in 2011, the army has found itself understaffed. So it came up with a creative plan to get into people's minds by using a cognitive bias called the mere exposure effect. This entails that we prefer things we encounter regularly over those that are out of our sight.

The solution to the public's lack of interest and appreciation was a partnership with the national rail service Deutsche Bahn (which is and has been struggling with a diminishing reputation). The army offered soldiers free rides on Germany's national rail service, but with one condition: that they wear their uniform on the train. Many may wonder how the army would benefit if soldiers wore their uniforms when traveling.

This strategy actually has a sound psychological explanation. If soldiers are out in public representing the army, people will be more exposed to the military institution. And since the mere exposure effect entails that more exposure equals more liking, people in Germany will begin to see the armed forces in a more favorable light. And if they have a better perception of the military, perhaps they'll be more interested in joining it, too. Based on the principles of the mere exposure effect, with this tactic, the German army will be visible to many people, who might as well start liking what being a soldier looks like.

Read this article about German soldiers getting free train travel

Smart Kids, Slim Odds: Can Brilliance Beat the Base Rate Fallacy?

March 13th

BASE RATE FALLACY

We fall prey to the base rate fallacy when we ignore general information in favor of information that is specific to a certain case, even if the general information is more important. We ignore the statistical base rate. This happens because we tend to think that information about an individual is more important than information about a group. This bias can make us perpetuate stereotypes and overgeneralize.

"Only 6% of people get into this university, but you'll definitely get in because you're brilliant." Some parents might overlook an important aspect if they view the situation this way. Most applicants to prestigious universities are already highly intelligent, as these institutions primarily attract top academic performers. Therefore, statistically speaking, being smart does not significantly alter your chances of acceptance relative to the average applicant at this level.

When making this judgment, we are committing a thinking error called the base rate fallacy. In this example, the proud parent focuses solely on the intelligence of their offspring, overlooking the general fact that the university's acceptance rate is low for everyone, including many other brilliant applicants. This disregard for the broader statistical context — that only 6 out of every 100 applicants are admitted — exemplifies the base rate fallacy. One reason this could happen is that we think our individual circumstances are more important or relevant than the information about the group.

Consider the case of former U.S. President Barack Obama, an individual of exceptional intelligence. Despite his brilliance, he was rejected by Swarthmore, a university with an acceptance rate of only 8%. This specific example may resonate more strongly than discussing statistics and base rates, demonstrating our tendency to favor individual anecdotes over broader statistical realities. Individual brilliance does not guarantee acceptance, and the base rate—the overall acceptance rate—is a more accurate indicator of the likelihood of acceptance.

This highlights a common pitfall: the allure of personal stories can often overshadow the importance of aggregate data.

*Is the Supernatural Real or
Are We Just Houdini-ed by Our Beliefs?*

March 14th

BELIEF BIAS

Belief bias distorts our evaluation of the logical strength of an argument because we judge it by the believability of the conclusion. In other words, when we believe the conclusion, we are inclined to believe that the method used to get the results must also be correct. Belief bias happens when we rely too much on what we remember and not enough on evaluating new information. Belief bias is more likely to happen when we really care about something.

Among Americans, more than four out of ten people believe in ghosts, demons, or other supernatural beings. Perhaps this widespread belief is why the psychic service industry has flourished in the last decade. Palm reading, tarot guidance, and fortune-telling are only a few of the spirituality services available to people, making the market for psychic services amount to $2.2 billion in the United States alone.

Yet the questionable nature of such services has long been recognized by notable figures throughout history. Harry Houdini, an American escape artist and magician who performed between 1885 and 1926, was particularly passionate about fighting against fraudulent spiritualists. He took extraordinary measures to expose their deceptions: infiltrating spiritualist societies with informants, having detectives spy on suspicious practitioners, and even attending séances in disguise. Houdini boldly declared that he could convincingly replicate any effect that a spiritualist displayed, and he publicly accused well-known spiritualists of fraud. While the entire spirituality business's reliance on belief bias may surprise many people today, Houdini recognized this phenomenon in the 1920s.

The belief bias keeps many people from questioning the validity of the conclusions made by psychic services. If we find a psychic's prediction believable, we tend not to question the validity of their arguments or methods. Our beliefs distort our judgment. However, as Houdini tried to demonstrate, psychic services aren't accurate simply because we believe them to be so.

Watch this video about Harry Houdini's crusade against spiritualism

Fear Factor: Are We Hardwired to Overreact to Disasters?

March 15th

AVAILABILITY BIAS

The availability bias is our tendency to make decisions based on information that comes to mind quickly and easily. It's a mental shortcut that gives more weight to information that was learned recently or that is easy to remember, for example, because it is an emotionally loaded memory. Our brain wants to save mental energy. So, we often go with the first information that comes to mind instead of putting in more mental effort to dig deeper.

Terrorism is an unfortunate reality in our modern world. As the media extensively covers terrorist attacks, our minds often focus on the horrors of these events. This can lead to an irrational fear of terrorism, which is an example of the availability bias.

When terrorism occurs, it often dominates media coverage. This intense focus can distort public perception, making it challenging to contextualize the true extent and frequency of terrorist acts. In 2017, close to 56 million people died, with just over 26,000 deaths caused by terrorism. This accounted for only 0.05% of all deaths. Terrorism consistently accounts for a very small fraction of global deaths. You are 3,000 times more likely to die from heart disease than from terrorism, for example.

However, the fear of terrorism can impact our behavior. More than a third of Americans say they are less willing to do certain activities because of terrorism. Research has shown that major terrorist incidents, like the 9/11 attacks, negatively impacted the willingness of people in the US to fly.

Terrorism receives media attention that is insanely disproportionate to its frequency. In 2016, The Guardian and the New York Times, for example, bloated up the coverage of terrorism by 3300% compared to the actual share of deaths. Media coverage of terrorist attacks is a key part of the terrorists' strategy because it creates fear. As terrorism continues to dominate media coverage, it's crucial to remember that the risk of falling victim to such an attack is extremely low.

Look at this statistic of causes of death in the US

Did You Think Amanda Knox Was Guilty?

March 16th

FUNDAMENTAL ATTRIBUTION ERROR

The fundamental attribution error refers to our tendency to assume that a person's behavior is a perfect reflection of their personality. We overestimate explanations that are due to the internal characteristics of a person and underestimate situational or environmental explanations. We do that simply because it saves mental energy to explain someone's behavior by attributing it to their personality rather than considering all possible situational and environmental factors.

The 2007 Amanda Knox case, in which the American student was accused of murdering her British roommate Meredith Kercher in Italy, serves as an excellent example of the fundamental attribution error. People, including the media and prosecution, rapidly judged Knox's character based on her behavior during the investigation and trial, often overlooking situational and environmental factors that may have influenced her actions.

For instance, when Knox was found kissing her boyfriend outside the crime scene, the public and media perceived her as cold and insensitive. This behavior was attributed to her personality, but the situational factor of needing support from her partner in a foreign country under immense stress was disregarded. Furthermore, Knox's inconsistent statements during police interrogation were seen as proof of her guilt and deceitfulness. The public and media didn't consider situational factors, such as intense pressure, language barriers, and the absence of legal representation, which could have contributed to these inconsistencies. The media's portrayal of Knox as the promiscuous and manipulative "Foxy Knoxy" intensified the fundamental attribution error. Unrelated aspects of her personal life were used to create the image of a calculating and malevolent individual, fueling public judgment of her character.

In a Netflix documentary about this case, you can see that, after years of legal battles, Knox was finally acquitted of all charges in 2015.

Watch the trailer of the Netflix series "Amanda Knox."

Driven to Stay in School: Can Losing Licenses Curb Dropouts?

March 17th

HYPERBOLIC DISCOUNTING

Hyperbolic discounting is our tendency to favor more immediate payoffs in comparison to later payoffs. We do prefer the immediate reward, even when it is objectively less valuable. We all make decisions today that we would have preferred not to have made in the future due to hyperbolic discounting. Our brains are hardwired to do so because immediate reward meant a better chance of survival in evolutionary terms.

Getting people to think about the long-term consequences of their actions is difficult. Unfortunately, our brains, by default, focus on instant gratification and short-term benefits. In many instances, we simply forget that we have a future we must prepare for. Yet, as we already know, all our decisions impact our future to varying degrees. Overeating cookies will affect the well-being of our future selves less than, for example, quitting school.

For the school dropout issue, authorities came up with creative solutions to get young people to rethink their decision to quit school. In the U.S., back in 1989, West Virginia passed a law stipulating that students under the age of 18 who chose to leave school would lose their driving licenses. Not surprisingly, the law proved effective; high school dropout rates fell by one-third. In their published paper, two well-known economists hypothesized that hyperbolic discounting bias was the reason for the law's success.

It may seem hard to believe that merely losing the ability to drive legally for one or two years would make such a big difference, but it demonstrates how we make decisions that focus only on short-term benefits rather than long-term goals. This one-third of potential school dropouts didn't stay in school because losing their driver's license made them suddenly aware of education's importance. They stayed because they valued the immediate ability to drive legally more than the long-term benefits of completing their education.

Can AI Really Think, or Are We Just Projecting Our Own Intelligence?

March 18th

ANTHROPOMORPHISM

Anthropomorphism is our natural tendency to attribute human traits, emotions, and intentions to non-humans, for example, animals, gods, natural forces, and the like. We do this because we naturally know more about human traits than non-human ones. Therefore, these come easier to mind, and that saves mental energy.

What is science fiction for some of us is already reality for others: machines and artificial intelligence that possess human-like consciousness. Google engineer Blake Lemoine, for example, publicly claimed that a chatbot has become sentient. The chatbot, called LaMDA, produces language based on data available on large sites such as Wikipedia and Reddit, but experts claim it doesn't understand its meaning yet. However, Lemoine was convinced that he was talking to a truly sentient being when he was chatting with Google's chatbot and received complex opinions on human rights, parenthood, and the third law of robotics. This led the Google engineer to present this as evidence that LaMDA was sentient.

A few weeks before Lemoine went public, his boss, Aguera Arcas, said in The Economist that he also felt more and more like he was talking to something intelligent when working with AI. Google, however, refuted Lemoine's claims that an AI developed sentience and claimed that these AI models only rely on pattern recognition and do not have more sophisticated cognitive abilities. Emily Bender, a professor at the University of Washington, said, "We now have machines that can mindlessly generate words, but we haven't learned how to stop imagining a mind behind them."

When the engineers claimed that the chatbot was sentient, it's possible that anthropomorphic bias played a role. If we see something acting like humans, anthropomorphic bias leads us to mistakenly attribute a human spirit to it.

Watch a video of Blake Lemoine making his sentient AI claim

Pandemic Panacea or Placebo?

March 19th

ILLUSORY TRUTH EFFECT

The illusory truth effect causes us to believe information is true if we hear it repeatedly, even when it's not. This happens because repeatedly hearing the same information makes it familiar, and our brain processes familiar things more easily. This ease is due to the activation of well-established neural pathways, which require less effort to process than new or unfamiliar information. When our brains process information with less effort, we tend to interpret this ease as a sign of truth. Thus, if something is easier to understand, we are more likely to believe it's true.

The COVID-19 restrictions led politicians and citizens alike into desperation. The mental pressure was so intense that everyone was waiting for treatment that could soon put an end to the pandemic stress. So, as soon as a promising medication called hydroxychloroquine was discovered, people, led by Donald Trump, were ready to spread the good news. For months, during his campaign, Trump preached on the effectiveness of this new medication, urging people to get it on prescription from their doctors. Even if there were barely any studies showing the effects of hydroxychloroquine in combating COVID-19, rumors about this magical treatment continued to spread in the media.

What made the news so popular, besides the collective desperation to end the pandemic, was the illusory truth effect. This entails that we are likely to believe statements that are easy to process and are encountered multiple times. So, if everyone shared the belief that hydroxychloroquine was the cure for COVID-19, why would we be the ones to say otherwise?

The fact that media personalities, such as Dr. Oz, who often appear as medical experts, supported the assertion only served to intensify the impact. Given how reliable this medication seemed on the surface, many people bought into it. A therapeutic advantage for COVID-19 from hydroxychloroquine was ultimately disproved. When the illusory truth effect is at play, we will take debatable facts as true and not bother to question them further.

What led to the Challenger disaster?

March 20th

GROUPTHINK

Groupthink is when our desire for harmony and conformity within a group leads to dysfunctional decision-making. Group members prioritize agreement over critical evaluation, resulting in a loss of individual creativity and thinking. This can lead to an inflated sense of confidence in the group's abilities, an undervaluation of opponents, group pressure, and potentially harmful actions towards outsiders.

The Challenger disaster occurred on January 28, 1986. The space shuttle tragically exploded just 73 seconds after liftoff, killing all seven crew members on board. The disaster was ultimately caused by a failure in the O-ring seal—a circular, rubber-like component designed to prevent leaks in the joints of the Space Shuttle's solid rocket boosters. The dynamics that led to this tragedy can be seen as an example of groupthink, particularly among the teams at NASA and Thiokol responsible for the shuttle's launch decision.

NASA management had an inflated sense of confidence in the shuttle program. Despite being aware of the risks associated with the O-rings and previous instances of O-ring damage, decision-makers chose to proceed with the launch. Morton Thiokol engineers, responsible for manufacturing the solid rocket boosters, expressed concerns over the O-rings' performance in cold weather. On the day of the launch, temperatures were a chilly 30 degrees Fahrenheit (-1 degree Celsius). Thiokol advised NASA to postpone the launch as the O-rings were deemed too fragile. In response, one NASA manager expressed shock at Thiokol engineers' recommendation.

A Thiokol engineer later claimed that pressure from NASA led Thiokol managers to override the engineers' concerns and greenlight the launch. NASA management's eagerness to adhere to an ambitious launch schedule resulted in the dismissal of all concerns. This scenario exhibits classic symptoms of groupthink, including peer pressure to conform to the group's opinion and a disregard for dissenting viewpoints.

Was Napoleon the Emperor of Excuses?

March 21st

SELF-SERVING BIAS

The self-serving bias is our tendency to take credit for good things that happen to us and blame other things or people for bad things that happen. We do that because we have the desire to feel good about ourselves. Being responsible for good things happening boosts our confidence and gives us a sense of control in our lives. When we blame external factors for bad things that happen to us, it can help us feel better about ourselves by protecting our ego.

Napoleon Bonaparte is often remembered as a legendary military leader and emperor who changed the course of European history. While his strategic genius is undeniable, he also serves as an excellent example of self-serving bias. This can be seen in how he attributed his victories to his strategic brilliance while attributing his defeats to external factors, such as bad weather or the incompetence of his subordinates.

Napoleon himself was known for taking credit for his successes. He once declared, "In war, three-quarters turns on personal character and relations," emphasizing his own importance. However, when it came to failures or setbacks, Napoleon was quick to blame external factors. For example, during the disastrous Russian campaign of 1812, he blamed the harsh winter conditions for his defeat. Napoleon lamented, "The winter was our disaster. We became the victims of Russia's climate," absolving himself of responsibility for the strategic mistakes.

Likewise, during the Battle of Waterloo in 1815, Napoleon attributed his defeat to his opponent's disregard for the rules, claiming that "by the rules of war I should have gained the battle." Additionally, he blamed his generals quite bluntly, declaring, "Had it not been for the imbecility of Grouchy, I should have gained the day," and insisting that "My generals were faint-hearted men." Another notable instance of Napoleon's self-serving bias emerged after the failed naval Battle of Trafalgar (1805), where he blamed Admiral Villeneuve's cowardice and incompetence for the devastating loss, rather than acknowledging the flaws in his own naval strategy against Britain.

Napoleon's tendency to take credit for victories and blame others for failures is a prime example of the self-serving bias in action.

Are Women Dodging the Bullet on Dating Apps?

March 22nd

RISK AVERSION

Risk aversion refers to your tendency to avoid things that might be dangerous. It is a personal preference, and everyone has a different level of it. Our level can be affected by our personalities, ages and stages of life, finances, education, and cultural or social norms. Risk aversion may have become hardwired into human behavior over time because it evolved as a way for individuals to protect themselves and increase their chances of survival.

Dating apps like Tinder attract numerous people because they offer endless options for dating partners. However, having so many chances at a great love story does come with a cost: the risk of collecting many failed date stories or bad experiences even before an actual date takes place. Some women describe their Tinder experiences like this: "I was often asked for a sexual favor before someone said hello, before someone told me their actual name." According to a Pew Research Center study, about one-third of users reported that their experiences were either extremely or very upsetting. Over time, it seems that women have realized these downsides more and more. The ratio of males to females fell from 62% males and 38% females in 2015 to about 72% males and 28% females in 2021.

Women's bad experiences with dating platforms and the stories about them circulating in peer groups and on social media have activated a bias called risk aversion. Risk aversion means that we would rather steer clear of situations that have a high degree of uncertainty. In the online dating world, women have learned that there is a risk of encountering weird or even emotionally harmful experiences. In fact, the risk of running into such people might be higher than the chance of bumping into people looking for a stable relationship or respectful, light-hearted fun.

Read some truly shocking stats and stories about online dating

A Draft Disaster That Stemmed from Overconfidence?

March 23rd

OVERCONFIDENCE EFFECT

We speak of the overconfidence effect when our subjective confidence in our judgments is higher than their objective accuracy. We can overestimate a variety of things, including our own performance or likelihood of success, our abilities in comparison to others, and the certainty of our answers or judgments.

Are you familiar with the NFL Draft? The NFL Draft is an annual event where teams select new players from college football, with the weakest team from the previous season picking first. Teams choose players in a fixed order over seven rounds, aiming to improve their rosters with fresh talent. They can also trade their draft picks with other teams for better positions, additional picks, or established players. This trading feature allows teams to improve strategically.

A notable example of overconfidence occurred during the 1998 NFL Draft. The New Orleans Saints were scheduled as the 12th overall pick in the draft. Their head coach, Mike Ditka, had his eyes on a new talent, Ricky Williams, a player from the University of Texas who had an outstanding college career and also set the NCAA record for rushing yards in 1998. Ditka was sure that Williams was a once-in-a-generation talent, like Walter Payton, and that the team's future success depended on getting him. He was willing to give up multiple first-round picks to get Williams. This means Ditka was prepared to trade away the Saints' top picks in several upcoming drafts, sacrificing potential future stars in exchange for securing Williams immediately.

The overconfidence effect in the story of Mike Ditka and Ricky Williams is evident in Ditka's strong belief that Williams was a once-in-a-generation talent, leading him to give up significant resources to acquire him. This excessive confidence in his judgment ultimately resulted in a trade that is remembered more for the assets surrendered than for Williams' eventual NFL career. In the end, Ricky Williams played just okay for the Saints for three seasons before he was traded to the Miami Dolphins.

Should We Gargle with Doubt Over Time-Honored Medical Treatments?

March 24th

BANDWAGON EFFECT

The bandwagon effect refers to the phenomenon in which a belief or behavior becomes more popular as more people adopt it. This can lead to a self-reinforcing cycle, as the increased popularity of the belief or behavior encourages more people to adopt it. The effect is caused by our desire to conform to social norms and our belief that the majority must be correct. It can also be caused by peer pressure and the fear of being left out or made fun of if we don't fit in.

Tonsils are two small, oval-shaped clusters of tissue tucked away at the back of your throat. They serve as a first line of defense in our immune system to catch incoming germs before they delve deeper into your body. But back in the 19th century and for much of the 20th, if these little warriors got infected or inflamed, the most common course of action was to remove them—a procedure known as a tonsillectomy.

Now, why did tonsillectomy gain such popularity? Was it because of irrefutable scientific proof of its effectiveness? Not quite. Like a meme going viral on social media, tonsillectomies became widespread, primarily because "everyone else was doing it." This phenomenon, where an idea or behavior gains traction simply because it's popular, is known as the bandwagon effect.

The bandwagon effect stems from our innate desire to fit into societal norms, convinced by the majority's wisdom and wary of the isolation that comes from dissent. Professor Layton F. Rikkers, an Emeritus of Surgery at the University of Wisconsin-Madison, fittingly dubbed tonsillectomy a "medical bandwagon." Countless doctors adhered to this surgical practice, with little to no scientific evidence to back its effectiveness.

What's even more interesting, or perhaps alarming, is that tonsillectomy is now associated with higher risks of allergic, respiratory, and infectious diseases later in life. So the next time you find yourself doing something because "everyone else is," stop and think: Are you boarding a bandwagon?

How Two Brothers' Rivalry Shaped a Town's Identity

March 25th

INGROUP BIAS

Ingroup bias is when we like and support people who are part of our own group more than people who are not part of our group. These groups can be divided based on seemingly trivial observable traits. This is rooted in the intrinsic human need for a group identity, which provides a sense of belonging and purpose. Additionally, we all have a desire to feel good about ourselves, and one way to achieve that is to see our own group as being superior to others.

The feud between two shoemaker brothers in the small German town of Herzogenaurach not only led to the creation of two of the world's biggest sports apparel companies, Adidas and Puma, but also serves as a remarkable example of ingroup bias. As the Dassler brothers' rivalry escalated around the time of World War II, it deeply influenced the social fabric of Herzogenaurach.

In this town, the allegiance to either Adidas or Puma went beyond mere workplace loyalty. Employees of the two companies, along with their families, developed a strong sense of identity tied to their respective firms. This was not limited to professional pride but extended to their social interactions and choices in daily life. Residents often avoided speaking to those affiliated with the rival company and patronized separate bars, bakeries, and barber shops, creating a distinct division within the community.

Such was the extent of this divide that people habitually looked at each other's shoes to ascertain their company's allegiance, earning Herzogenaurach the nickname "the town of bent necks." Choosing to wear shoes from Adidas or Puma was not just a matter of personal taste; it was a symbol of one's identity and group loyalty. This behavior exemplifies ingroup bias, where even trivial observable traits, like the brand of shoes one wore, became significant markers of group identity.

The consequences of the Dassler brothers' feud highlight the deep human need for belonging and identity and how this can significantly shape social interactions and communal structures.

Read more about Puma and Adidas' rivalry dividing a German town

Memory Makeover: Did You Really Predict That?

March 26th

HINDSIGHT BIAS

The hindsight bias is also called the "I-knew-it-all-along" effect. It describes the retrospective overestimation of predictability. In the present, it's hard to tell how something will turn out in the future, but is easy to understand how or why an event happened in retrospect. This bias happens because we mistakenly assume that we had the same understanding of an event before it happened as we do after it happened.

Many of us confidently declare, "I knew this would happen!" when things turn out a certain way. Even if we haven't voiced our predictions before the outcome, our inner Nostradamus comes out and claims victory. While this might seem like an ego boost, few of us realize that hindsight bias (the "I-knew-it-all-along" effect) also affects our memory of events.

The way in which hindsight bias changes how we store our predictions in memory was tested in several research studies. In 1991, an African American man named Rodney Glen King was the victim of police brutality. During the famous Rodney King civil rights trial, researchers surveyed 68 people to predict its outcome.

The same participants were then asked to remember their initial prediction at the end of the trial. Interestingly, some people remembered their predictions incorrectly, aligning with the actual outcome of the trial. More precisely, some of those who predicted that the verdict would be "the police officers in the trial are guilty" remembered that they had predicted "not guilty" (which was the actual verdict). Once they saw the results, their memories reconstructed their initial answers. This study shows that hindsight bias also has the power to distort our memory to match reality once we have new information.

For those unfamiliar with the historical significance of this case, the ruling in the Rodney King trial in 1992 led to riots that lasted six days and resulted in 63 fatalities and 2,383 injuries. In a separate civil rights case, two of the officers were found guilty and given jail sentences. The charges against the other two defendants were dismissed.

Heads or Tails: Do You Really Have a Handle on Chance?

March 27th

ILLUSION OF CONTROL

The illusion of control occurs when we believe we have more control over external events than we do. We frequently believe we have (or had) some control over events that are actually random. Researchers have found that people who feel in control will engage in healthier behaviors, feel less stress, and have better overall mental health. Therefore, this illusion makes us feel better about ourselves and the world around us, but it can also seduce us into relying on superstitions.

The illusion of control becomes stronger the more we think we have mastered a skill. For example, if you flip a coin several times and it lands on heads, you feel as if you have "mastered" this game and can therefore control which side the coin will land on. This occurred in an experiment that assessed the degree of control some people think they have over the outcome of flipping a coin. This simple game is a good example of the type of event we have no control over. You might get better at flipping a coin, but if you are playing fair, you cannot realistically predict the outcome.

However, this study showed a different angle: when the people taking part in the experiment had a consistent sequence of coins landing on heads, they felt that they had more chances of predicting the result of future sequences. An early and consistent pattern of successes leads to skill attribution and the illusion of control ("I now know the coin will land on heads"). Similarly, a consistent sequence of outcomes implies that the task is controllable, leading people to take credit for its success.

We are so motivated to see random events as controllable that any possible cue (such as a random sequence of wins) is sufficient to induce an illusion of control over a task as random as coin-flipping.

Singing Your Way to Dunning-Kruger's Got Talent?

March 28th

DUNNING–KRUGER EFFECT

The Dunning–Kruger effect describes our tendency to overestimate our own abilities in areas that we are unskilled in or lack knowledge in. This happens when we know just enough to think we are great but not enough to tell the difference between good and bad. We just don't know yet what we could do better. The effect also applies to society as a whole. The most uninformed citizens are often also the most confident ones.

TV talent shows are real-life demonstrations of what can happen when you overestimate your skills. Let's say you're an amateur singer with a part-time interest in music. Maybe you've tried singing at a few gigs, and people were generous with their feedback. So, you decide to take your new passion to the next level: you want to win the next "American Idol."

Except that you've never been in front of a large audience or sung complex songs. But this isn't even the real problem. The biggest issue is that you're not even aware that you don't yet have what it takes to carry out such a challenging performance. Given that you're relatively new to the world of music, you haven't had the chance to expose yourself to the limits of your talent. So, in your head, you imagine that you sound like the next Mariah Carey, but people's ears have an entirely different acoustic experience. This is the Dunning-Kruger effect at work, which is also called "the American Idol effect," particularly because of people who have overestimated their artistic talent enough to compete for the next "American Idol."

Believing in ourselves is great, but sometimes we have to be realistic about our knowledge and skills—especially when we're new to a career, hobby, or area of study. In fact, the first plunge into a new field is the most likely to trigger the Dunning-Kruger effect: the less we know of a subject, the more we think we do. This is because we lack exposure to the blind spots and gaps in our knowledge, which usually comes through deep immersion in a topic.

Watch this video of the worst American Idol auditions

Would Lady Luck Have Spared You from the Vietnam Draft?

March 29th

GAMBLER'S FALLACY

The gambler's fallacy arises from the mistaken belief that past events can affect the probability of future outcomes that are actually independent of the past. It is often manifested in the belief that a certain outcome is more or less likely to occur due to its frequency in the past, despite the fact that the probability remains the same. This fallacy is often driven by a desire for pattern-finding and prediction, as well as a dislike of uncertainty.

The Vietnam Draft Lottery, held during the height of the Vietnam War, was a source of anxiety and fear for many young American men. The draft determined who would be called to serve in the military. During this time, many Americans fell prey to the gambler's fallacy.

The Vietnam War draft lottery was based on birthdates and used a random process to select these dates. The process was as follows: 366 blue capsules, representing each day of the year including February 29, were placed in a glass container; all capsules were then drawn one after another. The first date drawn was assigned the number 1, the second received number 2, and so forth. The lower the assigned number, the higher the likelihood that men with that birthday would be called to serve. In 1970, all men with numbers 195 or lower were called for physical examinations. Draft lotteries were held again in 1970, 1971, and 1972, with the last one taking place on December 7, 1972.

The process employed by the Vietnam Draft Lottery to select young men for military service was entirely random. However, many people believed that certain birthdates were luckier than others or that the lottery was not truly random. This belief was a result of the gambler's fallacy. For example, some believed that certain birthdates were "overdue" to be chosen because they had not been selected in previous lotteries. This line of thinking, however, was flawed, as each lottery was an independent event, and the results of past lotteries had no influence on the outcome of subsequent ones.

Read more about how the draft worked

Are We Happier When We're Stuck with Our Decisions?

March 30th

COGNITIVE DISSONANCE

Cognitive dissonance describes the mental discomfort we experience when there is a conflict between our beliefs, actions, or perceptions. This discomfort often arises when our actions contradict our beliefs or when we hold two opposing beliefs simultaneously. To alleviate this discomfort, we may adjust our beliefs, perceptions, or actions to create a more consistent internal state. Achieving this internal consistency is crucial, as it helps maintain our sense of identity and coherence.

We humans are strange. We like having the chance to change our minds and to keep doors open rather than closed. But does that freedom to reconsider contribute to happiness?

A study conducted by two scientists offered two groups of photography students two contrasting options. Both groups were given the chance to take exactly one picture home from class. The first group had the option to change their minds later, while the other group was stuck with their initial choice without the option to reconsider. After a few weeks, the scientists asked both groups how happy they were with their choice.

Surprisingly, the group that was offered the chance to change their minds about the photograph was less satisfied with their final choice of photographs. Just the option to reverse one's decision raises FoBO—the fear of better options.

In theory, we are willing to pay for the option to change the outcome of our decisions. We prefer adjustable-rate mortgages, lease-purchase contracts, and prenuptial agreements. Yet, we are not always happy with the results. FoBO can induce cognitive dissonance when a we make a choice but continues to feel unsure or regretful, questioning whether we could have made a better decision. The mental discomfort arises from the conflict between our action (the choice we made) and the persistent belief that a better option might have been available.

For our happiness, we might be better off not having the option to change our minds too often.

Watch a TED Talk by Dan Gilbert about the science of happiness

Graded for Your (Un)lucky Genes?

March 31

HALO EFFECT

The halo effect is a type of cognitive bias in which our overall opinion of a person or brand affects how we feel about the specific qualities of that person or brand. If we have a good feeling about something as a whole, we are more likely to think that its individual parts are good as well. We do that because it saves cognitive effort to use our overall impressions as a shortcut to make judgments rather than evaluating each aspect of something separately.

Imagine a classroom where two students submit work of identical quality, yet one consistently receives higher grades. This discrepancy might not be due to favoritism but rather to a manifestation of the halo effect. This phenomenon occurs when teachers form positive opinions of a student based on factors unrelated to academic performance—such as background, physical appearance, or even the student's name.

Research has shown that students who are perceived as attractive inadvertently receive higher grades. The familiar saying "Don't judge a book by its cover" seems disregarded in these situations. This isn't intentional, but the halo effect subtly skews perception, leading teachers to unconsciously associate attractiveness with intelligence or greater effort. Moreover, the halo effect's influence extends beyond physical appearance. In one research study, two identical essays were assessed, differing only in their authors' names. One name was conventional and well-received; the other was unusual or possibly linked to certain stereotypes. Surprisingly, the former was graded more favorably, solely due to the name it carried. It's akin to viewing the work through colored lenses—the name itself shades the teacher's interpretation, despite the content, effort, and words remaining unchanged.

This isn't about blaming educators, since these biases are often subconscious. Rather, it's about heightening awareness and promoting fairness in grading practices. To address these issues, educational institutions could implement anonymous grading systems, where students' work is identified only by a random number or code during the evaluation process. This method minimizes the influence of personal biases related to the student's identity.

∞
APRIL

Did you hear of the Torrey Canyon oil spill?

April 1st

OSTRICH EFFECT OR NORMALCY BIAS

Normalcy bias, also known as "ostrich effect," makes us downplay warnings about dangers or ignore negative situations completely. We underestimate how likely it is that a disaster will happen and how it might affect us. We do that because we want to avoid an unpleasant emotional impact in the short term. The name comes from the popular (but false) belief that ostriches bury their heads in the sand when in danger.

The 1967 Torrey Canyon oil spill remains one of the most significant environmental disasters in history, with far-reaching impacts on marine ecosystems and coastal regions. The events leading up to the accident provide a compelling example of the normalcy bias, particularly in the decision-making process of the captain and crew aboard the SS Torrey Canyon before the ship ran aground on rocks off the UK coast.

Despite mounting evidence that the ship was heading towards disaster, the captain and crew persisted in following a risky course. The captain had chosen a route that, in hindsight, was far too tight for the massive oil tanker. The route was extremely close to the Scilly Isles, aiming to shorten the journey from the Persian Gulf to Milford Haven in Wales, where the oil was to be delivered.

As the evidence of an impending disaster continued to accumulate, the captain could have chosen to back out of the risky course but instead decided against it. This decision ultimately led to one of the largest oil spills in history. The captain and crew remained steadfast in their chosen route, even as the situation grew increasingly dire. This unwavering determination can be attributed to the normalcy bias, as the captain and crew downplayed all dangers and likely believed that, despite the warning signs, everything would work out fine, as it had in the past. They believed that the chosen route would not lead to disaster.

Overall, the leak released between 25 and 36 million gallons (94 and 164 million liters) of crude oil into the sea. That oil leak was among the worst in history, and it still ranks as the worst in the United Kingdom.

How to not stick to what we know

April 2nd

CONFIRMATION BIAS

Confirmation bias is our tendency to look for, acknowledge, favor, and remember information in a way that supports what we already think or believe. This bias occurs when we ignore information that contradicts our ideas or interpret ambiguous facts as evidence supporting our existing beliefs. Situations that involve emotionally charged topics, strongly held beliefs, or things we really want to happen are most susceptible to this bias.

The scientific method is a methodical way to learn about the world through critical thinking while avoiding confirmation bias as much as possible. Scientists do that by putting an emphasis on being willing to change their beliefs based on new evidence. But even very smart people may have trouble avoiding confirmation bias throughout their careers.

Researcher James Montier tested 300 professional fund managers with a riddle that asked them to check if a statement was true. The riddle goes like this: You are presented with four cards, each of which has a letter on one side and a number on the other. The four cards on the table are E, 4, K, and 7. Your task is to find out if the following statement is true: If a card has an E on it, it has a 4 on the opposite side. The question is, which two cards do you need to turn over to check if this statement is true? In fact, 95% of participants failed this question. Now, take a moment to think about which cards you would choose before reading further.

Most people answered E and 4, but the correct answer is E and 7. Why is that? The reason is that the statement is false if the card showing an E doesn't have a 4 on the other side. Also, if the back of the 7 card has an E, it shows that the statement is false. But if you flip over the card that says 4, you won't learn anything because your task is to check if an E should have a 4, not the other way around. The fund managers instinctively sought evidence that would confirm the statement. Had they approached the problem with a focus on disproving the statement, they would have been less prone to confirmation bias.

How Assertive Are You Really?

April 3rd

AVAILABILITY BIAS

The availability bias is our tendency to make decisions based on information that comes to mind quickly and easily. It's a mental shortcut that gives more weight to information that was learned recently or that is easy to remember, for example, because it is an emotionally loaded memory. Our brain wants to save mental energy. So, we often go with the first information that comes to mind instead of putting in more mental effort to dig deeper.

Think back to a time when you struggled to recall something important. Did it affect your confidence in your abilities? Believe it or not, how easily you remember something can influence the perception you have of yourself.

A study from 1991 tested how ease of recall influences people's perceptions of themselves. Participants were split into two groups: the first group was told to list six examples of assertive behaviors, and the second group was instructed to come up with 12 examples. At the end, individuals from both groups were told to rate their assertiveness on a scale from one to ten. Researchers found that people who were asked to list six examples of assertive behavior thought they were much more assertive than people who were asked to list 12 examples. Why?

Part of the explanation comes from the availability bias, which implies that we're more likely to form opinions with information that comes to mind quickly and easily. The participants, who only had to think of six assertive behaviors, could recall the examples quickly and easily, so they assumed they must be very assertive since it was so easy for them to identify examples of assertiveness.

In contrast, the other group had to think harder to list assertive behaviors. Since information did not come to mind as quickly and easily, they reasoned that perhaps they weren't so assertive after all. Instead of evaluating their genuine feelings about their assertiveness, they based their self-assessment on how quickly and easily they could generate examples.

How Can User Experience Design Be Peak-End Rule Friendly?

April 4th

PEAK–END RULE

The peak-end rule states that we tend to judge an experience based on the most intense moment as well as how the experience ended. The overall memory of the experience will be based on the average of the peak moment and the end. This bias happens because we remember events in snapshots rather than in their entirety. Furthermore, we remember things better when they are emotionally intense (the peak) or more recent (the end).

Last impressions last a lifetime. Some brands place a greater emphasis on this than others. While some apps or websites are a pleasure to navigate, others are not. Having a pleasant user experience that ends on a highly satisfactory note can make people come back to your website or app in the future. Our peak-end bias impacts how we remember past events, such as interactions with an online interface. Intense positive or negative moments (the peaks) and the final moments will have a strong impact on how we remember the experience with the app.

Duolingo is an example of a brand that has mastered the peak-end rule. The app, which gamifies the process of learning a language, provides the user with good interactive feedback throughout the learning process. For example, the app's cartoon mascot congratulates the user whenever they achieve a new peak performance (e.g., "Amazing! 10 correct words in a row!") as well as at the end of every single lesson. Thanks to this feature, the user leaves the app feeling like they have accomplished something valuable. Feedback during and at the end of a person's time with the app reinforces their learning and makes sure that they remember the experience in a positive light.

Designing interactions that follow the peak-end rule can help create positive and memorable experiences. This can make users enjoy using an app or website, feel more satisfied with their interaction, and be more likely to tell other people about it.

How Can Poverty Cloud Your Decision-Making Skills?

April 5th

DECISION FATIGUE

Decision fatigue is the mental exhaustion that comes from having to make a lot of complex decisions in a short amount of time. It is similar to using a muscle that becomes more fatigued the more we use it in a short period. This happens because our brain has a limited amount of mental energy and willpower to use for making decisions. This phenomenon can be caused by external factors such as stress and lack of sleep and can lead to difficulty concentrating, irritability, and impulsive behavior.

There is a common misconception that poor people are impoverished because they keep making bad decisions. However, current research shows that it's actually the reverse: poverty often leads to these poor decisions, not poor decisions leading to poverty.

One study found that the strain of consistently worrying about money is a barrier to efficient decision-making required to succeed in life. In other words, the poorer you are, the worse your decisions are. And the poorer your decisions are, the poorer you remain. For those who are wealthy, they may choose between ordering Italian or sushi for dinner. People who are financially disadvantaged must decide between buying food or medicine, paying for a school trip, or getting their car fixed. These choices are existential and put extra strain on their ability to make decisions. Another study found that being poor creates a mental strain similar to losing 13 IQ points.

This is a negative feedback loop that often keeps people with low socio-economic status from advancing in life. The study found evidence from low-income Americans and farmers in India that overthinking a financial decision impacted cognitive performance. For example, when asked to ponder an expensive car repair, low-income people performed worse on cognitive tests than higher-income people who were faced with the same scenario. However, this isn't because poor people aren't able to efficiently allocate their resources to a car repair; they are so fatigued by repeated decisions about where to spend their money.

Read this article about your brain on poverty

Is Your Expertise Foolproof Against Anchors?

April 6th

ANCHORING BIAS

Anchoring bias occurs when a specific reference point, or "anchor", influences our decision-making process. This anchor could be a number or any other kind of cue, even if it is completely unrelated to the decision at hand. Despite this, we often use the anchor as a starting point and adjust our decisions or judgments from there, without realizing it. As a result, our final estimates, decisions, or judgments can be significantly different from what they might have been without the influence of the anchor.

You may think that being an experienced professional means you won't be easily swayed by biases. However, studies show that this isn't true. Even seasoned experts can fall for biases, like anchoring, which can twist our thinking.

In a study, 54 amateur and 47 expert real estate agents were asked to guess the price of different houses. Before they gave their answers, they were given price suggestions by potential buyers. These suggestions were either very high or very low. The goal was to see if these suggested prices would change the agents' own price guesses. Interestingly, when the suggested prices were high, agents—both amateurs and experts—tended to estimate the house prices higher, and similarly, low suggestions led to lower estimates. This illustrates the anchoring effect, where the initial information (the price suggestion) serves as an anchor for subsequent judgments. After making their guesses, the agents were asked how much they thought the buyers' suggestions had influenced them. Only 19% of experts thought these suggestions had affected their guesses. However, 37% of the amateurs admitted that they were influenced by the anchor.

The study discovered that even experts are subject to anchoring bias within their own field. Additionally, experts are less likely than beginners to recognize or admit that they make judgments that are biased or skewed as a result of using very basic rules of thumb. It's not certain if experts' denial comes from not realizing they're relying on these rules or from not wanting to admit they're using inappropriate information.

So, the anchoring bias can affect us, no matter how expert we are. The real problem is not admitting it.

Do We Secretly Believe Victims Had It Coming?

April 7th

JUST WORLD HYPOTHESIS

The Just World Hypothesis is the belief that the world is just and fair, and that people get what they deserve. This means that if someone is experiencing bad things, it is because they have done something to deserve it and are punished. On the other hand, if someone is successful or happy, it is because they made good choices and are rewarded. This idea can be comforting because it gives us a sense of control over our lives and the belief that we can influence our own outcomes.

We are conditioned from birth to believe that the world is just, with good things happening to good people and bad things happening to bad people. For this reason, whenever something terrible happens to a person, there is often a sense that they must have done something to deserve it. This belief in a "just world" often comes into play in how we see victims of violent crimes.

When looking at stories of sexual assault, for example, there is often a tendency to assume that the victim is at least partially responsible due to making unwise choices that made them more vulnerable. This was evidenced in a study where subjects were presented with an account of a rape; those with a higher belief in a just world attributed more blame to the rape victim, reinforcing the idea that the victim must have done something to deserve their fate. Whether it was because the victim was a sex worker, had an active sexual history, was drunk, or walked through an unsafe neighborhood, victim-blaming is still quite common and can become an issue in court cases or media coverage of the crime.

For those believing in a "just world," such blaming of the victim helps them feel a little less uncomfortable about stories of physical or sexual assault, since they would otherwise need to accept that being "good people" won't protect them from disaster. It is also why people often say things like, "Why me?" when they are the victims of a crime.

*Framing the Debate: Are We Pro-Choice,
Pro-Life, or Pro-Compromise?*

April 8th

FRAMING EFFECT

The framing effect occurs when we draw different conclusions from identical information based solely on how that information is presented. This can happen when something is framed either positively or negatively, or as a gain versus a loss - we naturally tend to avoid losses in such situations. Our judgment can also shift depending on which features of the information are highlighted, even though the underlying facts remain exactly the same.

Abortion is a controversial and complicated topic. What makes it difficult to settle this ongoing dispute is that it involves two fundamental values that most people care about: the freedom to choose and the gift of human life. Because of the framing effect, we can perceive the two movements—pro-life and pro-choice—as perspectives that hold their own version of the truth.

The nuanced implications of the framing effect in shaping public discourse on abortion are vividly captured in a Mansfield Journal article. The article contains two unrelated stories on abortion. A woman who was glad to have had an abortion when she was a college student wrote the first story. She outlines women's fundamental right to make decisions for their bodies without impacting other people. Her story is presented through the "framing" of having the right to decide as a fundamental right for all free human beings ("pro-choice"). On the other hand, the second story is written purely from the perspective of preserving and cherishing human life ("pro-life").

Taken separately, both perspectives make sense. The fact that a woman should decide what happens to her body seems extremely plausible. So does the second perspective, which compels us to think about the importance of preserving life.

Both sides are "pro-something." Someone is pro-life and not anti-choice, or pro-choice and not anti-life. This implies that every side of the argument frames their position as standing up for something fundamentally good as opposed to being against something.

Did a Mummy's Curse Doom the Titanic?

April 9th

ILLUSIONS OF CAUSALITY

The illusion of causality occurs when we erroneously perceive a cause-and-effect relationship between two events. Assessing evidence requires cognitive effort, so our brain seeks mental shortcuts to expedite the process. This cognitive bias leads us to hastily infer a causal connection, even if there is none. This stems from our evolutionary need to comprehend the causes of events quickly in our surroundings for the sake of survival.

On the fateful night of April 14, 1912, the Titanic collided with an iceberg and sank, resulting in the loss of over 1,500 lives. This devastating event has inspired numerous books, films, and documentaries. One lesser-known aspect of the Titanic's tale is the connection some have drawn between the sinking and a curse related to a mummy on board.

In the early 20th century, newspapers often reported on supernatural occurrences. One such story is the infamous Curse of the Unlucky Mummy. The tale gained significant attention when the Washington Post published an article in 1912 claiming the Titanic's sinking was due to a mummy's curse. This ancient curse was thought to bring death, illness, and profound misery. After the Titanic catastrophe, rumors circulated that the curse had caused the ship's demise.

The story surrounding the mummy suggests that it brought only misfortune to its previous owner. He had displayed it in a drawing room in his English home. The following morning, every fragile object in the room had been shattered. The next night, the mummy was placed in another room, with the same outcome. An American collector later purchased the mummy and arranged for it to be shipped to America on board the Titanic.

The notion that the Titanic's fate was sealed by the presence of a cursed mummy aboard exemplifies the illusion of causality because it shows how easily unrelated events can be woven into a cause-and-effect narrative. Ultimately, the story of the mummy on board was revealed to be a hoax. The Unlucky Mummy remains on display, not on the ocean floor with the Titanic, but in the British Museum in London.

Watch a video to learn more about the mummy that sank the Titanic

Are You a Slave to Your Self-Image?

April 10th

CONSISTENCY BIAS

Consistency bias is our tendency to judge our own actions in specific situations based on our overall view of ourselves. Instead of objectively assessing our actions based on what actually happens, we often judge them according to our overall self-image, reinforcing a consistent view of ourselves. This bias motivates us to act in ways that are consistent with our self-image, ensuring that our future behaviors align with how we perceive ourselves.

We often assume that someone's past behavior is the greatest predictor of their future behavior. Why is that? The consistency bias suggests that people have a strong desire to be consistent with what they have already done. Once they have committed to a certain identity, they will feel pressure to act in accordance with it. Consistency bias often makes us act in predictable ways because it's easy to do what we have always done.

If you want to help someone change, get them to change how they view themselves. This is what a group of researchers wanted to test when they pretended to be the Community Committee for Traffic Safety and went door to door to promote a petition for safe driving. To create a control group, they skipped some homes.

Two weeks later, a different person from the committee went to the same neighborhood and asked people to install a large, unattractive sign in their front yard that said, "Drive Safely." This time, they went to all the houses.

Interestingly, only 17% of the homeowners who were skipped on the first petition visit agreed to have the sign installed. Meanwhile, 76% of those who received a visit and agreed to sign the petition during their first visit also agreed to install the sign.

The only thing that was different between the two groups was a previous commitment - or lack of it. Those who signed the safety driving petition saw themselves as promoters of safe driving. Therefore, they felt more motivated to accept that ugly sign in their yards and maintain the identity they created.

Are We Suffering from the 'Someone Like You' Syndrome?

April 11th

IMPACT BIAS

The impact bias is our tendency to think that events will have a stronger and longer-lasting effect on our future feelings than they actually will. We incorrectly believe that good things will make us happy forever, and bad things will make us miserable forever. We do that because we tend to focus on one event at a time, neglecting the future effects of unrelated events. Also, we don't realize how quickly our psychological immune system will reframe the events that happened.

One reason heartbreaks feel so dreadful is that they create a sense that the pain is unending. Similarly, when we're miserable in the present, we may project that misery onto our entire future. Conversely, we're often unrealistically optimistic about that one aspiration we believe will finally bring us lasting happiness and contentment.

These distortions in perception largely stem from our brain's susceptibility to impact bias. This cognitive tendency leads us to exaggerate the influence of specific events on our long-term emotional state more than they truly deserve. For instance, after a breakup, you might conclude that happiness will forever remain out of reach. However, this overlooks a crucial truth: your feelings and perspective about your former partner are likely to change significantly over time. Perhaps, in a few months, you'll begin recalling the disappointing vacations, the less-than-satisfying intimate moments, and the fundamental compatibility issues. Your psychological immune system has a remarkable ability to reshape narratives, eventually casting them in a more balanced light. Yet immediately following a breakup, your judgment is clouded by impact bias.

One effective strategy to mitigate this bias is to remind yourself that almost any situation can be interpreted from multiple perspectives. It can also be valuable to examine your assumptions by asking, "What is the probability that this event will truly leave a lasting imprint on my life?" The influence of a single occurrence, whether a heartbreak or a significant success, typically diminishes as time weaves new experiences into our life story.

Watch Dan Gilbert discuss 'What is Happiness?'

Did you try Crystal Pepsi?

April 12th

OUTCOME BIAS

We are subject to outcome bias when we judge a decision by its outcome. This is biased because we should rather base our judgment on the quality of the decision at the time it was made, given what was known at that time. We never have all the information we need, and every result has random and unpredictable parts. Bad outcomes are not always a sign of bad decision-making.

Crystal Pepsi was a caffeine-free, clear cola beverage introduced in the early 1990s as an innovative product that aimed to capitalize on the trend of "pure" products. Unlike traditional colas with their dark brown coloring, Crystal Pepsi maintained the familiar cola taste while appearing as clear as water. David Novak, then-Pepsi COO and the creator of Crystal Pepsi, considered it "the best idea I may have ever had in my career." Despite initial enthusiasm, Crystal Pepsi ultimately failed to gain widespread popularity and was discontinued within a few years. While there are many articles (and some pretty funny parodies) about why Crystal Pepsi was a bad idea, calling it a bad idea serves as a prime example of outcome bias in action.

Many factors contributed to the product's failure, including an unsuccessful marketing campaign and sabotage by Coca-Cola. Pepsi failed to effectively communicate the benefits and purpose of a clear cola to consumers. Additionally, the flavor of Crystal Pepsi led to disappointment among consumers who expected the taste of regular Pepsi. While it is easy to look back on Crystal Pepsi's failure and judge the decision to launch it as a bad one, this overlooks the factors that made the idea seem promising at the time. For example, from the late 1980s through the early 2000s, the "clear craze" was a marketing trend that associated transparency with purity. Several electrical devices (e.g., Gameboy) featured see-through casings, and personal hygiene items were reintroduced as clear, dye-free gels.

The eventual failure of Crystal Pepsi was primarily due to the poor execution of the marketing campaign and product positioning rather than the concept itself.

Watch the Crystal Gravy' spoof on Crystal Pepsi.

Did You Use Auto-Save in Microsoft Word?

April 13th

DEFAULT EFFECT

When offered a choice that has a pre-selected default option, we tend to choose this default option. This is called the default effect. Defaults are the options that take effect if we do nothing. Our brains try to save as much mental energy as possible. Accepting the default option saves energy because we don't have to think about the pros and cons of each choice.

Did you ever change the default side margin for your Word documents? The chances are very high that you did not. Most of us stick to the default settings of the applications and programs we use. Due to a bias with the same name—called the default effect—people rarely explore the settings of the software products they use other than the default one.

A survey wanted to find data on this phenomenon. They asked whether people customized their Microsoft Word version or kept the default settings. They asked and instructed people to send their settings file for Microsoft Word, which, interestingly, had over 150 settings that could be customized.

The survey found that most people had no clue about these settings in the first place. Less than 5% of the users they surveyed had changed any settings at all. More than 95% had kept them in the exact configuration that the program was installed in. Some people weren't even aware of some crucial functions, such as autosaving, which was disabled in some cases and had to be explicitly turned on to save one's work. Even the 95% of users who were running Word with autosave turned off didn't try to change the setting. They just assumed that was how Microsoft Word worked and made peace with that.

The survey results show that many software users miss out on important features and functions because they don't explore the default settings. Please dare to explore the settings of the software you use every day!

Did We Miss the Apocalypse?

April 14th

CLUSTERING ILLUSION

The clustering illusion is our tendency to give meaning to random patterns we perceive. We see these patterns because we see them in data sets that are very large or very small. For small data sets, it could be a winning-streak or a so-called "hot-hand" in sports. We think there is a pattern, but actually it is just coincidence. For very large datasets, random patterns will inevitably occur because of the sheer size.

In 2012, many people were captivated by dire predictions of an apocalypse, inspired by interpretations of the Mayan calendar that seemed to suggest Earth's imminent destruction. The ancient Mayan civilization, which thrived from 2000 BC to 1500 AD across what is now Mexico and Central America, developed an incredibly advanced calendar system. The focus of these apocalyptic theories was the Mayan Long Count calendar, organized into cycles lasting approximately 5,126 years each. December 21, 2012, marked the conclusion of the 13th cycle, which led some to believe that this date would also mark the catastrophic end of the world.

Proponents of this theory cited a series of natural disasters as signs pointing toward this conclusion. These included the 2009 H1N1 pandemic, the 2010 Haiti earthquake, and the 2011 Tōhoku earthquake and tsunami in Japan. These events were perceived as interconnected, heralding the approach of doomsday. However, such connections were coincidental; these were unrelated events that randomly occurred within a short time span.

The clustering illusion leads us to erroneously perceive a pattern or connection in random or unrelated data. Enthralled by this illusion, some people took drastic measures, including stockpiling food and constructing bunkers. The widespread fascination with this idea was further amplified by the media, leading to the production of documentaries like "Doomsday Preppers" and disaster films such as Roland Emmerich's "2012." Ultimately, December 21, 2012, passed without incident, and life continued as usual, debunking the myths surrounding the prophesied end of the world.

Read more about the Maya "Doomsday calendar."

How could you be motivated to do your cancer screening?

April 15th

DECOY EFFECT

The decoy effect describes how, when deciding between two options, adding a third, less appealing option (the decoy) can change how we feel about the two options we were originally considering. Decoys are much worse than one option, but only partially inferior to the second option. The decoy is there to nudge you towards one specific target option. Decoys work because they serve us as reference points that help us (unconsciously) justify our choices.

Very few people are particularly fond of health screenings. Some of us would even remain entirely oblivious to hidden health problems rather than face cancer screenings, such as colorectal cancer. A third of the US population, who should be screened, is not.

Naturally, hospitals have tried various methods to encourage people to undergo cancer testing. These methods have included offering free check-ups. However, let's examine a subtle but smart way of convincing people to attend their check-ups. In one study, patients were given three choices. The first option was to have their screening at their local hospital (the preferred option). Alternatively, they could be allocated to a random hospital, which might have been further away and might involve longer waiting times (the decoy). Of course, they could also opt not to go for the screening at all.

Initially, the decision was simply between going for a free screening at the local hospital or not going at all. The introduction of a third option, the random hospital, served as a decoy, making the local hospital appear much more convenient and appealing in comparison. At the end of the day, the procedure offered was the same, but this strategy effectively utilized the decoy effect. By presenting an option that was notably less convenient (the random hospital), the other choice—the local hospital—seemed much more desirable. Consequently, many participants felt they made a great choice by selecting their local hospital.

This clever use of options increased the likelihood of choosing a screening at the local hospital to about 60%. Interestingly, introducing a third, unappealing option increased screening rates compared to simply offering free screenings at the local hospital.

Can a Bad CEO Teach Us Good Leadership Lessons?

April 16th

SELF-SERVING BIAS

The self-serving bias is our tendency to take credit for good things that happen to us and blame other things or people for bad things that happen. We do that because we have the desire to feel good about ourselves. Being responsible for good things happening boosts our confidence and gives us a sense of control in our lives. When we blame external factors for bad things that happen to us, it can help us feel better about ourselves by protecting our ego.

A good leader takes accountability for their mistakes, even when doing so might compromise their reputation or public image. In contrast, poor leaders deflect blame onto others or external circumstances when facing negative results. When a company fails, they blame their employees; when it succeeds, they claim personal credit. This behavior exemplifies self-serving bias, which drives individuals to embrace favorable outcomes while distancing themselves from negative ones.

A striking example of self-serving bias emerges from the case of Warren Anderson, CEO of Union Carbide during the Bhopal disaster in India. The incident involved a catastrophic leak of over 40 tons of toxic gas from their chemical plant into the surrounding area. According to estimates, between 3,800 and 25,000 people died from direct exposure to the gas cloud, with up to 500,000 others suffering injuries – many of whom continue to experience health effects today. After being arrested in India and released on bail, Anderson fled to the United States to avoid prosecution.

Despite previously acknowledging that the plant operated below required safety standards, when questioned about the disaster's cause, Union Carbide shifted blame to a supposedly disgruntled employee. The company further deflected responsibility by criticizing the Indian government for allowing residential settlements near the plant. Anderson and his company never fully acknowledged their accountability in operating a facility that failed to meet basic safety requirements.

Watch NBC News on the Union Carbide Disaster in Bhopal

Who Is Captain Hindsight?

April 17th

HINDSIGHT BIAS

The hindsight bias is also called the "I-knew-it-all-along" effect. It describes the retrospective overestimation of predictability. In the present, it's hard to tell how something will turn out in the future, but is easy to understand how or why an event happened in retrospect. This bias happens because we mistakenly assume that we had the same understanding of an event before it happened as we do after it happened.

The interpretation of the COVID-19 pandemic evolved significantly as the crisis unfolded. Initially, judgments and decisions were made with limited information, leading to frequent revisions of strategies and opinions. In hindsight, we're all experts. We have all the answers and explanations.

In the second year of the pandemic, former UK prime minister Boris Johnson called opposition leader Sir Keir Starmer "Captain Hindsight" after he criticized Johnson for poorly handling rules for care homes. Sir Keir Starmer said better measures should have been taken to avoid the high number of deaths in the care homes. Boris Johnson replied that it's a lot easier to give advice in the immediate aftermath of incidents and disasters, which is what Keir Starmer did. In his defense, the former prime minister said that the mistakes made in the care homes were the result of not knowing a lot about the virus. He further accused Sir Keir of showing hindsight bias by stating, "Perhaps Captain Hindsight would like to tell us whether he knew that it was being transmitted asymptomatically."

Captain Hindsight is a reference to "South Park", an American animated sitcom. It's celebrated for its ability to address serious real-world issues with dark, often crude humor. In one episode, Captain Hindsight is a superhero character who arrives at disaster scenes and explains what should have been done to prevent the disaster after it has already occurred, rather than offering any real help. His "superpower" is, essentially, the ability to point out the obvious in retrospect, which is why his name is used to mock those who critically evaluate and critique past decisions with the benefit of knowing the outcome.

Trusting Your Gut with Finances?

April 18th

AFFECT HEURISTIC

The affect heuristic is a cognitive bias where decisions are based on emotions rather than objective information. This process allows for quick decision-making, which can be advantageous for survival by enabling fast reactions. However, it often leads to suboptimal choices by overshadowing more analytical thinking. When our emotions are strongly positive or negative, we might not seek further information or consider alternative options, limiting our decision quality.

Bernie Madoff was the leader of the biggest Ponzi scheme in history. A Ponzi scheme is a type of fraud that involves acquiring new investors and returning profits to previous investors using money from the newer ones.

For almost 20 years, Bernie Madoff convinced regulators and investors that he ran a legitimate investment company. After a series of investigations, he was found to have pulled off the largest Ponzi scheme in history, defrauding (directly and indirectly) 3 million people who lost $65 billion in total.

However, until his frauds were discovered, very few people questioned their trust in Madoff. He had a great financial track record, was an authority figure in the industry for years, and had influential links that made investors trust him. From the outside, Madoff looked and felt like a successful individual who sent out every possible trust signal to both novice and expert investors. He was entrusted with the money of major businesses, celebrities, and powerful individuals.

Author Andrew Miller proposes that due to the influence of the affect heuristic, investors in Madoff's company relied on their emotions stemming from their trust in Madoff. Naturally, their greed to earn a substantial profit also clouded their judgment. They neglected to thoroughly investigate the situation, as their gut instinct assured them that everything appeared to be in order. These emotions outweighed all the other shady details, such as the overly complicated and inaccessible language used in Madoff's documents, and the unrealistic high returns that Madoff promised.

Watch Malcolm Gladwell talk about how Bernie Madoff fooled everyone

Too Tired for Salad? How Ego Depletion Affects Our Choices

April 19th

EGO-DEPLETION

Ego depletion refers to the limited capacity of our mental willpower and self-control, which can be exhausted through demanding activities like decision-making, emotional restraint, or resisting temptations. When this psychological resource is depleted, our ability to maintain behavioral control diminishes. This mental fatigue can be triggered by stress, physical exhaustion, or insufficient sleep.

It's Friday evening, and you just finished work. Until this point in your day, you made several (un)conscious decisions. You decided to get out of bed instead of sleeping in, you heroically said no to the bakery on your street, you remained focused on numerous meetings. Finally, you also mustered the last ounce of motivation to make it to a gym class.

There were so many things your brain said "no" to—but, unfortunately, your mental resources aren't endless. At some point, you are likely to just give in to whatever opportunities for instant gratification present themselves to you. This is also known as ego depletion, a mental state in which we no longer have the resources to refrain from making decisions that make us feel good.

Ego depletion explains why we are more likely to order pizza on Friday night instead of Sunday afternoon or why a tiring house move results in pizza and beers instead of salads and smoothies. When we are too depleted to make decisions that require a degree of self-control, we will go with the option that feels the easiest and most aligned with our impulses.

Choosing satisfactory options when we are mentally depleted can be beneficial because it offers temporary relief from the demands of self-control. Indulging in less healthy foods or alcohol triggers a dopamine release, providing immediate pleasure and a sense of reward. While this approach does not truly replenish our mental resources in a sustainable manner, it does provide a temporary sense of ease and relief, making us feel momentarily recharged after a day filled with continuous demands and challenges.

Watch a TED Talk by Dan Ariely about self control

Why Was the Barnum Effect Named After the Master of Hoaxes?

April 20th

FORER EFFECT OR BARNUM EFFECT

The Forer effect, also known as the Barnum effect, describes the observation that people will give high accuracy ratings to personality descriptions that are supposedly tailored specifically for them. However, in reality, these descriptions are vague and general enough to apply to many people. This effect can help explain why some beliefs and practices, like astrology, palm reading, graphology, and some types of personality tests, are so popular.

The 2017 film "Greatest Showman" chronicles the life of Phineas Taylor Barnum, the man behind the so-called Barnum effect, with Hugh Jackman in the starring role as Barnum. Phineas Taylor Barnum was a renowned American showman who lived from 1810 to 1891. Barnum's extraordinary promotional skills and his talent for engaging audiences with his unconventional and often contentious acts gained him fame. In 1841, Barnum took control of the American Museum in New York and transformed it into one of the most spectacular entertainment attractions of the 19th century. He was unafraid of employing deception, staging contests, or fraud. For example, Barnum had an employee pose as a London doctor to prove the existence of the "Fiji mermaid," which was actually the upper body of a monkey skillfully attached to a fish's lower body.

The term "Barnum effect" was coined by Paul E. Meehl, who proposed the name to critique certain practices in psychological assessment. Meehl wrote, "I suggest—and I am serious—that we adopt the phrase Barnum effect to stigmatize those pseudo-successful clinical procedures in which personality descriptions from tests are tailored to fit the patient largely or wholly by virtue of their triviality." Meehl was critiquing the tendency within segments of the psychological community to use vague statements in clinical assessments that could seemingly apply to anyone. These assessments, he argued, were similar to the misleading tactics used by Barnum. Thus, Meehl drew a parallel between Barnum's deceptive practices and the superficial techniques he observed being used by some of his professional colleagues in psychology.

View the trailer for "The Greatest Showman"

Does Mother Earth Have a Mind of Her Own?

April 21st

ANTHROPOMORPHISM

Anthropomorphism is our natural tendency to attribute human traits, emotions, and intentions to non-humans, for example, animals, gods, natural forces, and the like. We do this because we naturally know more about human traits than non-human ones. Therefore, these come easier to mind, and that saves mental energy.

The Gaia Hypothesis is an interesting idea that has caught the attention of both scientists and non-scientists. It suggests that Earth's biosphere is a self-regulating, complex system that maintains conditions suitable for life. The Gaia Hypothesis can also be viewed as a great example of anthropomorphism.

Proponents of the theory describe Earth as a "living being" with intentions and a purpose. This characterization showcases our tendency to attribute human qualities to natural forces. James Lovelock, a chemist, and Lynn Margulis, a microbiologist, developed the Gaia Hypothesis in the 1970s. Lovelock called the idea "Gaia" after the Greek goddess Gaia, who was the personification of the Earth. The hypothesis proposes that living organisms interact with their inorganic surroundings on Earth to form a complex system that keeps the conditions on Earth suitable for life.

The Gaia Hypothesis has influenced various movements, including deep ecology and Gaianism. This movement posits that all life forms are part of a single living planetary being called Gaia. In Gaianism, Gaia made the atmosphere, seas, and Earth's crust on purpose to create that self-regulating system. The Gaia Hypothesis serves as a perfect example of how humans attribute human traits to non-human entities, in this case, the Earth itself. The Gaia Hypothesis has had a significant effect on how we think about the Earth's biosphere and on environmental movements. It also highlights the power of anthropomorphic thinking in shaping our perspective on the natural world.

Do You Remeber the Satanic Panic?

April 22nd

AVAILABILITY BIAS

The availability bias is our tendency to make decisions based on information that comes to mind quickly and easily. It's a mental shortcut that gives more weight to information that was learned recently or that is easy to remember, for example, because it is an emotionally loaded memory. Our brain wants to save mental energy. So, we often go with the first information that comes to mind instead of putting in more mental effort to dig deeper.

The "Satanic Panic" in the 1980s was a moral panic over cults performing child abuse and satanic rituals. It is a prime example of the availability bias. The Satanic Panic began with a few allegations that quickly spiraled into mass hysteria. The emotionally charged nature of the subject matter and the extensive media coverage made satanic ritual abuse very available in people's minds. As a result, people began to see Satanists everywhere, not because the allegations were substantiated but because the availability bias led them to overestimate the likelihood of such events.

Sensationalist media coverage and talk shows amplified fears of satanic ritual abuse. Michelle Smith and her psychiatrist wrote about Michelle's alleged memories of abuse at the hands of a satanic cult in their book "Michelle Remembers." The book became a bestseller and further fueled the panic. Law enforcement pursued allegations without a thorough investigation. Mental health professionals quickly accepted the existence of satanic ritual abuse, sometimes using "Michelle Remembers" as a training text. Many high-profile cases, like the McMartin Preschool case, received a lot of attention from the media and resulted in long trials.

Nearly 200 people were charged with crimes during the Satanic Panic, and dozens were convicted. Many of those convicted were eventually freed, some after spending years in prison. In 1994, officials found that none of the roughly 12,000 accusations of group cult sexual abuse based on satanic rituals could be substantiated.

Watch "McMartin Preschool: Anatomy of a Panic"

Why Did Liberty, Equality, and Fraternity Turn Into a Bloody Feast?

April 23rd

GROUPTHINK

Groupthink is when our desire for harmony and conformity within a group leads to dysfunctional decision-making. Group members prioritize agreement over critical evaluation, resulting in a loss of individual creativity and thinking. This can lead to an inflated sense of confidence in the group's abilities, an undervaluation of opponents, group pressure, and potentially harmful actions towards outsiders.

The French Revolution (1789-1799) was a period of radical change and upheaval in France, ultimately leading to the overthrow of the monarchy and the rise of Napoleon Bonaparte. One of the most infamous periods of the revolution, the Reign of Terror (1793-1794), saw the execution of thousands of people deemed to be enemies of the state. This bloody period serves as a chilling example of how groupthink can transform noble ideals into devastating actions.

During the French Revolution, various political factions competed to shape the future of France. The Jacobin movement, which included leaders like Maximilien Robespierre and Georges Danton, emerged as the most radical of these groups. While the Jacobins championed the ideals of liberty, equality, and fraternity, their absolute conviction in these principles and their implementation led to increasingly brutal measures and unwarranted violence. The group's collective mindset prioritized their shared revolutionary goals above all else, leading to the systematic suppression of dissenting voices, the dismissal of moderate positions, and violent actions towards perceived outsiders.

Robespierre's Committee of Public Safety received unprecedented power to detain and execute people suspected of participating in counter-revolutionary activities. This authority, combined with the group's rigid ideology, resulted in the arrest of over 300,000 people and the formal execution of approximately 17,000, including King Louis XVI and Queen Marie Antoinette. Up to 50,000 people died during this reign in total. The Reign of Terror finally came to an end in July 1794 when Robespierre himself was arrested and executed, a victim of the very system he had helped create.

Can You Outsmart the Market's Herd Mentality?

April 24th

BANDWAGON EFFECT

The bandwagon effect refers to the phenomenon in which a belief or behavior becomes more popular as more people adopt it. This can lead to a self-reinforcing cycle, as the increased popularity of the belief or behavior encourages more people to adopt it. The effect is caused by our desire to conform to social norms and our belief that the majority must be correct. It can also be caused by peer pressure and the fear of being left out or made fun of if we don't fit in.

A dramatic example of the bandwagon effect occurred during the "flash crash" on May 6, 2010. On this day, the Dow Jones, a key index tracking the performance of the U.S. stock market, experienced its largest drop in decades, plummeting 900 points (9%) within just five minutes. An astonishing two billion shares valued at $56 billion were exchanged. Navinder Sarao, a day trader from London, is believed to have triggered this 2010 flash crash in the U.S. stock market. He exploited the bandwagon effect by employing a tactic known as "spoofing."

Spoofing is a deceptive technique in which a trader, such as Sarao, places bets on a particular outcome and then manipulates the market in their favor. For example, Sarao bet on the S&P 500's price declining. The S&P 500, a broader index representing the value of the 500 largest U.S. corporations, was his target. He then created large fake orders in the opposite direction, selling numerous S&P 500 contracts. The market reacted with panic to this apparent massive sell-off, causing people to sell their holdings out of fear. More people jumped on this bandwagon, creating a self-reinforcing cycle that drove prices downward. In the end, Sarao, who orchestrated the fake orders, emerged victorious, as his initial bet was on lower prices.

Sarao was charged with 22 criminal counts, carrying a cumulative total of 380 years in prison. While in custody, it was revealed that the majority of his profits, approximately $50 million, had been lost. Given his diagnosis of Asperger's syndrome, his cooperation with authorities, and his non-greedy motives, the U.S. government showed leniency.

View a Bloomberg video about the Flash-Crash-Traders

Can confirmation bias explain the Salem Witch Trails?

April 25th

CONFIRMATION BIAS

Confirmation bias is our tendency to look for, acknowledge, favor, and remember information in a way that supports what we already think or believe. This bias occurs when we ignore information that contradicts our ideas or interpret ambiguous facts as evidence supporting our existing beliefs. Situations that involve emotionally charged topics, strongly held beliefs, or things we really want to happen are most susceptible to this bias.

In the late 17th century, the quiet town of Salem, Massachusetts, was gripped by a wave of hysteria fueled by superstition and fear. The residents believed that witchcraft was responsible for crop failures, illnesses, and even inexplicable deaths. During this period, known as the Salem Witch Trials, 20 innocent people were executed, and many others were imprisoned. The Salem Witch Trials are a stark example of confirmation bias in action.

The witch hunt in Salem began when a group of young girls exhibited seizures along with other strange and inexplicable behavior. Already steeped in superstition and fear of the supernatural, the community quickly blamed witchcraft. This initial conclusion set the stage for confirmation bias to take hold as people began to search for evidence to support their theory. Formal complaints were then lodged against those suspected of witchcraft, which brought them before local magistrates for pre-trial examinations. If deemed sufficient, the cases were escalated to formal trials.

As the trials progressed, the townspeople and authorities often dismissed any evidence that contradicted their existing beliefs. Confirmation bias fueled the hysteria and led people to find "evidence" of witchcraft even where none existed, creating a vicious cycle of accusations and fear. Much of this "evidence" was based on claims of witnesses having seen the accused's spirit or specter causing harm to victims. The community's fervent religious convictions and ignorance of the natural causes of various misfortunes increased its susceptibility to confirmation bias. The Salem Witch Trials serve as a chilling reminder of the power of confirmation bias and the consequences it can have.

Why Does Cupid's Arrow Attract More
When We're in Relationships?

April 26th

PRIMING EFFECT

The priming effect occurs when something we see or hear influences our thoughts or actions without us being aware of it. This can happen with words, pictures, or sounds we encounter. When our brain is primed, it becomes easier for us to think about, remember, and act on related information because the things we read, see, or hear activate connected information in the brain.

A perfect example of the priming effect can be observed when we enter a new romantic relationship. Normally, while single, attracting potential partners can feel challenging. However, once in a relationship, individuals often notice an increase in attention from others, as well as a heightened awareness of other potential romantic partners. This phenomenon was explored in a study involving 560 students who were asked to reflect on their experiences in two distinct roles: as someone in a new relationship noticing an increase in admirers, and as an admirer who feels more attracted to someone who has recently entered a relationship.

The results were striking. Over two-thirds of the participants reported a noticeable increase in the number of people showing interest in them once they were in a relationship. Conversely, about half of the respondents admitted to feeling more drawn to individuals who had just started dating someone else. Many attributed this increased interest to a sense of jealousy or a desire for something they couldn't have.

Interestingly, participants who recently entered a relationship did not believe that changes in their own behavior, such as increased confidence or improved appearance, played a significant role in attracting more admirers. Instead, it seems that the mere change in relationship status was enough to spark increased attention from others.

This study exemplifies the priming effect by showing how simple information, like someone's relationship status, can subconsciously influence our thoughts, emotions, and actions.

Would You Buy a Ticket Twice?

April 27th

SUNK COST FALLACY

The sunk cost fallacy is when we make a decision based on how much we have already invested in something rather than on whether it is the best choice for us right now. When we feel like we have already invested a lot in something, we feel like we would be losing something if we were to let it go. Another reason that the sunk cost fallacy occurs is because we tend to focus on the past rather than the present when we make decisions.

Sometimes, our financial decisions are irrational. Look at the following "lost ticket scenario" given to participants in a research study: "Imagine that you want to see a play where admission is $20. In your wallet, you have the ticket you already bought and another $20 bill. When you arrive at the theater, you discover that you lost the ticket." Before you read further, answer the following question: Would you use the $20 to buy a new ticket?

Participants were asked the same question, and more than half of them (54%) said no. Now, consider this small change in the scenario above: "You're on your way to a theater. In your wallet, you have two $20 bills. When you arrive at the theater, you discover that you've lost one of the bills."

When people were asked if they were willing to spend the remaining $20 on a ticket, the majority of them (88%) said yes. Yet, the amount of money lost is the same in both scenarios above. Regardless of whether you lost a ticket or a bill, you are still $20 poorer. However, people who have already bought a ticket perceive the loss differently because they have already invested financial resources. It seems we are not willing to pay twice for the same thing.

The main reason why there was such a massive difference in responses to the two scenarios is the sunk-cost fallacy. Because we've already made an investment, we feel that this should influence our decision-making. But in reality, the money is gone either way and cannot be recovered.

Iceland's Icarus: Flying Too Close to the Sun of Self-Belief?

April 28th

DUNNING–KRUGER EFFECT

The Dunning–Kruger effect describes our tendency to overestimate our own abilities in areas that we are unskilled in or lack knowledge in. This happens when we know just enough to think we are great but not enough to tell the difference between good and bad. We just don't know yet what we could do better. The effect also applies to society as a whole. The most uninformed citizens are often also the most confident ones.

A prime illustration of the Dunning-Kruger effect can be found in the political career of David Oddson, who served as Iceland's prime minister from 1991 to 2004. During his tenure, he took the fateful decision to privatize the nation's banks, inadvertently jeopardizing their stability. The privatization of banks in Iceland led to rapid financial sector expansion driven by external borrowing and speculative investments, with minimal regulatory oversight.

Subsequently, as governor of Iceland's central bank from 2005 to 2009, Oddson permitted the bank's balance sheets to swell to a staggering ten times the country's GDP. His apparent mismanagement sparked public outcry and protests, but he steadfastly refused to resign, ultimately leading to his removal by Parliament.

The privatization of banks, coupled with mismanagement during his tenure as the director of the central bank, led to a fragile financial system. This system ultimately collapsed during the 2008 global financial crisis, causing severe economic repercussions for Iceland. Time magazine went on to name David Oddson as one of the 25 individuals responsible for the global financial crisis.

Yet, in spite of this ignominious track record, Oddson's audacious ambitions remained undimmed. In 2016, he boldly announced his candidacy for the presidency of Iceland, asserting, "My experience and knowledge, which is considerable, could go well with this office." This statement serves as an exemplary demonstration of the Dunning-Kruger effect in action.

Read an article where Oddsson defends his role in Iceland's collapse

Change of Heart: Are We Ever Done Changing?

April 29th

END-OF-HISTORY ILLUSION

The end-of-history illusion refers to our tendency to underestimate the extent of personal changes that will occur in the future. While we acknowledge that our personalities, values, and tastes have evolved over time, we often believe that they will remain relatively stable going forward. This misconception persists regardless of age. The illusion arises because we find it hard to imagine personal changes and thus assume that such changes are unlikely to occur.

Do we ever stop growing up? On a certain level, we seem to believe we do. In a study that asked people how much they think they would change in the next 10 years, many reported that they would stay the same. Young people, middle-aged people, and older ones all believed they changed significantly in the past but wouldn't change much in the future.

In fact, it seems that many of us believe that we have reached a final version of ourselves that will remain relatively consistent for the rest of our lives. Because of this, we overpay for future opportunities that align with our current values and interests but do not consider natural changes to our personalities, preferences, or belief systems.

The "end-of-history illusion" explains this irrational belief that many of us subconsciously hold: that we changed more in the past than we will in the future. If someone had asked us 10 years ago how much we would change in the foreseeable future, we would have said "perhaps very little." Yet when looking at our past, the changes we have gone through are significant.

The end-of-history illusion has practical consequences for our lives. We invest in training and education based on our current interests. We marry people with whom our current version of ourselves is compatible and choose places to live based on temporary needs (such as a busy city suitable for someone aged 25–35). We omit that our professional course might take us on a different journey or that our current lifestyle and choice of partners are unsuitable for our future selves.

Eco-Friendly or Ego-Friendly?

April 30th

HALO EFFECT

The halo effect is a type of cognitive bias in which our overall opinion of a person or brand affects how we feel about the specific qualities of that person or brand. If we have a good feeling about something as a whole, we are more likely to think that its individual parts are good as well. We do that because it saves cognitive effort to use our overall impressions as a shortcut to make judgments rather than evaluating each aspect of something separately.

Many brands communicate how socially responsible they are in one way or another. For example, Google adds a green leaf icon to many of their services, whether it's in Maps or their cloud services, to indicate the environmentally friendly option. Another notable example is Apple, which showcased its efforts through the "Mother Nature" ad. Despite being criticized for its humor, the ad effectively drew attention to Apple's environmental initiatives. Corporate social responsibility (CSR) is admirable and noble, but what is behind all of this?

If we were to speculate about the hidden reasons why corporations invest so much in these programs, many of us would immediately see this: CSR is good for the environment and the world at large, but it also undoubtedly benefits the companies themselves. When someone does a wonderful deed, our opinion of them improves. This is known as the halo effect, where specific traits influence the way we perceive a brand.

One study tested whether the positive initiatives taken by large companies had an effect on their public image after some negative news about them. Not surprisingly, social responsibility actions attenuate the public's inclination to take negative action against a company. In other words, companies can convince people to turn a blind eye to their mistakes if they have previously shown concern for a wider problem in the world. Another study found that companies with extensive CSR programs tend to receive more lenient court decisions in unrelated corruption cases.

Watch Apple's "Mother Nature" ad

∞
MAY

Can Trusting Tech in Medicine be a Deadly Dose of Misjudgment?

May 1st

AUTOMATION BIAS

Automation bias means that we are likely to follow the advice of automated systems, like those in airplane cockpits or on your phone (think autocorrect, Google Maps). We tend to ignore contradictory information made without automation, even if it is correct. In decision-making, we like to take the path of least cognitive effort. We are happy to accept the answers that automated systems give us because it is often easier than having to think for ourselves.

You've probably never heard of the Therac-25, a radiation therapy machine. Between 1985 and 1987, accidents involving these machines showed how dangerous automation bias can be in the field of medicine. Medical professionals trusted an automated system, which resulted in six incidents of massive radiation overdoses.

The Therac-25 was the company's third radiation therapy machine and was made to work only with computer control. The Therac-25 relied only on software for safety and didn't have any hardware interlocks or supervisory circuits that could shut down the machine or trigger an alarm. Between 1985 and 1987, six patients were exposed to massive overdoses of radiation. The accidents led to severe injuries, and four of the patients died as a result. Operators of the machine ignored warning signs, assuming the computer must be accurate. After the incidents, a thorough investigation was done, and it was found that there were two main causes: software bugs and the fact that safety was based on the computer in charge. The Therac-25 depended solely on its software for safety measures, lacking any physical safety mechanisms such as hardware interlocks that could intervene to shut down the machine in case of an error. This over-reliance on software, coupled with the inexperience of the programmers who were not well-versed in coding for real-time systems, left the machine vulnerable to critical failures.

The Therac-25 was declared defective, and the producer issued software and hardware updates, allowing the machine to return to service. However, another patient was exposed to an overdoses of radiation in 1987 due to a new software issue. The patient died three months later.

When Should Homeopathy Take a Backseat?

May 2nd

ILLUSION OF CONTROL

The illusion of control occurs when we believe we have more control over external events than we do. We frequently believe we have (or had) some control over events that are actually random. Researchers have found that people who feel in control will engage in healthier behaviors, feel less stress, and have better overall mental health. Therefore, this illusion makes us feel better about ourselves and the world around us, but it can also seduce us into relying on superstitions.

In the United States, homeopathy has expanded into a $1.2 billion industry, with projections suggesting a growth of 12.5% in 2023. Although once perceived as a practice favored by the 'hippie' community, homeopathy has gained widespread acceptance and is frequently employed as an alternative, or even a replacement, for conventional medical treatments. The increasing popularity of homeopathic medicine can largely be attributed to the powerful placebo effect it often induces, offering individuals an illusion of control and leading them to feel they can manage their illnesses. This effect leads patients to experience real improvements in their symptoms, even though the treatment itself has no direct therapeutic properties.

However, there is a perilous aspect to homeopathy that becomes evident when it's used recklessly. A tragic instance of this occurred in Sydney, involving a couple's decision to solely rely on natural remedies to treat their 9-month-old daughter's severe skin disorder. The baby's father, a lecturer in homeopathy, sought help exclusively from fellow practitioners of natural medicine. Despite the baby's progressively worsening condition, evident when her black hair turned white, the parents persisted in their aversion to mainstream medicine.

Ultimately, their daughter became malnourished, and her health declined irreversibly. By the time she was brought to a hospital, it was too late for any intervention, and she passed away three days later. The parents were subsequently convicted of manslaughter and received several years of imprisonment. This heartbreaking event underscores the potential dangers of overestimating one's control over serious medical conditions through alternative remedies.

Possession Obsession: Are We Overvaluing What's Ours?

May 3rd

ENDOWMENT EFFECT

The endowment is the idea that when we own an object, we tend to value it more than we would if it were someone else's. The mere feeling of ownership makes us value it more. One reason for this effect is that we are loss-averse. We really dislike losing things. Ownership therefore influences how we value an object and how much we are willing to accept in exchange for it.

Owning something makes us value it more than if we didn't own it, and the longer we possess something, the more valuable we perceive it to be. By the same token, people often request a higher price to give up an object they possess than they would be willing to pay. The discrepancy between these two situations is the essence of the endowment effect.

In a popular experiment, a student group was endowed with coffee mugs. Later on, they were offered the choice to trade them for a chocolate bar. A second group was endowed with a chocolate bar, which they could also swap for a coffee mug later. Finally, the third group wasn't endowed with either and was just told to make a choice between mugs or chocolate bars.

The third group didn't show a particular trend in their preferences: 56% chose the coffee mug, and 44% went for the chocolate bar. This balanced division indicates that, absent any prior ownership, the items held more or less equal value to the participants. Given the nearly even split in preferences of the third group, one might expect that individuals would be similarly inclined to switch their initial choices when presented with the option to trade. However, the behavior of the first two groups, who were initially endowed with either a mug or a chocolate bar, contradicted this expectation.

Instead, the first two groups showed high resistance to swapping the mug for chocolate and vice versa: out of all those given the coffee mug, 89% decided to keep it and only 11% exchanged it for chocolate. Similarly, only 10% of the students who got the chocolate bar first decided to change it to a mug. This experiment shows that possessing something does influence our perception of an object's value. The mere idea that it belongs to us makes it a lot more valuable.

Head in the Sand: Do Investors Ignore Bad News?

May 4th

OSTRICH EFFECT OR NORMALCY BIAS

> *Normalcy bias, also known as "ostrich effect," makes us downplay warnings about dangers or ignore negative situations completely. We underestimate how likely it is that a disaster will happen and how it might affect us. We do that because we want to avoid an unpleasant emotional impact in the short term. The name comes from the popular (but false) belief that ostriches bury their heads in the sand when in danger.*

When you anticipate receiving bad news, your natural inclination might be to resist absorbing the details. If you know something is going to ruin your day, why delve deeper into it? This reasoning results from the ostrich effect, which makes us "stick our heads in the sand" instead of confronting a difficult situation.

Even professional investors are vulnerable to this. A Scandinavian research study tested the hypothesis that investors check the value of their portfolios more frequently in rising markets but "put their heads in the sand" when markets are flat or failing. The study found that investors will collect more information following favorable news and avoid information following neutral or bad news. For example, depending on the information they receive about the stock market, they will decide whether to check their personal portfolios.

This avoidance behavior isn't entirely irrational. In their case, the ostrich effect is used to shield oneself from upsetting information. Given the volatile nature of investing, controlling which information to seek and which to avoid is a form of managing one's emotions and preventing impulsive behaviors, such as making hasty decisions to buy or sell in a panic.

Just as with investors, all humans exhibit this bias. It helps control what information they pay attention to. Burying your head in the sand can seem useful in the short term. It can serve as an emotional regulation tool to avoid impulsive decisions. However, it's not a sustainable long-term strategy. Continuous avoidance of difficult situations can lead to larger problems in the end.

Mirror, Mirror on the Wall:
Does Our Group Shape Our Self-View After All?

May 5th

STEREOTYPING

Stereotypes exist when we think that a category of people always has certain characteristics or behaviors. The brain has a natural tendency to put things into groups. By grouping into categories, we can process our environments more efficiently. It is a mental shortcut that saves time and mental energy. Because of that, we might assume that certain stereotypes apply to a certain member of a group even though we know nothing about that individual.

Stereotyping affects not only how we view members of other groups but also how we perceive ourselves. When you have always belonged to a certain social group, it can be difficult to define yourself outside of that group's default characteristics. Moreover, when you are repeatedly exposed to information about a group you feel a sense of belonging to, you gradually internalize these characteristics and make them part of your identity.

Research illustrates this self-stereotyping effect. For example, studies show that both men and women often define their career trajectories based on cultural beliefs about which jobs "are a good fit for their gender." These cultural beliefs significantly influence individuals' perceptions of their own competence and their career-related decisions. Consider how women, when faced with the stereotype that they underperform in mathematical skills compared to men, might not even attempt to excel in scientific careers. Consequently, people no longer make objective decisions about their careers because their perception of their own competence has been shaped by stereotypes. How society views the group you belong to ultimately influences how you view yourself.

The impact of such stereotypes on self-perception becomes particularly evident in global contexts. According to the World Value Survey, almost 70% of Bangladeshis believe men to be better business executives than women. As a result, women in Bangladesh may unintentionally internalize this bias, stifling their own ambitions and inadvertently perpetuating the very stereotype that holds them back.

More effort, more love?

May 6th

IKEA EFFECT

The IKEA effect refers to our tendency to place a disproportionately high value on objects that we helped create, such as IKEA furniture. We do that regardless of the quality of the end product. This bias helps us to feel better about ourselves in two ways. First, we want to feel that our effort was well invested and that we did not waste our time but instead created something of value. Secondly, creating things makes us feel more competent.

To many in the West, the concept of arranged marriage seems akin to a lifelong relationship lottery. How can one forge a fulfilling, enduring bond when the choice of partner wasn't theirs to begin with? However, a closer examination reveals that arranged marriages aren't necessarily a recipe for discontent. Astonishingly, they boast lower divorce rates and, perhaps more surprisingly, higher levels of marital satisfaction. One study in particular highlights that Indian couples in arranged marriages residing in the U.S. report greater satisfaction than American couples who married for love.

If these statistics surprise you, it may be because you struggle to understand satisfaction in the absence of personal choice. We often assume that the sheer freedom to select our life partners will pave the way for perpetual happiness. Yet reality suggests otherwise. This paradox can be partially explained by the IKEA effect: the notion that our investment of time and resources in creating something amplifies our appreciation for it.

In arranged marriages, individuals are often compelled to invest more effort to nurture the relationship. Knowing they didn't handpick their spouse, they tend to exert additional effort to understand their partner, harmonize their interests, and navigate conflicts. This intensive investment is no easy feat. And here, the IKEA effect comes into play: the more effort we (have to) dedicate to building something, the more we value the end result.

Remember That Techno-Apocalypse That Never Occured?

May 7th

ILLUSION OF VALIDITY

The illusion of validity is a cognitive bias where we overestimate our ability to understand and predict an outcome based on the information we have. When analyzing new information, we rely on things we already know, for example, stereotypes and prior beliefs. When we assume that what we know is valid enough to predict what will happen in different contexts, we make confident predictions that can turn out to be utterly inaccurate.

The Y2K scare, which occurred between 1999 and 2000, is a perfect example of the illusion of validity. The Y2K (short for "year 2000") bug was a problem with dates in computer programs. In some cases, programs used only the last two digits to show the year—for example, "99" instead of "1999." People were worried that this flaw could lead to widespread technological failures because computers could mistake "00" for "1900" instead of "2000."

Many experts predicted that technology would fail all over the world because of the "Y2K bug," which caused widespread panic. As the year 2000 approached, concerns about the Y2K bug grew exponentially. Experts, news media, and government officials warned of dire consequences, such as financial crises or power outages. People around the world prepared for the worst, stocking up on supplies and taking precautions to safeguard their computer systems.

In reality, the Y2K bug had a minimal impact on computer systems and infrastructure. There were no major technological failures or disruptions. In fact, countries that had done little to prepare for Y2K, such as Italy, Russia, and South Korea, experienced no more problems than those that had invested millions of dollars in combating the issue. This outcome demonstrates the illusion of validity at work. Using their knowledge of computer systems and programming, many experts were convinced that widespread technology failures would occur. They made these predictions because they believed they understood enough about the problem to make accurate forecasts.

All In with the House Money?

May 8th

FRAMING EFFECT

The framing effect occurs when we draw different conclusions from identical information based solely on how that information is presented. This can happen when something is framed either positively or negatively, or as a gain versus a loss - we naturally tend to avoid losses in such situations. Our judgment can also shift depending on which features of the information are highlighted, even though the underlying facts remain exactly the same.

Information is rarely perceived objectively. Instead, we filter it through personal lenses, which psychologists recognize as the framing effect. As a result, people often draw vastly different conclusions from the same basic information, depending on their perspective and how the information is presented.

This cognitive bias manifests particularly strongly in our relationship with money. In gambling, for instance, players frame wins and losses according to their overall performance that day. While a $300 loss represents the same monetary value regardless of context, the framing effect influences how people interpret this loss. Consider winning $1,000 before losing $300 - most people would view that loss merely as a reduction in their gains rather than an actual loss.

This psychological phenomenon gave rise to the term "house money," which refers to money that a gambler has won from the casino (the "house") rather than the money they brought to the gambling table. The house money effect leads people to become more risk-seeking after a prior gain since they perceive potential losses as merely reduced gains. This mindset is especially prevalent when a potential loss is significantly smaller than the original gain. The effect extends beyond gambling to other financial situations, such as investing, where individuals may take greater risks with profits from previous investments.

Thus, the framing effect can serve as a powerful rationalization tool for gambling behavior. It distorts our perception of money, even though the reality remains simple: we're either losing or winning actual money, regardless of its source or how we frame it.

Are Referendums Failing to Capture the Full Story?

May 9th

BINARY BIAS

Binary bias is our tendency to categorize things or people into two distinct categories, often based on their perceived characteristics or attributes. This can lead to oversimplification, stereotyping, and discrimination. We do that because it helps us make sense of the world around us quickly. From an evolutionary perspective, we need to quickly distinguish between potential allies and threats, categorizing people as friends or foes.

Political referendums are, by their very nature, binary propositions. They ask voters to make a choice between two opposing options, often on highly complex issues. While this approach may appear straightforward, it can lead to the oversimplification of multifaceted topics.

The 2016 Brexit referendum serves as a prime example of the dangers of binary bias. The question of whether the United Kingdom should remain a member of the European Union or leave was reduced to a simple "Leave" or "Remain" choice. This approach didn't consider the many complicated economic, political, and social factors that go into making decisions. Media headlines and campaign slogans became the dominant sources of information. The slogan "Take back control," for example, effectively combined the promise of a bright future with the assertion that something rightfully belonged to the British people. Another compelling slogan, "We send the EU £350 million a week. Let's fund our NHS instead," played on financial concerns by suggesting a redirection of funds to the National Health Service (NHS).

The 2014 Scottish independence referendum is another case in which binary bias shaped public opinion. Voters were asked to decide between two options: "Yes" for independence or "No" to remain part of the United Kingdom. This simplistic choice did not capture the intricate historical, economic, and cultural factors at play. The referendum was often framed as a choice between an independent Scotland and a United Kingdom under English rule, despite the existence of many other dimensions to the debate.

In both cases, the binary nature of referendums led to dangerously oversimplified answers to difficult questions.

Cheat Now, Rationalize Later:
Are We Fooling Ourselves into Morality?

May 10th

COGNITIVE DISSONANCE

Cognitive dissonance describes the mental discomfort we experience when there is a conflict between our beliefs, actions, or perceptions. This discomfort often arises when our actions contradict our beliefs or when we hold two opposing beliefs simultaneously. To alleviate this discomfort, we may adjust our beliefs, perceptions, or actions to create a more consistent internal state. Achieving this internal consistency is crucial, as it helps maintain our sense of identity and coherence.

Plagiarism scandals have been particularly damaging for German politicians, often resulting in career-ending embarrassment. In Germany, a mistake in a doctoral thesis can have severe consequences, unlike scandals common in other countries involving shady backroom deals or extramarital affairs. These scandals were notably prevalent in Angela Merkel's cabinet, where plagiarism scandals were the number one reason for politicians' departure. Even though these politicians say they stand for values like integrity and honesty, they cheated. This conflict between their actions and proclaimed values undoubtedly leads to cognitive dissonance. How do politicians and others who cheat reconcile the discomfort of dishonesty with their desire to see themselves as good people?

A research study from 2021 showed how people who cheat rationalize their behavior. In this experiment, participants were provided with questions and the correct answers displayed in small, upside-down print in the corner of a screen in front of them. They also received explicit instructions not to look at these answers; however, this setup presented a perfect opportunity to cheat. Participants who were given the chance to cheat in this test were more likely to later state in an interview that they knew the answers all along. Through this self-deception, cheaters are able to reduce the cognitive dissonance.

Politicians caught in plagiarism scandals likely engage in similar cognitive gymnastics. They delude themselves into believing that their accomplishments were earned through genuine knowledge to uphold their image of integrity, despite the contradiction in their actions.

Do Trending Topics Dictate Political Decisions?

May 11th

AVAILABILITY BIAS

The availability bias is our tendency to make decisions based on information that comes to mind quickly and easily. It's a mental shortcut that gives more weight to information that was learned recently or that is easy to remember, for example, because it is an emotionally loaded memory. Our brain wants to save mental energy. So, we often go with the first information that comes to mind instead of putting in more mental effort to dig deeper.

Political decision-making is often assumed to be a straightforward reaction to global events: something happens, and policymakers respond. However, this process is far more complex and susceptible to cognitive biases than it may appear. Political elites, despite their access to extensive resources and knowledge, are not immune to the influence of biases that can distort decision-making.

A striking example of such bias is the prevalence of 'availability bias' among political elites. This cognitive shortcut leads individuals to rely on information that is most immediate and memorable, rather than what is necessarily most appropriate. This phenomenon was clearly illustrated in a 2018 study examining policy decisions in Latin America.

When Chile implemented a pioneering pension scheme in 2007, it inadvertently set a precedent for nearby countries. These nations, influenced by the proximity and recency of Chile's reforms, adopted similar pension policies. Instead of delving into detailed legislative research or tailoring unique solutions to fit their specific needs, these countries opted for the path of least resistance: emulating a model that was readily observable and straightforward to implement.

An interesting finding from the study is that despite their susceptibility to availability bias, political elites are less likely to resort to these mental shortcuts than ordinary citizens, thanks to their greater resources and knowledge. This suggests that while biases are a universal human trait, the capacity to mitigate their impact varies significantly across different levels of decision-making authority. To say it in the words of the researchers, the "difference between political elites and ordinary citizens is one of degree, not kind."

What Are the Secret Ingredients in the Recipe for Success?

May 12th

SELF-SERVING BIAS

The self-serving bias is our tendency to take credit for good things that happen to us and blame other things or people for bad things that happen. We do that because we have the desire to feel good about ourselves. Being responsible for good things happening boosts our confidence and gives us a sense of control in our lives. When we blame external factors for bad things that happen to us, it can help us feel better about ourselves by protecting our ego.

Almost all CEOs, founders, and successful people will tell you that hard work is the key to achievement. Just read any personal development book, interview, or story of a high-achiever, and many will say similar things. In a netsuite.com article on the recipe for success, you read things like "it's 20% luck and 80% grind," or "I'd say it's about 88% skill and hard work, 12% luck."

Personal effort is a prerequisite for building anything worthwhile. Yet perhaps achievement depends on far more factors than this. Besides hard work and luck, there are other advantages like privilege, family support, or the societal base you were born into. Those successful entrepreneurs who think almost everything is down to their hard work might as well be slightly biased. Self-serving bias makes people interpret and explain outcomes in ways that have favorable implications for themselves. For example, thinking that your business is profitable just because you're smart and hardworking is a typical case of self-serving bias.

If you're successful, this means you had an entire ecosystem of resources that helped you reach your goal. Perhaps you lived in a good place with access to education and safety, not only for you but also for the employees of the company that helped grow the business. Perhaps you were even born into a wealthy family. Maybe you also lived in a society with an initial market large enough to sell your product. All these external factors are contributing factors that are easily overlooked.

Read 13 entrepreneurs' views on luck vs. skill in startup success

Fortune Favors the Bold: Do Entrepreneurs Make Their Own Luck?

May 13th

HINDSIGHT BIAS

The hindsight bias is also called the "I-knew-it-all-along" effect. It describes the retrospective overestimation of predictability. In the present, it's hard to tell how something will turn out in the future, but is easy to understand how or why an event happened in retrospect. This bias happens because we mistakenly assume that we had the same understanding of an event before it happened as we do after it happened.

Entrepreneurship is often perceived as a journey marked by strategic decisions, calculated risks, and flawless execution. However, the reality is far more nuanced and complex. The success of an entrepreneur is often the result of a unique combination of factors, some within their control and others beyond it.

Because of hindsight bias, we often think that successful entrepreneurs always knew what they were doing, did a great job, and that their actions were the result of good planning and foresight. But this is because, when we look back, we can see that each step that led to success made sense and was the right choice. It's possible that the choices were very risky at the time and that the entrepreneur was just lucky. Doubters and critics seem wrong now, but back then, they might have been right to point out the overly risky behavior. Daniel Kahneman, the researcher who introduced the idea of cognitive biases, said that we, as a society, tend to reward luck as if it were skill.

Consider Elon Musk, CEO of Tesla, Neuralink, SpaceX and owner of Twitter. When Elon Musk invested in Tesla, the electric car industry was far from the mainstream. In fact, Tesla faced multiple near-bankruptcy moments, particularly during the development of its first model, the Roadster. Musk also took a chance by launching SpaceX, a company that aimed to revolutionize the aerospace industry. Despite facing serious financial risk in the past, SpaceX has managed to survive, including failed launches that nearly led to the company's closure.

Musk continues to be regarded as one of the biggest innovators of our times, as many of the risks he undertakes, in hindsight, appear to have paid off, contributing to his enduring legacy.

Why do you make terrible life choices?

May 14th

HYPERBOLIC DISCOUNTING

Hyperbolic discounting is our tendency to favor more immediate payoffs in comparison to later payoffs. We do prefer the immediate reward, even when it is objectively less valuable. We all make decisions today that we would have preferred not to have made in the future due to hyperbolic discounting. Our brains are hardwired to do so because immediate reward meant a better chance of survival in evolutionary terms.

We humans have a tendency to prefer short-term rewards over longer-term gains. For example, many of us would rather take $50 now than $60 in one month. The cognitive bias that describes this behavior is called hyperbolic discounting. We favor immediate payoffs over later benefits.

Procrastination itself is a form of hyperbolic discounting. We procrastinate in all areas of our lives: our health, wellness, finances, work, and social lives. We delay getting a medical check-up until it's too late; we leave physical activity for next week, and we tell ourselves we're going to start saving for retirement soon. Instead, we choose to remain in our comfort zones today, splurge our money on a night out rather than invest it, and make choices we might regret a year from now. We delegate all problems to future-me.

Procrastinating those uncomfortable behaviors happens for an obvious reason: we don't want to feel discomfort, loss, or pain now. In fact, our brains are wired to seek out what feels good and pleasurable now. Our ancestors had to make decisions in shorter time frames, such as where to get the next meal, how to avoid becoming prey for wild animals, and where to rest safely. However, as time passed, society and our personal lives changed a great deal, but our brains did not to the same extent.

Life today is a lot more about renunciation that should have benefits later: studying now to earn more later, working hard now to be more free later, and so on. We pay a price in the long term for failing to do what's uncomfortable today.

Are We Falling Prey to the Illusory Truth Effect of Diet Trends?

May 15th

ILLUSORY TRUTH EFFECT

The illusory truth effect causes us to believe information is true if we hear it repeatedly, even when it's not. This happens because repeatedly hearing the same information makes it familiar, and our brain processes familiar things more easily. This ease is due to the activation of well-established neural pathways, which require less effort to process than new or unfamiliar information. When our brains process information with less effort, we tend to interpret this ease as a sign of truth. Thus, if something is easier to understand, we are more likely to believe it's true.

Almost everyone has been the victim of social media diet advice at least once in their lives. Frequently, health influencers promote new ideas promising weight loss or health problem cures. For example, Paleo diet supporters claim that eating like our ancestors—fruits, meat, eggs, and starchy veggies, while avoiding grains—will make us healthier because our bodies are evolutionarily adapted to this diet, having eaten this way since the Stone Age. This sounds logical at first glance, but it's often the illusory truth effect at work: statements that are easy to grasp and frequently repeated are more likely to be perceived as true.

A more recent example of how the illusory truth effect shapes diet trends can be seen in the celery juice phenomenon. Health influencers claimed it could cure chronic illnesses like allergies, despite no medical evidence supporting these claims. Doctors dismissed the trend, noting that celery juice offers no substantial benefits beyond hydration. However, by the time medical professionals spoke out, the misinformation had already spread.

The dangers of such trends became evident in 2023 when a TikTok creator went viral by promoting "raw meat healing." Claiming that eating exclusively raw meat could cure various ailments, the trend gained significant traction through repeated exposure on social media. Several followers who attempted this dangerous diet required hospitalization due to severe bacterial infections and food poisoning. So next time a new diet trend floods your social media feed, remember: repetition doesn't make it true.

Read this article about the viral Instagram "cure" celery juice

Mirror, Mirror on the Car:
Are We Really the Best Drivers of Them All?

May 16th

OVERCONFIDENCE EFFECT

We speak of the overconfidence effect when our subjective confidence in our judgments is higher than their objective accuracy. We can overestimate a variety of things, including our own performance or likelihood of success, our abilities in comparison to others, and the certainty of our answers or judgments.

Confidence is a trait that appears very desirable to us. However, in certain cases, such as driving, it can be too much of a good thing.

Think of how you would rate your driving abilities in comparison to other people's. You might be another one of us who experienced the overconfidence effect if your first thought was "better than average." Because of the overconfidence effect we show excessive confidence in certain abilities or knowledge and build an inaccurate view of ourselves. The overconfidence effect leads us to make unrealistic and inaccurate evaluations of ourselves. For example, we may overestimate our performance or skills, leading to an exaggerated perception of how well we're doing in reality.

In a research study, 88% of participants rated their driving ability as "above average," which, if you think about it, is rather impossible from a statistical standpoint. There are not enough people left to be below-average drivers. If 88% of people consider themselves to be better than the average driver, this means that we're suffering from the overconfidence effect.

Unfortunately, overconfidence is an important consideration because it can lead drivers to underestimate risky situations, which in turn fuels risky behaviors like speeding and accidents. While we shouldn't go to the opposite extreme (where we devalue ourselves) to drive safely, it would be useful to admit that it's better to recognize our limits, especially in risky situations on the road.

Read more about the study

From Touchdowns to Lockdowns:
How Far Will You Go for Your Team?

May 17th

INGROUP BIAS

Ingroup bias is when we like and support people who are part of our own group more than people who are not part of our group. These groups can be divided based on seemingly trivial observable traits. This is rooted in the intrinsic human need for a group identity, which provides a sense of belonging and purpose. Additionally, we all have a desire to feel good about ourselves, and one way to achieve that is to see our own group as being superior to others.

If you've ever been to a sporting event, you've probably seen the craziness that fans create firsthand. When two famous teams play each other, their fans become as enthralled as if they were personally involved in the game. Psychologists have been studying these strong attitudes toward the rivals of their favorite sports teams for a long time. Part of what drives the division between two sports teams is the in-group bias.

According to this, we see the members of our group (e.g., the football team) in more positive terms than others. This explains why the fans of two rival teams occasionally dislike each other so intensely. Consider one of the most ferocious rivalries in baseball and all of American sports: the New York Yankees versus the Boston Red Sox. The competition, which stretches well over 100 years, has been the focus of the media and tabloids in the US for almost the same length of time. The fans of the two teams hate each other so much that numerous violent incidents between them have been recorded in the past. In 2008, a New York Yankees fan was charged with second-degree murder after running her car into a group of people and killing a Boston Red Sox fan. This is, of course, just one isolated example of the conflicts between the two sports teams' fans.

In-group bias manifests strongly in sports. Fans develop such a strong attachment to their favorite team that they are willing to harm others simply because they are not part of their group.

How Can Seeking Confirmation Lead to Deception?

May 18th

CONFIRMATION BIAS

Confirmation bias is our tendency to look for, acknowledge, favor, and remember information in a way that supports what we already think or believe. This bias occurs when we ignore information that contradicts our ideas or interpret ambiguous facts as evidence supporting our existing beliefs. Situations that involve emotionally charged topics, strongly held beliefs, or things we really want to happen are most susceptible to this bias.

One reason people fall for scams is that they're looking for confirmatory evidence that the person they're trusting is legitimate. Scam artists know this and come prepared to give people all the evidence they need. All that matters is that the victim develops the first theory that they're making a good decision, and the rest is just confirmation bias. This is why scammers appear well-dressed and articulate.

Take, for example, the famous case of Marc Dreier, who is serving a 20-year sentence for investment fraud involving a Ponzi scheme. Dreier owned a law firm and lived an expensive lifestyle. He stole over $740 million by selling fake bonds. Bonds are loans investors give to a company with the promise of getting their money back, plus interest, after a certain period. However, in Dreier's case, these bonds were completely fabricated. He created and sold these nonexistent bonds, which were supposedly issued by a real company owned by one of his clients. As the profits from his law firm were not sufficient to repay the money he had borrowed, he issued more fake bonds to pay off the old debts and to bring in new funds. To make people believe in these fake bonds, Dreier even hired someone to impersonate an executive from his client's company, who then confirmed that Dreier's offer was legitimate.

An important aspect of financial fraud is establishing some form of confirmation for the victims. Most people tend to seek evidence supporting their initial beliefs, making it crucial to instill that initial trust. Therefore, a good way to avoid fraud is not to seek evidence proving something, but rather to be vigilant for evidence that disproves it.

Watch the trailer of the movie about Marc Dreier

Can Purchase Limits Make Us Soup-er Spenders?

May 19th

ANCHORING BIAS

Anchoring bias occurs when a specific reference point, or "anchor", influences our decision-making process. This anchor could be a number or any other kind of cue, even if it is completely unrelated to the decision at hand. Despite this, we often use the anchor as a starting point and adjust our decisions or judgments from there, without realizing it. As a result, our final estimates, decisions, or judgments can be significantly different from what they might have been without the influence of the anchor.

Would you buy more bananas tomorrow if you were told that you were only allowed to buy five? Perhaps you never even thought of buying so many bannas in the first place, but now that there's a limit in place, you start having second thoughts. The anchoring effect is sometimes used in sales to boost purchasing behavior, just as it did in the following study.

When people get anchored on a detail, like a limit to how much they can buy, their buying behavior changes. This was found in a study where a supermarket had a promotion on Campbell soups. The retailer limited soup purchases to a maximum of 4 or 12 cans to see when the shoppers would purchase more cans on average. The result?

When there was no limit, people purchased 3.3 cans on average. When the limit was 4, people purchased slightly more, 3.6 cans per person. But when the limit went up to 12 cans, the anchored shoppers purchased 7 cans per person! Let this sit for a moment. People could have bought 20 cans when there was no limit, but they decided to purchase just 3.3 cans. Once a high anchor was around, the purchase limit of 12 cans, this anchor influenced the decision-making of the soup fanatics and soup sales went up by more than 100%.

While the single item price of the soup remained the same — and so did the quality and appeal of the product — people were likely to buy more when there was an anchor to estimate how much they could purchase. Remember this story next time you are faced with a purchase limit in a supermarket.

Is Karma Really a B*tch?

May 20th

JUST WORLD HYPOTHESIS

The Just World Hypothesis is the belief that the world is just and fair, and that people get what they deserve. This means that if someone is experiencing bad things, it is because they have done something to deserve it and are punished. On the other hand, if someone is successful or happy, it is because they made good choices and are rewarded. This idea can be comforting because it gives us a sense of control over our lives and the belief that we can influence our own outcomes.

The Just World Hypothesis posits that good things happen to good people and bad things to bad people. Hence, our experiences, whether positive or negative, are the direct results of our actions. A research study found a strong correlation between beliefs in the Just World Hypothesis and religious attitudes. This isn't entirely surprising. Many religious teachings suggest that our actions in the world directly influence our fate.

Take, for example, the stories from the Bible such as the destruction of Sodom and Gomorrah, the deaths of Ananias and Sapphira, and the demise of King Herod Agrippa. In Genesis, the cities of Sodom and Gomorrah were obliterated by sulfur and fire because of their widespread wickedness, which included grave violations of hospitality, sexual violence, and a lack of compassion towards the needy, demonstrating a direct and severe consequence for their collective moral failure. In the Acts of the Apostles, Ananias and Sapphira lied about their donations to the church and were struck dead, emphasizing the fatal outcomes of deceit. Similarly, King Herod Agrippa, who accepted divine honors for himself, was struck down and died gruesomely, punished for his arrogance and blasphemy. These stories underscore the idea that we live in a moral universe where goodness and justice are met with rewards, and wrongdoing with swift retribution.

On the other hand, the Book of Proverbs teaches that wisdom and righteousness lead to life and prosperity, reinforcing the Just World Hypothesis by advocating that moral integrity and fear of the Lord result in divine favor and protection.

Watch a summary of the Book of Proverbs

Can Basketball Players Really Get on a 'Hot Streak'?

May 21st

GAMBLER'S FALLACY

The gambler's fallacy arises from the mistaken belief that past events can affect the probability of future outcomes that are actually independent of the past. It is often manifested in the belief that a certain outcome is more or less likely to occur due to its frequency in the past, despite the fact that the probability remains the same. This fallacy is often driven by a desire for pattern-finding and prediction, as well as a dislike of uncertainty.

How accurate and valid are the beliefs about "the hot hand" and "streak shooting" in basketball? If you ask basketball players and fans alike, they will confidently tell you that a player's chances of hitting a shot are greater after a hit than after a miss on the previous shot.

Logically speaking, it makes no sense why the hit or miss on the previous shot would influence the next outcome. However, beliefs in phenomena such as "the hot hand" seem to derive from a fallacious belief in "the law of small numbers." According to this, basketball fans are convinced that players are more likely to make the next shot when on a "hot streak." In other words, the outcome of a previous shot would influence the next one's chances of success.

Unfortunately, scientific evidence does not support this bias. Detailed analyses of the shooting records of the Philadelphia 76ers found no correlation between the outcomes of successive shots in basketball games. Records from the Boston Celtics and a shooting experiment with Cornell's teams helped support the conclusion. As it turns out, there is no correlation between successive shots. Every single shot's chance of success is not related in any way to the previous one's outcome; therefore, they have no effect on the player's performance.

Although the "hot hand" is nothing but a myth, sports fans can nevertheless enjoy the rush of adrenaline and excitement it brings.

Bullet holes, aircrafts, and survivorship

May 22th

SURVIVORSHIP BIAS

Survivorship bias is the mental short-cut we take when we focus on a certain subgroup that made it through a selection process—the survivors—and ignore the ones that didn't—the failures. Because we don't pay equal attention to both survivors and failures, we might mistakenly assume that a shared trait of the survivors caused their survival. This seduces us to mistake correlation for causation.

During World War II, American airplanes flying over Germany frequently returned with severe damage. The U.S. military, eager to reduce these losses, closely analyzed the damage patterns on the aircraft that returned. They observed that the tails and wings were often the most damaged parts of these planes. The initial solution seemed straightforward: reinforce these areas with extra armor.

Abraham Wald, a highly skilled mathematician associated with the Statistical Research Group, saw a significant flaw in this strategy. He introduced a crucial perspective that shifted the entire approach. Wald pointed out that making decisions based solely on the aircraft that returned was a mistake. He argued that this limited viewpoint missed vital information from the planes that didn't survive the journey. Wald argued that the military was misinterpreting the data. The lack of damage on certain parts of the returning planes (like the engines) didn't mean these areas were less vulnerable. In fact, it was likely the opposite. Planes hit in these areas probably didn't return at all.

Wald's famous advice was, "Gentlemen, you need to put more armor plates where the holes aren't, because that's where the holes were on the planes that didn't return." This insightful observation may seem obvious in hindsight, but it underscores a common oversight in decision-making: survivorship bias can easily skew our understanding by focusing only on the survivors, neglecting the full scope of evidence.

Big Brother or Brain Trick?

May 23rd

FREQUENCY ILLUSION OR BAADER–MEINHOF PHENOMENON

The frequency illusion is when you notice something, you start to notice it every time it happens. This makes you think it happens a lot, even though it doesn't. This bias is also known as the Baader–Meinhof phenomenon. It happens when heightened awareness of something creates the impression that it is happening more frequently than it actually is.

Does the following scenario sound familiar to you? One of your friends tells you about a cool new gadget they just bought. Later on, you scroll through Facebook, Instagram, TikTok, or any other social media platform, and you notice an ad for the exact product your friend just mentioned!

So, naturally, you draw the obvious conclusion: "Big Brother is watching me! This platform is reading my chats and listening to my conversations to hack into my private life."

As sensational as this explanation seems, there might be something else going on: you might be experiencing the frequency illusion. In reality, the ad was shown to you a few times already, but you just did not notice it. We are more likely to notice a product if it is familiar to us. We see around 4,000 to 10,000 ads each day, many of which go unnoticed. Now that you are aware of the product, you are more likely to notice it.

Another, more technical explanation for your sudden awareness of the product ads might be a marketing strategy called "look-alike audiences." Social media platforms identify potential buyers, like you, to whom they can show the ads based on similarities with people who have already bought the product, such as your friend. This means you start seeing ads for the same product not because the platform is spying on you, but because it recognizes shared interests between you and your friend.

Therefore, Big Brother might not pay that much attention to your private conversations after all. The frequency illusion just took over your brain.

Are You Brand-Washed?

May 24th

MERE EXPOSURE EFFECT

The mere exposure effect says the more we are exposed to something, the more we like it. Familiarity breeds liking. When asked to make a choice, we tend to prefer what is familiar, even if this is not the optimal choice. One reason for this behavior is that evolution has taught us to be careful around new things. Everything unfamiliar could be potentially dangerous. When we see something over and over again without any bad results, we assume it is safe.

What's the difference between a highly popular brand and a lesser-known but equally efficient one? In many cases, it comes down to effective marketing. When we're highly familiar with a certain brand, we're more likely to choose it while making decisions at the supermarket. This choice isn't always based on thorough research comparing its quality to that of less well-known brands. The popular brand simply comes to mind more easily. We unknowingly make decisions based on the mere exposure effect in many situations. This mental shortcut suggests that we are more likely to develop a preference for things or people that are more familiar to us.

It's no surprise, therefore, that popular brands advertise their products everywhere. They aim to increase exposure so that the next time we're searching for a product, we're already familiar with it and more likely to select it over other, less familiar options. Consider your preferences for beverages, laptops, cellphones, or cars. The frequency with which you've seen a certain brand likely has a significant impact on how you feel about it. Coca-Cola spends more than $2.3 billion on advertising annually, despite being known by 94% of the world's population. Coca-Cola doesn't spend that much money to reach the remaining 6%; rather, they spend it to stay in the minds of those who already know the brand.

One significant issue with the mere exposure effect is that it leads us to make decisions based on very limited information instead of conducting proper research to determine the best product.

Is Performance-Support Bias Fueling the Gender Pay Gap?

May 25th

GENDER BIAS

Gender bias refers to a widely held set of implicit biases that discriminate against one gender. These biases include stereotypes like men being more logical and women more emotional. When there are no gender indicators, people often default to assuming subjects are male. Gender bias also manifests in double standards used to judge behavior - for instance, when men are praised for their sexual activities while women are derogated.

The gender pay gap has been decreasing in many occupations. Yet, there are still some professional roles where men might be favored over women through a set of work practices that feed our gender bias. For example, people working in financial services, such as stockbrokers, experience one of the highest gender pay gaps among sales occupations. The gender pay gap here is around 6.4 percent, even after adjusting for variables such as age, education, experience, location, occupation, job title, and company, according to a study by Oliver Wyman. This gap is one of the largest among the industries analyzed in the study. So, what are the reasons behind this?

The answer might be found in a concept named "performance-support bias," which was debated in a 2012 study. The concept refers to the idea that the pay gap exists because of the inequality of support offered to men and women working in financial services. Despite the fact that both genders are equally paid based on commission rates, the efforts that men and women have to invest to achieve the same performance are not equal, which results from company practices.

For example, women receive inferior assignments compared to men, such as accounts with lower historic commissions. So even if the pay criteria look fair in theory, the assignment of sales makes it more difficult for women to achieve the same performance as men. In other words, women work longer hours to be paid the same commission that men are paid for simpler assignments. Therefore, even if some companies have fair salary policies, they might display a subtle performance-support bias which is reflected in the unfair distribution of sales opportunities.

Why are the gods angry again?

May 26th

ANTHROPOMORPHISM

Anthropomorphism is our natural tendency to attribute human traits, emotions, and intentions to non-humans, for example, animals, gods, natural forces, and the like. We do this because we naturally know more about human traits than non-human ones. Therefore, these come easier to mind, and that saves mental energy.

Historically, people sought supernatural explanations for the myriad events unfolding around them. They were so captivated by natural phenomena that they felt compelled to weave stories that rendered these occurrences comprehensible. Thus, in Greek lore, Helios was revered as the god of the sun, while thunderstorms and lightning were perceived as divine indicators of the gods' moods.

In truth, these correlations were merely attempts to distill the overwhelming complexity of the unknown world into something more digestible. This human tendency reveals a notable bias, known as anthropomorphism. This means we have a predisposition to assign uniquely human characteristics and emotions to inanimate objects, animals, and abstract concepts. Consequently, ancient societies often believed in gods with human-like forms.

Consider the Greek god Zeus. Mythology recounts that he commanded the thunder, implying that any resounding storm was a sign of his distress. When hurricanes struck people sought meaning in the chaos. Lacking logical interpretations for phenomena like thunder and lightning, they conjured up divine beings to account for these events. These gods were characterized by distinctly human attributes and behaviors: Zeus was temperamental and amorous, Dionysos had a penchant for indulgence, and Hades was notably reclusive.

Highlighting this bias, the Greek philosopher Xenophanes observed that if horses had gods and the capacity to create art, they would undoubtedly depict their gods like horses: "If cattle and horses, or lions, had hands, or were able to draw with their feet and produce the works which men do, horses would draw the forms of gods like horses, and cattle like cattle, and they would make the gods' bodies the same shape as their own."

Did you know about the Children's Crusades?

May 27th

GROUPTHINK

Groupthink is when our desire for harmony and conformity within a group leads to dysfunctional decision-making. Group members prioritize agreement over critical evaluation, resulting in a loss of individual creativity and thinking. This can lead to an inflated sense of confidence in the group's abilities, an undervaluation of opponents, group pressure, and potentially harmful actions towards outsiders.

The Children's Crusades of the early 13th century, although a largely forgotten chapter in history, provide a poignant example of the dangers of groupthink.

A young shepherd named Nicholas of Cologne in Germany led the popular movement that emerged in Europe in 1212. The movement believed they had been divinely chosen to lead a crusade to retake the Holy Land from Muslim control without bloodshed. The young people's group developed a strong sense of groupthink, despite the pope and other church leaders not being in favor of the movement.

The group believed that children's innocence and purity would ensure their success. About 20,000 children, teenagers, and adults joined the movement, many of them drawn in by religious fervor and the promise of divine favor. The belief in divine protection and the purity of the participants contributed to an inflated sense of confidence among the crusaders. The group's faith in their ability to succeed despite their lack of experience and resources is an example of groupthink. The Children's Crusades were also characterized by a simplistic view of the enemy, with Muslims being portrayed as inferior. The undervaluation of opponents is also a common feature of groupthink, as it allows a group to maintain its cohesion and sense of purpose while minimizing the need for critical analysis.

Unfortunately for those who joined, the crusades ended disastrously before even reaching the Holy Land, with most participants either dying from hunger, disease, or experiencing other misfortunes, such as being sold into slavery.

Watch this video to learn more about the Children's Crusade

Do you know the most handsome killer in history?

May 28th

HALO EFFECT

The halo effect is a type of cognitive bias in which our overall opinion of a person or brand affects how we feel about the specific qualities of that person or brand. If we have a good feeling about something as a whole, we are more likely to think that its individual parts are good as well. We do that because it saves cognitive effort to use our overall impressions as a shortcut to make judgments rather than evaluating each aspect of something separately.

The case of Ted Bundy, one of the most notorious American serial killers, provides an excellent example of the halo effect in action. Bundy, who confessed to over 30 murders, was able to deceive those around him due to his good looks, charm, and intelligence. This "halo" of positive qualities led many people to overlook his dark side, enabling him to continue his killing spree for years.

Eight women had vanished before witnesses could describe a suspect and his car. The police put up posters around King County. Four people who recognized Bundy's sketch and vehicle identified him as a suspect. However, the police officers did not believe that a good-looking, well-groomed law student with no prior convictions could be the perpetrator.

Later, the media also played a significant role in perpetuating the halo effect surrounding Bundy. Newspapers and television news programs often highlighted Bundy's physical attractiveness, charm, and educational background, with some even referring to him as "the handsome killer." Even after his conviction, the halo effect persisted, leading to a continued fascination with Bundy's life and crimes. Numerous books, documentaries, and films about Bundy have focused on his charm, intelligence, and good looks, often overshadowing the brutality of his crimes.

The case of Ted Bundy serves as a chilling reminder of the power of the halo effect. His attractive appearance and intelligence created a deceptive "halo" that allowed him to evade suspicion and manipulate others.

Are We Trading Our Opinions for Acceptance?

May 29th

BANDWAGON EFFECT

The bandwagon effect refers to the phenomenon in which a belief or behavior becomes more popular as more people adopt it. This can lead to a self-reinforcing cycle, as the increased popularity of the belief or behavior encourages more people to adopt it. The effect is caused by our desire to conform to social norms and our belief that the majority must be correct. It can also be caused by peer pressure and the fear of being left out or made fun of if we don't fit in.

People want to feel part of a group so much that they're willing to set aside their real thoughts and feelings. A famous experiment showed that people were more likely to give wrong answers to a simple task when they were in a group compared to when they were by themselves. In this experiment, a group of people were asked to compare the length of two lines. What they didn't know was that most of the people in the group were actors who were purposely giving the wrong answers.

To see how being around others affected the participants' answers, the researchers also set up a different scenario where none of the actors gave wrong answers on purpose. The results showed that when the actors gave the wrong answer, a lot of the real participants also gave the wrong answer, even though they knew it wasn't right. This occurred because the participants did not want to stand out from the group. The experiment illustrates that people may conform to group norms to feel included and avoid the discomfort of being ostracized, even at the expense of their own beliefs.

The desire to be liked can lead to things like the bandwagon effect. This is when we decide to go along with popular beliefs or ideas instead of coming up with our own. When a person's opinion is different from the group's, the person will often give up their opinion to agree with the group. We seem to prefer acceptance in a group over being correct.

Watch the original Asch conformity experiment

How Much Does Yesterday's Kiss or Clash Tint Your Love Goggles?

May 30th

AVAILABILITY BIAS

The availability bias is our tendency to make decisions based on information that comes to mind quickly and easily. It's a mental shortcut that gives more weight to information that was learned recently or that is easy to remember, for example, because it is an emotionally loaded memory. Our brain wants to save mental energy. So, we often go with the first information that comes to mind instead of putting in more mental effort to dig deeper.

How do you feel about your relationship? How does your answer change if someone asks this question right after an intense argument? And what about if you evaluate it right after the perfect, honeymoon-like holiday?

Without even realizing it, recent events in our lives have a big impact on how we judge our romantic relationships. This was the conclusion of a study that asked participants to rate their relationship's stability twice, eight months apart. During the second assessment, participants were also asked to describe how they remembered the quality of their relationship eight months prior. The results revealed that the current quality of a relationship (good or bad) influences how people think they felt about it in the past. For example, if someone goes through a turbulent time with their partner, the availability of this recent event in their memory leads them to think their relationship has always been problematic. The availability of this information in their minds biases their judgment. Conversely, if a relationship is great in the present moment, it feels natural to think it has always been this way.

Therefore, it's hard for us to remain objective when looking back at our previous interactions with people; what has recently happened (and the emotional charge it carries) will always influence our perception. Keep that in mind during your next argument with your partner. Things might feel dire, but they will likely fade away quickly after your next joyful encounter.

Fun fact: Research revealed the "magic ratio" for relationship success—couples who remember at least five positive interactions for every negative one tend to be happier in their relationships.

Why Do We Flee from Checkups Like Ostriches on the Run?

May 31st

OSTRICH EFFECT OR NORMALCY BIAS

Normalcy bias, also known as "ostrich effect," makes us downplay warnings about dangers or ignore negative situations completely. We underestimate how likely it is that a disaster will happen and how it might affect us. We do that because we want to avoid an unpleasant emotional impact in the short term. The name comes from the popular (but false) belief that ostriches bury their heads in the sand when in danger.

If your health is at risk, the doctor's office should probably be the last place you'd want to avoid, in theory. But since you're a human being, you might just do that. You have solid reasons for doing so, and running away from bad news is the biggest one. For mortals like us, coping with difficult emotions is not an easy task. This is why we ignore our health problems, sweep relationship issues under the rug, and stay away from the doctor's office.

The phenomenon explaining this behavior is called the ostrich effect. According to this cognitive bias, we downplay problems in our lives by pretending they don't exist. We stick our heads in the sand, like ostriches are wrongly accused of doing when they face danger. Of course, we don't do this purposefully but rather in an unconscious attempt to protect ourselves from emotional discomfort. This might explain why people with higher health risks are often the ones most likely to avoid medical examinations. A survey of U.S. adults found that avoiding doctor visits was more common among those who feared they might get cancer or were worried about cancer in general. Specifically, 29.4% of people over 50 and 40.4% of people under 50 reported avoiding medical visits. People typically don't want to learn about things that might stress them out, such as discovering they might have a serious illness. If they don't know about it, they can pretend it isn't real.

Hence, it's a natural tendency for us to slip into "ostrich mode" when we're about to confront difficult news. But the problem is that ignoring health issues won't make them disappear, so we'd better gather our courage and make that doctor's appointment.

∞
JUNE

Serving Up Overconfidence:
Do Men Think They Can Score on Serena?

June 1st

DUNNING–KRUGER EFFECT

The Dunning–Kruger effect describes our tendency to overestimate our own abilities in areas that we are unskilled in or lack knowledge in. This happens when we know just enough to think we are great but not enough to tell the difference between good and bad. We just don't know yet what we could do better. The effect also applies to society as a whole. The most uninformed citizens are often also the most confident ones.

Self-delusion is not uncommon in the world of hobby sports. As in other fields, those who know little are more likely to consider themselves more skilled than they actually are. Likewise, amateur players will overtly exaggerate their skills, sometimes to ridiculous proportions.

An online survey carried out by the British market research firm YouGov asked people to respond as to how they thought they'd perform in a match against Serena Williams. Surprisingly, one in every eight men (12%) who responded to the poll said they could win a point in a tennis match against the multiple Grand Slam winner. This percentage reflects a significant overestimation of their tennis abilities, given Serena Williams' skill level. These respondents are average men who occasionally play tennis for fun. Yet they are confident enough in their abilities to think they can score against one of, if not the best, tennis players in the world. In response to the survey results, Serena Williams humorously challenged these overly confident men, saying, "Well, any day, I'm ready. We should start doing a big challenge. Come over to my house, and I will take them down one at a time."

In another interview, Serena Williams noted that the comparisons between amateur and professional tennis players shouldn't extend to matchups between male and female professionals. She explained that men's and women's tennis are almost like two distinct sports due to differences in speed, power, and gameplay. Serena remarked that a match against a male professional like Andy Murray would likely result in a swift defeat for her, highlighting the physical differences. Andy Murray had previously proposed such a match, to which Serena responded that he would probably beat her 6-0, 6-0 in roughly ten minutes.

Does a Happy Ending Excuse Questionable Actions?

June 2nd

OUTCOME BIAS

We are subject to outcome bias when we judge a decision by its outcome. This is biased because we should rather base our judgment on the quality of the decision at the time it was made, given what was known at that time. We never have all the information we need, and every result has random and unpredictable parts. Bad outcomes are not always a sign of bad decision-making.

Very often in life, we are evaluated based on results rather than on the quality of our decisions. This was also the conclusion of a study conducted at Harvard Business School, which asked a group of participants to evaluate some ethically questionable behaviors based on the results. Participants were given a series of stories describing different unethical behaviors carried out by a scientist who was looking to prove the efficacy of a drug they were testing. They were either told that a positive result was obtained (e.g., the drug was found efficient) or a negative result followed (e.g., the drug was found dangerous).

The findings were quite revealing. Participants were more likely to judge a behavior as less ethical if it resulted in a negative outcome. They also assigned more blame and demanded harsher punishment for these actions. Interestingly, even when participants initially deemed the behavior acceptable, they revised their judgment to be less ethical if the outcome was negative.

This outcome bias can have serious implications. It may lead to unjust blame and punishment for individuals who made rational decisions but were simply unlucky with the outcomes. Conversely, it may also lead to unethical individuals escaping blame due to positive outcomes.

Got Guts? How Default Laws Impact Organ Donation Rates

June 3rd

DEFAULT EFFECT

When offered a choice that has a pre-selected default option, we tend to choose this default option. This is called the default effect. Defaults are the options that take effect if we do nothing. Our brains try to save as much mental energy as possible. Accepting the default option saves energy because we don't have to think about the pros and cons of each choice.

Are you registered as an organ donor? If you are an organ donor, did you actively say, "Yes, I would like to be an organ donor"? If you are not registered as an organ donor, did you actively say, "No, I do not want to be an organ donor" at some point?

To put things in perspective, the United States, for example, has a critical shortage, with more than 45,000 people dying while waiting for a suitable organ donor. While most Americans approve of organ donation, less than half decide to donate. The same applies in other countries, such as Germany, Spain, and Sweden. In Germany, for example, 39% of the population is registered as an organ donor. Other countries, such as Austria and France, have extremely high organ donation rates, such as 99.98% in the case of Austria. Are the people in countries with a high organ donor rate more conscientious about organ donation? Are they just better people?

The explanation for this difference in donation rates is that countries with high donation rates have laws that make organ donation the default choice. In other words, applicants must formally state that they choose not to become donors; otherwise, they are.

According to the default effect, people are more likely to stick to the default decision that has been made for them. If more countries were to adopt a policy where being an organ donor is the default option, and opting out requires an action, organ donor rates would surely increase drastically, which would save and improve many lives.

View Dan Ariely's TED Talk about this.

How would you spend 18 years in prison?

June 4th

BELIEF BIAS

Belief bias distorts our evaluation of the logical strength of an argument because we judge it by the believability of the conclusion. In other words, when we believe the conclusion, we are inclined to believe that the method used to get the results must also be correct. Belief bias happens when we rely too much on what we remember and not enough on evaluating new information. Belief bias is more likely to happen when we really care about something.

The West Memphis Three case is a prime example of how belief bias can produce awful outcomes. In this case, three teenagers, Damien Echols, Jason Baldwin, and Jessie Misskelley, were wrongfully convicted of brutally murdering three young boys in West Memphis, Arkansas, in 1993. The prosecution's case hinged on the argument that the teenagers were involved in satanic rituals, despite the lack of solid evidence.

The prevailing societal belief in the existence of satanic cults significantly impacted the prosecution. For example, the prosecution presented evidence such as Damien Echols' interest in the occult and his black clothing, which they argued was indicative of satanic involvement. The conclusion was that these three boys must be guilty. This was very credible to many, not because the argument was very logical but because the narrative made sense to them. The belief bias also affected the jury's evaluation of the case. Many jurors were already predisposed to believe in the dangers of satanic practices and the guilt of those associated with them. As a result, they were more likely to accept the prosecution's conclusion that the teenagers were guilty simply because they were involved in satanic rituals. Also, the brutal murders of three young boys evoked strong emotions and a desire for justice.

In 2011, after new DNA evidence surfaced and issues with the jury's impartiality were revealed, the West Memphis Three were released after serving 18 years in prison. Their wrongful convictions were based on a flawed argument that relied on the jurors' existing beliefs rather than a logical evaluation of the evidence.

Watch to learn more about the "West Memphis Three" case.

Do Numbers Hold the Key to so Many Secrets?

June 5th

CLUSTERING ILLUSION

The clustering illusion is our tendency to give meaning to random patterns we perceive. We see these patterns because we see them in data sets that are very large or very small. For small data sets, it could be a winning-streak or a so-called "hot-hand" in sports. We think there is a pattern, but actually it is just coincidence. For very large datasets, random patterns will inevitably occur because of the sheer size.

If you've never heard of Gematria, you're missing out on some key knowledge. Gematria is an ancient practice that assigns a numerical value to names, words, and phrases. Believers then search for patterns and connections between those values.

In an Instagram video that The Daily Show posted, a young woman convincingly explains how this works. She pulls out her phone and goes to a Gematria app to explain the theory. She calculates the numbers for Michael Jackson's last concert, which was "This is it." The number 113 pops up. She says this means "not true," subtly implying that Michael Jackson's death is just an illusion.

Another interesting example: The word "Trump" translates to the number 88, which is the same number that corresponds to "J. Kennedy." When the interviewer asks her if she implies that Trump and Kennedy are the same person, she responds insinuatingly, "That is what Gematria says." The number 88 also has significance in Neo-Nazi and white supremacist symbolism. It is used as a code to represent the phrase "Heil Hitler," because "H" is the eighth letter of the alphabet, so "88" can be interpreted as "HH" or "Heil Hitler." How does that relate to Trump and Kennedy? Probably not at all, because the conclusions drawn from numbers given to words are arbitrary and based on personal interpretations. Believers see patterns that are just the result of the clustering illusion. Because of the sheer size of the dataset at hand, which consists of all existing words, random patterns will inevitably occur.

Watch this hilarious clip about Gematria

Swipe Right or Have You Been Decoyed?

June 6th

DECOY EFFECT

The decoy effect describes how, when deciding between two options, adding a third, less appealing option (the decoy) can change how we feel about the two options we were originally considering. Decoys are much worse than one option, but only partially inferior to the second option. The decoy is there to nudge you towards one specific target option. Decoys work because they serve us as reference points that help us (unconsciously) justify our choices.

Did a string of disappointing swipes on Tinder lead you to lower your attractiveness standards, or was it merely the decoy effect at play? The influence of the decoy effect extends to online dating, where our judgments of attractiveness might not be as accurate as we believe. Dating platforms offer an endless array of potential partners with varying levels of appeal.

An intriguing experiment sheds light on this phenomenon. Participants were shown photographs of two individuals, Tom and Jerry, and asked whom they would prefer to go on a date with. The experimenters then introduced a less attractive version of either Tom or Jerry to half of the participants. The results showed that when the less attractive version of Jerry was presented, Jerry's popularity increased, and the same occurred for Tom. This clearly demonstrates the impact of the decoy effect on our perception of attractiveness.

In the realm of online dating, we often (unconsciously) assess people's attractiveness by comparing them to others. For instance, after swiping through a series of unappealing potential dates, you may perceive someone with a decent dating profile as more attractive due to the contrast with the less desirable options. So, be cautious when evaluating your dates as smarter, better looking, or kinder simply because your previous experiences were subpar. Although it's tempting to use others as a frame of reference, strive to resist the innate decoy effect and perceive individuals independently of your past partners or dates.

Watch Dan Ariely on this topic in a TED Talk

What Are the Reasons for Your Success?

June 7th

SELF-SERVING BIAS

The self-serving bias is our tendency to take credit for good things that happen to us and blame other things or people for bad things that happen. We do that because we have the desire to feel good about ourselves. Being responsible for good things happening boosts our confidence and gives us a sense of control in our lives. When we blame external factors for bad things that happen to us, it can help us feel better about ourselves by protecting our ego.

Scott Galloway, a renowned professor at NYU Stern School of Business, has built an impressive career as a bestselling author, podcast host, and entrepreneur. He has founded multiple thriving companies and served on the boards of several businesses. Galloway has earned recognition as one of the World Economic Forum's "Global Leaders of Tomorrow." He currently co-hosts the podcast "Pivot" alongside Kara Swisher and hosts "The Prof G Show," which he previously presented on the CNN+ streaming platform. By many measures, Scott Galloway has achieved remarkable success.

In a conversation with Steven Bartlett on the podcast "The Diary Of A CEO," Galloway demonstrates a striking absence of self-serving bias. Rather than claiming personal credit, Galloway attributes his accomplishments to external factors. He openly states that "a lot of my success is not my fault," highlighting two primary reasons. Firstly, he acknowledges his privileged position of being born a white heterosexual male in California during the 1960s, describing it as "hitting the lottery." Secondly, he credits his mother's unwavering dedication and passion for his well-being as a crucial factor in his success.

In contrast to the typical manifestation of self-serving bias, where individuals attribute their achievements primarily to personal effort, Galloway recognizes external factors as the main contributors to his accomplishments. What do you think? Are his statements a humble brag or indeed a compelling example of how to avoid self-serving bias?

Listen to the exact part in the interview

Framing the War on Drugs: A Sobering Look at Fear Tactics?

June 8th

FRAMING EFFECT

The framing effect occurs when we draw different conclusions from identical information based solely on how that information is presented. This can happen when something is framed either positively or negatively, or as a gain versus a loss - we naturally tend to avoid losses in such situations. Our judgment can also shift depending on which features of the information are highlighted, even though the underlying facts remain exactly the same.

During the 1970s, President Richard Nixon launched the infamous "war on drugs" campaign to decrease substance use in the U.S. He mobilized the global military and police, ultimately leading to an investment of over $1 trillion, and strategically injected fear into the masses about the consequences of drug use.

"If we cannot destroy the drug menace in America, then it will surely in time destroy us," Nixon told Congress in 1972. Through this rhetoric, drug use was portrayed as an imminent danger that warranted any sacrifice to stop. Nixon deliberately framed drug users as criminals rather than viewing drug use as an addiction, where users would be seen as individuals needing help and support. This choice of framing had far-reaching consequences.

The "war on drugs" initiative proliferated violence around the world and contributed to mass incarceration in the United States. While the campaign achieved limited success in temporarily reducing drug abuse, the consequences were overwhelmingly negative. Overall, drug use remained a persistent problem in the U.S., and the campaign did more harm than good in its supposed mission of creating a safer society.

The reason Nixon's measures gained such widespread acceptance lies in his masterful use of the framing effect: he presented drugs as an existential threat to society's well-being and deliberately instilled fear in the population. This demonstrates how the same basic information ("people use drugs in our country") can lead to radically different conclusions and policy responses depending on how it is framed and presented to the public.

Explore the article on how President Nixon linked addiction to crime

177

Why Do Misfortunes Seem Obvious Only in the Rearview Mirror?

June 9th

HINDSIGHT BIAS

The hindsight bias is also called the "I-knew-it-all-along" effect. It describes the retrospective overestimation of predictability. In the present, it's hard to tell how something will turn out in the future, but is easy to understand how or why an event happened in retrospect. This bias happens because we mistakenly assume that we had the same understanding of an event before it happened as we do after it happened.

Hindsight bias often leads us to believe that an event was predictable after it has occurred, distorting our perception of foresight. This cognitive bias significantly impacted the case of the Italian scientists convicted of manslaughter for failing to predict a devastating earthquake.

In 2009, six Italian scientists were told to anticipate the possibility of a large earthquake after a series of small tremors affected the L'Aquila region. Their response was that it was nearly impossible to predict such an event since they were missing important details. Unfortunately, the major earthquake did happen, shaking L'Aquila six days later and killing more than 300 people. To the scientists' misfortune, they were accused of manslaughter and sentenced to six years in prison for failing to prevent the risk. In the authorities' view, the scientists should have seen the tragedy coming, just as they were able to see it after its occurrence.

The initial court that convicted the scientists in 2012 appeared to be influenced by hindsight bias, believing that the scientists should have anticipated the earthquake based on the information available before the event. However, in 2014, an appeals court overturned the judgment, recognizing the inherent unpredictability of earthquakes and the limitations of the scientists' risk assessments. This decision was further upheld in 2015 by Italy's highest court, which fully acquitted the scientists. These higher courts acknowledged the complexity of seismic prediction and rejected the notion that the scientists could be held criminally responsible for failing to foresee the disaster, thus correcting the earlier judgment influenced by hindsight bias.

Familiarity Breeds Liking

December 24th

MERE EXPOSURE EFFECT

The mere exposure effect says the more we are exposed to something, the more we like it. Familiarity breeds liking. When asked to make a choice, we tend to prefer what is familiar, even if this is not the optimal choice. One reason for this behavior is that evolution has taught us to be careful around new things. Everything unfamiliar could be potentially dangerous. When we see something over and over again without any bad results, we assume it is safe.

While this phenomenon had been observed throughout human history, it wasn't until the late 1960s that it received rigorous scientific investigation. Robert Zajonc first investigated the mere exposure effect in depth in 1968.

In one of Zajonc's experiments, participants were shown a series of nonsense words and Chinese characters. They weren't asked to learn these or even understand their meaning. Instead, they were simply exposed to these symbols multiple times. Interestingly, without any logical reason, the participants started to develop a favorable attitude towards these previously meaningless words and symbols compared to new symbols they had not seen before. It's like hearing a song for the first time and not thinking much of it, but then starting to like it after hearing it over and over again. Familiarity breeds liking.

Another experiment took this idea into a more everyday context. Participants were shown different brands of nylon stockings, each associated with a nonsense symbol they had been exposed to previously. Without any actual difference in the quality of the stockings, people tended to prefer the brand associated with the symbol they had seen more frequently.

This study was revolutionary because it showed that our preferences could be influenced without our conscious awareness. We tend to like things more simply because they are familiar to us. This insight has profound implications for how we make decisions in our daily lives, from the products we buy to the people we trust, and continues to influence fields ranging from marketing to social psychology today.

Can We Manifest Our Dreams and Control Our Destiny?

June 11th

ILLUSION OF CONTROL

The illusion of control occurs when we believe we have more control over external events than we do. We frequently believe we have (or had) some control over events that are actually random. Researchers have found that people who feel in control will engage in healthier behaviors, feel less stress, and have better overall mental health. Therefore, this illusion makes us feel better about ourselves and the world around us, but it can also seduce us into relying on superstitions.

Have you ever found yourself writing down your dreams repeatedly, convinced that putting them on paper will somehow make them come true? Or perhaps you've heard of the millions using specific "manifestation sounds" on TikTok, believing that listening daily will attract their desires? While it might sound far-fetched, this practice has exploded in popularity, especially since the pandemic when Google searches for "manifesting" increased by a whopping 600%.

The fascinating thing about manifestation is how it intertwines with our tendency to seek control. People create rituals - from the "3-6-9 method" of writing desires three times in the morning, six times in the afternoon, and nine times at night, to using specific crystals meant to amplify their manifestation power. Practitioners swear by their success stories, from manifesting job opportunities to romantic relationships.

But here's where it gets interesting: while manifestation can be a powerful tool for focusing our minds and intentions, it's crucial to understand that thoughts alone don't create reality. The real power lies in how manifestation practices can inspire action. When we actively focus on our goals through manifestation, we're more likely to notice opportunities, take concrete steps, and maintain the motivation needed to achieve them. It's like creating a mental radar that helps us spot relevant opportunities - but we still need to act on them.

Research shows that people who combine positive thinking with concrete action plans are significantly more likely to achieve their goals. Perhaps the real value of manifestation lies not in its mystical promises, but in its ability to help us focus, plan, and persist in pursuing what matters to us.

Why Did So Many Roll with the Toilet Paper Craze?

June 12th

ZERO RISK BIAS

The Zero Risk Bias is a mental shortcut that makes us prefer a risk-free option, even if this choice is not the most rational or beneficial one. In uncertain situations, the mere possibility of something happening is emotionally more important than how likely it is to happen. So, we'd rather get rid of the possibility all together.

You probably found yourself buying unnecessary things "just in case." Many people, for example, keep all types of medication in their bathroom cabinets for all sorts of medical conditions. Even if they rarely get those conditions, they still want to be prepared.

This tendency to over-prepare was glaringly evident at the beginning of the COVID-19 pandemic, when people were stocking up on toilet paper. Looking from the outside, this hoarding behavior seemed exaggerated. The Internet was flooded with images of empty toilet paper shelves, funny memes, and social media videos on that topic. After all, why would a virus cause a global shortage of toilet paper? Many people probably knew there was no reason to stock up on such items. Yet they still did. One bias that could explain this type of irrational behavior is the zero-risk bias, which makes us do crazy things to eliminate tiny amounts of risk. Even when the risks are low, we still want to eliminate them completely and be certain we are ready for the worst.

During the toilet paper craze, perhaps people wanted to eliminate the potential threat of not being able to wipe their behinds at home due to a lack of resources. Although this appears to be somewhat bizarre and outlandish behavior, it could be interpreted as a strategic action to control at least one aspect of the multifaceted threat—one less thing to be concerned about. One way of tackling complex threats is to eliminate one threat at a time in its entirety.

Laugh at these 18 quarantine toilet paper memes

How Can Tweaking Feedback Order Make Feedback More Pleasant?

June 13th

PEAK–END RULE

The peak-end rule states that we tend to judge an experience based on the most intense moment as well as how the experience ended. The overall memory of the experience will be based on the average of the peak moment and the end. This bias happens because we remember events in snapshots rather than in their entirety. Furthermore, we remember things better when they are emotionally intense (the peak) or more recent (the end).

Most of our memories are false. Not in the sense that we remember made-up facts, but rather that we choose which aspect of a specific memory to remember best. It can be shocking to check the factual details of an event and see how subjective you are. One cause that leads to memory distortions is the peak-end rule. According to this, we remember past events through the lenses of their peak moments and endings. The resulting memory is a simplification of the original event, which is reduced to the most intense moment and its ending.

The peak-end rule is also applied in education, especially when teachers offer students feedback. You have probably noticed that assessment feedback usually follows a certain structure. Often, they start or end with some positive feedback. Vincent Hoogerheide, an educational psychologist and researcher, developed this strategy. He conducted many studies to see how different forms of feedback impact children's learning. In one of the studies, children received two different versions of the same feedback. Some of them received feedback with a negative rating at the end, while others received feedback with a moderately positive rating. Students remembered the second type of feedback better and found it easier to process. Hoogerheide concluded that teachers should structure their feedback by ending with the best or more positive part of the assessment.

The peak-end rule doesn't have to be perceived as a thinking flaw. Instead, it can be used to facilitate learning and receptiveness to feedback.

Feeling cold changes how you perceive people

June 14th

PRIMING EFFECT

The priming effect occurs when something we see or hear influences our thoughts or actions without us being aware of it. This can happen with words, pictures, or sounds we encounter. When our brain is primed, it becomes easier for us to think about, remember, and act on related information because the things we read, see, or hear activate connected information in the brain.

One of the first things you notice about someone is whether they are "warm" or "cold". This trait either encourages us to get to know a person better or keeps us reserved around them. An intriguing research finding demonstrates that our own physical warmth or coldness affects how warm we feel from others. In other words, feeling physically cold will make you see people as less friendly and open. This happens because of the priming effect. According to this, our sensorial experiences, such as what we hear, see, or feel, influence our thought process without us being aware of it. Because our brains connect information and draw their own conclusions, stimuli like temperature prime us to make certain decisions.

A study conducted with two experiments provides insightful examples of how physical warmth can influence perceptions and behavior. In the first experiment, participants were asked to hold either a hot or an iced cup of coffee and then rate another person's personality. Those holding the warm cup judged the target person as having a warmer personality. In the second experiment, participants were again asked to hold a hot or an iced cup of coffee. This time, they had to choose a gift, and those holding the warm cup were more likely to select a gift for a friend rather than for themselves. The only variable that differed between these two experiments was the temperature of the cup participants held.

These experiments are a good example of how priming works: your baseline emotional state or physical sensations will determine ("prime") how you perceive the people around you or how you feel about certain things. Therefore, next time you make judgments about someone, ask yourself if there's a chance you primed yourself in some way.

Did Trump's Loss Lingo Win Him the White House?

June 15th

LOSS AVERSION

Loss aversion means that the perceived loss of value from losing an object is greater than the perceived value of getting it. The pain of losing is twice as strong as the pleasure of gaining. The factors that influence this bias have been extensively researched. Among others are cultural factors (collectivist cultures have less loss aversion than individualist cultures) and socio-economic factors (powerful and wealthy people are less loss-averse).

Whether you admire or despise him, Donald Trump wielded significant political influence during his presidential campaign and tenure. He possessed an uncanny ability to resonate with both supporters and opponents through carefully chosen words. Trump's use of language allowed him to draw attention and secure votes.

By closely examining his tweets and speeches, one can observe Trump's frequent use of "loss" as a central theme. He deliberately painted grim scenarios involving loss and its consequences, instilling fear in the public. This tactic is a prime example of employing loss aversion in public oratory. The psychological impact of losing is perceived to be twice as powerful as the comparable pleasure of winning.

Trump liberally employed the concept of "loss" in his rhetoric: "We're losing to the Chinese, we're losing to the Mexicans, we're losing our country..." By stoking fear through hypothetical situations related to loss, Trump effectively gained votes. In this context, personal character becomes secondary to concerns over job security, financial stability, or basic safety. Trump's highlighted political repercussions linger in the minds of many, reinforcing the sense of urgency and fear he aimed to instill.

Undeniably, Trump capitalized on loss aversion to great effect. This cognitive bias contributed to his presidential victory, demonstrating the potency of the fear of loss in mobilizing the masses.

Hungry for Justice: Can Meal Breaks Impact Parole Decisions?

June 16th

DECISION FATIGUE

Decision fatigue is the mental exhaustion that comes from having to make a lot of complex decisions in a short amount of time. It is similar to using a muscle that becomes more fatigued the more we use it in a short period. This happens because our brain has a limited amount of mental energy and willpower to use for making decisions. This phenomenon can be caused by external factors such as stress and lack of sleep and can lead to difficulty concentrating, irritability, and impulsive behavior.

Consider the following cases of three prisoners who appeared before a parole board. Each prisoner had completed two-thirds of their sentence, and although their cases appeared similar, only one was granted parole:

Case 1, a man serving a 30-month sentence for fraud — heard at 8:50 a.m.

Case 2, a man serving a 16-month sentence for assault — heard at 3:10 p.m.

Case 3, a man serving a 30-month sentence for assault — heard at 4:25 p.m.

These cases illustrate a broader phenomenon uncovered by researchers in a study examining 1,000 rulings by eight judges. They discovered that the factors influencing parole decisions weren't related to the prisoners' backgrounds or sentencing details. Instead, the decisions were mainly influenced by the timing of the hearings. Prisoners who appeared early in the morning were given parole 65% of the time. In contrast, those heard later in the day or before lunch break were only 10% likely to be paroled, before their chances spiked back up to 65% after a meal or snack break that replenished mental energy.

In our example, the prisoner who was seen at 8:50 a.m. wasn't favored for other characteristics, nor was his case less severe. Just by chance, the hearing was in the early part of the day before judges had to sit through a number of challenging decisions. A researcher from Stanford stated that the judgment error was simply a consequence of decision fatigue, which occurs after making repeated decisions. The depletion of mental resources impaired judges' ability to make accurate decisions.

Read more about judges being more lenient after taking a break

BlackBerry's Key to Failure:
Was Their Physical Keyboard Their Undoing?

June 17th

SUNK COST FALLACY

The sunk cost fallacy is when we make a decision based on how much we have already invested in something rather than on whether it is the best choice for us right now. When we feel like we have already invested a lot in something, we feel like we would be losing something if we were to let it go. Another reason that the sunk cost fallacy occurs is because we tend to focus on the past rather than the present when we make decisions.

The sunk cost fallacy frequently plagues all kinds of businesses, which, due to significant resources invested, continue to pour money into their product or service even when it's clear they won't make much progress. A prime example of this is BlackBerry, a once-dominant smartphone brand that first made waves in 1998. They revolutionized the mobile industry with their innovative device featuring a unique, ergonomic arched keyboard that made typing on a phone easier.

However, as the mobile industry evolved, touchscreen displays began gaining popularity. BlackBerry, on the other hand, refused to adapt and remained stubbornly committed to their keyboard-centric devices. Their unwavering dedication to the original product idea can be attributed to the sunk cost fallacy. BlackBerry's extensive investment in research and development for their physical keyboard technology made it more difficult for them to abandon everything they had already invested so much in. Eventually, BlackBerry's stubbornness led to a decline in sales and market share, ultimately forcing the company out of the smartphone business.

In contrast, other businesses that didn't fall victim to the sunk-cost fallacy are now still thriving because they decided to change their business model. YouTube started as a video dating site, but it was transformed into a video platform for all kinds of videos as soon as the founders had evidence that their idea wasn't working. If BlackBerry did not hold on too tightly to the product they invested resources in, perhaps they would still play a role in the smartphone market now.

Read about the interesting story behind YouTube's history as a dating site

Ever Heard of the 1954 Windshield Pitting Epidemic?

June 18th

AVAILABILITY BIAS

The availability bias is our tendency to make decisions based on information that comes to mind quickly and easily. It's a mental shortcut that gives more weight to information that was learned recently or that is easy to remember, for example, because it is an emotionally loaded memory. Our brain wants to save mental energy. So, we often go with the first information that comes to mind instead of putting in more mental effort to dig deeper.

In 1954, a strange thing happened in the Pacific Northwest. People in Bellingham, Seattle, and other cities in Washington State said that their windshields were damaged. This event, now known as the Seattle windshield pitting epidemic, provides an excellent example of the influence of availability biases in shaping public perception.

At first, the strange pitting was thought to be the work of vandals. As more and more damage was reported, though, people started to blame a wide range of strange things, from sand flea eggs to nuclear bomb tests. The message started spreading among citizens quickly, and this widespread speculation caught the attention of the media. Soon, the issue became a topic of public concern. Figures such as the governor of Washington, university scientists, and even President Dwight D. Eisenhower were notified about the phenomenon.

The epidemic crossed state lines and even reached Canada, with sightings of damaged windshields being reported in at least nine states. However, after an extensive investigation, law enforcement officials ruled out vandalism and radioactive fallout as potential causes, attributing the reports to "public hysteria" instead. It became clear that a lot of the windshield damage that was being reported wasn't new. Instead, people were just noticing flaws in their windshields that they hadn't noticed before. This is availability bias at its best. They just started noticing the damage because they heard about damaged windshields in the news.

The pitting suddenly stopped in April 1954. It was concluded that the reports were largely due to collective delusion.

Read more about the windshield pitting epidemic

Is the IKEA Effect the Secret Ingredient to Loving Healthy Food?

June 19th

IKEA EFFECT

The IKEA effect refers to our tendency to place a disproportionately high value on objects that we helped create, such as IKEA furniture. We do that regardless of the quality of the end product. This bias helps us to feel better about ourselves in two ways. First, we want to feel that our effort was well invested and that we did not waste our time but instead created something of value. Secondly, creating things makes us feel more competent.

Do you find the food you prepare yourself more satisfying than food cooked by someone else? Due to the IKEA effect, we place more value on things and products that we were at least partially involved in creating. This is also why we find it more difficult to let go of things we put significant effort into assembling.

A study with 119 female participants showed that the mere fact that a dish is self-made increases its enjoyment. Researchers tested this with two groups. Group one had to prepare a milkshake by themselves, while group two received the very same milkshake, made with the same ingredients and method, but prepared by the researchers. Additionally, they tested a healthy versus an unhealthy milkshake variant.

Healthy food, in particular, received better ratings overall from the participants in this study. Furthermore, at least in this study, the participants did not state that the unhealthy milkshake tasted better when they made it themselves.

Given that the IKEA effect makes us perceive self-made objects as more valuable, it influences our perception of the taste of healthy food when it is prepared by ourselves. This shows that the effort, time, and attention we put into preparing our food are good investments, making us enjoy our food even more than we would enjoy ready-made dishes.

Can Fund Managers Really Predict the Market?

June 20th

ILLUSION OF VALIDITY

The illusion of validity is a cognitive bias where we overestimate our ability to understand and predict an outcome based on the information we have. When analyzing new information, we rely on things we already know, for example, stereotypes and prior beliefs. When we assume that what we know is valid enough to predict what will happen in different contexts, we make confident predictions that can turn out to be utterly inaccurate.

Fund managers are well-paid professionals whom investors trust to (hopefully) achieve investment returns that are higher than the average returns of the stock market by picking the best stocks. It is assumed that fund managers have more information than individual investors and are seen as experts.

Few fund managers, such as Peter Lynch and T. Rowe Price Jr., have shown phenomenal stock-selecting ability and consistently produced great returns over a longer period of time. However, their specific performance is the exception and not the rule.

A group of researchers conducted a study to find out if mutual funds that performed well in one year would do well in the next year as well. A mutual fund is a type of investment where a group of people pool their money together, and a professional manages it to make more money out of it.

They analyzed numerous mutual funds over a 12-year period. The study found that mutual funds that performed well in one year did not consistently perform well in the following year. This suggests that the past performance of a mutual fund is not a reliable indicator of its future performance. However, past performance is an important reason for investors to invest their money in a fund because it provides a tangible track record that can instill confidence in the fund manager's ability to generate returns.

This is a perfect example of the illusion of validity. In the case of mutual funds, investors may overestimate the ability of fund managers to consistently pick winning stocks based on their past performance, even though this performance is not a reliable indicator of future success.

Is the Spotlight Effect Serving Up Unnecessary Anxiety?

June 21st

SPOTLIGHT EFFECT

The spotlight effect is our tendency to think that other people are paying more attention to us than they really are. It makes us feel like we are always "in the spotlight." This happens because our brains are wired to pay more attention to ourselves than to others. Additionally, we are more aware of changes concerning ourselves compared to others. The effect occurs in both positive (like a personal success) and negative situations (like something we are embarrassed of).

The spotlight effect is one of the main reasons people are afraid of doing things alone, such as eating out or going to the cinema by themselves. There is a persistent fear of being judged for being alone. This fear is so common that even the popular TV show "Friends" addressed it in one episode. When Monica asks, "Excuse me, what is wrong with a woman eating alone?" Chandler responds, "Well, obviously something. She's eating alone!" While this attitude is more prevalent in some cultures than others, we must ask: is this fear of being "alone in the spotlight" stronger in our imagination than in reality?

If we're examining the spotlight effect, this is what the bias entails: the illusion of being at the center of everyone's attention is often out of proportion to the outside reality. Most people are too occupied with their own concerns to pay attention to everyone they encounter. Yet, we don't realize this when we're out doing things alone and cringing at the thought of everyone seeing us as social outcasts for getting dinner in our own company.

The spotlight effect also activates a confirmation bias, where our fears of being noticed make us selectively perceive elements in the environment that support this fear. In the scenario of eating out alone, believing that everyone judges us creates an anxiety cycle where we misinterpret casual looks, innocent gestures, or brief glances as signs of judgment. Of course, these perceived judgments exist primarily in our minds.

Watch the scene from "Friends."

Is There a Middle Ground in the US Gun Control Debate?

June 22st

BINARY BIAS

Binary bias is our tendency to categorize things or people into two distinct categories, often based on their perceived characteristics or attributes. This can lead to oversimplification, stereotyping, and discrimination. We do that because it helps us make sense of the world around us quickly. From an evolutionary perspective, we need to quickly distinguish between potential allies and threats, categorizing people as friends or foes.

The U.S. leads the world in gun ownership, with an astonishing 120.5 firearms per 100 residents as of 2024, making it the only country in the world with more civilian-owned firearms than people. This unique situation shapes the national conversation about gun control.

Existing federal legislation provides a foundation for gun control by determining who can purchase, sell, and use specific firearms, with states retaining the power to impose additional restrictions. Licensed dealers must conduct background checks on buyers to prevent sales to "prohibited persons," such as felons or those with a history of domestic violence. However, this requirement doesn't extend to private sellers at gun shows or online marketplaces.

The U.S. gun control debate is often portrayed as being split between two opposing positions: those who support unrestricted gun ownership based on the Second Amendment, and those who want to stop gun violence by banning all guns. This makes it difficult to discuss policy because any compromise is seen as either a violation of constitutional rights or as capitulating to dangerous ideas.

With less binary thinking in the discussion, there would be various practical ways to address gun violence without infringing on the Second Amendment. These include implementing universal background checks for all gun sales, enacting "red flag" laws to temporarily remove firearms from potentially dangerous individuals, and imposing mandatory waiting periods between purchasing and possessing a firearm to reduce impulsive violence.

Watch Obama's response on restricting "good" gun owners

Is Cognitive Dissonance Driving Your Purchases?

June 23rd

COGNITIVE DISSONANCE

Cognitive dissonance describes the mental discomfort we experience when there is a conflict between our beliefs, actions, or perceptions. This discomfort often arises when our actions contradict our beliefs or when we hold two opposing beliefs simultaneously. To alleviate this discomfort, we may adjust our beliefs, perceptions, or actions to create a more consistent internal state. Achieving this internal consistency is crucial, as it helps maintain our sense of identity and coherence.

Some salespeople know that inserting some dissonance here and there can be highly effective, especially when the dissonance affects the buyer's self-image. You would be surprised to find out that people are willing to go to great lengths to maintain a respectable image in front of others.

For example, let's say that you consider yourself a savvy automotive enthusiast. While visiting a high-end auto dealership, the salesperson says to you, "Unfortunately, too many people aren't sophisticated and knowledgeable enough to understand that this car is a great buy." Maybe it doesn't look obvious, but the salesperson just planted a new thought in your mind—even if you weren't even thinking of buying the car. On the one hand, you feel the need to resist their cringe-worthy sales pitch (you can't be so naive and give in to their offer right away). However, you also feel that by declining their proposal, you could be perceived exactly like the unsophisticated customer they were talking about.

The fight between these two ideas is intense. One way to reduce the cognitive dissonance is to fall for the salesperson's trick. You might decide to buy the car to maintain your self-image as a savvy and knowledgeable automobile enthusiast. By doing so, you avoid being perceived as someone who can't recognize a great car when they see it, aligning your actions with the salesperson's perception. Alternatively, you could reevaluate the purchase and start thinking that your expertise is greater than the salesperson's, who is just trying to sell you something. By reaffirming your self-confidence and trusting in your own knowledge and judgment, you can resist the sales pitch without feeling that your expertise is being questioned.

Did you see "The Butterfly Effect"?

June 24th

ILLUSIONS OF CAUSALITY

The illusion of causality occurs when we erroneously perceive a cause-and-effect relationship between two events. Assessing evidence requires cognitive effort, so our brain seeks mental shortcuts to expedite the process. This cognitive bias leads us to hastily infer a causal connection, even if there is none. This stems from our evolutionary need to comprehend the causes of events quickly in our surroundings for the sake of survival.

The 2004 movie "The Butterfly Effect," starring Ashton Kutcher, is a science-fiction thriller that presents a gripping tale of time travel and the consequences of trying to change one's past. While it is an entertaining and thought-provoking movie, it also serves as a great example of the illusion of causality.

The premise of "The Butterfly Effect" revolves around the idea that small actions or events can have significant consequences in the future. However, the film takes this idea to the extreme, presenting a distorted and exaggerated view of causality.

Throughout the movie, the protagonist, Evan Treborn, repeatedly travels back in time and alters his past to create different futures for himself and his friends, Kayleigh and Tommy. Each time he makes a change, the events that follow are portrayed as directly and causally linked to his actions. For example, when Evan prevents Kayleigh's father from sexually abusing her, it leads to a chain reaction of events. Kayleigh's brother Tommy becomes more unhinged, Evan kills him in self-defense, and is sentenced to prison. The film suggests that Evan's actions are the sole cause of these following events, which is an illusion of causality.

In reality, the connection between events is often far more complex and multifaceted than what the movie portrays. Life is a web of interconnected and interdependent events, and it is rarely possible to trace a single cause for any given outcome. By oversimplifying and exaggerating the link between cause and effect, the movie uses the illusion of causality to tell a coherent and very captivating story.

Watch the trailer for the great movie "The Butterfly Effect."

Is it Attraction or an Arousal Mix-Up?

June 25th

MISATTRIBUTION OF AROUSAL

Misattribution of arousal occurs when we experience physical symptoms of arousal, such as a fast heartbeat or sweaty palms, and incorrectly attribute these symptoms to the wrong cause. This phenomenon arises because various triggers—like fear or romantic excitement—can produce similar physical responses. Our brains, trying to find patterns and make sense of these signals, may link the arousal to an incorrect source.

Can we confuse fear with sexual attraction? After all, feeling afraid has little to do with liking someone, right? However, fear does manifest in a similar biological way: our heart rate increases, our brain chemicals go crazy, and we get sweaty palms. This is the reason psychologists coined a term for it: misattribution of arousal.

If you're not fully convinced yet, consider this research experiment. Two groups of men were allocated to two groups: the first group was asked to walk across a very shaky suspension bridge, while the other group walked across a more solid wood bridge. At the end of the bridge, an attractive woman awaited the male participants. After that, she conducted interviews with all of the men. After the interview, she gave them her number in case they needed to contact her (wink).

Here are the results: More men from the group who walked on the shaky suspension bridge made use of the phone number and called the female interviewer (50%), compared to men who walked on the easy-going bridge (12%).

The shaky bridge induced anxiety in the men who crossed it: increased heart rate, sweaty palms, and so on. The men attributed these symptoms incorrectly. Their brain created a storyline attributing the arousal to the attractive woman in front of them, not the shaky bridge. That is why the men on the shaky bridge were way more likely to call the female interviewer after the experiment. They accepted the story that they must find the women very attractive since they felt so aroused.

Do Pretty Faces Make Products and Services Shine?

June 26th

HALO EFFECT

The halo effect is a type of cognitive bias in which our overall opinion of a person or brand affects how we feel about the specific qualities of that person or brand. If we have a good feeling about something as a whole, we are more likely to think that its individual parts are good as well. We do that because it saves cognitive effort to use our overall impressions as a shortcut to make judgments rather than evaluating each aspect of something separately.

If you usually consult a product's reviews before making a purchase, you probably think that you just pay attention to the content of the review. Since you don't know any of those people, all their opinions should theoretically weigh equally in your decision. But what if you, in fact, subconsciously approach those reviews differently, based not just on what they say but also on who writes them?

A research study shows that the attractiveness of the reviewers actually influences the way you evaluate a product. For instance, you'll give someone's online review more weight if it comes with a picture rather than one without a picture. Additionally, a review with a picture of an attractive person is generally seen as more credible than one written by a less attractive person. However, this is only valid in the case of positive reviews. If the evaluation is negative, the attractiveness of the reviewers doesn't impact the product evaluation as strongly.

The reason for this effect is the halo effect. This heuristic makes us evaluate people and objects based on one of their strongest attributes or features. In this case, a highly attractive person's review would be considered more credible for a variety of reasons. For instance, the halo effect could make you think that someone who is particularly attractive is also more intelligent or has more pertinent opinions. Since they have such credible qualities, they must know what they're talking about when recommending the product you want to purchase.

Therefore, be careful when letting online reviews influence your purchases.

Is Ignorance Bliss When Facing Financial Fears?

June 27th

OSTRICH EFFECT OR NORMALCY BIAS

Normalcy bias, also known as "ostrich effect," makes us downplay warnings about dangers or ignore negative situations completely. We underestimate how likely it is that a disaster will happen and how it might affect us. We do that because we want to avoid an unpleasant emotional impact in the short term. The name comes from the popular (but false) belief that ostriches bury their heads in the sand when in danger.

Saying that we don't have time for urgent issues is one of the biggest ways we lie to ourselves. A more honest thing to say is that we simply don't take the time to do them.

"I didn't have the chance to sort out my finances this year," says a post-graduate student covered in debt. But is it really a lack of time that prevents us from taking a deeper look at our finances?

A better way to approach the answer is that we're simply not ready to deal with some uncomfortable truths. A postgraduate afraid to face the huge interest added to their loan would do anything to avoid checking their account. If they did, they'd probably have a lot to deal with, including the financial stress they already face, worries related to savings, and other big expenses. Keep in mind that in 2021, thirty percent of all adults, representing over 4 in 10 people who went to college, incurred at least some debt for their education. The reminder of being tied to this debt for a big part of their lives—none of these are light things to think about. They bring a huge emotional cost, which many people simply cannot afford, especially when they're in a difficult place in their lives.

Refusing to confront an obviously urgent situation is a classic case of the ostrich effect. This refers to the idea that we'd rather "stick our heads in the sand" than deal with something requiring our attention. The ostrich effect often affects our ability to manage our finances, such as when we refuse to see how much money we've spent over the years or don't let ourselves think about the interest added to our mortgage.

Therefore, instead of pushing those urgent issues to the back of our minds, let's make a brave choice and face them.

Do We Really Like It, or Is It Just Familiarity?

June 28th

MERE EXPOSURE EFFECT

The mere exposure effect says the more we are exposed to something, the more we like it. Familiarity breeds liking. When asked to make a choice, we tend to prefer what is familiar, even if this is not the optimal choice. One reason for this behavior is that evolution has taught us to be careful around new things. Everything unfamiliar could be potentially dangerous. When we see something over and over again without any bad results, we assume it is safe.

Think about the advertisements and product placements you encounter every day. Are your preferences for certain products or brands based on their inherent qualities, or are they the result of repeated, brief exposure?

According to the mere exposure effect, we tend to have stronger attachments and more positive emotions towards things that are familiar to us because we have been exposed to them frequently. A theory based on evolutionary psychology suggests that we are wired to be cautious of new things since they could potentially harm us. When we repeatedly observe the same thing and nothing terrible happens, we begin to learn that there is nothing to fear. The mere exposure effect occurs because we feel more comfortable with something familiar than with something new (and potentially dangerous).

The process of getting used to things around us happens without us even realizing it. In a fascinating study, participants were shown pictures under two different conditions: one group of images was displayed for a brief duration of 5 milliseconds, and the other group for 500 milliseconds.

The 5-millisecond exposure is so fleeting that it is almost impossible for the conscious mind to register. After these exposures, participants were asked to rate their preference for the images. Surprisingly, the participants showed a higher preference and ability to recognize the images they had seen for just 5 milliseconds. This means that even if you are exposed to something subliminally, such as a quick glimpse of a brand logo in a movie or TV show, you are still likely to recognize it and develop a preference for it.

People Don't Mind Their Own Business, but I Do!

June 29th

BASE RATE FALLACY

We fall prey to the base rate fallacy when we ignore general information in favor of information that is specific to a certain case, even if the general information is more important. We ignore the statistical base rate. This happens because we tend to think that information about an individual is more important than information about a group. This bias can make us perpetuate stereotypes and overgeneralize.

Secretly, we might all feel a bit better than others at times. For example, back in 1998, during Bill Clinton's presidency and his famous scandal, a CBS News poll provided an interesting example of this. The poll sought to determine how interested Americans were in the juicy details of Clinton's private life. Surprisingly, only a few people admitted they were fascinated (7%), while most claimed they weren't interested at all (50%). However, when asked how interested they thought others were, the numbers changed: more people believed others were fascinated (25%), and fewer thought others weren't interested (18%). This discrepancy suggests that many people might not have been honest about their own curiosity, possibly to present themselves as more morally upright than they actually were. It highlights how we often see ourselves as different and even morally superior to others.

It's not just about being cynical about others; it also shows we think too highly of ourselves. It shows how we tend to put our personal views above general facts, leading to a skewed perspective. This is the manifestation of the base rate fallacy. We are unwilling to consult population base rates when predicting our own behavior, but we use this diagnostic information about ourselves more readily when predicting others.

Especially when we think about moral choices, we focus a lot on what we believe about ourselves and our character, ignoring what's usually true for most people. This makes us think we're more moral or helpful than others. However, when evaluating others, we don't apply this same optimistic lens, making our judgments about others more realistic than those about ourselves.

"My Teddy Bear is Upset!"

June 30th

ANTHROPOMORPHISM

Anthropomorphism is our natural tendency to attribute human traits, emotions, and intentions to non-humans, for example, animals, gods, natural forces, and the like. We do this because we naturally know more about human traits than non-human ones. Therefore, these come easier to mind, and that saves mental energy.

Children form special bonds with their toys, often treating them as important members of the family. These toys become essential companions during playtime, meals, and even trips. This common anthropomorphism, where toys are treated like best friends or younger siblings, highlights that our tendency to anthropomorphize is inherent. The significant role of toys in children's lives from an early age demonstrates that this behavior is deeply ingrained in us.

"Is my teddy bear tired?" "I won't leave it at home today; it will be lonely!" are things young children say. Anthropomorphism seems to be the default way in which we think about the world. It's not learned or acquired later in life, which is often the case with other biases. Instead, it comes from the unconscious assumption that everything in the world operates like us.

American researchers found that young children are more likely to anthropomorphize attachment objects with human-like features (faces) than they are to anthropomorphize similar favorite toys. For example, they would rather attribute their mental states and emotional lives to their beloved teddy bear than to their favorite blanket. This means that people anthropomorphize objects and animals more when they have a minimum degree of similarity to them.

The researchers suggest that this behavior is typical for children aged 2–7. During this time, they can represent objects and ideas symbolically. However, their thinking is still not fully logical, and they are egocentric, meaning they have difficulty taking others' perspectives. Thus, the tendency to anthropomorphize reflects their developmental stage and cognitive limitations rather than learned or acquired biases.

∞
JULY

Understanding the Human Face of Atrocity

July 1st

GROUPTHINK

Groupthink is when our desire for harmony and conformity within a group leads to dysfunctional decision-making. Group members prioritize agreement over critical evaluation, resulting in a loss of individual creativity and thinking. This can lead to an inflated sense of confidence in the group's abilities, an undervaluation of opponents, group pressure, and potentially harmful actions towards outsiders.

The haunting events of the Holocaust are often attributed to the actions of fanatical leaders, but the reality is more complex. The Reserve-Polizei-Bataillon 101, a unit comprised of ordinary German men, serves as a chilling testament to the dangers of groupthink. These men, many from Hamburg, weren't fervent Nazis or seasoned soldiers. They were ordinary people with everyday jobs such as dock workers, truck drivers, and office clerks. They were generally too old to be drafted into the regular army and had little prior experience with military service. Despite their regular lives and families, they participated in the mass murder of Jews in Poland during World War II.

A particularly striking example of this groupthink occurred at the very outset of their mission. Major Wilhelm Trapp, the commander of the battalion, addressed his men before their first mass execution in Józefów. He spoke of the unpleasant task they were ordered to perform and, understanding the difficult nature of this assignment, offered any man who felt unable to participate the chance to literally just make a step out of the group. Remarkably, out of approximately 500 men, only 12 chose to opt out. This moment encapsulates the overwhelming power of groupthink: the pressure to conform and the fear of standing out.

Many members of the battalion initially hesitated or felt uncomfortable participating in the mass shootings. However, the overwhelming desire to conform and not appear "different" or "weak" to their peers often overrode their personal reservations. While some did refuse to participate in the killings, their objections were often silenced or marginalized, with the group's cohesion taking precedence over individual moral standpoints.

Watch the trailer for "Ordinary Men: The Forgotten Holocaust."

How Can Price Anchors Bake Sales Success?

July 2nd

ANCHORING BIAS

Anchoring bias occurs when a specific reference point, or "anchor", influences our decision-making process. This anchor could be a number or any other kind of cue, even if it is completely unrelated to the decision at hand. Despite this, we often use the anchor as a starting point and adjust our decisions or judgments from there, without realizing it. As a result, our final estimates, decisions, or judgments can be significantly different from what they might have been without the influence of the anchor.

Did you ever wonder about the purpose of price contrasts in sales and marketing? The anchoring bias that marketers use to sway consumer behavior is a factor in this well-researched strategy.

For example, by offering promotional sales, stores encourage customers to compare the discounted price against the original one (the "anchor") so that they believe they're getting a bargain. In general, people feel more confident purchasing a product when comparing its price to an existing alternative.

This was also the case for the famous $279 bread maker sold by Williams-Sonoma. When they initially launched a single model of the product on the market in the 1990s, barely anyone bought it. So they cleverly applied the anchoring bias to increase its popularity. But they didn't lower the product's price as you would have expected. Instead, they added a more expensive version of the bread maker, which cost no less than $429. "But this makes no sense," you might think to yourself. Adding a product twice as expensive when you can barely sell the first model? This smart move doubled the sales of the original, less expensive model.

The contrast in the prices of the two models led customers to view the first breadmaker model more favorably because of its lower price. The deluxe version merely acted as an anchor for potential customers to compare prices. When there was no other product to compare it to, $279 seemed like a lot to pay for a bread maker. But adding a significantly more expensive one made the first price seem reasonable.

Read a case study about the Williams-Sonoma bread maker

Do We Really Reap What We Sow?

July 3rd

JUST WORLD HYPOTHESIS

The Just World Hypothesis is the belief that the world is just and fair, and that people get what they deserve. This means that if someone is experiencing bad things, it is because they have done something to deserve it and are punished. On the other hand, if someone is successful or happy, it is because they made good choices and are rewarded. This idea can be comforting because it gives us a sense of control over our lives and the belief that we can influence our own outcomes.

We like to use expressions like "what goes around comes around" or concepts like "karma" because they simplify life. They provide a simple explanation of why certain things happen to us: If our lives go really well, it must be because of our good past deeds.

However, if you look a bit closer, you'll see that the world is much more complex than this. Good things happen to people for many other reasons besides their inherent goodness. Yet, it's a lot easier to use this mental shortcut and assume that everything we experience comes down to our previous actions or character. The bias responsible for this thinking error is called the just world hypothesis. This makes us assume that the world is a fair place, where good things happen to good people and the evil ones are punished by fate.

This bias has wider implications, such as how we perceive some leaders in power. One very interesting study indicated that people with high scores on belief in a just world were more likely to approve of and trust major political institutions, such as the US Congress, the Supreme Court, and the military. Incidentally, this study was carried out during the Watergate Scandal, where the Nixon administration was accused of organizing a break-in to the Democratic National Committee office. Those who had a strong believe in the just world hypothesis were less likely to see President Nixon as guilty.

Participants thought that someone with Nixon's level of success would have a strong character and moral compass, so they didn't think he would do something like that.

Can You Bank on a CEO's Self-Serving Bias?

July 4th

SELF-SERVING BIAS

The self-serving bias is our tendency to take credit for good things that happen to us and blame other things or people for bad things that happen. We do that because we have the desire to feel good about ourselves. Being responsible for good things happening boosts our confidence and gives us a sense of control in our lives. When we blame external factors for bad things that happen to us, it can help us feel better about ourselves by protecting our ego.

John Stumpf is the former CEO of the financial services company Wells Fargo. As CEO, he emphasized an aggressive cross-selling strategy, internally called "Eight is Great," aiming for each individual customer to hold eight different Wells Fargo products. Under intense pressure to meet unrealistic sales targets and facing the threat of being demoted or fired, employees resorted to opening 1.5 million unauthorized accounts and 500,000 credit card applications without customer consent to fulfill their quotas. These practices went on for years until fraud investigations discovered in 2016 that at least 5,300 employees were involved in them.

The bank's reputation was tainted by this widespread fraud scandal, and it was fined around $185 million. Mr. Stumpf shifted the blame to lower-level employees within regional banking. Senator Warren addressed Mr. Stumpf's self-serving bias with drastic words in a committee hearing: "When it all blew up, you kept your job, you kept your multimillion-dollar bonuses, and you went on television to blame thousands of $12-per-hour employees who were just trying to meet cross-sell quotas that made you rich."

By shifting blame onto lower-level employees while denying his own responsibility in creating the aggressive sales culture, John Stumpf exhibited self-serving bias by attributing the company's failures to others rather than acknowledging his own role. Despite many calls for criminal charges, Stumpf ultimately left the banking industry with over $130 million in compensation as a free man by paying a $17.5 million fine.

Watch this video of Senator Elizabeth Warren grilling Wells Fargo CEO John Stumpf

Can Cognitive Biases Convict the Innocent?

July 5th

CONFIRMATION BIAS

Confirmation bias is our tendency to look for, acknowledge, favor, and remember information in a way that supports what we already think or believe. This bias occurs when we ignore information that contradicts our ideas or interpret ambiguous facts as evidence supporting our existing beliefs. Situations that involve emotionally charged topics, strongly held beliefs, or things we really want to happen are most susceptible to this bias.

Cognitive biases are particularly important in criminal investigations because they can severely impact investigators' ability to make accurate decisions about suspects. For instance, when a police officer becomes convinced that a suspect is the perpetrator, they may unconsciously search for evidence that confirms their suspicion. Investigators can develop tunnel vision due to confirmation bias, leading them to dismiss or minimize evidence that supports a suspect's innocence while actively building their case for conviction.

The confirmation bias likely played a significant role in the wrongful conviction of Dennis Oland for the murder of his father, millionaire Richard Oland, who was violently killed in his office in Saint John, New Brunswick. After discovering Richard's body, police quickly focused on Dennis as their primary suspect. They interpreted his nervous body language during questioning – his visible discomfort and tendency to shrink away from the detective – as signs of guilt. Once convinced of Dennis's guilt, investigators, influenced by confirmation bias, actively sought evidence to support their theory while overlooking or minimizing contradictory evidence.

Richard's son was sentenced to life in prison in 2015, but he maintained his innocence and appealed the verdict. In 2019, he was finally acquitted when his defense team presented compelling evidence demonstrating that Dennis could not have been at the crime scene when the murder occurred. Meanwhile, the true killer remains unidentified and has never been caught.

Watch this video of Dennis Oland's retrial

Is the Crypto Craze Just a Bandwagon Gone Bad?

July 6th

BANDWAGON EFFECT

The bandwagon effect refers to the phenomenon in which a belief or behavior becomes more popular as more people adopt it. This can lead to a self-reinforcing cycle, as the increased popularity of the belief or behavior encourages more people to adopt it. The effect is caused by our desire to conform to social norms and our belief that the majority must be correct. It can also be caused by peer pressure and the fear of being left out or made fun of if we don't fit in.

In November 2022, FTX, then the second-largest cryptocurrency exchange, declared bankruptcy. Its CEO, Sam Bankman-Fried, faced charges of unauthorized and deceptive use of client assets. This led to significant financial losses and caused a ripple effect across the entire cryptocurrency sector. The accusations against Bankman-Fried cast doubt on the trustworthiness of cryptocurrency companies in general.

In the past, Sam Bankman-Fried was seen as a charismatic tech founder who won over powerful investors with his trading company, Alameda Research, which he operated alongside FTX. Once he gained the trust of a few key individuals, a bandwagon effect was triggered. More and more investors became attracted to his companies, FTX and Alameda Research. This led to a surge in investments in both the crypto market and his enterprises, turning them into widespread trends.

This is how the bandwagon effect manifests in practice: when people see a product or idea gaining popularity, they tend to join the trend without questioning its legitimacy. They assume that if everyone supports that idea or person, it must be good. While the bandwagon effect contributed to the popularity of cryptocurrencies, it is also the reason why people lose faith in them, causing significant downturns in the market. The FTX scandal created a negative bandwagon effect. The crypto industry often moves in cycles, and scandals like this have historically led to periods where prices fall because investor confidence drops.

In 2024, Bankman-Fried was sentenced to 25 years in prison. He caused the company's bankruptcy by misappropriating customer funds to cover losses and to make risky investments at Alameda Research.

Why Can We Easily Get Into a Car but Fear Taking Flight?

July 7th

AVAILABILITY BIAS

The availability bias is our tendency to make decisions based on information that comes to mind quickly and easily. It's a mental shortcut that gives more weight to information that was learned recently or that is easy to remember, for example, because it is an emotionally loaded memory. Our brain wants to save mental energy. So, we often go with the first information that comes to mind instead of putting in more mental effort to dig deeper.

Your chances of dying in a car accident are 1 in 107. The odds of dying in a plane crash are estimated to be around 1 in several million, depending on the source and methodology. This number varies by region, type of aircraft, and other factors, but it is clear that the odds are significantly lower than those for a car accident. Yet, there are fewer people who are afraid of getting in a car than have flying anxiety.

What makes the idea of flying so terrifying that it causes people to have panic attacks just thinking about it? Perhaps one of the reasons is how we remember rare incidents of plane crashes. Whenever such a tragedy happens, the news is almost everywhere, and it causes a real shock among people. Because the shock of this event is strong, the memory is also encoded differently in our minds than a normal road accident. As a result of this, we remember it more vividly and allow it to take up more space in our minds. Whenever we speak of plane crashes, we usually experience strong emotions like shock, fear, compassion, and helplessness. These accompanying emotions will make the memory of the plane crash news a lot more vivid and emotionally charged, ultimately making it more available.

Food poisonings, lightning, horses, and fireworks are all more deadly than plane crashes. Therefore, our fear of flying is indeed irrational, at least from a statistical point of view. In case you have flying anxiety, I hope this story has given you a way to cope with it a little better.

Can You Trust Your Memory?

July 8th

HINDSIGHT BIAS

The hindsight bias is also called the "I-knew-it-all-along" effect. It describes the retrospective overestimation of predictability. In the present, it's hard to tell how something will turn out in the future, but is easy to understand how or why an event happened in retrospect. This bias happens because we mistakenly assume that we had the same understanding of an event before it happened as we do after it happened.

Whenever global conflict breaks out, you can be sure that many will come out boasting about how they saw it coming for a long time. We're all familiar with that excess of confidence that occurs alongside hindsight bias. But is there more to our hindsight than mere confidence?

A research study found that looking at an event in retrospect can cause people to remember things incorrectly. When asked to predict the outcomes of the 1998 German Bundestag election, participants in a study showed significant errors when they had to remember their estimates. Two months after the election ended, the average participant remembered making predictions that were one-quarter closer to the actual election results than the original estimates were. It is interesting to note that the participants all remembered their estimates incorrectly in the same direction: they all remembered being more correct than they actually were. For example, a participant who initially predicted a party would receive 30% of the vote (the actual result was 40%) later recalled their estimate as 35%, making their remembered prediction closer to the outcome. No one remembered being further away from the results than they actually were. Perhaps their strong desire to be right led their minds to distort the accuracy of the facts surrounding the predictions they made in the past.

The results of this study can be explained through hindsight bias, which leads to the false belief that we could have predicted an event after it occurred. But it seems there is more to it than just false confidence. Our memory actually distorts the facts to support our belief that we could have predicted an outcome better than we actually did.

Is Nuclear Power a Clean Dream or Radioactive Nightmare?

July 9th

FRAMING EFFECT

The framing effect occurs when we draw different conclusions from identical information based solely on how that information is presented. This can happen when something is framed either positively or negatively, or as a gain versus a loss - we naturally tend to avoid losses in such situations. Our judgment can also shift depending on which features of the information are highlighted, even though the underlying facts remain exactly the same.

The portrayal of nuclear power in the media serves as an excellent example of the framing effect. Nuclear power can be seen as either a clean, efficient energy source or a dangerous, environmentally harmful technology, depending on how the media frames the issue.

When nuclear power is framed as a clean, efficient energy source, the focus falls on its low carbon emissions and minimal land footprint. It is praised for its ability to generate massive amounts of power while having a significantly smaller environmental impact compared to fossil fuels. Proponents emphasize its role in protecting air quality and its efficient use of space for power generation.

Conversely, when nuclear power is framed as a dangerous, environmentally harmful technology, attention shifts to the potential risks and downsides. This negative framing emphasizes issues such as nuclear waste management, nuclear proliferation, and national security concerns. The risk of accidents and potential health impacts, such as increased cancer rates near nuclear power plants and among industry workers, become central to the discussion.

The framing effect significantly influences public opinion on nuclear power. When presented with a positive frame, people tend to support the expansion of nuclear power as a solution to climate change and reduced dependence on fossil fuels. However, when confronted with the negative frame, the same people may oppose nuclear expansion due to perceived risks and environmental concerns, despite the underlying facts remaining unchanged.

Can You Band-aid Ignorance?

July 10th

DUNNING–KRUGER EFFECT

The Dunning–Kruger effect describes our tendency to overestimate our own abilities in areas that we are unskilled in or lack knowledge in. This happens when we know just enough to think we are great but not enough to tell the difference between good and bad. We just don't know yet what we could do better. The effect also applies to society as a whole. The most uninformed citizens are often also the most confident ones.

Which is worse—exaggerating the knowledge you do have, or pretending to know what you're talking about when asked about things that don't even exist?

A funny story from Jimmy Kimmel's "Lie Witness News" demonstrated that people are ready to fake knowledge they don't actually possess. During the annual music festival South by Southwest, Kimmel sent a camera crew to the streets of Austin and questioned people about their opinions on nonexistent bands. The names of these bands were completely fabricated, featuring humorous titles such as "Contact Dermatitis" and "Tonya and the Hardings." Although the bands weren't real, this didn't stop concertgoers from telling the camera crew how much they enjoyed their music.

Most people who attend regular concerts and festivals take great pride in their knowledge of artists and new bands. In this video, people not only claimed they knew these fake bands, but they also formed elaborate opinions about them and made up stories about their experiences with the music. Viewers witnessed very confident people sharing strong opinions about new bands and their latest albums, as if they had been listening to those bands all their lives.

Of course, this represents a new level of the Dunning-Kruger effect, as most people in this video didn't merely exaggerate existing knowledge but fabricated facts that weren't real. However, the underlying intention remained similar: to appear confident in their knowledge and overestimate their expertise.

Watch this video on YouTube

Instant Gratification or Long-Term Success: Which Path Do You Choose?

July 11th

HYPERBOLIC DISCOUNTING

Hyperbolic discounting is our tendency to favor more immediate payoffs in comparison to later payoffs. We do prefer the immediate reward, even when it is objectively less valuable. We all make decisions today that we would have preferred not to have made in the future due to hyperbolic discounting. Our brains are hardwired to do so because immediate reward meant a better chance of survival in evolutionary terms.

Would you prefer to amass wealth rapidly or cultivate a sustainable, long-term business or career over an extended period? Naturally, many of us gravitate towards immediate gratification: we aspire to win the lottery, gamble at casinos, or seek short-term financial gains. Although these approaches are not inherently flawed, they lack efficiency in securing long-term success.

Amazon founder Jeff Bezos once asked Warren Buffett, "You're the second-richest guy in the world. Your investment thesis is so simple. Why don't more people just copy you?" He replied, "Because people don't want to get rich slowly." While the road to wealth may be more intricate, it reveals a fundamental truth: our innate drive for swift outcomes often overpowers our patience for persistent and consistent efforts.

Recently, there has been a surge in self-proclaimed "get-rich-quick" coaches who emerge like mushrooms in a forest, peddling courses on drop shipping, affiliate marketing, and the like. These individuals frequently assert that rapid wealth accumulation can be achieved without complex work or significant effort. By exploiting our propensity for hyperbolic discounting, these schemes entice us with the promise of instant fortune just a few clicks away.

Understanding hyperbolic discounting empowers us to make more rational decisions by recognizing and mitigating our innate biases toward immediate gratification. Instead of succumbing to the allure of quick wealth, we can consciously shift our focus to long-term growth and stability.

Did the Illusory Truth Effect Rig Many Minds in 2020?

July 12th

ILLUSORY TRUTH EFFECT

The illusory truth effect causes us to believe information is true if we hear it repeatedly, even when it's not. This happens because repeatedly hearing the same information makes it familiar, and our brain processes familiar things more easily. This ease is due to the activation of well-established neural pathways, which require less effort to process than new or unfamiliar information. When our brains process information with less effort, we tend to interpret this ease as a sign of truth. Thus, if something is easier to understand, we are more likely to believe it's true.

The "Stop the Steal" movement, which emerged following the 2020 United States presidential election, serves as a prime example of the illusory truth effect in action. Despite multiple audits, investigations, and court rulings that found no evidence of widespread voter fraud, millions of Americans continue to believe the claims that the election was stolen. According to recent polls, approximately 60% of Republican voters still believe that Biden's victory in 2020 was not legitimate.

In the context of the "Stop the Steal" movement, Donald Trump's relentless repetition of the false claim that the election was rigged significantly influenced public opinion. As president and leader of the Republican Party at the time, Trump was a trusted source for millions of Americans. His continuous assertions about election fraud, amplified by conservative media outlets and prominent Republican figures, helped cement this narrative in the public consciousness.

The illusory truth effect becomes particularly potent when trusted sources or members of one's social circle repeat a statement. This power lies in the human tendency to equate familiarity with truth; the more we are exposed to a claim, the more likely we are to accept it as true. Despite substantial evidence refuting claims of widespread election fraud, the "Stop the Steal" movement has persisted largely due to the illusory truth effect. As Trump, his supporters, and certain conservative media outlets continue to repeat this false narrative, it becomes increasingly entrenched in the minds of those exposed to it.

Discover what Republicans think about the 2020 election through this poll

Fires, Fortunes, and Failures

July 13th

OVERCONFIDENCE EFFECT

We speak of the overconfidence effect when our subjective confidence in our judgments is higher than their objective accuracy. We can overestimate a variety of things, including our own performance or likelihood of success, our abilities in comparison to others, and the certainty of our answers or judgments.

Marcus Licinius Crassus, a man of immense wealth and power in ancient Rome, serves as a perfect example of the overconfidence effect. Crassus's fortune was so immense that he was as rich as Bill Gates in 2024 in today's money. Crassus was not only wealthy but also politically influential, forming the First Triumvirate—a political alliance of three powerful men—with Julius Caesar and Pompey to control Roman politics. Crassus demonstrated his canny yet ruthless business acumen through schemes like his private firefighting company. In the fire-prone city of Rome, he capitalized on disaster by offering to purchase burning properties at minimal prices. Only after securing the deal would his firefighters extinguish the flames, salvaging the property for its new owner—himself.

Emboldened by his vast wealth and influence, Crassus aspired to conquer the Parthian Empire (modern-day Iran) to expand Rome's eastern dominion, despite having limited military experience. His overconfidence led to a series of strategic blunders, including underestimating the Parthian army. Moreover, he ignored valuable advice from his officers and local allies, convinced that his wealth and power would guarantee victory. After his disastrous defeat at Carrhae, the Parthians captured Crassus and killed him by mockingly pouring molten gold down his throat. Only 10,000 of his 50,000 men managed to return to Roman territory, with the rest killed or captured.

Crassus's downfall highlighted the limits of wealth and power when not paired with wisdom and humility. Marcus Licinius Crassus's campaign against the Parthian Empire offers a cautionary tale about the perils of overconfidence. Despite his extraordinary wealth and influence, his hubris led to a disastrous defeat and a humiliating end for both himself and his army.

Why is it always "us" versus "them"?

July 14th

INGROUP BIAS

Ingroup bias is when we like and support people who are part of our own group more than people who are not part of our group. These groups can be divided based on seemingly trivial observable traits. This is rooted in the intrinsic human need for a group identity, which provides a sense of belonging and purpose. Additionally, we all have a desire to feel good about ourselves, and one way to achieve that is to see our own group as being superior to others.

Have you ever noticed how quickly people form "us versus them" mindsets, even over trivial differences? This tendency to favor our own group while excluding others is a deeply rooted psychological phenomenon. To explore how in-group bias develops and affects behavior, psychologist Muzafer Sherif conducted a landmark study in 1954 known as the "Robbers Cave" experiment.

In the study, 22 11-year-old boys were sent to a summer camp, where they were split into two groups. During the camp, they took part in activities and a four-day series of competitions. Once the two teams engaged in competitive activities, they immediately started displaying prejudice against the other group, both physically and verbally. Physical clashes included looting the opposing group's cabin and stealing personal items. After this stage, they were asked to describe the members of the other group. The boys tended to characterize their in-group in very favorable terms and their out-group in very unfavorable terms. The only thing that reduced the prejudice between the teams was encouraging them to work together for common goals. These goals involved engaging both groups of boys in cooperative tasks—such as restoring the camp's water supply, pulling a stuck truck, and pooling resources for a movie—that required them to work together to solve shared problems.

These conclusions apply well in real life. For example, rival political parties may view each other with suspicion due to conflicting ideologies, but working together on bipartisan issues can reduce hostility. Similarly, nations competing over trade or influence can ease tensions through international cooperation on global challenges.

Is Your Loan Approval a Victim of the Gambler's Fallacy?

July 15th

GAMBLER'S FALLACY

The gambler's fallacy arises from the mistaken belief that past events can affect the probability of future outcomes that are actually independent of the past. It is often manifested in the belief that a certain outcome is more or less likely to occur due to its frequency in the past, despite the fact that the probability remains the same. This fallacy is often driven by a desire for pattern-finding and prediction, as well as a dislike of uncertainty.

The gambler's fallacy is a bias that runs deeper than our rational thinking. It can affect our judgment even in situations where we are supposed to be logical and objective.

One example of this erroneous thinking was found among loan officers working in banks. Theoretically, whether someone approves or denies your loan application should be based on objective data such as your credit history, employment details, and so on. You would never think that whether you get a loan or not depends on something as ridiculous as how many people have been offered the loan before you.

The bad news is that this does happen. Studies have found steady evidence that loan officers avoid approving several loans in a row because they assume sequential events cannot occur by chance. In other words, these officers do not assess each application totally independently of the others, as they think they do. They might reject a strong application if they've approved several applications in a row, falling into the trap of thinking that after a streak of "good" applications (say, four or five), a "bad" one is statistically due. This flawed reasoning leads them to believe that approving too many loans consecutively is improbable and that there must inevitably be a "bad apple" among the applications, even when this contradicts the objective data before them.

While every loan is entirely unrelated to the next, the decision-making process of these officers is often compromised by the gambler's fallacy, which inadvertently makes them assume that all applications are somehow connected.

Are We Kicking Logic Aside in Football Penalty Shootouts?

July 16th

OUTCOME BIAS

We are subject to outcome bias when we judge a decision by its outcome. This is biased because we should rather base our judgment on the quality of the decision at the time it was made, given what was known at that time. We never have all the information we need, and every result has random and unpredictable parts. Bad outcomes are not always a sign of bad decision-making.

In normal situations, we should distinguish a decision-making process from its outcome. Most decisions take place in an uncertain world, so a good decision may lead to poor consequences, while a poor decision can yield positive outcomes. However, most of us don't approach our judgments this way. We wrongly assume that if an outcome is good, the initial thought process that led to it was the right one. Psychology calls this "outcome bias," which makes us judge the quality of a decision by its consequences.

This occurs frequently in football, particularly during penalty shootouts. If a team wins a match on penalties, fans tend to forget about a poor overall performance and rate the team more favorably. This happens even though the penalty shootout is separate from the main game and doesn't necessarily reflect the team's overall play. Surprisingly, this positive bias extends to the entire winning team, not just those involved in the shootout. Studies have found that even when the penalty-takers are excluded from the analysis, people still overrate the whole team's performance - including players who didn't score or even participate in the shootout.

This means that a whole team of players could bask in the victory of two exceptional ones thanks to the outcome bias. We make the same error by assuming that someone who made it this far in life always made really good decisions. But don't let yourself be blinded by outcomes. Instead, try to separate the process from the outcome.

Depressed or Realist?

July 17th

ILLUSION OF CONTROL

The illusion of control occurs when we believe we have more control over external events than we do. We frequently believe we have (or had) some control over events that are actually random. Researchers have found that people who feel in control will engage in healthier behaviors, feel less stress, and have better overall mental health. Therefore, this illusion makes us feel better about ourselves and the world around us, but it can also seduce us into relying on superstitions.

All of us suffer from a degree of illusion of control. We think we can control our future, people's feelings towards us, or our health to a greater extent than we actually do. However, ultimately, full control over our lives remains a mere illusion. Not everyone experiences this illusion to the same degree, though, and mental health plays a significant role in shaping our sense of control. Studies show that depressed people are less likely than non-depressed individuals to succumb to the illusion of control. Depression is characterized by feelings of guilt or poor self-worth as well as reduced enjoyment of life.

One study used a dice game to demonstrate how depression affects perceptions of control. In this experiment, an equal number of depressed and non-depressed undergraduates placed bets on the results of a game of dice. Sometimes the player threw the dice, and sometimes a casino employee did. The study found that non-depressed people felt more confident about winning when they threw the dice themselves. Depressed people, on the other hand, felt more confident about winning when the casino employee threw the dice.

This experiment illustrates a broader pattern in how depressed and non-depressed individuals judge control. When it comes to depression and judgments of control, depressed people think they have little to no influence on the outcome of a situation, while non-depressed people overestimate how much they can influence it. In contrast, depressed people overestimate how much control others have, while non-depressed individuals think that others have little to no control over their lives. In other words, non-depressed people succumb to the illusion of control—but only for themselves, not for others.

Do you like the song "Pumped Up Kicks"?

July 18th

COGNITIVE DISSONANCE

Cognitive dissonance describes the mental discomfort we experience when there is a conflict between our beliefs, actions, or perceptions. This discomfort often arises when our actions contradict our beliefs or when we hold two opposing beliefs simultaneously. To alleviate this discomfort, we may adjust our beliefs, perceptions, or actions to create a more consistent internal state. Achieving this internal consistency is crucial, as it helps maintain our sense of identity and coherence.

Are you aware of the true topic behind the catchy and upbeat song "Pumped Up Kicks" by Foster the People? In 2010, the song quickly gained popularity due to its infectious melody. However, beneath the catchy tune lies a disturbing story about a school shooting. The song presents a great example of cognitive dissonance.

At first listen, "Pumped Up Kicks" might seem like just another feel-good tune. However, the lyrics reveal a sinister narrative. The song tells the story of Robert, a troubled youth who finds his father's gun and plans a violent attack: "Robert's got a quick hand… He found a six-shooter gun in his dad's closet… he's coming for you." The chorus, repeated throughout the song, paints a chilling image of the potential victims, urging them to run faster than the bullets: "All the other kids with the pumped-up kicks, you better run, better run, outrun my gun… You better run, better run, faster than my bullet."

The stark contrast between the song's upbeat melody and its dark lyrics creates cognitive dissonance in listeners, who find themselves enjoying the tune while simultaneously being repulsed by the subject matter. To resolve this cognitive dissonance, listeners can change either their beliefs or their actions. For those who reject the song, consistency is achieved by aligning their actions (not listening) with their beliefs about the inappropriateness of the content. Those who continue to enjoy the song maintain consistency by adjusting their perception of the lyrics, perhaps viewing them as metaphorical or as a form of social commentary rather than a literal narrative about violence.

Listen to "Pumped Up Kicks" from Foster The People

Are You Saving for Your Golden Years?

July 19th

DEFAULT EFFECT

When offered a choice that has a pre-selected default option, we tend to choose this default option. This is called the default effect. Defaults are the options that take effect if we do nothing. Our brains try to save as much mental energy as possible. Accepting the default option saves energy because we don't have to think about the pros and cons of each choice.

Given that many people worldwide are not saving sufficient money for their retirement, some governments have created policies to boost these funds. One country that has acted to increase retirement funds is the US, where the government is enrolling all employees in a default retirement savings account. This is a highly efficient action because many people don't question default options due to the default effect, which makes us accept a preselected default option because it takes the least cognitive effort.

Automatic pension plans are a good example of how the default effect works. If the default option is to save for retirement, people apparently do not question or even revert to it. In the US, the introduction of automatic pension saving enrollment in 2012 has increased participation in workplace pension schemes by 36%. After only 3 years of this policy change, the number of private sector employees who were supposed to be automatically enrolled in a workplace pension scheme reached 88%. Compared to other countries around the world, where participation in pension schemes is much lower, this figure is quite impressive.

The only difference between the pension schemes in the US and those in other countries is that the former are introduced automatically when an employee starts to get paid. In other words, they are offered a default choice, which they can opt out of, but the chances of them making this cognitive effort are small.

This small tweak in policy—making retirement savings the default option—can have drastic positive consequences for wealth in retirement. By leveraging the default effect, governments can nudge citizens towards more financially secure futures without restricting their freedom of choice.

Who's the Real Loser?

July 20th

FUNDAMENTAL ATTRIBUTION ERROR

The fundamental attribution error refers to our tendency to assume that a person's behavior is a perfect reflection of their personality. We overestimate explanations that are due to the internal characteristics of a person and underestimate situational or environmental explanations. We do that simply because it saves mental energy to explain someone's behavior by attributing it to their personality rather than considering all possible situational and environmental factors.

Little Miss Sunshine, a 2006 comedy-drama film, brilliantly illustrates the concept through its characters. The film follows a dysfunctional family on a cross-country road trip to support their young daughter, Olive, in her bid to win the Little Miss Sunshine beauty pageant. The behavior of the character Richard particularly presents a compelling example of the fundamental attribution error.

Richard, played by Greg Kinnear, is the brother-in-law of Frank, portrayed by Steve Carell. Frank's character is introduced as a man who recently attempted suicide after losing his job and his partner. Instead of empathizing with Frank, Richard immediately assumes that Frank's actions stem from a weak personality and labels him a "loser." This reflects the fundamental attribution error, as Richard disregards the situational factors that contributed to Frank's crisis.

A particularly striking example of the fundamental attribution error occurs when Richard responds to Frank's sarcasm. He declares, "Sarcasm is the refuge of losers," suggesting that Frank's use of sarcasm is merely indicative of his "loser" personality. In reality, sarcasm can be a coping mechanism for dealing with emotional pain and difficult situations, as evident in Frank's character. Richard's attribution of Frank's sarcasm to his personality rather than his circumstances demonstrates an instance of his fundamental attribution error. While the filmmakers exaggerated Richard's character for comedic effect, the film masterfully illustrates how the fundamental attribution error can blind us to the complex circumstances that shape human behavior, making us quick to judge and slow to understand.

Watch the trailer for the movie "Little Miss Sunshine."

Can We Really Trust Personality Tests for Hiring the Right Fit?

July 21th

FORER EFFECT OR BARNUM EFFECT

The Forer effect, also known as the Barnum effect, describes the observation that people will give high accuracy ratings to personality descriptions that are supposedly tailored specifically for them. However, in reality, these descriptions are vague and general enough to apply to many people. This effect can help explain why some beliefs and practices, like astrology, palm reading, graphology, and some types of personality tests, are so popular.

Personality tests exist largely because of the Barnum effect, which refers to the tendency of people to accept general personality descriptions as uniquely applicable to themselves. Unfortunately, hiring processes are often subject to this cognitive bias through the widespread use of personality tests. In fact, studies show that 76% of organizations with more than 100 employees rely on personality tests for external hiring.

The Barnum effect's influence on personality tests has been well-documented through various studies. One notable experiment captured this phenomenon in action. A group of hiring managers were administered personality tests and told they would receive a report with their scores. However, the reports they received, which contained general statements like "You have a tendency to be critical of yourself," weren't scientifically validated. Instead, researchers provided identical, fabricated results to all participants—without their knowledge.

The results were striking: when asked to rate how accurate the reports were in describing their personalities, 50% of the hiring managers marked the fake description as "amazingly accurate." The remaining participants rated the accuracy as "rather good" (40%) or "about half and half" (10%).

These findings reveal a significant issue: if half of people consider a fake personality report to be "amazingly accurate," similar misconceptions likely occur with "real" personality tests in hiring. The Barnum effect leads people to believe these tests capture their personality traits, when the descriptions could apply to almost anyone.

Watch this trailer of HBO's "Persona."

I Did Not Like That Toy Anyway

July 22nd

COGNITIVE DISSONANCE

Cognitive dissonance describes the mental discomfort we experience when there is a conflict between our beliefs, actions, or perceptions. This discomfort often arises when our actions contradict our beliefs or when we hold two opposing beliefs simultaneously. To alleviate this discomfort, we may adjust our beliefs, perceptions, or actions to create a more consistent internal state. Achieving this internal consistency is crucial, as it helps maintain our sense of identity and coherence.

Leon Festinger, the founding father of cognitive dissonance, demonstrated this concept through several experiments.

In one, he first asked children to rate several toys, identifying pairs they found equally desirable. Then, in a second step, the children were asked to choose between two toys they had previously rated as equally appealing. After making their choice, the children were asked to rate the toys again. Interestingly, they now showed a stronger preference for the toy they had chosen while devaluing the toy they had rejected. This adjustment in attitude after making the choice was interpreted as a mechanism to reduce the dissonance between their action (choosing one toy) and their original belief (liking both toys equally).

In another experiment, Festinger recruited students to complete an intentionally tedious task. After completing it, some students were paid $20 (a substantial sum at the time) while others received only $1 to tell the next participant that the task was actually enjoyable and interesting. Surprisingly, those who received $1 were more likely to later rate the task as genuinely interesting compared to those who received $20. Festinger explained this counterintuitive result through cognitive dissonance: The students who received $20 had a clear external justification for their lie ("I did it for the money"), while those who received only $1 needed to resolve the uncomfortable disconnect between their actions and beliefs. To reduce this dissonance, they unconsciously adjusted their opinion of the task to match what they had told others.

These experiments show how people often change their attitudes to reduce the mental discomfort of conflicting beliefs and actions.

How Funny Are You?

December 26th

DUNNING–KRUGER EFFECT

The Dunning–Kruger effect describes our tendency to overestimate our own abilities in areas that we are unskilled in or lack knowledge in. This happens when we know just enough to think we are great, but not enough to tell the difference between good and bad. We just don't know yet what we could do better. The effect also applies to society as a whole. The most uninformed citizens are often also the most confident ones.

Justin Kruger and David Dunning's "Unskilled and Unaware of It" presents groundbreaking research that explores what we now know as the Dunning-Kruger effect.

The foundation of this effect is vividly illustrated in an experiment where participants took a logical reasoning test and then estimated their performance. Interestingly, the poorest performing students (those scoring in the lowest 25%) not only overestimated their logical reasoning skills but also their test performance. This pattern highlighted a key aspect of the Dunning-Kruger effect: those with the least skill often lack the ability to recognize their own incompetence, leading to inflated self-assessments.

Building on this insight, another study took a more lighthearted approach: analyzing humor recognition. First, professional comedians rated a series of jokes on an 11-point scale, establishing a baseline for humor quality. Then, participants were shown these same jokes and asked to rate their humor. Finally, participants were asked to assess their own ability to recognize what's funny compared to the average student. The results mirrored those of the logical reasoning study: individuals with poorer humor recognition significantly overestimated their ability to discern good comedy.

Through these experiments, Kruger and Dunning identified a widespread cognitive bias and illuminated the complexities of self-assessment.

*From Passion to Payment:
Are We Selling Out Our Favorite Activities?*

July 24th

OVERJUSTIFICATION HYPOTHESIS

The overjustification hypothesis predicts that rewards delivered by an external agent to engage in an activity reduce subsequent, internal, motivation to engage in that activity after explicit extrinsic rewards have been discontinued.

Can we decrease someone's motivation to engage in their favorite activity if we offer them an external reward like money? Unfortunately, a research study has shown that the answer is yes.

It's important to first understand two types of motivation: intrinsic (doing something for personal enjoyment) and extrinsic (doing something for external rewards or to avoid punishment). In a field experiment study, children who expected to be rewarded for drawing showed less intrinsic motivation to engage in this favorite activity in the future. More specifically, those who were told they would receive a financial reward before drawing were less motivated to engage in it when the external reward was not present anymore. Over the course of the study, intrinsic motivation did not decrease in children who did not anticipate being offered money for drawing.

While the results of this study may seem perplexing, the underlying explanation is simple. When an external reward is present, we shift our focus from the enjoyment of the activity and derive our satisfaction only extrinsically. This is also what happened in the experiment with children: until they were offered money for drawing, their only source of satisfaction for engaging in this activity originated intrinsically. However, after the financial reward was offered and discontinued, they no longer found drawing to be that much fun. This happened because their minds formed a new association between drawing and a financial reward, which deactivated the role of intrinsic motivation.

Be cautious when using money to motivate activities that should be driven by personal enjoyment, as it may unintentionally reduce the genuine passion behind them.

Watch a TED Talk about motivation by Dan Pink

Who Will You Become in a Decade?

July 25th

END-OF-HISTORY ILLUSION

The end-of-history illusion refers to our tendency to underestimate the extent of personal changes that will occur in the future. While we acknowledge that our personalities, values, and tastes have evolved over time, we often believe that they will remain relatively stable going forward. This misconception persists regardless of age. The illusion arises because we find it hard to imagine personal changes and thus assume that such changes are unlikely to occur.

"Most people overestimate what they can do in one year and underestimate what they can do in ten years," Bill Gates once observed. This insight extends beyond achievements – it applies equally to our personal growth. We tend to believe we've reached a stable point in our lives, assuming our current selves represent our final form.

Studies consistently show that the changes we remember experiencing are far greater than the changes we anticipate making. This disconnect isn't merely a memory error but rather a fundamental prediction error. For instance, when people are asked to identify who their best friends will be in ten years, they typically name their current friends. However, when others are asked to compare their present friendships with those from a decade ago, they often reveal significant changes in their social circles.

In a groundbreaking study, psychologist Daniel Gilbert explored this phenomenon in depth. He asked participants to predict their future preferences in areas like music, friendships, and personal values over the next decade. The participants overwhelmingly believed these aspects would remain largely unchanged. However, when Gilbert surveyed a separate group – now at the age the first group had predicted for – about their changes over the previous decade, a different picture emerged. This second group reported substantial transformations across all areas, from shifting musical preferences to evolving personal values.

Assuming you've reached a stable phase in life where nothing about yourself will surprise you anymore is precisely what the end-of-history illusion warns against. The reality is that personal growth and change remain constant companions throughout our lives.

Are You Afraid of Sharks?

July 26th

AVAILABILITY BIAS

The availability bias is our tendency to make decisions based on information that comes to mind quickly and easily. It's a mental shortcut that gives more weight to information that was learned recently or that is easy to remember, for example, because it is an emotionally loaded memory. Our brain wants to save mental energy. So, we often go with the first information that comes to mind instead of putting in more mental effort to dig deeper.

The 1975 blockbuster film "Jaws" not only took the world by storm but also ingrained an irrational fear of sharks into the public's psyche. The availability bias continues to distort the truth about shark attacks and their actual threat to humans. "Jaws" changed the way we see and feel about sharks forever, making us think they are more dangerous than they really are.

Scientists have been researching the public's fear of sharks, often referring to it as "The Jaws Effect." According to psychologists, media portrayals of sharks as dangerous, bloodthirsty predators particularly contribute to the learning and social reinforcement of shark fear. The popularity of "Jaws" and its subsequent sequels, as well as other shark-related media, has ensured that images of shark attacks remain readily available in the public's consciousness. As a result, people tend to overestimate the likelihood of shark attacks by a lot. In reality, shark attacks are exceedingly rare. In 2022, there were only 57 registered shark attacks worldwide, with only five of them being lethal. To put this into perspective, a person is more likely to win the lottery than to suffer a shark attack.

This overestimation is largely due to the fact that visual images are more readily available in our minds. The vivid, emotionally charged scenes from "Jaws" and similar media become powerful mental references, overshadowing less memorable information about the actual frequency of shark encounters. Both Peter Benchley, the author of the novel that inspired "Jaws," and Steven Spielberg, the director of the movie, later regretted fueling public fear, acknowledging that the idea of a rogue shark developing a taste for human flesh is a myth.

Are Healthier Fast Food Choices Just a Calorie-Loaded Illusion?

July 27th

HALO EFFECT

The halo effect is a type of cognitive bias in which our overall opinion of a person or brand affects how we feel about the specific qualities of that person or brand. If we have a good feeling about something as a whole, we are more likely to think that its individual parts are good as well. We do that because it saves cognitive effort to use our overall impressions as a shortcut to make judgments rather than evaluating each aspect of something separately.

Have you ever chosen Subway over McDonald's, thinking it's a healthier option? When we're short on time, a brand's healthy image can easily mislead us. Subway, for example, presents itself as diet-friendly with multigrain breads and veggie options. Their famous campaign featuring Jared Fogle, who reportedly lost 220 pounds eating Subway, strengthened this healthy image.

However, real-world data paints a different picture. A study from 2011 looked at 26 wealthy countries and found an interesting pattern: places with more Subway restaurants tended to have higher rates of obesity. For example, the United States and Canada, which have lots of Subway shops, also have more overweight people. On the flip side, countries like Japan and Norway, which have fewer Subways, also have fewer obese people. It's important to note, though, that just because these things happen together doesn't mean one directly causes the other. There could be other factors at play.

One possible explanation lies in how we perceive these "healthier" fast food options. The health claims made by these restaurants often lead consumers to underestimate the number of calories in the dishes they order and even compensate for their supposedly healthy choices with high-calorie desserts or drinks. This phenomenon may stem from our tendency to generalize a single aspect of a brand (e.g., fewer calories) to everything it offers. Consequently, we might reason that: Subway = fewer calories, therefore, I can eat more here than at McDonald's without gaining weight. As a result, the "health halo" effect can lead to overeating and undermine our weight loss goals.

Watch a Subway commercial with Jared Fogle from 2006

Does Disconfirmatory Info Break Bias or Cement Convictions?

July 28th

CONFIRMATION BIAS

Confirmation bias is our tendency to look for, acknowledge, favor, and remember information in a way that supports what we already think or believe. This bias occurs when we ignore information that contradicts our ideas or interpret ambiguous facts as evidence supporting our existing beliefs. Situations that involve emotionally charged topics, strongly held beliefs, or things we really want to happen are most susceptible to this bias.

An antidote to thinking more critically about our views is to sit with disconfirming information. In theory, this is supposed to widen our perspective and challenge our existing assumptions. But is this always effective and possible? In one captivating study, proponents and opponents of a highly complex social issue - capital punishment - were exposed to identical information on the topic. The information offered both support and disconfirmation for their views (e.g., "this is why capital punishment prevents crime" versus "why it doesn't"). This strategy aimed at making participants more critical of their opinions.

However, the experiment results showed that exposure to opposing evidence does not always change our minds. Depending on participants' beliefs, they either accepted the information or looked for reasons to reject it. If the information matched participants' existing beliefs, they accepted it, and if it contradicted their views, they looked for flaws in it. For instance, a pro-capital punishment participant might accept statistics showing crime reduction in states with the death penalty, but question the methodology of studies suggesting it doesn't deter crime. An opponent might do the reverse, readily accepting evidence against its effectiveness while scrutinizing supportive data.

Participants remembered the strengths of the confirming evidence and the weaknesses of the disconfirming evidence. They regarded the flaws in the data of opposing evidence as a sign that their views were correct. Because of confirmation bias, participants' perceptions of capital punishment didn't shift much. Instead, they processed the information on this topic in a way that solidified their views and discarded the opposing facts even more.

What Prevents Us From Owning Traffic Mistakes?

July 29th

SELF-SERVING BIAS

The self-serving bias is our tendency to take credit for good things that happen to us and blame other things or people for bad things that happen. We do that because we have the desire to feel good about ourselves. Being responsible for good things happening boosts our confidence and gives us a sense of control in our lives. When we blame external factors for bad things that happen to us, it can help us feel better about ourselves by protecting our ego.

Self-driving cars offer a compelling promise: to dramatically reduce road accidents and fatalities by eliminating human error, which is responsible for the vast majority of traffic incidents. Interestingly, public perception doesn't align with this promise, as three out of four Americans believe self-driving cars are less safe than human-operated vehicles.

This skepticism may actually stem from self-serving bias. A striking example of this bias is that 75% of drivers involved in road accidents assume someone else should be blamed for the accident, rather than accepting responsibility themselves. A recent study highlighted the impact of this bias on attitudes toward self-driving cars. Researchers evaluated 531 drivers on their degree of self-serving bias and found that those with higher levels of self-serving bias tended to underestimate the potential of self-driving cars to reduce road accidents.

The explanation for this correlation lies in how people attribute responsibility. Those with strong self-serving tendencies rarely take responsibility for their mistakes, making it difficult for them to acknowledge the potential benefits of autonomous vehicles. To fully appreciate the efficiency of self-driving cars, one must first recognize their own role in contributing to road accidents.

Consequently, individuals with significant self-serving bias often perceive self-driving technology as a potential cause of accidents while overlooking its role in preventing mishaps. This skewed perspective arises because such individuals tend to attribute successful outcomes to their own driving abilities, while conveniently placing blame on external factors like autonomous driving systems when things go awry.

Are Algorithms Amplifying Our Social Biases?

July 30th

AUTOMATION BIAS

Automation bias means that we are likely to follow the advice of automated systems, like those in airplane cockpits or on your phone (think autocorrect, Google Maps). We tend to ignore contradictory information made without automation, even if it is correct. In decision-making, we like to take the path of least cognitive effort. We are happy to accept the answers that automated systems give us because it is often easier than having to think for ourselves.

Using automated translation tools can lead to serious misunderstandings and potentially dire consequences if not carefully verified. This was the case with the news of a Palestinian arrested in Israel in 2017 because Facebook incorrectly translated "good morning" automatically to "attack them."

The man, a construction worker at the West Bank settlement of Beitar Ilit near Jerusalem, innocently posted a picture of himself leaning against a bulldozer, a vehicle that has been used in previous hit-and-run terrorist attacks. He captioned the picture "Good morning" in Arabic. Facebook's automatic translation software mistakenly translated this as "hurt them" in English and "attack them" in Hebrew. The Judea and Samaria District Police were quickly notified of the post and urged the man to be immediately arrested. In the end, Facebook recognized the translation error, and the police admitted their mistake.

This incident highlights how automation bias can intersect with algorithmic errors to amplify existing social tensions. The mistranslation was likely influenced by the regional context, demonstrating how algorithms may inadvertently reinforce societal prejudices. The quick escalation to arrest without sufficient human verification showcases a concerning over-reliance on automated systems. What began as an innocent social media post nearly resulted in wrongful arrest, illustrating the real-world impact of algorithmic mistakes and the critical need for human oversight in automated decision-making processes, especially in sensitive contexts like law enforcement or international relations.

Watch Timnit Gebru talk about the limitations of AI

Did Someone See 9/11 Coming?

July 31st

HINDSIGHT BIAS

The hindsight bias is also called the "I-knew-it-all-along" effect. It describes the retrospective overestimation of predictability. In the present, it's hard to tell how something will turn out in the future, but is easy to understand how or why an event happened in retrospect. This bias happens because we mistakenly assume that we had the same understanding of an event before it happened as we do after it happened.

The 9/11 Commission report, officially titled "The National Commission on Terrorist Attacks Upon the United States," was a comprehensive government investigation into the September 11, 2001 terrorist attacks on the United States. Commissioned by President George W. Bush and Congress, the report was released on July 22, 2004, providing a detailed account of the events leading up to the attacks, the attacks themselves, and recommendations for preventing future terrorist incidents. The eleventh chapter of this report is titled "Foresight and Hindsight." The officials composing this report were very much aware of the dangers of hindsight bias that would make them step into the "We-knew-it-all-along" trap. You need to read the first paragraph.

"In composing this narrative, we have tried to remember that we write with the benefit and the handicap of hindsight. Hindsight can sometimes see the past clearly—with 20/20 vision. However, the path of what happened is so brightly lit that it places everything else more deeply into shadow. Commenting on Pearl Harbor, Roberta Wohlstetter found it "much easier after the event to sort the relevant from the irrelevant signals. After the event, of course, a signal is always crystal clear; we can now see what disaster it was signaling since the disaster has occurred. But before the event, it is obscure and pregnant with conflicting meanings."

The quoted Roberta Wohlstetter was a military historian known for her analysis of the Pearl Harbor attack. Her work on intelligence failures and the difficulty of interpreting signals before a crisis has been influential in understanding surprise attacks. The 9/11 Commission's explicit acknowledgment of hindsight bias serves as a powerful reminder of the importance of context in historical analysis.

∞
AUGUST

Is Our Primate Brain Making Us Irrationally Attached?

August 1st

ENDOWMENT EFFECT

The endowment is the idea that when we own an object, we tend to value it more than we would if it were someone else's. The mere feeling of ownership makes us value it more. One reason for this effect is that we are loss-averse. We really dislike losing things. Ownership therefore influences how we value an object and how much we are willing to accept in exchange for it.

You've probably noticed that you value your possessions a lot. This is why you might be inclined to sell something you own for a higher price than, objectively speaking, it is worth. This phenomenon is known as the endowment effect.

This effect is rooted in primate brain structures that make quick but often irrational decisions. A research study demonstrated that capuchin monkeys exhibited the same tendencies toward the endowment effect. The researchers found that capuchin monkeys value things they own more highly than things they don't, even if the things they don't own are just as good as the things they already own.

In the experiment, the researchers gave capuchin monkeys two different types of treats: fruit discs and cereal chunks. They made sure that each monkey liked both types of treats equally. Then, they gave each monkey one type of treat and offered them the opportunity to trade it for the other type of treat. The researchers found that the monkeys were much less likely to trade their treat for the other treat if they already owned it. In other words, they valued their treat more highly than the other treat, even though both treats were equally good. The study also ruled out other explanations, such as the time it takes to trade or eat the food.

Capuchin monkeys exhibit the endowment effect like humans, implying this bias is rooted in primitive cognitive systems. So, if you ever wonder why you perceive your possessions to be more valuable than they actually are, it might be due to our primate brain.

Is Your Culture Making You a Lone Dollar Ranger?

August 2nd

PRIMING EFFECT

The priming effect occurs when something we see or hear influences our thoughts or actions without us being aware of it. This can happen with words, pictures, or sounds we encounter. When our brain is primed, it becomes easier for us to think about, remember, and act on related information because the things we read, see, or hear activate connected information in the brain.

We all know that different cultures emphasize different values. If you grow up in the heart of New York City, you are less likely to hold community as your primary value than someone who has lived all their lives in a village in Turkey.

The priming effect explains how our exposure to cues, like messages about money, influences our values and behavior. This was demonstrated in a series of experiments where participants were "primed" with money-related cues, such as Monopoly money, dollar bill screensavers, or money-related phrases. They then took part in activities involving social interactions or choices. Interestingly, the effects were similar whether using real money, play money, or just images of money, highlighting the power of even symbolic reminders of money.

In one experiment, participants primed with money spent more time trying to solve a difficult puzzle alone before asking for help. In another, they picked up fewer pencils to help someone who had spilled them. The results were revelatory: people exposed to money-related cues were less likely to ask for help, more stubborn to persevere alone, and less likely to help others. They also maintained greater physical distance from others and preferred being alone. In one particularly telling experiment, researchers found that participants primed with money donated less to a student fund compared to those not primed.

Researchers termed this effect "self-sufficiency," describing a state where people prefer to be free of dependency and dependents. Even subtle reminders of money led to more self-sufficient and less cooperative behavior. While this research doesn't directly prove long-term effects, it suggests that repeated exposure to money-related concepts might influence our behavior and social interactions over time.

Ponzi or Not Ponzi: How Ignorance Fueled a Financial Fiasco?

August 3rd

OSTRICH EFFECT OR NORMALCY BIAS

Normalcy bias, also known as "ostrich effect," makes us downplay warnings about dangers or ignore negative situations completely. We underestimate how likely it is that a disaster will happen and how it might affect us. We do that because we want to avoid an unpleasant emotional impact in the short term. The name comes from the popular (but false) belief that ostriches bury their heads in the sand when in danger.

One striking example of the ostrich effect is the case of Bernie Madoff. His wealth management business was eventually exposed as a massive Ponzi scheme, a fraudulent investment operation where the operator promises high returns with little risk, but instead of generating legitimate profits, pays existing investors using funds from new investors. This scheme requires a constant influx of new investments to sustain itself.

Harry Markopolos, an American securities industry executive, recognized the red flags in Madoff's operation and repeatedly alerted the U.S. Securities and Exchange Commission (SEC) from 2000 to 2005. Using mathematical and logical arguments, Markopolos demonstrated that Madoff's claimed 1-2% monthly returns were impossible to achieve consistently. Despite Markopolos' efforts, the SEC either ignored his evidence or conducted only superficial investigations. It took nearly eight years from Markopolos' first warning before Madoff's fraud was finally exposed in 2008, resulting in Madoff's 150-year prison sentence for orchestrating the largest Ponzi scheme in history.

The most intriguing aspect of this case is how the entire finance sector failed to recognize the scheme. Despite obvious warning signs, the financial community exhibited a classic ostrich effect, metaphorically burying their heads in the sand and refusing to acknowledge that one of Wall Street's most prominent figures was running a fraudulent operation. This collective denial may have stemmed from an unwillingness to accept the possibility of such a massive financial catastrophe. This case illustrates how the ostrich effect allows fraudulent activities to persist even in the face of clear evidence.

Watch a trailer of the movie "The Wizard of Lies" about Bernie Madoff

Can Objects Be Your New BFF?

August 4th

ANTHROPOMORPHISM

Anthropomorphism is our natural tendency to attribute human traits, emotions, and intentions to non-humans, for example, animals, gods, natural forces, and the like. We do this because we naturally know more about human traits than non-human ones. Therefore, these come easier to mind, and that saves mental energy.

Loneliness can transform any object into a trusted friend. In the movie "Castaway," FedEx employee Chuck Noland gets stranded on an island after his plane crashes over the Pacific Ocean during a storm. As the sole survivor of the flight, Chuck has to learn how to survive on the island for years. However, survival, as he soon finds out, isn't the only challenge he has to face. Without another human being, Chuck makes a volleyball his best friend, advisor, and empathic listener.

One of the most emotional moments of the movie is when Wilson floats away from Chuck, who is forced to let it go to survive. Those watching the movie might find themselves attached to the inanimate volleyball as well, which initially might sound odd, but when looking closer, one can understand why it happens.

Human beings are social creatures. We need to be in contact with others; if this contact is denied, we will create it. Due to loneliness, we form close bonds with animals or even invent imaginary friends. That's what Chuck does on the island: he invents Wilson to accompany him and have someone to talk to.

At the root of this behavior is anthropomorphism. When we anthropomorphize, we attribute human-specific traits to non-humans and transform them into something that could replace a real person. When Chuck loses his volleyball, he doesn't lose an object; he loses his best friend at this point.

Watch the scenes from Castaway

Would You Tell President Nixon He Was Mistaken?

August 5th

GROUPTHINK

Groupthink is when our desire for harmony and conformity within a group leads to dysfunctional decision-making. Group members prioritize agreement over critical evaluation, resulting in a loss of individual creativity and thinking. This can lead to an inflated sense of confidence in the group's abilities, an undervaluation of opponents, group pressure, and potentially harmful actions towards outsiders.

The Watergate scandal remains one of the most infamous political events in American history. In 1972, members of President Richard Nixon's reelection campaign orchestrated a break-in at the Democratic National Committee headquarters. This event not only led to the resignation of President Nixon but also exposed a culture of corruption and criminal activity within the highest levels of government. Most importantly, it serves as an illustrative example of groupthink.

The Watergate scandal showcases the inflated sense of confidence often found in groupthink situations. The Committee to Re-Elect the President (commonly known as CREEP) felt that they were above the law and that all actions were justified to secure Nixon's re-election. They believed they were invincible, which only encouraged further criminal activities, such as the break-in and subsequent cover-up. The Nixon administration and CREEP members also exhibited a tendency to stereotype outsiders, particularly the media and political opponents. They dismissed journalists as "enemies" and portrayed them as biased and untrustworthy. This mindset further reinforced the group's belief in their righteousness and the justness of their actions.

Within the circle, groupthink created an atmosphere of conformity and false loyalty that prevented the group from reassessing their actions. When John Dean, the White House Counsel, realized that higher-ups were setting him up to be the scapegoat, he lost loyalty to the inner circle, was eventually fired, and turned into a crucial witness in the trial.

Listen to John Dean, the designated scapegoat

Can You Trust the Buzz?

August 6th

BANDWAGON EFFECT

The bandwagon effect refers to the phenomenon in which a belief or behavior becomes more popular as more people adopt it. This can lead to a self-reinforcing cycle, as the increased popularity of the belief or behavior encourages more people to adopt it. The effect is caused by our desire to conform to social norms and our belief that the majority must be correct. It can also be caused by peer pressure and the fear of being left out or made fun of if we don't fit in.

There's something powerful about viral posts that makes us read, share, like, and engage with them. We consider the information to be more credible if many people support it. We are vulnerable to this because the bandwagon effect exists in all of us, making us follow the actions of others simply because everyone else is doing the same.

However, before you trust a highly popular tweet, Facebook post, or news article, there's something you should consider about what made them go viral. One possibility is that social media bots, which are algorithmically driven entities that mimic human behavior on social media platforms, are manipulating them. They are present in controversial contexts, such as political debates, to damage people's reputations or exaggerate the importance of an issue to make it look like many other people agree with someone's opinion.

Emilio Ferrara, a data scientist, discovered that bots produced nearly 19% of all retweets about the election US in 2016. Also, during the 2020 political election, bots were a huge issue. They were used to spread misinformation, such as conspiracy theories or depicting COVID-19 as a liberal scam.

So if you wondered why the articles on these topics received so much attention, remember that there might have been a vicious circle at play. Unfortunately, social media popularity does not always entail reliability, which is why we should question our instinctual bandwagon effect critically.

Watch this video on how social bots work

Was the Maginot Line a Costly Monument to Misjudgment?

August 7th

SUNK COST FALLACY

The sunk cost fallacy is when we make a decision based on how much we have already invested in something rather than on whether it is the best choice for us right now. When we feel like we have already invested a lot in something, we feel like we would be losing something if we were to let it go. Another reason that the sunk cost fallacy occurs is because we tend to focus on the past rather than the present when we make decisions.

France constructed the Maginot Line, a line of fortifications, between 1929 and 1940 to protect itself from potential invasions from Germany after World War I. Despite being built with impressive conviction and $9 billion in today's currency, the Maginot Line was a strategic failure during World War II. The line spanned approximately 280 miles and included numerous forts, underground bunkers, minefields, and gun batteries. Today, it serves as a prime example of the sunk cost fallacy.

The significant advancements in tanks with enhanced speed and firepower, the evolution of aircraft capable of long-range bombing and deploying airborne troops, and the introduction of mobile artillery and portable anti-tank weapons underscored the shift towards mobility and adaptability in warfare. It became apparent that the static defenses of the Maginot Line were becoming obsolete. However, due to the sunk costs and a desire to defend their previous choices, the French government continued to invest in the Maginot Line. French leaders focused on the amount of money already spent on the project and were reluctant to abandon it.

When World War II broke out, the Maginot Line was of little use. In 1940, the German army circumvented the line and invaded through the Ardennes Forest in Belgium, an area thought to be too difficult to traverse and therefore left unguarded. The German blitzkrieg, a planned, quick-moving attack that utilized tanks, infantry, and air support, caught the French military off guard because it heavily relied on the Maginot Line as a defense.

*From Apu to Yunioshi:
Do TV and Film Characters Reinforce Prejudices?*

August 8th

STEREOTYPING

Stereotypes exist when we think that a category of people always has certain characteristics or behaviors. The brain has a natural tendency to put things into groups. By grouping into categories, we can process our environments more efficiently. It is a mental shortcut that saves time and mental energy. Because of that, we might assume that certain stereotypes apply to a certain member of a group even though we know nothing about that individual.

Stereotyping saves time and mental energy, but it also leads to misjudgments and perpetuates problematic beliefs. Movies and television series often employ stereotypes to make their narratives easier to understand, as viewers need to think less to comprehend the story. Let's look at three popular examples.

In the long-running animated series "The Simpsons," Apu Nahasapeemapetilon is an Indian-American convenience store owner characterized by a heavy accent. The character of Mr. Yunioshi in "Breakfast at Tiffany's" is a caricature of a Japanese man. Played by Mickey Rooney, the character's exaggerated accent, appearance, and behavior perpetuates stereotypes about Japanese people. The classic movie "Gone with the Wind" portrays African American slaves in a manner that perpetuates the stereotype of the "happy slave." This depiction simplifies the harsh reality of slavery and presents a distorted, inaccurate representation. HBO Max recently removed "Gone With the Wind" from its streaming service due to its racist stereotypes and whitewashing of the horrors of slavery, with plans to reintroduce it with added historical context.

Stereotyping in movies and series may make narratives easier to understand, but it comes at the cost of the perpetuation of outdated and possibly problematic beliefs. What do you think? Is the removal of a movie like "Gone with the Wind" from streaming platforms a correct approach to addressing these issues, or is it an overreaction?

Watch Breakfast at Tiffany's' Mr. Yunioshi

How Did Shreddies Turn a 45-Degree Twist into a Marketing Masterpiece?

August 9th

FRAMING EFFECT

The framing effect occurs when we draw different conclusions from identical information based solely on how that information is presented. This can happen when something is framed either positively or negatively, or as a gain versus a loss - we naturally tend to avoid losses in such situations. Our judgment can also shift depending on which features of the information are highlighted, even though the underlying facts remain exactly the same.

There are many great marketing campaigns out there, but this one will blow your mind. Shreddies, a popular cereal brand in Canada, Britain, and New Zealand, decided in 2008 to relaunch the product. Their strategy was pure innovation: the square-shaped cereals became diamond-shaped cereals. How? Just turn the square-shaped cereal 45 degrees on the image on the carton, and you have a diamond. To make sure everyone knew about the change, Shreddies even changed their product name to Diamond Shreddies.

The results of the campaign were impressive even from the first month: Shreddies' baseline sales rose 18%, according to the company's analysis, and brand recognition was 52% greater than the competition. Yes, that's right - all those results came just from rotating the square-shaped cereal and adding the word "diamond" to the product name. There is a video recording of customers comparing the new Diamond Shreddies against the old ones. Their conclusion is that the new ones even taste better. Genius, right?

The true genius of this campaign lay in its clever exploitation of the framing effect. Shreddies did exactly that, both figuratively and literally. By giving their product a new angle—45 degrees to be precise—they made customers see their cereal in a new light. This simple yet ingenious approach not only revitalized the brand but also demonstrated how powerful perception can be in marketing. Without altering the product itself, Shreddies managed to change how consumers viewed—and even tasted—their cereal.

Watch this genius move of Diamond Shreddies

Are You Really a Wine Connoisseur?

August 10th

DUNNING–KRUGER EFFECT

The Dunning-Kruger effect describes our tendency to overestimate our own abilities in areas that we are unskilled in or lack knowledge in. This happens when we know just enough to think we are great but not enough to tell the difference between good and bad. We just don't know yet what we could do better. The effect also applies to society as a whole. The most uninformed citizens are often also the most confident ones.

There's a difference between thinking that you're a wine expert and actually being one. Having a bit of knowledge of wine makes you more likely to use fancy terms such as "crisp," and "tannic" in front of your friends while positioning yourself as a real wine connoisseur. However, subjective knowledge—what you think you know—is not always the same as objective knowledge (what you actually know).

In fact, the difference between the two types of knowledge often lies in the Dunning-Kruger effect. Novice learners are more likely to overestimate their knowledge and skills than experts, who will constantly second-guess everything they know. In one study, being an expert in wine was shown to be an illusion for many people. In the study, researchers tested people's actual wine knowledge with a quiz about grape varieties, wine regions, and winemaking. They also asked participants to rate how much they thought they knew about wine. To round things out, the researchers gathered information on how often people drank wine and how much they typically spent on it. This clever setup allowed them to compare what people really knew about wine with what they thought they knew, revealing some interesting patterns.

The results were pretty eye-opening. People who knew the least about wine often thought they knew more than they actually did. They were confident in their wine knowledge, even though they didn't score well on the quiz. On the flip side, the real wine experts tended to underestimate how much they knew. They scored high on the quiz but were more modest about their expertise.

The findings do not just apply to wine - in many areas of life, a little knowledge can make us overconfident, while true expertise often comes with a healthy dose of humility

Why Do We Get More Satisfaction from Work Than Leisure Activities?

August 11th

IKEA EFFECT

The IKEA effect refers to our tendency to place a disproportionately high value on objects that we helped create, such as IKEA furniture. We do that regardless of the quality of the end product. This bias helps us to feel better about ourselves in two ways. First, we want to feel that our effort was well invested and that we did not waste our time but instead created something of value. Secondly, creating things makes us feel more competent.

We often have mixed feelings about our jobs. Sometimes, we claim to hate the arduous and unpleasant nature of tasks we have to perform for a paycheck. However, work also provides meaning and purpose in our lives. Research studies consistently support this claim. One particular study found that people rank their jobs or spending time with children among the least enjoyable but most rewarding activities.

This research revealed that people generally find physical activity, watching TV, eating, and reading more pleasurable than work or spending time with their children. However, when it comes to feeling rewarded, only work scored higher than spending time with children, while activities like watching TV, resting, eating, or shopping were all less rewarding.

The simultaneously rewarding and unpleasant nature of work or raising children has been explained by researchers through the concept of "effort justification." This principle suggests that the more effort people invest in something, the more they come to value it. Labor alone is sufficient to increase one's appreciation for the result – the very definition of the IKEA effect.

Perhaps we experience the same psychological phenomenon with our jobs and our children. Even if we don't like all aspects of our work, we feel accomplished when we complete our tasks at the end of the day. And just like our jobs, even if some moments with our children are challenging, nothing can replace the immense gratification we experience from watching them grow and learn, reinforcing that the most rewarding endeavors in life often require the most effort.

A Side Hustle Gone Wrong?

August 12th

ILLUSION OF VALIDITY

The illusion of validity is a cognitive bias where we overestimate our ability to understand and predict an outcome based on the information we have. When analyzing new information, we rely on things we already know, for example, stereotypes and prior beliefs. When we assume that what we know is valid enough to predict what will happen in different contexts, we make confident predictions that can turn out to be utterly inaccurate.

Human behavior is never easy to predict. In fact, making predictions about someone's behavior based on a single thing we know about them can turn out to be a massive error. By doing this, we're setting ourselves up for the illusion of validity, which makes us overestimate our ability to foresee an outcome based on the limited information we have..

This tendency to overestimate our predictive abilities isn't limited to individuals; it can affect entire governments and lead to unintended consequences. A striking example of this occurred in 18th century France, where the illusion of validity led to a costly and counterproductive policy. At the time, there were too many squirrels roaming the country, which was a bothersome problem. The authorities then decided to come up with an intelligent solution—or so they thought. They announced that anyone who kills a squirrel will be awarded a monetary prize if they bring back the tail. Bonus points if you brought in extra ones.

The public was very receptive. In fact, the number of squirrel hunters increased annually. But there was one issue there: the squirrel issue actually became worse. Upon closer investigation, French authorities got to the root of the mystery. The reason squirrels multiplied despite aggressive hunting was that some people started squirrel farms as a way to earn money from the government.

The authorities clearly didn't see that coming. The government's inability to foresee this unintended consequence stemmed from their misplaced confidence in their predictions. For better or worse, human creativity knows no boundaries.

Are Judges Rolling the Dice on Criminal Sentencing?

August 13th

ANCHORING BIAS

Anchoring bias occurs when a specific reference point, or "anchor", influences our decision-making process. This anchor could be a number or any other kind of cue, even if it is completely unrelated to the decision at hand. Despite this, we often use the anchor as a starting point and adjust our decisions or judgments from there, without realizing it. As a result, our final estimates, decisions, or judgments can be significantly different from what they might have been without the influence of the anchor.

You might think that judges base sentencing decisions solely on solid facts. However, research shows that judges, like everyone else, are susceptible to cognitive biases. One particular striking study demonstrates the effect of anchoring bias in legal settings.

In this experiment, legal professionals made sentencing decisions for a hypothetical shoplifting case. Before deciding, they were exposed to a "prosecutor's demand" determined randomly by dice rolls. Despite knowing the number was random, it significantly influenced their sentencing decisions.

The results were startling. Judges who saw a low random number gave shorter sentences, around 5 months on average. Those who saw a high random number gave longer sentences, almost 8 months on average. That's nearly a 3-month difference in jail time, just because of a meaningless number! Even experienced judges fell for this trick. Experts were just as easily swayed as judges with less experience.

The study also found that casual conversations could affect sentencing. When researchers mentioned higher numbers in pretend phone calls with journalists, judges tended to give longer sentences. This happened even when judges knew these numbers weren't related to the case at all.

These findings highlight how even trained legal professionals can be unconsciously swayed by irrelevant information when making critical decisions. The study shows that random numbers can alter sentencing decisions by up to 48%, raising important questions about judicial objectivity and emphasizing the need for safeguards against such biases in our legal system.

The Media's Focus on the Negative Makes Us Unnecessarily Pessimistic

August 14th

AVAILABILITY BIAS

The availability bias is our tendency to make decisions based on information that comes to mind quickly and easily. It's a mental shortcut that gives more weight to information that was learned recently or that is easy to remember, for example, because it is an emotionally loaded memory. Our brain wants to save mental energy. So, we often go with the first information that comes to mind instead of putting in more mental effort to dig deeper.

If you spend some time reading the news, you would most likely think that the world is doomed. Most headlines outline the most negative aspects of the world, such as natural disasters, economic crises, and violent conflicts, which influence our perception of reality. Due to availability bias, we get the impression that the world is a dire place, The author of the book "Factfulness" as well as the futurist Ray Kurzweil suggest that the vast majority of people are unnecessarily pessimistic.

"Factfulness" emphasizes that many people still think about the world in terms of developed and developing countries. Instead, the authors suggest a simpler way to look at the world. They group countries based on how much money people typically earn each day. This approach shows that in most countries, people now live on up to $32 a day. The percentage of the world's population living in extreme poverty went from 35% in 1994 to 10% in 2018.

Futurist Ray Kurzweil asked 24,000 people in a poll how they think the proportion of the world population living in extreme poverty had changed in the last 20 years. 70% said it increased by 25 or even 50%, and just 1% said they believed that it decreased by 50%, which is actually the correct answer.

Both examples perfectly show the gap between perception and reality. The mainstream media focuses overly on bad news, which makes it more readily available in our minds when we think about the state of the world. This is the availability bias at work, shaping our worldview in ways that often don't align with factual improvements in global conditions.

Listen to Ray Kurzweil speak about extreme poverty statistics with Lex Fridman

Fortune Favors the... Ideologue?

August 15th

JUST WORLD HYPOTHESIS

The Just World Hypothesis is the belief that the world is just and fair, and that people get what they deserve. This means that if someone is experiencing bad things, it is because they have done something to deserve it and are punished. On the other hand, if someone is successful or happy, it is because they made good choices and are rewarded. This idea can be comforting because it gives us a sense of control over our lives and the belief that we can influence our own outcomes.

What type of beliefs do you have about money and wealth? Do you think wealth is fairly achieved as a result of your work and efforts? Or perhaps you think it is something entirely left to chance that we have no control over?

According to a scientific measurement of people's perception of money, called the "Causal Attributions of Financial Uncertainty" (CAFU), people relate to money in three main ways. Some think that money is "rewarding" (as a result of individual effort), "rigged" (reliant on external factors such as favoritism and discrimination), or "random" (entirely determined by chance). Interestingly, a study that examined these beliefs found that they often align with someone's political ideology.

For example, conservatives are more likely to fit in the "rewarding" category, meaning that they see money as a fair consequence of personal efforts and abilities. This worldview is in line with the Just World Hypothesis. When we perceive reality through its lenses, we assume the world is a fair place where everything that happens to us is the result of our actions. However, if you've been around for a while, you know this isn't always the case. The liberal perception, on the other hand, is a lot more complex; they seem to rather subscribe to the "rigged" and "random" nature of money, which also takes external forces into account.

The reality of wealth and money is rarely black and white, but rather shades of gray. While personal effort matters, external factors and chance also play significant roles. It's a complex interplay of rewarding, rigged, and random elements.

Are We Melting the Middle Ground in
Climate Change Conversations?

August 16th

BINARY BIAS

Binary bias is our tendency to categorize things or people into two distinct categories, often based on their perceived characteristics or attributes. This can lead to oversimplification, stereotyping, and discrimination. We do that because it helps us make sense of the world around us quickly. From an evolutionary perspective, we need to quickly distinguish between potential allies and threats, categorizing people as friends or foes.

Are opinions on climate change as divided as the media claims they are? If you read an article on this topic, it may seem that everyone is either a believer in this phenomenon or a brutal denier. This is the binary view: it's either 1 or 0.

This polarity leads us to forget that there are people who approach climate change differently, beyond the categories of believers and skeptics. In fact, the number of those who completely reject climate change is not as high as we might imagine. Only 12% of people clearly dismiss the existence of any climate change issues. However, because of the press coverage they receive, we may overestimate their prevalence.

This phenomenon can be partly attributed to binary bias, which makes us ignore the opinions that do not sit at either end of the belief spectrum. We tend to overestimate how common extreme views are. We also focus disproportionately on the two extremes (believers versus skeptics). In reality, data shows that the majority of people sit somewhere in the middle of the two ends of the belief spectrum. This means that while many do not have a strong opinion on climate change, they are open to new information and approach the discussion with curiosity.

Unfortunately, splitting the world into two opposing dimensions seems more entertaining to the media. It is undoubtedly more fascinating to put those with extreme views on climate change in the spotlight and either criticize or praise them, instead of showing that most people do not have a clear opinion on this matter. As a result, we are left with a distorted view of the world and humanity.

Survival of the Foodiest: Are We Blind to Fallen Culinary Ventures?

August 17th

SURVIVORSHIP BIAS

Survivorship bias is the mental short-cut we take when we focus on a certain subgroup that made it through a selection process—the survivors—and ignore the ones that didn't—the failures. Because we don't pay equal attention to both survivors and failures, we might mistakenly assume that a shared trait of the survivors caused their survival. This seduces us to mistake correlation for causation.

It's Friday night. You venture downtown and walk by all the shiny, fully-packed restaurants on the main street. "What a profitable business this is," you're thinking to yourself.

The next thing you know, a new business idea takes shape in your mind. "If all these restaurants are doing so well, why couldn't I make a lot of money doing the same thing? People are always eating out, and people are willing to spend money on good food." While this is not wrong, you have failed to consider all the ventures that have closed their doors because those people eating out had too many options to choose from. Of course, why would you even be thinking about them? They are rarely in sight. However, every third restaurant closes within the first year after opening, and 80% of newly opened restaurants do not make it past their fifth birthday party.

This is a classic example of survivorship bias, which leads us to make decisions based on success stories and neglect the ones that didn't stand the test of time, recession, or the natural selection process. The thriving restaurants on the main street will always be a great example of why you should pursue a restaurant business, but you may overlook the ones that close three months after opening.

This bias doesn't just affect restaurant owners; it pervades all industries. Take the tech world, for instance. We constantly hear about the rise of companies like Amazon, Apple, or more recently, OpenAI. But for every successful tech startup, thousands of others never make it. In fact, according to recent studies, about 90% of startups fail. Yet, aspiring entrepreneurs look at these outliers and believe their chances of building the next billion-dollar company are far greater than they actually are.

Watch a TED Talk on survivorship Bias

How Could the Swedish Police Miss the Elk in the Room?

August 18th

CONFIRMATION BIAS

Confirmation bias is our tendency to look for, acknowledge, favor, and remember information in a way that supports what we already think or believe. This bias occurs when we ignore information that contradicts our ideas or interpret ambiguous facts as evidence supporting our existing beliefs. Situations that involve emotionally charged topics, strongly held beliefs, or things we really want to happen are most susceptible to this bias.

In the realm of criminal investigations, the pursuit of truth is paramount. Investigators are trained to follow the evidence, no matter where it leads. However, human psychology can sometimes interfere with this objective pursuit, leading to flawed conclusions.

The case in question revolved around Agneta Westlund and her husband, Ingmar Westlund, from southern Sweden. In 2008, Ingmar was accused of murdering his wife. From the outset, the police were convinced of his guilt. They had a theory that the husband had used a sit-on-mower to commit the crime. Their belief was so strong that even when presented with evidence that contradicted this theory, such as other DNA traces and hairs found on the victim's body, they chose to disregard it. In an attempt to validate their theory, the police conducted experiments where they drove a sit-on-mower over a deceased pig to see if the injuries matched those of the wife. The results did not support their theory. Yet, instead of re-evaluating their stance, this only spurred them on to find alternative ways the husband could have committed the crime.

The police overlooked clear evidence because it did not fit their narrative, missing out on crucial leads that could have solved the case much earlier. The accused suffered immensely, both emotionally and reputationally. He was viewed as a murderer by his community, leading him to relocate, all because of a flawed investigation. The real cause of the woman's death — an attack by an elk — was only discovered much later, prolonging the agony for the victim's family and delaying closure for all involved.

Do Doctors Have Diagnosis Déjà Vus?

August 19th

"FREQUENCY ILLUSION OR BAADER–MEINHOF PHENOMENON"

The frequency illusion is when you notice something, you start to notice it every time it happens. This makes you think it happens a lot, even though it doesn't. This bias is also known as the Baader–Meinhof phenomenon. It happens when heightened awareness of something creates the impression that it is happening more frequently than it actually is.

When we discover a new concept or idea, there are high chances that we will begin to notice it everywhere. However, many times, we notice these new ideas because we now have a mental representation of them in our minds, not necessarily because they're present everywhere.

This so-called "frequency illusion" often happens in medical diagnoses. To keep up with the latest discoveries in healthcare, doctors have to constantly read journals and research articles. Reading new information helps them discover new symptoms of a disease, but this also has a downside: it can erroneously lead doctors to see the symptoms everywhere, even in patients who do not display them. A medical student, Kush Purohit, wrote a letter to the editor of the Academic Radiology journal about his experience with the frequency illusion effect.

Having just learned about a new condition called "bovine aortic arch" from a patient who displayed all the symptoms of this rare disease, the medical student went on to diagnose five other people with the same condition within the next 24 hours. Because the new condition and its symptoms were fresh in his mind, he was more likely to see them in similar manifestations, even if, in reality, they were symptoms of an entirely different disease. Therefore, the medical student wrongly diagnosed people with a new condition he would otherwise have ignored. The editor of the journal that received this story published the case because many more clinicians might be affected by the frequency illusion and not be aware of it.

The letter quickly spread among medical professionals, catching the attention of numerous practitioners who recognized this phenomenon in their own experiences.

Familiarity Breeds Sobriety: Can Pop Culture Save Lives?

August 20th

MERE EXPOSURE EFFECT

The mere exposure effect says the more we are exposed to something, the more we like it. Familiarity breeds liking. When asked to make a choice, we tend to prefer what is familiar, even if this is not the optimal choice. One reason for this behavior is that evolution has taught us to be careful around new things. Everything unfamiliar could be potentially dangerous. When we see something over and over again without any bad results, we assume it is safe.

The mere exposure effect is a powerful tool for positive change, especially in public health. By placing messages in highly visible locations, campaigns increase familiarity with important concepts, often leading to greater public acceptance and adoption.

A stellar example of the genius application of the mere exposure effect lies in the rapid and widespread adoption of the "designated driver" concept, originally from Scandinavia. A designated driver is a person who agrees not to drink alcohol at a social event and instead stays sober to drive the others in their group home safely. The mastermind behind this campaign, Jay Winsten, went above and beyond by collaborating with major Hollywood studios to disseminate the message. Winsten brought the anti-drunk driving movement to the forefront of American culture in the late '80s and early '90s. He did this by incorporating the idea of a "designated driver" into about 160 popular TV shows, such as "The Simpsons," and by getting celebrities to endorse it.

By 1991, over 90% of Americans were familiar with the designated driver concept, contributing to a 24% decrease in alcohol-related traffic fatalities between 1988 and 1992, with about 37% of Americans reporting they had acted as a designated driver by 1993. Utilizing mass media and pop culture, Winsten effectively promoted the "designated driver" concept, leading to its widespread acceptance. As people became more familiar with the "designated driver" concept and, therefore, with the anti-drunk driving movement, they began to view it more favorably.

Watch a video about the "Designated Drivers" program

Is Your Work Review Unfairly Biased?

August 21st

GENDER BIAS

Gender bias refers to a widely held set of implicit biases that discriminate against one gender. These biases include stereotypes like men being more logical and women more emotional. When there are no gender indicators, people often default to assuming subjects are male. Gender bias also manifests in double standards used to judge behavior - for instance, when men are praised for their sexual activities while women are derogated.

Work performance evaluations are rarely fun. They sometimes seem like a long list of reasons why you haven't met corporate standards yet or why you'll never make your boss truly happy. One reason most people dislike being assessed at work is that they sense the evaluator cannot be fully accurate about their performance. They're not far from the truth. People are biased. Based on whether you're a man or woman, your skin color, or your evaluator's preference for blue or hazel eyes, they're going to associate you with some prejudices they hold internally.

The Harvard Business Review published a report demonstrating that gender bias had an impact on the performance evaluations they examined. Even if, in theory, the assessments are standardized, their ambiguity leaves a lot of room for biased thinking. In this report, researchers found that women are more likely to receive vague feedback that gives no guidance on how to improve. Women were more likely to be instructed to "do more work in person," for example, without being informed of the problem to be solved or the change's intended outcome. Women, in particular, received feedback that often focused on communication skills as opposed to the technical skills emphasized in men's reviews.

The inconsistencies found in evaluations were not unexpected to many managers. A mere 15% of female managers and 24% of male managers expressed confidence in the performance evaluation system. The majority perceived it as being overly subjective and fraught with ambiguity.

Read this article about why most performance evaluations are biased

How to Make People Feel Flattered After Donating Blood?

August 22nd

PEAK–END RULE

The peak-end rule states that we tend to judge an experience based on the most intense moment as well as how the experience ended. The overall memory of the experience will be based on the average of the peak moment and the end. This bias happens because we remember events in snapshots rather than in their entirety. Furthermore, we remember things better when they are emotionally intense (the peak) or more recent (the end).

Getting people to donate blood is tough. Besides the noble feeling of doing a good deed, there's not much else to take home. For many, that's not enough incentive, especially since there's no guarantee their blood will be put to good use.

This is why Sweden revamped the blood donation process. Instead of letting donors wonder, Swedish hospitals send them a text message informing them who received their blood. This establishes a sense of connection with the recipient and ends the donation experience on a high note, filled with altruism. The text campaign leverages the peak-end rule bias. The end of the donation experience is elevated by the text message, which not only provides closure but also a sense of accomplishment and connection. This positive ending likely enhances donors' overall perception of the experience, making them more likely to donate again in the future. A field experiment showed an increase in subsequent donations due to these messages of up to 6.5%.

The initiative also generated social media buzz, enhancing community engagement and encouraging more people to donate blood. It's part of a broader effort to battle blood shortages and promote recurring donations. Now, donors in Sweden walk away knowing their donation had a direct impact, rather than just hoping for the best. Knowing exactly who you helped adds a personal touch that's far more satisfying. As a result, donors are more likely to view their experience positively and, consequently, are more likely to donate again in the future. This strategy has not only led to an increase in blood donations but also created a community-driven movement, embracing a holistic approach to tackle blood shortages.

Why Do Golf Skills Drive CEO Salaries?
A Hole-in-One Misconception

August 23rd

HALO EFFECT

The halo effect is a type of cognitive bias in which our overall opinion of a person or brand affects how we feel about the specific qualities of that person or brand. If we have a good feeling about something as a whole, we are more likely to think that its individual parts are good as well. We do that because it saves cognitive effort to use our overall impressions as a shortcut to make judgments rather than evaluating each aspect of something separately.

Deciding the criteria for CEO salary compensation can be a difficult task for companies. A study by French and Spanish researchers suggests that the golfing abilities of a CEO are actually a great predictor of his or her salary. The study discovered a strong correlation between CEO pay and handicap, with golfers earning more than non-golfers and pay rising with golfing skills. CEOs who play golf earn an average of 15% more than those who don't. Most likely, being a good golfer is perceived as a positive attribute in the boardroom environment where the CEO's salary gets decided. Furthermore, golf clubs offer settings where the involved actors can mingle and assess one another on a range of criteria.

The researchers hypothesize that boardroom members' assumption of a positive correlation between golfing ability and leadership skills is attributable to the "halo effect." This bias makes us assume that one single positive trait in someone will trickle down to other attributes of the person. In other words, boardroom members mistakenly assume that better golfers make better leaders.

The halo effect can make us assume that performance in one area of work translates into excellent abilities in another one when, in reality, this is far from the truth. The study found that being good at golf doesn't actually mean someone is a better CEO. In fact, another study even found that CEOs who were better at golf tended to be less effective leaders. This shows us how dangerous it can be to judge someone's abilities in one area based on how well they perform in a completely different area.

Are We Merit Magnets or Fault Dodgers?

August 24th

SELF-SERVING BIAS

The self-serving bias is our tendency to take credit for good things that happen to us and blame other things or people for bad things that happen. We do that because we have the desire to feel good about ourselves. Being responsible for good things happening boosts our confidence and gives us a sense of control in our lives. When we blame external factors for bad things that happen to us, it can help us feel better about ourselves by protecting our ego.

After a grueling job-hunting process, you finally get the call: You're hired. Amidst your unparalleled excitement and hopes for a new chapter, another feeling stands out: an evident pride in being selected among many talented candidates. If you were the chosen one, you reason, there must be something exceptional about you. Since you made it through the selection, the merits must be yours alone. It's easy to place a magnifying glass on our qualities and achievements when the odds are in our favor. Yet how difficult it becomes to maintain this self-examination when we face rejection.

How often have you heard people blame everyone but themselves after being laid off? "The company culture was toxic." "They got rid of all the good people," or "They had to fire everyone on our team—including me." Rarely do we hear someone admit, "I was fired because I was undertrained for the job" or "I didn't meet the position's requirements."

The tendency to claim credit for positive outcomes while deflecting blame for negative ones stems from self-serving bias. This bias helps maintain and enhance self-esteem by attributing personal successes to our own characteristics and failures to external circumstances. Moreover, it helps us align reality with our self-image and others' expectations.

While we all experience self-serving bias, and to some degree it contributes to our mental well-being, it's crucial to maintain an accurate evaluation of our merits and shortcomings by viewing ourselves objectively.

Lucky Tycoon or Gentleman Gangster?

August 25th

HINDSIGHT BIAS

The hindsight bias is also called the "I-knew-it-all-along" effect. It describes the retrospective overestimation of predictability. In the present, it's hard to tell how something will turn out in the future, but is easy to understand how or why an event happened in retrospect. This bias happens because we mistakenly assume that we had the same understanding of an event before it happened as we do after it happened.

In the tapestry of American history, Cornelius Vanderbilt stands out as a titan of rail and steam, often celebrated for his entrepreneurial spirit. Cornelius Vanderbilt's wealth in 1877 made up about 1.15% of the U.S. economy, while Jeff Bezos' wealth was around 0.88% of the U.S. economy in 2021. So, even though Bezos' fortune is much larger in absolute terms, Vanderbilt's share of the economy was actually bigger at his time. However, a closer examination through the lens of hindsight bias reveals a more morally ambiguous character.

Vanderbilt started out in the steamboat business. He was very tough, and he often chose to fight his battles outside of the courtroom. He once said, "Gentlemen, you have undertaken to cheat me. I won't sue you, for the law is too slow. I'll ruin you." This shows he was ready to do whatever it took to win, even if it meant ignoring the rules. When he moved into the railroad business, he kept using bold strategies. He once said to someone, "My God, John, you don't suppose you can run a railroad in accordance with the statutes of the State of New York, do you?" These actions and words paint Vanderbilt as someone who thought he was above the law and didn't need to follow the same rules as everyone else. His success was partly because he was smart in business but also because he was willing to just break the law.

Nowadays, people often look back at Vanderbilt and think of him as a great business genius. But this is an example of hindsight bias. Looking back, it's easy to see his success as something that was bound to happen. But in reality, during his time, many of his actions could have been seen as wrong and even illegal. Vanderbilt was at least as lucky as he was smart, for he narrowly escaped major conflicts with the law that could have otherwise destroyed his empire.

Fashion Faux-pas or Brainpower Boost?

August 26th

DECISION FATIGUE

Decision fatigue is the mental exhaustion that comes from having to make a lot of complex decisions in a short amount of time. It is similar to using a muscle that becomes more fatigued the more we use it in a short period. This happens because our brain has a limited amount of mental energy and willpower to use for making decisions. This phenomenon can be caused by external factors such as stress and lack of sleep and can lead to difficulty concentrating, irritability, and impulsive behavior.

Have you ever wondered if the world's most successful people spend their mornings in front of the mirror wondering if their shoes match their ties? Probably not, and there's a good reason for that.

We humans only have a limited amount of brainpower reserved for our daily decision-making process. The more we navigate choices, whether complex or insignificant, the more mentally fatigued we get. Like a muscle that weakens with overuse, our decision-making ability deteriorates throughout the day.

This is precisely why many successful people wear the same outfit for years. Take Mark Zuckerberg, who rarely deviates from his iconic gray Brunello Cucinelli t-shirt, or Steve Jobs, who was known for his signature black turtleneck and sneakers combination. Even Barack Obama addressed this directly in an interview: "You'll see I wear only gray or blue suits. I'm trying to pare down decisions. I don't want to make decisions about what I'm eating or wearing. Because I have too many other decisions to make."

Of course, these leaders might swap colors now and then, but the staples of their outfits remain the same. And this isn't because they can't afford a stylist to create the right outfits for them. They simply decide to save their brainpower for more important decisions. Since we have limited mental energy to spend on making efficient choices, it makes sense to save it for things that truly matter to us.

Read this article about why Obama and Zuckerberg wear the same thing every day

Can Herbs Sniff Out the Black Death?

August 27th

ILLUSION OF CONTROL

The illusion of control occurs when we believe we have more control over external events than we do. We frequently believe we have (or had) some control over events that are actually random. Researchers have found that people who feel in control will engage in healthier behaviors, feel less stress, and have better overall mental health. Therefore, this illusion makes us feel better about ourselves and the world around us, but it can also seduce us into relying on superstitions.

One of the most poignant examples of the illusion of control is the widespread reliance on superstitions during the outbreak of the Black Death, which ravaged Europe between 1347 and 1351, causing immense suffering and millions of deaths.

In the face of the terrifying illness, various superstitions emerged as supposed protections against the spread of the disease. Theories about witchcraft, devilish operations, and plots to spread the plague through venom circulated widely. The belief that God's wrath had fallen upon them led many to become more religious, engage in self-punishment, and persecute Jews, who were wrongly accused of poisoning wells.

In their quest for control and protection against the Black Death, individuals turned to a variety of strange and ineffective precautions. Some thought they could avoid contracting the disease by only opening their windows to the north or not sleeping during the day. It was common practice to carry flowers, herbs, or spices while walking about, often held up to the nose. This was believed to help protect against the disease by removing bad smells, which were considered a cause of the plague. Doctors at the time believed that herbs would counteract the "evil" smells of the plague and prevent them from becoming infected.

In reality, Yersinia pestis, a type of bacteria, is believed to have caused the Black Death. It's thought that it spread to humans from rats via flea bites - a mechanism far beyond the understanding or control of medieval Europeans. The widespread reliance on superstitions during this pandemic vividly illustrates how, when faced with uncontrollable and terrifying situations, people often resort to illusory means of regaining a sense of control.

Keep Calm and Go Swimming, Mayor Vaughn?

August 28th

OSTRICH EFFECT OR NORMALCY BIAS

Normalcy bias, also known as "ostrich effect," makes us downplay warnings about dangers or ignore negative situations completely. We underestimate how likely it is that a disaster will happen and how it might affect us. We do that because we want to avoid an unpleasant emotional impact in the short term. The name comes from the popular (but false) belief that ostriches bury their heads in the sand when in danger.

The normalcy bias can often have detrimental consequences, as individuals may downplay the severity of a situation or fail to take the necessary precautions to prevent a disaster. One prime example of this can be found in the behavior of Mayor Larry Vaughn in the classic film "Jaws."

In the 1975 blockbuster "Jaws," a great white shark terrorizes the small beach town of Amity Island. Despite evidence of the shark's presence and multiple deadly attacks, Mayor Vaughn, played by Murray Hamilton, refuses to close the beaches for fear of damaging the local economy. Chief Martin Brody, portrayed by Roy Scheider, repeatedly urges Mayor Vaughn to prioritize public safety, but his warnings are neglected.

The subsequent quote from Mayor Vaughn demonstrates a strong presence of normalcy bias: "Martin, it's all psychological. You yell barracuda, and everybody says, 'Huh? What?' You yell shark, we've got a panic on our hands on the Fourth of July." In this statement, Mayor Vaughn attempts to justify his choice to keep the beaches open, even when faced with undeniable signs of danger. By contrasting the shark with the less-threatening barracuda, he minimizes the seriousness of the situation.

Mayor Larry Vaughn's behavior in "Jaws" is a textbook example of the normalcy bias. By ignoring the evidence and Chief Brody's warnings, he chooses to avoid facing the danger and what might happen as a result. This denial of reality ultimately leads to more shark attacks and tragedies in the movie.

View a scene featuring Mayor Vaughn in 'Jaws'

Why Can't We Face the Change in Climate Change

August 29th

COGNITIVE DISSONANCE

Cognitive dissonance describes the mental discomfort we experience when there is a conflict between our beliefs, actions, or perceptions. This discomfort often arises when our actions contradict our beliefs or when we hold two opposing beliefs simultaneously. To alleviate this discomfort, we may adjust our beliefs, perceptions, or actions to create a more consistent internal state. Achieving this internal consistency is crucial, as it helps maintain our sense of identity and coherence.

Climate change is an undeniable issue that has already turned millions into climate refugees and raised concerns about our planet's future. Despite awareness of the problem and necessary actions, we consistently fail to act, both individually and collectively.

The "doom and gloom" messaging often used by climate change activists, scientists, and the media plays a significant role in creating cognitive dissonance. This type of messaging focuses on worst-case scenarios, often using alarming language and imagery to convey the urgency of the climate crisis. While intended to motivate action, this approach can overwhelm people, presenting a future so dire that it conflicts with their desire for a positive outlook. As a result, many experience cognitive dissonance: they understand the severity of climate change but find it difficult to reconcile with their hope for the future as well as their current way of life.

To resolve this dissonance, we often employ psychological coping mechanisms that allow us to acknowledge the reality of climate change while minimizing personal responsibility and maintaining our current lifestyles. A common approach is adjusting our thinking instead of taking concrete action. We generate narratives like "I am too small to have an impact" or "Humanity will solve this problem somehow with technology." These stories allow us to shift blame and rationalize our inaction.

By employing this mechanism, we alleviate the cognitive dissonance caused by the stark contrast between our understanding of climate change and our daily behaviors.

Watch a video about why humans are so bad at thinking about climate change

What Is Responsible for Website Sales and What Is Not?

August 30th

ILLUSIONS OF CAUSALITY

The illusion of causality occurs when we erroneously perceive a cause-and-effect relationship between two events. Assessing evidence requires cognitive effort, so our brain seeks mental shortcuts to expedite the process. This cognitive bias leads us to hastily infer a causal connection, even if there is none. This stems from our evolutionary need to comprehend the causes of events quickly in our surroundings for the sake of survival.

In the fast-paced world of digital marketing, it's essential for businesses to make data-driven decisions. However, even with the best intentions, marketing professionals can sometimes fall prey to illusory correlations.

Imagine you own a company called "SuperShoes." You decide to pay for ads on Google so that when people search for "SuperShoes," your website appears at the top of the results. This seems like a good idea – the more visible you are, the better, right?

After running these ads for a while, you check your Google Ads dashboard. The software shows that many people who clicked on your ads went on to make purchases on your website. It's tempting to think, "Great! The Google ads are working! Look at all these sales they're generating!" But here's where the illusion of causality might trick you:

Many of these customers might have already known about SuperShoes from other sources, like a friend's recommendation or a TV commercial. They searched for "SuperShoes" because they were already planning to buy. The Google ad didn't create a new customer; it just caught someone who was already interested.

The danger is that you might think, "We should spend more money on these Google ads!" when in reality, that money might be better spent on other ways to spread the word about SuperShoes.

This scenario illustrates how the illusion of causality can impact business decisions. Our brains are quick to draw connections between events, like seeing ad clicks lead to sales, and assume a direct cause-and-effect relationship. However, in complex situations like marketing, many factors are often at play.

Lunacy or Just Loony: Are We Really Swayed by Lunar Cycles?

August 31st

BELIEF BIAS

Belief bias distorts our evaluation of the logical strength of an argument because we judge it by the believability of the conclusion. In other words, when we believe the conclusion, we are inclined to believe that the method used to get the results must also be correct. Belief bias happens when we rely too much on what we remember and not enough on evaluating new information. Belief bias is more likely to happen when we really care about something.

If you enter the astrologers' bubble, you will see that the full moon craze is real. So much of what's going wrong in the world is attributed to the Earth's natural satellite. Within these circles, you'll encounter a variety of firmly held convictions: "My boyfriend got all mental at me for no reason; surely the full moon must have affected him." These convictions exemplify the lunar theory, which implies that there is a direct correlation between moon cycles and human behavior.

While it is tempting to blame human error and emotional volatility on the moon, research studies point to a different reality. Researchers analyzed many studies and found that the moon's phases have very little influence on human behavior. When looking at things like hospital admissions or crime rates, changes in the moon's appearance can only account for about 1% of the variations at most, meaning that 99% or more of these changes are due to other factors unrelated to the moon. Although some statistically significant relationships did emerge in the study, the effects were so weak that they couldn't possibly explain a direct correlation between the full moon and abnormal behavior.

Yet some beliefs are so embedded in our views of the world that we aren't willing to listen to the opposing evidence. This is a classic example of belief bias in action. People who firmly believe in the moon's influence may dismiss or rationalize away the scientific evidence because it doesn't align with their preexisting beliefs, judging the validity of the research based on how well it matches their conclusions rather than on the strength of the methodology. Of course, there will always be unfortunate incidents that happen on a full moon night, but that doesn't mean we have to blame the moon.

∞
SEPTEMBER

Was It German Accuracy?

September 1st

CLUSTERING ILLUSION

The clustering illusion is our tendency to give meaning to random patterns we perceive. We see these patterns because we see them in data sets that are very large or very small. For small data sets, it could be a winning-streak or a so-called "hot-hand" in sports. We think there is a pattern, but actually it is just coincidence. For very large datasets, random patterns will inevitably occur because of the sheer size.

Have you ever found yourself seeing patterns in random events? There are many cases in which we perceive patterns and correlations that aren't there, and the clustering illusion is a perfect example of this.

Psychologist Thomas Gilovich studied the experience of Londoners during WWII, who strongly believed that German missiles were targeting specific areas of the city. American newspapers at the time published maps showing strikes from German missiles in Central London. The bombing targets appeared to be clustered near Regent's Park, which made Americans worried that bombing campaigns were more precise than they had expected. This fear led to another irrational assumption: that areas relatively untouched by bombs must be harboring German spies.

In reality, the German army had limited accuracy over central London, and any location in the city was as likely to be struck as any other. Some studies even conducted statistical analyses to determine whether there was indeed a pattern in London's bombing, but the apparent clusters were attributed solely to the clustering illusion. While at first glance the map may not look random, statistical analysis reveals that it actually is. Unfortunately for conspiracy theorists, the Germans had no secret plan to destroy specific areas of London. Our brains' innate propensity to detect patterns where none exist had created the illusion of bombing clusters.

See an image of the London "cluster."

Feeling Lucky? The Lottery Reality Check

September 2nd

AVAILABILITY BIAS

The availability bias is our tendency to make decisions based on information that comes to mind quickly and easily. It's a mental shortcut that gives more weight to information that was learned recently or that is easy to remember, for example, because it is an emotionally loaded memory. Our brain wants to save mental energy. So, we often go with the first information that comes to mind instead of putting in more mental effort to dig deeper.

Sir William Petty, an English economist, once referred to the lottery as "a tax upon unfortunate self-conceited fools; men that have a good opinion of their luckiness, or that have believed some fortune-teller or astrologer, who had promised them great success about the time and place of the lottery." Despite this critique from 1662, nearly half of the nations worldwide currently operate lotteries, and more than $115 billion in lottery tickets are sold globally each year. This staggering figure surpasses the entire GDP of Kenya.

Most people are likely aware that the odds of winning the lottery are far from favorable. While these odds vary depending on the type of lottery, the chances of winning are approximately 1 in 14 million. One major reason why playing the lottery remains popular is the prevalence of winners' stories and the absence of losers' accounts. After all, when we witness numerous people winning, it's easy to believe that we could be the next fortunate winner. However, we rarely encounter interviews with lottery losers.

This phenomenon serves as an excellent example of the availability bias in action. We are exposed to more stories about lottery winners than losers, which makes these success stories more readily available in our memory. This selective exposure influences our perception of the likelihood of winning. To put things in perspective, consider that the following events have a higher probability of happening than winning a million-dollar jackpot: being struck by a meteorite, getting wrongfully convicted of a crime, becoming a movie star or an astronaut.

Watch Dan Gilbert speak about why we make bad decisions

Can a Third Wheel Swing an Election? The Decoy Effect in Action

September 3rd
DECOY EFFECT

The decoy effect describes how, when deciding between two options, adding a third, less appealing option (the decoy) can change how we feel about the two options we were originally considering. Decoys are much worse than one option, but only partially inferior to the second option. The decoy is there to nudge you towards one specific target option. Decoys work because they serve us as reference points that help us (unconsciously) justify our choices.

The 2000 US presidential election, in which George W. Bush narrowly defeated Al Gore, offers an intriguing case study for exploring the decoy effect in politics. Multiple sources suggest that the third, lesser-known candidate Ralph Nader impacted the outcome. Analyzing this election through the lens of the decoy effect provides a compelling way to understand how this phenomenon might manifest in political contexts.

In this election, Ralph Nader ran as the Green Party candidate alongside Bush and Gore. Some critics argue that Nader's presence might have inadvertently influenced the outcome in a manner similar to a decoy. Bush won by a slim margin of 537 votes in Florida, leading to speculation about Nader's impact on the result. Critics claim that in a direct comparison, Bush did not appear more competent than Gore. However, they suggest that for some undecided voters, Bush seemed more appealing when compared to both Gore and Nader. The argument posits that these voters may have perceived Nader as entirely inferior to Bush but only slightly inferior to Gore, potentially making Bush appear as the dominant option.

This perception might have been influenced by the fact that both Nader's and Gore's campaigns focused on progressive issues, such as environmental concerns, making them appear similar. In contrast, Bush's platform was distinctly different, potentially benefiting from the comparison. However, this interpretation simplifies a complex election. Factors like ideology, ballot design, and vote counting disputes all significantly influenced the 2000 outcome.

Watch a video of Ralph Nader on this

Medicine that is Too Good to Be True?

September 4th

OPTIMISM BIAS

Optimism bias is our tendency to overestimate the likelihood of positive events occurring in our lives and to underestimate the likelihood of negative events occurring. This can lead us to make overly optimistic predictions about the future, causing us to underestimate the risks and challenges that we may face. This occurs due to our desire to feel good about ourselves and the future, and can be influenced by social norms and cultural values that encourage positive thinking.

When it comes to developing new treatments and therapies, it's natural to want to believe that they will be effective. However, in the field of clinical research, this leads to what is known as the optimism bias. This bias can manifest in several ways, such as by selectively citing positive studies and underrepresenting negative results.

Optimism bias in clinical research can have serious consequences. For example, in a 1990 study on a new radiotherapy treatment for head and neck cancer, clinicians surveyed before the study was conducted predicted a 30% reduction in the mortality rate. However, the final results of the study showed no such reduction. This bias towards optimism can lead to unrealistic expectations for patients as well as their doctors and can even result in poorly designed or unnecessary trials.

Another group of researchers looked at 57 different ways to treat cancer using radiation. They studied these treatments for 34 years and looked at the results of almost 13,000 patients. They found that new treatments were as likely to be inferior to established treatments as they were to be superior.

Another interesting aspect of this bias is that it is more likely to happen in research projects sponsored by industry than in publicly funded research. Industry-sponsored research tends to exhibit more optimism bias compared to publicly funded studies, potentially due to financial incentives and conflicts of interest.

Next time you hear of a new "miracle cure" or read an article about a new treatment, take a moment to consider whether the results might be too good to be true.

Free Love and Fishing—What Could Go Wrong?

September 5th

AUTHORITY BIAS

Authority bias is our tendency to attribute greater accuracy and credibility to the opinions of people in positions of power, regardless of the content of their statements. This makes people give more weight to the opinions of those in power, which makes it more likely that they will follow orders. There is an evolutionary benefit to authority bias. It helped people stick together and stay alive as a group.

While there is an evolutionary advantage to authority bias, as it fosters group cohesion and survival, it can also lead to dangerous consequences when the authority figure is manipulative or misguided. One striking example of authority bias is the infamous Children of God cult.

David Berg founded the religious cult The Children of God, which is now known as The Family International, in 1968. The cult propagated unconventional beliefs and practices, such as free love, the imminent apocalypse, and spiritual elitism. Berg, also known as Moses David, claimed to receive divine revelations and communicated these through his writings, referred to as the "Mo Letters." Followers were expected to live in communes, cut ties with their families, and devote their lives to spreading the cult's message. By linking himself and his messages directly to God, he bolstered his position of ultimate power, further amplifying authority bias.

Berg's followers never questioned his authority as the cult's prophet and leader. They believed he had a direct connection to God. This led to a culture of blind obedience, where members would follow his instructions without questioning the morality or consequences of their actions. For example, Berg introduced a practice called "flirty fishing," where female members were encouraged to engage in sexual acts with potential converts as a means of spiritual recruitment. Between 1971 and 1987, over 200,000 men were "fished," and over 10,000 babies were born to cult women as a result.

Watch these recordings of the Children of God cult

What Game of Thrones Character Are You?

September 6th

FORER EFFECT OR BARNUM EFFECT

The Forer effect, also known as the Barnum effect, describes the observation that people will give high accuracy ratings to personality descriptions that are supposedly tailored specifically for them. However, in reality, these descriptions are vague and general enough to apply to many people. This effect can help explain why some beliefs and practices, like astrology, palm reading, graphology, and some types of personality tests, are so popular.

If you're itching to figure yourself out, personality quizzes on social media are just the ticket. They claim to reveal your perfect job match or how your name reflects who you are. Still not convinced? Try some of the more unconventional quizzes. Find out which Game of Thrones character you are, or which Hogwarts house you'd call home. Intriguing, right? Once you dive in, there's no going back. Your view of yourself will forever change.

These quizzes are based on broad descriptions that can fit just about anyone. Though most of us wouldn't put much stock in them, we're still oddly drawn to their promise of quick and easy insight into who we are. Take that Game of Thrones quiz that pegged you as Ned Stark, the loyal family man. Sound like you? Just remember, it was designed to sound like everyone.

This phenomenon, known as the Barnum effect, tricks us into believing that these vague personality descriptions are a perfect fit for us. Our brains are wired to seek out evidence that confirms our beliefs rather than contradicts them. So, if you're reading a test result thinking, "Wow, this is so me!" just remember there are millions out there thinking the exact same thing. The tests aren't as insightful as they appear. Instead, it's our brains that are good at finding the connections, making us believe we're just like Ned Stark or whoever the quiz tells us we are.

While these quizzes can be entertaining, it's important to approach them with a critical eye and not take their results too seriously.

How Can We Outsmart Our Impulsive Brains
for a Comfy Retirement?

September 7th

HYPERBOLIC DISCOUNTING

Hyperbolic discounting is our tendency to favor more immediate payoffs in comparison to later payoffs. We do prefer the immediate reward, even when it is objectively less valuable. We all make decisions today that we would have preferred not to have made in the future due to hyperbolic discounting. Our brains are hardwired to do so because immediate reward meant a better chance of survival in evolutionary terms.

Saving money for the future is difficult when temptations to splurge are everywhere around us. Our brains act on impulse and immediate reward rather than long-term planning. The bias responsible for those impulsive choices is called hyperbolic discounting, and it refers to our default preferences for immediate rewards.

Since getting people to save for retirement is very difficult, particularly because of this bias, researchers in behavioral economics have tried to find ways to make saving money easier. They tested an interesting solution that they called "Save More Tomorrow." The suggestion was to make people commit in advance to allocating a portion of their future salary increases to retirement savings. For example, someone could commit 15% of all future pay raises. That means people do not have to sacrifice money now; they just committed to doing it for future money. The actual disposable income never declined because the only thing that happened was that 85% of the pay raise was added to the disposable income.

The idea was very successful among employees. A high proportion (78%) of those offered the plan joined it, and 80% of those who joined it remained in it through the fourth pay raise. Besides, the average savings rate increased from 3.5% to 13.5%.

The main thing that made the program successful was the reduction of people's hyperbolic discounting. The power of this approach underscores that if we want to change our financial future, we must learn to make present commitments that work with our biases rather than fight them.

Will Robots and AI Deserve Social Responsibility?

September 8th

ANTHROPOMORPHISM

Anthropomorphism is our natural tendency to attribute human traits, emotions, and intentions to non-humans, for example, animals, gods, natural forces, and the like. We do this because we naturally know more about human traits than non-human ones. Therefore, these come easier to mind, and that saves mental energy.

Robots and artificial intelligence are rapidly advancing, and so is our interaction with them. The way we relate to these smart machines is more complex, personal, and dynamic than it used to be. Recent advances make it seem very likely that we will no longer treat them as empty machines with no brains or souls.

Part of this is due to our inherent anthropomorphic bias. A good example of this bias comes from a study that looked into how people responded to robots carrying out social interactions. Participants were divided into two groups. One group was told the robot was acting autonomously, while the other group was told that the robot was pre-programmed. In reality, both robots were pre-programmed, but the participants were given different information about the robots' capabilities for the purposes of the study.

The first group believed that robots could act on their own, so they gave the robots more social responsibility and treated them more like living beings. In contrast, the other group attributed less competence, agency, and responsibility to the robots when they were told that they were simply acting in response to pre-programmed behaviors.

The results of this study might also provide some insights into how we relate to artificial intelligence. If we think that AI is just a bunch of complicated statistics and code written by people, we won't see it as autonomous. However, if we get the feeling it acts autonomously, we are more likely to perceive it as a possible threat.

A recent striking example was the media response to Chaos-GPT, a version of ChatGPT programmed to be "destructive and manipulative." The public reaction highlighted how perceived AI autonomy can influence our response, despite knowing it's human-created.

Read more about Chaos-GPT

Deja Vu and True? How Familiarity Breeds Believability

September 9th

ILLUSORY TRUTH EFFECT

The illusory truth effect causes us to believe information is true if we hear it repeatedly, even when it's not. This happens because repeatedly hearing the same information makes it familiar, and our brain processes familiar things more easily. This ease is due to the activation of well-established neural pathways, which require less effort to process than new or unfamiliar information. When our brains process information with less effort, we tend to interpret this ease as a sign of truth. Thus, if something is easier to understand, we are more likely to believe it's true.

What makes popular stories so persuasive? Repetition may be one way that false claims are passed forward as supreme truth. Recurring examples are political propaganda, science myths, or conspiracy theories.

According to the illusory truth effect, information that is repeated frequently is more likely to be rated as true than information that has never been heard before. This was also the conclusion of a study reporting that familiarity with false news increases its perceived truthfulness among recipients. In this study, experimenters also tested whether familiar false stories led people to create false memories of them.

Participants who were exposed to fake news stories rated them as more plausible than participants who hadn't been exposed to them. Moreover, some participants also created false memories about the source of their stories. They mistakenly believed they had encountered the false information from legitimate sources rather than from the study, further reinforcing the perceived credibility of the misinformation. Another study added an equally interesting valence: repeating false information can increase its perceived truthfulness even among those who have prior knowledge of that specific topic.

Unfortunately, this is partly why fake news keeps going around: the more it is repeated, the more plausible and truthful it seems. And the more we rate it as true, the more we repeat it. And the more we repeat it, the more accessible it becomes. It is a vicious cycle that keeps us from separating truth from lies.

Watch a video on the psychology behind fake news

Did You Know About the Speedo-Wearing Spiritual Guru?

September 10th

GROUPTHINK

Groupthink is when our desire for harmony and conformity within a group leads to dysfunctional decision-making. Group members prioritize agreement over critical evaluation, resulting in a loss of individual creativity and thinking. This can lead to an inflated sense of confidence in the group's abilities, an undervaluation of opponents, group pressure, and potentially harmful actions towards outsiders.

The 2016 documentary "Holy Hell" provides an unsettling glimpse into the Buddhafield, a spiritual group formed in the 1980s in West Hollywood, California. Its enigmatic leader, Jaime Gomez, called Michel, promised enlightenment and spiritual growth. However, the Buddhafield ultimately transformed into a manipulative cult, with groupthink perpetuating its leader's harmful actions.

Buddhafield members considered themselves spiritually superior, on a unique path compared to outsiders, resulting in inflated group confidence. Like many cults, the Buddhafield group also promoted conformity and discouraged dissent. Members were expected to unquestioningly follow Michel's teachings, with doubters often ostracized or dismissed. This fostered a mentality of prioritizing agreement over critical evaluation, facilitating Michel's control and manipulation. Members faced immense group pressure. For example, they were required to work out to ensure their bodies were perfect specimens because the cult leader himself made a point of looking good in the Speedos he always wore. Will Allen, the director of "Holy Hell," describes how the loss of individual thinking was accepted: "surrendering to the guru, dropping your ego... we didn't think of it as giving our power, we thought of it as empowering."

The group's collective mindset reinforced Michel's perceived divine status. Members rationalized his abusive actions, including sexual misconduct, as part of their shared spiritual journey. This collective justification silenced individual doubts, with the group prioritizing harmony over questioning their leader's behavior, enabling his continued manipulation.

Watch the trailer for the documentary "Holy Hell."

Does Your Birthplace Predict Your Saving Behaviour?

September 11th

RISK AVERSION

Risk aversion refers to your tendency to avoid things that might be dangerous. It is a personal preference, and everyone has a different level of it. Our level can be affected by our personalities, ages and stages of life, finances, education, and cultural or social norms. Risk aversion may have become hardwired into human behavior over time because it evolved as a way for individuals to protect themselves and increase their chances of survival.

Every person has their own degree to which they are risk-averse. Some people tend to be risk-seekers, while others prefer to avoid risks. A study from 2018 confirmed that risk aversion is a strong predictor of one's financial behavior with savings. Interestingly, this study also found that your aversion to risk is likely to depend on where you were born.

How risk-averse you are determines what you will do with your savings. Highly risk-averse people will keep their money in safer options with a low but guaranteed interest rate, such as a savings account, while those who can bear a higher degree of uncertainty will choose to invest in higher-risk, potentially higher-reward options. These might include stocks, real estate investment trusts, commodities, or even more volatile assets like cryptocurrencies.

The aforementioned study analyzed attitudes toward financial risk across 15 different countries. The study found that people living in Germany, Austria, and the Netherlands are most risk-averse, while those in the US, Turkey, Australia, and the UK are more accepting of risk. In Germany, in particular, only 16.2% of people invest in stocks, and 36.5% of these stockholders are over 60 years old. The rest of the people choose low-interest bank deposits and insurance savings accounts.

In the US, people seem to be a lot less risk-averse. Data from 2022 reports that around 58% of Americans own stock. This is quite a difference from some European countries, which are at the other end of the spectrum. These statistics further support the study's findings on the cultural influences on risk aversion, demonstrating significant differences in financial behavior across countries.

Saving Lives or Losing Them?

September 12th

FRAMING EFFECT

The framing effect occurs when we draw different conclusions from identical information based solely on how that information is presented. This can happen when something is framed either positively or negatively, or as a gain versus a loss - we naturally tend to avoid losses in such situations. Our judgment can also shift depending on which features of the information are highlighted, even though the underlying facts remain exactly the same.

Facts are important. However, how you present them also matters. This is just as crucial as the factual information itself. Let's consider the following experiment:

Researcher James Montier presented a group of managers with two different scenarios of a disease outbreak in a village of 600 people. Their task was to choose the scenario that is most likely to combat the outbreak based on the probabilities they received. The first scenario entailed two programs, A and B. Program A would certainly save 200 lives. Program B could potentially save 600 lives, but the success probability is just 1/3. The second scenario also had two programs, C and D. Program C would certainly lead to 400 deaths. Program D would lead to 600 deaths, with a probability of 2/3. How would you choose?

Basically, the programs A and C (and also B and D) are the same; they are just framed differently. All programs ensure the safety of 200 people and have an outcome where 400 are at risk. In the experiment, people's preferences changed significantly, with a higher percentage of people choosing a certain option when it was framed as saving lives than when it was described as killing people.

Why did people change their minds? It comes down to how we think about gains and losses. When talking about saving lives, people played it safe and chose the sure thing (Program A). But when it was about avoiding deaths, they took a risk to try and prevent any losses (Program D). This change happened even though the end results were the same in both cases. It shows how powerful words can be – just by describing the same situation differently, we can completely change how people make decisions.

Why Do We Cling to Beliefs Despite Contradictory Evidence?

September 13th

CONFIRMATION BIAS

Confirmation bias is our tendency to look for, acknowledge, favor, and remember information in a way that supports what we already think or believe. This bias occurs when we ignore information that contradicts our ideas or interpret ambiguous facts as evidence supporting our existing beliefs. Situations that involve emotionally charged topics, strongly held beliefs, or things we really want to happen are most susceptible to this bias.

In a perfectly rational world, people would readily adjust their beliefs when encountering evidence that challenges their assumptions. In reality, this rarely happens.

Instead, even when presented with alternative views, people often reject new evidence and actively search for reasons to justify their existing beliefs. This is how confirmation bias manifests: we hold on to what we know and selectively accept and seek out information that aligns with our beliefs.

Confirmation bias is particularly evident in controversial issues and political beliefs. A striking example comes from a global analytics company that polled 1,029 adults in June 2003 about Iraq's weapons of mass destruction (WMD). In the initial evaluation (before the war), 93% of Americans believed Iraq possessed WMDs. Later, new evidence emerged showing no proof that Iraq had such weapons or facilities to create them. Yet when researchers reassessed people's beliefs after these facts became public, the number of people who thought Iraq had WMDs only dropped to 86%. The new evidence had minimal effect on their convictions.

People neither acknowledged, remembered, nor cared about the new facts. This phenomenon showcases the resilience of confirmation bias and the challenge of changing deeply held beliefs, underscoring how perceptions can persist even in the face of contradicting information.

Read about Americans' views on Iraq's weapons of mass destruction

When Does Confidence Become a Risky Business?

September 14th

OVERCONFIDENCE EFFECT

We speak of the overconfidence effect when our subjective confidence in our judgments is higher than their objective accuracy. We can overestimate a variety of things, including our own performance or likelihood of success, our abilities in comparison to others, and the certainty of our answers or judgments.

The image of a successful investor often evokes confidence and bravado. However, true investment mastery lies not in unwavering self-assurance, but in careful risk management. Many tasked with managing others' fortunes overestimate their abilities, their perceived skills far exceeding reality. This disconnect sets the stage for exploring a critical pitfall: the overconfidence effect.

A study by researcher James Montier that involved 300 experienced fund managers beautifully illustrates this effect. When asked to rate their own investing abilities, a staggering 74% considered themselves above average, while the rest thought they were just average. However, statistically speaking, this can't possibly be true. It's intriguing to observe the frequency with which fund managers believe they're the exception to the rule, thinking, "Yes, everyone believes they're above average, but in my case, it's true."

The overconfidence effect is likely at play for a substantial chunk of these 74%, causing them to significantly overestimate their abilities and knowledge relative to others. Confidence may be an asset in some arenas, but in the high-stakes world of investing, it often proves to be a liability. Take it from Ray Dalio, the man who started the world's largest hedge fund, Bridgewater & Associates; he credits a significant portion of his success to consciously avoiding the trap of overconfidence.

As Dalio wisely states: "If you're not worried, you need to worry. And if you're worried, you don't need to worry." This mindset encourages investors to remain cautious in good times and confident in their preparation during challenges, fostering more balanced decision-making in the unpredictable world of finance.

Would You Trade Land for a Tulip?

September 15th

BANDWAGON EFFECT

The bandwagon effect refers to the phenomenon in which a belief or behavior becomes more popular as more people adopt it. This can lead to a self-reinforcing cycle, as the increased popularity of the belief or behavior encourages more people to adopt it. The effect is caused by our desire to conform to social norms and our belief that the majority must be correct. It can also be caused by peer pressure and the fear of being left out or made fun of if we don't fit in.

People today are amazed by the soaring prices of cryptocurrencies like Bitcoin. If individuals from 1637 could witness this, they would feel a strong sense of familiarity. Back in the 17th century, the Dutch Tulip Mania made tulip bulbs more valuable than gold. The Dutch Tulip Mania and the current enthusiasm for digital currencies share many similarities, both being great examples of the bandwagon effect.

Tulips arrived in Europe in the late 16th century from Central Asia and quickly became popular in the Netherlands. Their unique appearance, combined with the country's newfound prosperity during its Golden Age, turned the tulip into a sought-after luxury item. Certain tulip varieties, particularly those with intricate lines and vivid streaks, were in high demand. As the prices of tulip bulbs skyrocketed, professional growers and speculators joined the market. Instead of physically trading bulbs, many engaged in speculative contracts and futures trading, betting on future prices without even handling the actual bulbs. The cost of rare bulbs kept increasing, and by 1636, even ordinary bulbs commanded extravagant prices. According to later reports, many people sold their belongings to invest in the tulip market. One rare bulb (yes, just one) was traded for five hectares of land and another one was purchased for 2,500 florins. While challenging to convert accurately, this sum could be worth around $50,000 today.

The perceived value of tulips skyrocketed as more people joined the craze simply because others had done so before them. In February 1637, the tulip market crashed when buyers suddenly refused to pay the exorbitant prices, causing a rapid sell-off and collapse in value, making it the first known example of a speculative bubble.

Can You Spot the Difference?

September 16th

INGROUP BIAS

Ingroup bias is when we like and support people who are part of our own group more than people who are not part of our group. These groups can be divided based on seemingly trivial observable traits. This is rooted in the intrinsic human need for a group identity, which provides a sense of belonging and purpose. Additionally, we all have a desire to feel good about ourselves, and one way to achieve that is to see our own group as being superior to others.

People often note that the facial features of individuals from the same ethnic or cultural groups look similar to their own. Conversely, they can discern subtler differences in features among those from their own group, a skill that seems less prevalent when viewing faces from other backgrounds. This well-documented phenomenon is known as "the other-race effect."

Part of why this happens lies in our ingroup bias. This bias predisposes us to view members of our own social or cultural groups more favorably than those outside of them. This preference is often unconscious. Studies found that we tend to perceive faces from our own ethnic or cultural group holistically, allowing us to detect patterns and recognize individuals more effectively. In contrast, our ability to detect such patterns in the facial features of individuals from different backgrounds is less precise. We focus on specific features, such as the shape of the nose or eyes, rather than seeing the face as a whole. Holistic perception allows us to see individuals beyond mere physical characteristics. Conversely, our reduced ability to distinguish the facial features of individuals from different backgrounds might lead us to perceive them as "the others."

On a deeper level, these disparities in facial perception might contribute to the social divisions that exist between people from diverse backgrounds. We tend to perceive individuals from our own ethnic group with more detail, while individuals from a different group might be viewed as just another face in the crowd.

Watch this video featuring Koreans attempting to distinguish Westerners

Doc, Are You a Pro or Just a Show?

September 17th

DUNNING–KRUGER EFFECT

The Dunning–Kruger effect describes our tendency to overestimate our own abilities in areas that we are unskilled in or lack knowledge in. This happens when we know just enough to think we are great but not enough to tell the difference between good and bad. We just don't know yet what we could do better. The effect also applies to society as a whole. The most uninformed citizens are often also the most confident ones.

Have you ever met someone who thinks they are an expert in a certain field but, in reality, doesn't have a clue? This phenomenon is known as the Dunning-Kruger effect.

According to a recent study (details of which should be provided), doctors are not immune to this effect. The study found that doctors often have poor self-awareness and are not good at judging their own abilities. Researchers examined several papers about doctors' self-assessment and found little association between how knowledgeable doctors think they are versus how knowledgeable they actually are. The study also found that age and experience didn't seem to play a role in doctors' ability to self-assess.

The study came to a concerning conclusion: the least skilled doctors were often the most confident, even though they were the worst at judging their own abilities. This is especially troubling because other research has shown that the more confident someone appears, the more we tend to believe them. Unfortunately, confidence is an unreliable indicator of actual skill.

This research highlights the importance of using objective measures, rather than just perceived confidence, when judging the skills and abilities of doctors. It also serves as a reminder to seek second opinions on important medical decisions.

Is the Gambler's Fallacy Tipping the Scales of Justice?

September 18th

GAMBLER'S FALLACY

The gambler's fallacy arises from the mistaken belief that past events can affect the probability of future outcomes that are actually independent of the past. It is often manifested in the belief that a certain outcome is more or less likely to occur due to its frequency in the past, despite the fact that the probability remains the same. This fallacy is often driven by a desire for pattern-finding and prediction, as well as a dislike of uncertainty.

Our cognitive biases influence our daily micro-decisions, but they can also have significant, life-altering impacts, especially when our decisions affect others, necessitating clear and moral thinking.

A research study tested whether U.S. judges in refugee asylum cases are more likely to deny or grant asylum after granting or denying asylum to the previous applicant. They wanted to see if the outcome of a previous decision influenced the following ones. The researchers thought that judges who make decisions about the cases of asylum seekers might be susceptible to the gambler's fallacy because they would feel bad about rejecting or accepting many cases in a row.

In line with this assumption, a 2016 research study found that judges are up to 3.3% more likely to reject the current case if they approved the previous one. On the other hand, if the judge denied asylum to the previous applicant, he or she is 3.3% more likely to grant asylum to the current applicant. The researchers employed statistical techniques to ensure that extraneous factors, such as the specifics of the case, did not skew the results. Thus, the 3.3% difference can be solely attributed to the gambler's fallacy.

While 3.3% may not seem like a significant figure at first glance, it's crucial to remember that this represents real people whose lives are profoundly impacted by these decisions. In the context of asylum cases, this means that for every 1000 people seeking refuge, 33 individuals may face life-altering consequences due to this cognitive bias.

Who's to Blame?

September 19th

SELF-SERVING BIAS

The self-serving bias is our tendency to take credit for good things that happen to us and blame other things or people for bad things that happen. We do that because we have the desire to feel good about ourselves. Being responsible for good things happening boosts our confidence and gives us a sense of control in our lives. When we blame external factors for bad things that happen to us, it can help us feel better about ourselves by protecting our ego.

You are probably familiar with the sight of an angry child adamantly denying responsibility for their mistakes. Many children will instinctively protest, "I didn't do anything," when their parents intervene in a conflict. This reflexive denial of responsibility reveals much about our innate thinking processes.

When children become upset, they naturally lash out and deflect blame onto others. This reaction occurs involuntarily as a response to overwhelming emotions. Rather than confronting the complexity of guilt, they adopt an defensive stance, pointing fingers at those around them while maintaining an expression of perfect innocence. As the saying goes, the best defense is a good offense.

This behavior can be traced to our innate self-serving bias, which leads us to interpret situations in ways that cast us in the most favorable light. In successful outcomes, we readily claim credit, but in failures, we seek external causes. A study examining siblings between 4 and 9 years old demonstrated this strong self-serving bias in action. The children consistently denied wrongdoing and shifted blame to their siblings. They eagerly claimed credit for positive events while rarely acknowledging their siblings' contributions. Even when forced to admit mistakes, they quickly provided justifications to minimize their responsibility.

This pattern suggests that our desire to maintain positive impressions has been ingrained since childhood. While this universal human tendency to seek approval is understandable, the self-serving bias that serves as a protective mechanism in childhood can become an obstacle to genuine self-awareness in adulthood.

Could a Presidential Shortcut Have Prevented 9/11?

September 20th

HINDSIGHT BIAS

The hindsight bias is also called the "I-knew-it-all-along" effect. It describes the retrospective overestimation of predictability. In the present, it's hard to tell how something will turn out in the future, but is easy to understand how or why an event happened in retrospect. This bias happens because we mistakenly assume that we had the same understanding of an event before it happened as we do after it happened.

Hindsight bias can often cause us to look back at events and question why warning signs were missed. This phenomenon is not limited to individuals but can also be seen in the actions of important organizations. An example of this can be found in Daniel Kahneman's book "Thinking Fast and Slow," where he cites a quote from The Washington Post on the 9/11 attacks.

The newspaper reported on how the CIA had information about a potential attack, but instead of bringing it directly to President Bush, they went to National Security Advisor Condoleezza Rice. The Washington Post criticized the CIA's actions, stating, "It seems elementary that if you have the story that is going to dominate history, you might as well have gone directly to the president." This criticism, however, fails to acknowledge a crucial fact: at the time, no one could have known that this particular piece of intelligence would become a pivotal moment in history.

The CIA, like other intelligence agencies, receives countless reports and threats daily. In the days and weeks before the attacks, they were dealing with a large amount of information, trying to distinguish between credible threats and false alarms. It's only in hindsight that we can easily see the connections and patterns that were overlooked at the time. The criticism of the CIA's actions by The Washington Post is a perfect example of hindsight bias – judging past actions based on information that wasn't available then.

When examining events like 9/11, it's crucial to consider the situation and the information that was available at the time, rather than judging actions based on what we know now.

Rule of Thumb Or More Like Rule of Numb?

September 21st

CONFIRMATION BIAS

Confirmation bias is our tendency to look for, acknowledge, favor, and remember information in a way that supports what we already think or believe. This bias occurs when we ignore information that contradicts our ideas or interpret ambiguous facts as evidence supporting our existing beliefs. Situations that involve emotionally charged topics, strongly held beliefs, or things we really want to happen are most susceptible to this bias.

Peter Wason's pioneering experiment on confirmation bias in 1960 unveiled fascinating insights into human reasoning processes. Participants in the experiment were told the numbers "2, 4, 6" conform to a simple rule, and their task was to identify the rule by proposing sets of three numbers to test. After each proposal, Wason would merely inform them whether the numbers did or did not fit the rule, which was actually just "any ascending order of numbers."

Most participants quickly formed hypotheses about the rule, typically assuming it was "consecutive even numbers increasing by 2" based on the initial example. However, this assumption led them down a narrow path of investigation. They were unable to let go of their initial presumptions and continued to look for evidence to support their theories, suggesting sequences like "8, 10, 12," while ignoring crucial disconfirming examples. To falsify an insufficiently narrow hypothesis, participants needed only to test sequences that violated their assumed rule while still being in ascending order, such as "3, 5, 7."

This tendency to seek confirming evidence rather than potentially disproving information was striking. Simple sequences that could have disproven their theories were consistently overlooked. For example, numbers like "3, 5, 7" or "20, 22, 24" followed the correct "ascending order" rule while contradicting participants' incorrect assumptions. Participants seemed driven by a confirmation bias, relentlessly accumulating affirmative instances for their flawed hypotheses rather than testing for potential counterexamples.

Can Looking Smart Boost a Political Career?

September 22nd

HALO EFFECT

The halo effect is a type of cognitive bias in which our overall opinion of a person or brand affects how we feel about the specific qualities of that person or brand. If we have a good feeling about something as a whole, we are more likely to think that its individual parts are good as well. We do that because it saves cognitive effort to use our overall impressions as a shortcut to make judgments rather than evaluating each aspect of something separately.

You might think your voting decisions are based on rational considerations like a candidate's competence, and experience. But would you believe that something as seemingly trivial as appearance could influence such an important decision? Surprisingly, research shows we often judge a person's competence simply by looking at their face.

The halo effect, which causes us to form a general opinion about someone based on one of their specific attributes, is primarily to blame for this. This happens without us noticing. We often unknowingly let someone's face influence the opinions we form about their character.

A study found that people judge how competent a political candidate is by their facial features alone. In a series of experiments, researchers showed participants photographs of pairs of political candidates from real U.S. congressional races. Participants were asked to judge which candidate in each pair looked more competent, based solely on the facial photographs and without any other information about the candidates. These rapid competence judgments, made after viewing the faces for as little as one second, predicted the actual election outcomes at rates significantly better than chance. For example, in the 2004 Senate races, the candidates judged as appearing more competent based on facial photographs won 68.8% of the time. Across multiple election cycles, the facially "competent" candidate won in 71.6% of Senate races.

In short, our voting decisions are heavily influenced by rapid, unconscious judgments. We form impressions about competence from facial appearances in mere seconds, and these snap judgments can significantly sway our votes, despite our intentions to make rational choices.

Yanny or Laurel?

September 23rd

PRIMING EFFECT

The priming effect occurs when something we see or hear influences our thoughts or actions without us being aware of it. This can happen with words, pictures, or sounds we encounter. When our brain is primed, it becomes easier for us to think about, remember, and act on related information because the things we read, see, or hear activate connected information in the brain.

In 2018, there was a viral phenomenon called Yanny/Laurel that divided the nation of Internet users. An audio illusion released on Reddit played one single word that many people heard either as "Yanny" or "Laurel." The viral phenomenon is the audio version of "The Dress," which people could perceive in two different colors.

Scientists found two explanations for why we hear two different variations of the same word. The first one has to do with the frequency of the sounds. The words "Yanny" and "Laurel" contain a mix of high and low-frequency sounds, allowing for different auditory interpretations. High frequencies are associated with "Yanny", low frequencies with "Laurel". Individual hearing capabilities and audio equipment quality influence which word is perceived. Younger people often hear "Yanny", while older individuals tend to hear "Laurel".

The second explanation, however, has to do with priming. If you first see the word "Laurel" on the screen, this is going to prime your perception to hear the same word. According to the priming effect, the introduction of one stimulus influences how we respond to or perceive a subsequent stimulus. It occurs by activating an association or representation in memory right before another stimulus is presented.

Many people who heard either "Laurel" or "Yanny" in that viral effect might have just been primed because they read or heard the word. If most of your friends told you they definitely heard "Yanny," your brain has already been primed to hear the same sounds as well. Check what you hear: Yanny or Laurel? While this debate might sound a bit silly, it does a great job of showing that we perceive reality according to how we have been primed to see it.

Will you bury your head in the sand until the sand is too hot?

September 24th

OSTRICH EFFECT OR NORMALCY BIAS

Normalcy bias, also known as "ostrich effect," makes us downplay warnings about dangers or ignore negative situations completely. We underestimate how likely it is that a disaster will happen and how it might affect us. We do that because we want to avoid an unpleasant emotional impact in the short term. The name comes from the popular (but false) belief that ostriches bury their heads in the sand when in danger.

Many who dismiss the reality of climate change or downplay its consequences are demonstrating the ostrich effect. The recent Intergovernmental Panel on Climate Change (IPCC) report starkly illuminates the profound impacts of climate change on our world's biodiversity and ecosystems, underscoring the pressing call for intervention.

Climate change is reshaping biodiversity and ecosystems as rising temperatures and extreme events challenge species' adaptive limits. Agriculture, fisheries, and human well-being stand in the crosshairs of these changes, which manifest as drastic alterations in spatial patterns and severe repercussions for diverse flora and fauna. Extreme climatic events are triggering mass die-offs and extinctions, propelling ecosystems towards points of no return. As global warming escalates, habitats like coral reefs, kelp forests, and rainforests face heightened extinction risks. This compromises the ecosystems' climate-regulating functions, setting off a feedback loop that exacerbates climate change. The IPCC report isn't a mere projection; it's a consensus among global scientists on the immediate and tangible threats of climate change.

The reluctance to acknowledge these findings, despite overwhelming evidence, is a textbook case of the ostrich effect. By ignoring or downplaying the clear signs and consensus on climate change, individuals are choosing short-term emotional comfort over confronting an unsettling reality, much like the myth of the ostrich burying its head in the sand.

Is The Price Right?

September 25th

ANCHORING BIAS

Anchoring bias occurs when a specific reference point, or "anchor", influences our decision-making process. This anchor could be a number or any other kind of cue, even if it is completely unrelated to the decision at hand. Despite this, we often use the anchor as a starting point and adjust our decisions or judgments from there, without realizing it. As a result, our final estimates, decisions, or judgments can be significantly different from what they might have been without the influence of the anchor.

One of the most notable examples of Anchoring Bias in action can be found in the popular '80s TV game show "The Price is Right." The show's format highlights how anchoring bias affects contestants' guesses and decision-making, with the first contestant's bid often serving as an unintentional anchor.

"The Price is Right" is a TV game show that gained widespread popularity during its revival in the '80s. The show requires contestants to guess the prices of various consumer products without going over the actual retail price. The contestant who comes closest to the correct price without exceeding it wins the item. The show's format, which involves contestants taking turns bidding on items, provides a perfect setting to observe the impact of anchor bias on contestants' judgments.

The first contestant's bid for a product serves as an anchor that influences the subsequent contestants' guesses. Although this initial bid is often based on the individual's own perception of the product's value, it significantly affects the decision-making process of the other contestants. For example, if the first contestant bids $600 for a refrigerator, the following contestants are likely to adjust their guesses around that anchor, perhaps suggesting $650 or $700. However, if the initial bid were $800, their guesses would likely be higher.

While "The Price is Right" resembles a flashy infomercial with its prominent display of various products and brands, it serves as a great example of anchoring bias.

Do Different Cultures Have Different Views on Financial Responsibility?

September 26th

JUST WORLD HYPOTHESIS

The Just World Hypothesis is the belief that the world is just and fair, and that people get what they deserve. This means that if someone is experiencing bad things, it is because they have done something to deserve it and are punished. On the other hand, if someone is successful or happy, it is because they made good choices and are rewarded. This idea can be comforting because it gives us a sense of control over our lives and the belief that we can influence our own outcomes.

The World Values Survey, a comprehensive research initiative conducted every six years across 90 countries, provides valuable insights into how different cultures view financial responsibility and success. This extensive study examines various aspects of society, including poverty, education, health, and social tolerance, revealing fascinating patterns in cultural differences and similarities across societies.

Our cultural background and socioeconomic status fundamentally shape our worldview, particularly regarding beliefs about financial success and responsibility. These influences become especially apparent when examining attitudes through the lens of the Just World Hypothesis, which suggests that our life circumstances directly reflect our actions and choices.

Analysis of the World Values Survey data reveals striking contrasts in attitudes towards wealth and poverty across different cultures. For example, 60% of Americans view poor people as lazy, compared to only 26% of Europeans. Conversely, 54% of Europeans attribute income levels to luck, while only 30% of Americans share this belief. These disparities demonstrate how cultural contexts influence people's susceptibility to the Just World Hypothesis.

The survey data particularly highlights how Americans demonstrate a stronger tendency to embrace the Just World Hypothesis compared to Europeans. This notable difference emphasizes how cultural factors significantly influence how people perceive and justify social and economic inequalities in their societies, ultimately affecting their views on financial responsibility and success.

Billions Down the Drain: When Should You Abandon a Costly Project?

September 27th

SUNK COST FALLACY

The sunk cost fallacy is when we make a decision based on how much we have already invested in something rather than on whether it is the best choice for us right now. When we feel like we have already invested a lot in something, we feel like we would be losing something if we were to let it go. Another reason that the sunk cost fallacy occurs is because we tend to focus on the past rather than the present when we make decisions.

Have you ever felt you've spent too much time or money on a project and thought, "This is not worth it," but "because all the work would have been for nothing," you decided yet again to continue investing time and effort? Well, you shouldn't feel too bad unless, like the British and French governments, you've overspent billions of dollars on a single project.

This is what happened in the 1960s when Concorde, a supersonic airliner, saw its development budget go from $400 million to $2 billion. In today's money, this is a difference of over 11 billion dollars! While it was clear that the increasing costs would upset any potential financial gains, the two governments kept pushing it. The Concorde's trademark sonic boom, which is created when an object surpasses the speed of sound, generated a lot of noise complaints from people on the ground, leading to restrictions on its flight routes. The 2000 crash of a Concorde aircraft resulted in 113 fatalities and ultimately contributed to the decline in public confidence and the eventual retirement of the entire Concorde fleet in 2003.

This is a typical example of a sunk cost fallacy, where one believes that if they have already invested time, effort, or money into a project, it's best to finish the project no matter what. The manufacturers and governments followed through on the project because they had already made significant financial investments and dedicated a lot of time to it.

Be aware that sometimes you're fighting a losing battle, and it's time to stop instead of continuing.

View a scene from "Better Call Saul" that exemplifies the sunk cost fallacy

Cracking the Cake Code:
Are We Hardwired to Love Handmade Treats?

September 28th

IKEA EFFECT

The IKEA effect refers to our tendency to place a disproportionately high value on objects that we helped create, such as IKEA furniture. We do that regardless of the quality of the end product. This bias helps us to feel better about ourselves in two ways. First, we want to feel that our effort was well invested and that we did not waste our time but instead created something of value. Secondly, creating things makes us feel more competent.

In the mid-1950s, cake mix sales began to flatten, causing concern among manufacturers. General Mills was and still is a major American food manufacturing company.. Seeking to understand the flattening trend sales, they hired psychologist and marketing specialist Ernest Dichter to survey women and analyze their attitudes towards cake mixes. Dichter discovered that women felt guilty for not contributing more to the baking process, making them reluctant to use cake mixes.

Dichter's research led to a change in marketing strategy, which promoted cake mixes as just one step in the baking process. Women were encouraged to personalize their cakes with icing and decorations, tapping into their creativity and making the cakes feel like their own creations. This change in perception proved to be a crucial turning point for the cake mix industry.

Food historian Laura Shapiro observed that this decorating obsession sold the idea that by adding decorations and icing, women were making the cakes their own. Advertisements, recipes, and homemaking magazines showcased elaborate cake designs, further fueling the trend and empowering women to express their creativity through baking.

The introduction of decorations and icing not only revived cake mix sales but also redefined the meaning of home baking. As Shapiro noted, women began to consider using cake mixes as baking from scratch. The increased involvement in the cake-making process allowed women to feel a sense of accomplishment and ownership over their creations, illustrating the power of the IKEA effect.

Read an article about history of boxed cake mix

Is Your Crystal Ball Deceiving You?

September 29th

ILLUSION OF VALIDITY

The illusion of validity is a cognitive bias where we overestimate our ability to understand and predict an outcome based on the information we have. When analyzing new information, we rely on things we already know, for example, stereotypes and prior beliefs. When we assume that what we know is valid enough to predict what will happen in different contexts, we make confident predictions that can turn out to be utterly inaccurate.

You will often be tempted to make predictions based on the things you know. For example, you might assume that a male leader will win an election simply because men have historically dominated presidential roles. However, doing this might trap you in the illusion of validity. This bias describes our tendency to predict outcomes based on information we have, even when that information may not be relevant. Even if the information is valid in some situations, it doesn't necessarily mean it will predict future events correctly.

A compelling example comes from the founding father of behavioral economics, Daniel Kahneman. As an Israeli, he had to do military service. One of his duties was to assess candidates for officer training. To evaluate them, he and his colleagues set up a challenge for a group of soldiers. They believed that the leadership skills displayed by the soldiers in this situation would indicate how well they would perform in officer training school.

However, the reality proved quite different: the soldiers' performance in the task had no correlation with how they performed in the actual training school. In fact, Kahneman himself admitted that their predictions were "better than blind guesses, but not by much." The team had to acknowledge that they had succumbed to what they called the "illusion of validity." Even though their observations of leadership skills as officers were valid, this didn't mean they could predict how officers would perform in school. Their confidence in the validity of their data had led them to make incorrect predictions.

Watch this video of Daniel Kahneman talking about his experiences

Are You a Winner or a Loser?

September 30th

BINARY BIAS

Binary bias is our tendency to categorize things or people into two distinct categories, often based on their perceived characteristics or attributes. This can lead to oversimplification, stereotyping, and discrimination. We do that because it helps us make sense of the world around us quickly. From an evolutionary perspective, we need to quickly distinguish between potential allies and threats, categorizing people as friends or foes.

In the film "Little Miss Sunshine," Richard Hoover, the father of the dysfunctional Hoover family, serves as a prime example of how binary bias can shape one's worldview and interactions with others, often leading to misunderstandings, miscommunications, and prejudiced beliefs.

At the beginning of the film, Richard appears as a narrow-minded and arrogant character, perpetually fixated on success and the need to be perceived as a winner. He makes his worldview clear by repeatedly stating, "There are two kinds of people in this world: winners and losers. You know what the difference is? Winners don't give up." This mindset perfectly demonstrates his binary bias, as he divides all of humanity into two simplistic categories.

However, the film also illustrates the potential for personal growth and change, as Richard eventually abandons his black-and-white worldview in favor of a more nuanced understanding of life and the complexities of human nature. Through a series of transformative events, including the unexpected death of his father and his daughter's unconventional performance at the beauty pageant, Richard is forced to confront the limitations of his binary thinking. He ultimately learns the value of empathy and understanding, discovering that human worth cannot be reduced to simple categories of winners or losers. For anyone interested in exploring the pitfalls of binary thinking and the beauty of personal growth, "Little Miss Sunshine" offers a heartwarming and thought-provoking journey that challenges our preconceptions about success and failure.

Watch Greg Kinnear in "Little Miss Sunshine" talk about winners

∞
OCTOBER

How to Control a Lifeline Beyond the Grave?

October 1st

ILLUSION OF CONTROL

The illusion of control occurs when we believe we have more control over external events than we do. We frequently believe we have (or had) some control over events that are actually random. Researchers have found that people who feel in control will engage in healthier behaviors, feel less stress, and have better overall mental health. Therefore, this illusion makes us feel better about ourselves and the world around us, but it can also seduce us into relying on superstitions.

There is a saying that goes, "different strokes for different folks," meaning that different cultures have their own unique traditions. These traditions can include ceremonies and rituals that are practiced during various life events, such as birthdays, weddings, holidays, and funerals. These ceremonies often hold great significance for those who participate in them and can serve as a way to connect with one's community and maintain a sense of control over life's uncertainties.

Some traditional ways of healing involve ceremonies or rituals that people believe will help them get better. For example, in some cultures, healing dances or chants are performed to cure illness or promote fertility. One reason why cultures maintain these ceremonies is that they provide a sense of control over unpredictable events. This sense of control, while often illusory, serves an important psychological purpose. In Ghana, for example, people celebrate death by placing deceased individuals into fantasy coffins. These caskets are masterfully crafted in the form of ships, animals, or cars and are beautifully painted.

The idea behind this ritual is that death is the beginning of a different form of life, which continues on the other side. In the afterlife, the deceased will continue with their profession. By placing the dead in such coffins, Ghanaian people believe they can influence some of the uncertainty surrounding death and what happens afterward. In the face of life's greatest mystery, rituals like Ghana's fantasy coffins provide a comforting illusion of control. Even if it's just an illusion, this celebration of life reflects humanity's resilient spirit.

Read more about Ghana's fantasy coffins

Politics and Math: A Divisive Formula for Logic?

October 2nd

COGNITIVE DISSONANCE

Cognitive dissonance describes the mental discomfort we experience when there is a conflict between our beliefs, actions, or perceptions. This discomfort often arises when our actions contradict our beliefs or when we hold two opposing beliefs simultaneously. To alleviate this discomfort, we may adjust our beliefs, perceptions, or actions to create a more consistent internal state. Achieving this internal consistency is crucial, as it helps maintain our sense of identity and coherence.

In the realm of human cognition, political identities often exert a profound influence. This phenomenon was strikingly illustrated in a 2013 study involving over 1,100 American adults. Participants were given a math test with two types of questions: one neutral, involving skin cream and rashes, and the other contentious, relating to gun control and crime rates.

While participants generally answered the neutral question correctly, their responses to the contentious question revealed a significant sway of political beliefs, even among those with strong math skills. Liberals tended to solve the problem correctly when the data suggested that gun control reduced crime, whereas conservatives were more accurate when the data indicated the opposite. At this point, the brain deliberately introduces an error, aligning cognitive outcomes with pre-existing political beliefs and overriding logical reasoning. It's as if the mind intentionally misinterprets data to avoid conflicting with deeply held political convictions.

Political identities affiliate us with social groups, which can lead to cognitive dissonance when group beliefs conflict with factual information. In the study's gun control question, individuals experienced a clash between the correct, logical answer and their political leanings. This conflict often resulted in adjusting answers to align with political beliefs rather than accepting factual information. These findings reveal a critical intersection between political identity and cognitive processing, underscoring the challenge of maintaining objectivity in the face of personal beliefs.

View a TED talk about the dangers of the partisan brain

How Many Innocents Served Time for a Crime They Didn't Commit?

October 3rd

CONFIRMATION BIAS

Confirmation bias is our tendency to look for, acknowledge, favor, and remember information in a way that supports what we already think or believe. This bias occurs when we ignore information that contradicts our ideas or interpret ambiguous facts as evidence supporting our existing beliefs. Situations that involve emotionally charged topics, strongly held beliefs, or things we really want to happen are most susceptible to this bias.

Before relying on forensic science, the criminal justice system used eyewitness accounts as the main source of information in a prosecutor's case. However, human beings can be quite unreliable information providers due to our predisposition for confirmation bias.

In the famous murder case of Dorka Lisker, detectives were convinced that the suspect was her son, Bruce Lisker, whose hands were covered in blood when police arrived. He also appeared to be high on methamphetamine and had a history of fights with his mother. When you put this information together, all the evidence seems to fit the story of the murder. Or so the detectives thought.

Despite Bruce Lisker's innocence, he tragically spent 26 years in prison as a result of investigators succumbing to confirmation bias. Initially overlooked, crucial evidence later emerged that exonerated him, including the fact that his shoes did not match the footprints at the crime scene. Furthermore, an alternative suspect, Mike Ryan, was discovered to have lied about his alibi, and a phone call made from Lisker's home to his mother at the time of the murder further cast doubt on his guilt. Unfortunately, all of this evidence was initially ignored, leading to Lisker's wrongful imprisonment.

The investigators confirmation bias about someone whose hands are covered in blood (and who is also on drugs) led them to look at all the evidence that this person is guilty of the crime. They discarded all the arguments why he shouldn't have been ruled out as a suspect.

Read an article about Bruce Lisker's case

Is Exposure to Gay TV Characters the Remote Control for Tolerance?

October 4th

MERE EXPOSURE EFFECT

The mere exposure effect says the more we are exposed to something, the more we like it. Familiarity breeds liking. When asked to make a choice, we tend to prefer what is familiar, even if this is not the optimal choice. One reason for this behavior is that evolution has taught us to be careful around new things. Everything unfamiliar could be potentially dangerous. When we see something over and over again without any bad results, we assume it is safe.

Television has the potential to generate positive societal impacts, including reducing prejudice. Thoughtfully crafted television programming can play a meaningful role in fostering greater understanding and acceptance of LGBTQ+ individuals within society. This connection between exposure and acceptance becomes particularly evident when examining popular media's influence on social attitudes.

The groundbreaking sitcom "Will & Grace," which introduced the first gay leading characters in the history of television, serves as a prime example of the mere exposure effect in action, as noted by "Cognitive Bias" podcast host David Dylan Thomas. The show brought these relatable gay characters into the homes of millions of Americans. A 2006 study discovered that exposure to TV shows like this had the power to substantially decrease sexual prejudice. Intriguingly, the study found that watching gay characters on TV was just as effective at reducing prejudice as having direct personal interactions with gay individuals. This supports other research that shows that contact between minority and majority groups can lessen prejudice within the majority group.

The mere exposure effect facilitated a greater familiarity with gay relationships among the general public. By showcasing two gay men, "Will & Grace" enabled a conversation about a subject that many people had never encountered before. As President Joe Biden once noted, "Will & Grace probably did more to educate the American public than almost anything anyone has done so far." The show's impact on American society is a testament to the power of the mere exposure effect.

Watch Joe Biden speak about Will & Grace

Are You Committing to Success or Falling for a Sales Pitch?

October 5th

CONSISTENCY BIAS

Consistency bias is the tendency to choose information or actions that fit with what you already believe, value, or do. This bias can lead individuals to reject new information or evidence that contradicts their existing views, or to selectively interpret and remember information in a way that supports their preexisting beliefs.

You hear about the importance of staying committed to your goals in many personal development videos and books. But have you ever thought that perhaps your commitment is part of someone's sales strategy? According to consistency bias, we are more likely to take actions that align with our previous behavior. This is because we want to maintain a sense of coherent identity. If we acted differently on a day-to-day basis, we would question who we are.

In an investing workshop I attended, we were encouraged to fill out a "promise card." This card was designed to help people stay focused on achieving financial security and pursue activities that would help them reach this goal. Many participants were eager to fill out this promise card—strictly for their psychological fulfillment. However, this tactic wasn't random at all. A few days later, workshop attendees started receiving calls from the organizers, who were promoting a trading course. They positioned themselves as being motivated to help participants reach their financial goals, reminding them of the promise card they had written to themselves. The organizers simply wanted to help participants stay committed to their goals—while selling their trading course.

Do you really think these workshop organizers were unaware of the power of consistency bias? Of course not! They deliberately used it as a sales strategy by aligning people's mindset (their desire to attain financial freedom) with a specific behavior (buying their trading course).

Are Money-Back Guarantees the Ultimate Sales Hack?

October 6th

ZERO RISK BIAS

The Zero Risk Bias is a mental shortcut that makes us prefer a risk-free option, even if this choice is not the most rational or beneficial one. In uncertain situations, the mere possibility of something happening is emotionally more important than how likely it is to happen. So, we'd rather get rid of the possibility all together.

You're watching an ad on your favorite social media platform and are already convinced to buy the product. It looks like a deal you shouldn't miss out on, but what if you won't be happy with it? Don't worry! The seller has got you covered. Just when you think they couldn't sweeten the deal any more, they offer to give all your money back if you're not fully satisfied with what you're getting. Now all your concerns are gone — if you can simply return the product if you don't like it, what have you got to lose?

When retailers offer a "money-back guarantee," it means that they're capitalizing on our zero-risk bias. Our natural tendency is to prefer options with lower or no risk over those with higher risk due to high uncertainty. Many sellers are aware of this, which is why they promise people that they have nothing to lose when making a purchase. The money-back guarantee is a marketing tool that eliminates the risk of making the wrong purchasing decision. One of people's main worries when buying something is that they will regret the purchase later. "Buyer's remorse" is the technical term for this. Retailers make sure that potential buyers' remorse is eliminated from the start.

If you're wondering whether this strategy affects a retailer's profit, know that it actually has the opposite effect. One study showed that offering a money-back guarantee can increases customer satisfaction by 98.4%, boosts profits by 7.36%, and allows retailers to charge 1.81% more for new products.

This way, you can make that impulse purchase without worrying about it, while retailers get to boost their sales and profits.

Pay Now or Pay Later: What Motivaes More?

October 7th

LOSS AVERSION

Loss aversion means that the perceived loss of value from losing an object is greater than the perceived value of getting it. The pain of losing is twice as strong as the pleasure of gaining. The factors that influence this bias have been extensively researched. Among others are cultural factors (collectivist cultures have less loss aversion than individualist cultures) and socio-economic factors (powerful and wealthy people are less loss-averse).

Losing the money you already have can be a powerful motivator. Recently, a study applied this bias in an educational setting to see whether teachers are more motivated by the money they're given upfront than the ones promised as future bonuses.

This experiment utilized loss aversion, which states that people are generally more motivated by the idea of losing than by the prospect of gaining. To motivate teachers to increase learning performance, an experiment conducted in a Chicago school district offered a $4,000 upfront payment to new teachers and asked them to sign a contract stating they would return the money if the children's school grades did not improve. To control the results, the study also included a control group of teachers who were not offered any upfront money and were promised a bonus later in the future.

Both groups of children (the ones supervised by the teachers who were paid in advance and the ones in the "traditional" teaching group) were assessed on their math knowledge before and after the experiment. The results of the study are highly supportive of the loss aversion: children supervised by teachers with the upfront bonus improved their math grades three times, while the ones in the other group stayed the same.

The upfront payment served as an incentive for teachers to motivate students to perform so they would not lose the bonus they had already received. It is more painful to lose something we own than to never gain something we hope for. Therefore, if we can't motivate ourselves to do something by thinking about the benefits we can gain, we can think about what we can lose if we don't act.

Are You Really the Center of Attention?

October 8th

SPOTLIGHT EFFECT

The spotlight effect is our tendency to think that other people are paying more attention to us than they really are. It makes us feel like we are always "in the spotlight." This happens because our brains are wired to pay more attention to ourselves than to others. Additionally, we are more aware of changes concerning ourselves compared to others. The effect occurs in both positive (like a personal success) and negative situations (like something we are embarrassed of).

We often perceive ourselves as the center of our universe, but others don't see us that way. While we're highly conscious of our own mistakes and actions, others often don't notice them. What feels mortifying to us, like an awkward mistake on a first date or mispronouncing a word during a speech, might go completely unnoticed by others. Many of these awkward situations exist only in our imagination.

Researchers conducted a series of experiments to explore the spotlight effect in action. Participants were asked to wear a T-shirt displaying either an embarrassing image or a picture of a well-known figure. In one experiment, participants wore T-shirts with an embarrassing image of Barry Manilow, while in another, they chose from shirts depicting figures they felt good about, such as Martin Luther King Jr. The researchers examined whether participants overestimated how noticeable their appearance was to others, regardless of whether the T-shirt was potentially embarrassing or not.

The results were striking and consistent across all experiments. The spotlight effect caused participants to significantly overestimate the attention they received from others. Participants wearing either type of T-shirt consistently misjudged how much they were noticed by others in public. For instance, in the Barry Manilow T-shirt study, participants estimated that 46% of observers would identify the singer on their shirt, when in reality, only 23% did.

These findings highlight an important truth: even when we believe we are the center of attention during an extraordinary or embarrassing moment, in reality, most people are preoccupied with their own lives and are similarly influenced by their own spotlight effect.

Are Sporty Getaways the Secret to Boosting Birth Rates?

October 9th

MISATTRIBUTION OF AROUSAL

Misattribution of arousal occurs when we experience physical symptoms of arousal, such as a fast heartbeat or sweaty palms, and incorrectly attribute these symptoms to the wrong cause. This phenomenon arises because various triggers—like fear or romantic excitement—can produce similar physical responses. Our brains, trying to find patterns and make sense of these signals, may link the arousal to an incorrect source.

When natality rates were significantly dropping in Denmark, a travel company came up with an innovative idea: lure couples into booking sports holidays. What is the reasoning behind this? There is a strong scientific argument behind this initiative, which has to do with a term called "misattribution of arousal." This is the notion that physiological arousal may appear to originate from a source other than the one that really caused it. When actually experiencing physiological responses due to sport (sweat, increased blood pressure, and heart rate), people could easily understand those responses as sexual arousal.

The travel company in Denmark seems to know exactly how to use the concept of misattribution of arousal to boost birth rates. In their viral video "Do it for Denmark," they state that exercising with your partner increases sex drive. In the video, the narrator says, "You sweat, your heart beats faster, and you lose your breath. Symptoms we know from being in love and feeling aroused." To back up their promise, the Danish company also offered three years of baby supplies besides a "child-friendly" holiday if the couple could show that they conceived during their holiday.

Following this campaign, Denmark launched another one called "Do it for Mom," which played on mothers' desire to have grandchildren and had the same purpose in mind. They also launched a campaign called "Do it forever" to promote sex for older couples because of its increased health benefits.

By the way, after the advertising campaign, the birth rate actually increased by about 6% from 2014 to 2016.

Watch the video 'Do It For Denmark!'

Feeling Down or Just Well-Informed?
The Curious Case of Depression Ads

October 10th

AVAILABILITY BIAS

The availability bias is our tendency to make decisions based on information that comes to mind quickly and easily. It's a mental shortcut that gives more weight to information that was learned recently or that is easy to remember, for example, because it is an emotionally loaded memory. Our brain wants to save mental energy. So, we often go with the first information that comes to mind instead of putting in more mental effort to dig deeper.

The more exposed you are to information about depression, the more common it may seem. This is due to the availability bias, which means that the accessibility of certain information determines how likely it is to pop up in your thought processes.

Several studies have shown that TV advertising can influence viewers' perceptions of the outside world. One particularly interesting finding was that people are more likely to think that many individuals suffer from depression if they are exposed to advertisements for depression medication. In this study, respondents had to answer questions such as, "What percentage of adult American people do you think suffer from depression?" and "Do you recall seeing or hearing an advertisement for anti-depression drugs in the last six months?"

The results revealed a clear connection between ad exposure and perception of depression prevalence. People who remembered advertisements for antidepressants tended to think that depression was more common than it actually is. This perception comes from seeing these ads often, even if we don't pay close attention to them. Interestingly, when people were asked to think about where they got their information before guessing about depression rates, this effect disappeared.

This demonstrates the availability bias in action: participants used these ads to make assumptions without questioning if they were a reliable source of information. Because the ads were readily available in the participants' memories, they tended to rely on them when estimating how common depression is.

Can You Afford That?

October 11th

FRAMING EFFECT

The framing effect occurs when we draw different conclusions from identical information based solely on how that information is presented. This can happen when something is framed either positively or negatively, or as a gain versus a loss - we naturally tend to avoid losses in such situations. Our judgment can also shift depending on which features of the information are highlighted, even though the underlying facts remain exactly the same.

The price of a $100 pair of shoes, objectively speaking, is the same for everyone. However, its perceived value differs, not just based on how much money you have but also on your financial goals.

Because of the framing effect, we can perceive, interpret, and use a particular piece of information in entirely different ways. We can also frame something as simple as making a purchase in various ways, depending on our approach to money and saving at that particular time. You may have heard about "mental accounting," which is the process of categorizing and evaluating financial outcomes based on personal priorities.

With mental accounting, you create mental "accounts" for different types of expenses or financial goals and allocate resources to these accounts. This practice activates your framing effect, specifically in how you look at a purchase. For example, if your goal is to save as much as possible for your emergency account, you won't look at a bonus or monetary gift in the same way as someone who prioritizes immediate pleasure. You will perceive that extra cash as funding for difficult times rather than as an opportunity for current enjoyment.

The framing effect can help you understand why, for example, a vacation might be entirely affordable for you but an impossible stretch for your friends. Or why you might splurge on nights out some months and barely leave the house in others. It's all about how you frame these expenses in your mind.

Do You Underrate Your Emotional Resilience?

October 12th

IMPACT BIAS

The impact bias is our tendency to think that events will have a stronger and longer-lasting effect on our future feelings than they actually will. We incorrectly believe that good things will make us happy forever, and bad things will make us miserable forever. We do that because we tend to focus on one event at a time, neglecting the future effects of unrelated events. Also, we don't realize how quickly our psychological immune system will reframe the events that happened.

The psychological immune system is our mind's way of coping with negative emotions, but most people don't realize they have this system. This lack of awareness leads to what scientists call impact bias - the tendency to overestimate how long we'll feel bad after something unpleasant happens. To demonstrate this phenomenon, researchers conducted six studies examining impact bias in various situations, including romantic breakups, the death of a child, and job rejections.

One notable experiment focused on job interviews. Participants were divided into two groups: an "unfair decision" group, where a single MBA student determined the hiring outcome, and a "fair decision" group, where a team of MBA students unanimously decided. Before the interview, participants in both groups predicted how they would feel immediately after learning whether they got the job, and then how they would feel ten minutes later. Interestingly, both groups accurately predicted their immediate emotional reactions to the news. However, ten minutes after hearing the results, everyone felt much better than they had anticipated, clearly demonstrating impact bias.

This pattern held true across all six studies. Participants consistently overestimated the duration of their negative emotional reactions, failing to account for their psychological immune system's ability to help them bounce back. Despite the varying nature and severity of the situations studied, people wrongly assumed their negative emotions would persist equally in each case. This oversight highlights how the psychological immune system operates beneath our conscious awareness, quietly helping us cope with life's setbacks more effectively than we might expect.

Why Do We Save Species That Are Simiar To Us?

October 13th

ANTHROPOMORPHISM

Anthropomorphism is our natural tendency to attribute human traits, emotions, and intentions to non-humans, for example, animals, gods, natural forces, and the like. We do this because we naturally know more about human traits than non-human ones. Therefore, these come easier to mind, and that saves mental energy.

Consider the following thought experiment: You must decide which species the government should prioritize for increased protection efforts. How would you choose between dogs and cows? What about dogs versus bees? And how would you compare sunflowers and seaweed?

Our perception of an organism's worthiness for protection is often influenced by anthropomorphic thinking. Research has demonstrated that people tend to allocate more resources to protect animals than plants and vertebrates over invertebrates, irrespective of the organism's importance to the ecosystem. This bias also extends to government decision-making, with species that resemble humans in appearance receiving a larger share of policy attention and conservation funding.

In essence, the greater the morphological and behavioral similarity between animals and humans, the more inclined we are to attribute human-like mental states to non-human species. This tendency to project our own mental states onto other species is not exclusive to humans; it is also found in other primates. It is suggested that this anthropomorphism bias has evolutionary roots, predating the emergence of modern humans.

To ensure the preservation of our ecosystems, we must prioritize the ecological significance of a species rather than basing our decisions on their resemblance to human behavior, acknowledging that while dogs may melt our hearts, bees and algae play a far more crucial role in sustaining life on Earth.

Read an article about 11 surprising species with high ecological significance

Could You Have Resisted the Nazi Nonsense?

October 14th

GROUPTHINK

Groupthink is when our desire for harmony and conformity within a group leads to dysfunctional decision-making. Group members prioritize agreement over critical evaluation, resulting in a loss of individual creativity and thinking. This can lead to an inflated sense of confidence in the group's abilities, an undervaluation of opponents, group pressure, and potentially harmful actions towards outsiders.

The National Socialist German Workers' Party (NSDAP) and the Nazi movement under Adolf Hitler provide a striking example of groupthink in action. The desire for conformity within the party led to the suppression of dissenting opinions, the acceptance of extremist ideologies, and ultimately, catastrophic consequences for millions of people. The NSDAP was united in its goals of national pride, territorial expansion, and the creation of a racially pure society. This common purpose reinforced the groupthink mentality, as members prioritized these shared goals over critically evaluating the party's actions.

The belief in a utopian future under Nazi rule further solidified the group's cohesion and resistance to alternative viewpoints. Central to the Nazi ideology was the concept of the Aryan race as a kind of "Übermensch," or superior human. This belief led to an inflated sense of confidence in the group's abilities and a dangerous underestimation of those deemed inferior or oppositional.

The Nazi regime's control over the flow of information and suppression of dissenting opinions created an echo chamber that further solidified the groupthink mentality. Members of the NSDAP who questioned the leadership or deviated from the party line faced severe pressure, including harsh consequences such as imprisonment or execution. This fear of punishment reinforced the groupthink mentality and discouraged dissent. It also fostered a culture of complicity, where individuals were too intimidated to speak out or confront the party's actions, even when they recognized blatant moral atrocities.

The Nazi regime exemplifies how groupthink can lead to catastrophe, highlighting the crucial need for critical thinking and the courage to question authority.

Who's to Blame: Teachers, Students, or Self-Serving Bias?

October 15th

SELF-SERVING BIAS

The self-serving bias is our tendency to take credit for good things that happen to us and blame other things or people for bad things that happen. We do that because we have the desire to feel good about ourselves. Being responsible for good things happening boosts our confidence and gives us a sense of control in our lives. When we blame external factors for bad things that happen to us, it can help us feel better about ourselves by protecting our ego.

When we think back to our school days, we probably attributed our successes to our own brilliance while blaming teachers for our failures. But teachers aren't immune to this bias either.

A fascinating study investigated how students and teachers attributed success and failure to themselves. The researchers conducted two clever experiments: one in a controlled setting where college students played the roles of teachers, students, and observers, and another in a real-world university setting. In the controlled experiment, "teachers" prepared lessons, "students" took tests, and everyone tried to explain why the students succeeded or failed. In the real-world study, actual university teachers, students, and staff recalled recent high and low grades and explained what caused them.

The results showed that both, students and teachers are prone to self-serving bias, taking credit for successes and deflecting blame for failures. When asked to explain the reasons behind the outcomes of the test, both teachers and students credited themselves if the results were positive. However, they attributed the negative results to either the teacher's lack of skills or the students' lack of effort.

Surprisingly, the study found that students and teachers were pretty good at predicting each other's biases. This suggests that we're not as oblivious to each other's thought processes as we might think!

Often, schools take pride in their students' exceptional achievements but hesitate to accept full responsibility when those same students fail to meet expectations.

Are You a True Fan or Just Riding the Bandwagon Wave?

October 16th

BANDWAGON EFFECT

The bandwagon effect refers to the phenomenon in which a belief or behavior becomes more popular as more people adopt it. This can lead to a self-reinforcing cycle, as the increased popularity of the belief or behavior encourages more people to adopt it. The effect is caused by our desire to conform to social norms and our belief that the majority must be correct. It can also be caused by peer pressure and the fear of being left out or made fun of if we don't fit in.

Bandwagon behavior is evident in many aspects of sports, particularly when people become fans of a popular team without genuine interest in the sport itself.

For example, the Golden State Warriors, an American professional basketball team, struggled to get public attention in the 1980s. It wasn't until Stephen Curry joined the team that they achieved a historic feat in the 2015-2016 season: winning 73 games and losing only 9 out of their 82-game regular season. This record-breaking performance sparked interest among millions of people.

The bandwagon effect can be seen in the sales statistics of point guard Stephen Curry's jersey. Curry's total merchandise sales in the first two weeks of the 2015–2016 season were 453% higher than in the first two weeks of the 2014–2015 season, including a 581% increase in sales just for his jersey. Following these record sales, his merchandise became a top seller in 38 of the 50 U.S. states. The Warriors merchandise was the best-selling of any NBA team.

Part of this growth was just the result of the bandwagon effect. Many people bought Warriors merchandise simply because they saw others doing it. Even though the team's popularity was also due to its merits and successes, this created a snowball effect that got them even more fans and admiration.

X-Ray Vision: Are We All Expert Radiologists in Retrospect?

October 17th

HINDSIGHT BIAS

The hindsight bias is also called the "I-knew-it-all-along" effect. It describes the retrospective overestimation of predictability. In the present, it's hard to tell how something will turn out in the future, but is easy to understand how or why an event happened in retrospect. This bias happens because we mistakenly assume that we had the same understanding of an event before it happened as we do after it happened.

Nir Eyal, the author of "Hooked," presents a classic case of hindsight bias through the following anecdote: In 2000, a 69-year-old man sought medical advice for a persistent cough. During an X-ray examination, the radiologist identified a large tumor in his chest, which would lead to lung cancer. Three years prior, the same radiographic examination had not found anything unusual, and the patient was told he was in perfect health.

The patient, questioning why the radiologist missed early tumor signs but found advanced lung cancer three years later, decided to sue the doctor. During the trial, the doctor's lawyer showed the initial X-rays to other radiologists in the court, who could all identify the tumor. Moreover, they claimed that the tumor was so obvious that the patient had suffered a serious case of medical malpractice.

The radiologist's lawyer argued that the reason it was so easy for the other doctors to see the tumor was that they were intentionally looking for it. They knew there was something abnormal to find in the scans, so they had better chances of detecting it. Therefore, the other radiologists' opinions were formed as a result of hindsight bias. One expert supported this idea, stating, "I've never had an attorney bring me a normal radiograph. Whenever an attorney shows or sends me radiographs, the first and only question that comes to my mind is, 'What was missed on these films?'"

The jury, however, found the defendant radiologist guilty of malpractice and granted $872,000 in compensation to the deceased patient's family.

Is Your Driving Confidence Steering You Toward Danger?

October 18th

DUNNING–KRUGER EFFECT

The Dunning–Kruger effect describes our tendency to overestimate our own abilities in areas that we are unskilled in or lack knowledge in. This happens when we know just enough to think we are great but not enough to tell the difference between good and bad. We just don't know yet what we could do better. The effect also applies to society as a whole. The most uninformed citizens are often also the most confident ones.

If you asked people to rate their driving abilities, almost everyone would think they're "above-average" drivers. Few will see themselves as one of the best drivers in the world, but not many will show a realistic self-assessment either. Yet, from a statistical point of view, it's impossible that the majority of us are better drivers than the average, because by definition, the average represents the middle point of all drivers' abilities. The reason we make such bold claims has to do with the Dunning-Kruger effect. According to this, we are highly inclined to overestimate our abilities.

In one very interesting study, half of the participants believed they were among the safest 20–30% of drivers in their group. Similarly, most of the participants regarded themselves as more skilled drivers.

The study also suggests why this might be an issue. Our self-image can influence how willing we are to take risks and how much effort we put into finding information about potential risks and safety measures. For example, if we have a positive self-image and see ourselves as confident and capable drivers, we may be more willing to take risks and be less concerned about safety measures. On the other hand, if we have a more realistic view of ourselves and think we are not sure how good a driver we are, we may be more careful and more likely to learn about the risks and safety measures.

Nearly 3,700 people die every day in traffic accidents around the world. If more people were aware that the Dunning-Kruger effect has an impact on their driving abilities, we might be able to lower these numbers.

Did Outcome Bias Pull the Plug on Dell's Reputation?

October 19th

OUTCOME BIAS

We are subject to outcome bias when we judge a decision by its outcome. This is biased because we should rather base our judgment on the quality of the decision at the time it was made, given what was known at that time. We never have all the information we need, and every result has random and unpredictable parts. Bad outcomes are not always a sign of bad decision-making.

In 2005, Dell Computer topped Fortune magazine's list as the World's Most Admired Company, boasting revenues exceeding $55 billion. By 2007, Dell's stock had plummeted nearly 50%, leading analysts and the media to speculate on the reasons for the downturn, such as over-reliance on PCs and a lack of innovation. The media's coverage of big companies like Dell holds significant sway, as it can shape investor sentiment and perceptions, thereby directly influencing stock prices and the overall market's confidence in the company's strategies and future prospects.

In this case, the media's behavior in dissecting Dell's decline provides a classic example of outcome bias in action. The general assumption among journalists was that a poor outcome was a direct result of poor decision-making. This was evident in the criticism Dell received when it attempted to diversify its product line. However, this criticism ignored the fact that Dell, like any company, needed to evolve to maintain competitiveness. It's worth mentioning that Michael Dell and his team had foreseen that their dominance in the PC market would not last indefinitely, prompting them to explore other avenues as early as the late 1990s. They tried to leverage Dell's manufacturing efficiency in the production of printers and televisions.

Despite industry experts acknowledging Dell's diversification as a wise move, outcome bias led to public perception skewing against Dell. Decisions with unfavorable outcomes were deemed poor, regardless of the initial strategy's merits.

Till Death Do Us Part or Just a Change of Heart?

October 20th

END-OF-HISTORY ILLUSION

The end-of-history illusion refers to our tendency to underestimate the extent of personal changes that will occur in the future. While we acknowledge that our personalities, values, and tastes have evolved over time, we often believe that they will remain relatively stable going forward. This misconception persists regardless of age. The illusion arises because we find it hard to imagine personal changes and thus assume that such changes are unlikely to occur.

"Until death do us part" is the phrase that many couples innocently agree to at the altar. They want—or at least they hope—to be just as deeply in love with their partner as they are on their wedding day. In the U.S., approximately 45% of marriages end in divorce. While divorce rates vary significantly across the world, one thing is certain: no marriage carries an absolute guarantee of lasting forever.

However, we still approach marriage as if it's one of those constants that will accompany us until the end of our days. The end-of-history illusion deludes us into believing that we won't change in the future as much as we did in the past. So when we love someone today, we commit ourselves in marriage, assuming our feelings will remain equally passionate. Not anticipating personal growth and change during a marriage can result in profound disillusionment. There is a significant possibility that the person we will become in ten years may not be compatible with the person our partner evolves into during that time.

Just as we fail to anticipate our own changes, we also underestimate our partner's potential transformation over the years. Similarly, our relationship dynamics today might shift considerably in the future—for better or worse.

This isn't to say that getting married is a bad idea. However, approaching it as an unchangeable commitment is perhaps overly romantic and unrealistic.

Health Halo:
Do Organic Labels Feed Your Brain More Than Your Body?

October 21st

HALO EFFECT

The halo effect is a type of cognitive bias in which our overall opinion of a person or brand affects how we feel about the specific qualities of that person or brand. If we have a good feeling about something as a whole, we are more likely to think that its individual parts are good as well. We do that because it saves cognitive effort to use our overall impressions as a shortcut to make judgments rather than evaluating each aspect of something separately.

The organic food label provides a compelling example of the halo effect in action. A revealing study examined how organic labels fundamentally alter our perception of food products.

In this study, researchers asked participants to evaluate three different foods (yogurt, potato chips, and juice) under two conditions: in their homes and in a controlled test location. The researchers presented identical food pairs, labeling one as regular and the other as organic, though the products were exactly the same. The findings revealed that the organic label not only made people rate the food more favorably but also increased their willingness to pay more and led them to estimate lower calorie content. Additionally, participants reported different taste experiences for the supposedly organic juice and yogurt.

Remarkably, the organic label's influence on food perception remained consistent across both testing environments, demonstrating the halo effect's powerful role in shaping our preferences and choices.

Our minds automatically make associations: organic equals lower calories, higher nutritional value, and better health outcomes, making it seem superior to non-organic products. A simple organic label and attractive packaging can make us overlook a product's potential drawbacks. While these assumptions are often unfounded, the halo effect leads us to attribute positive qualities to a product based solely on one favorable characteristic (in this case, being organic). The significant danger of this halo effect lies in its potential to make us underestimate the caloric content of organic foods, which can lead to less optimal dietary choices.

Are AI Face Recognition Tools Discriminating by Design?

October 22nd

AUTOMATION BIAS

Automation bias means that we are likely to follow the advice of automated systems, like those in airplane cockpits or on your phone (think autocorrect, Google Maps). We tend to ignore contradictory information made without automation, even if it is correct. In decision-making, we like to take the path of least cognitive effort. We are happy to accept the answers that automated systems give us because it is often easier than having to think for ourselves.

Software using artificial intelligence (AI) is built by humans, which means it can reflect our biases, social prejudices, and judgment errors. Automation bias leads us to trust AI systems, even when they're flawed. Two major issues arise: First, AI can be as biased as we are. The quality of AI depends heavily on its input data. Often, the data used to train AI is biased, and this bias may be made worse by the unconscious biases of the programmers and software architects developing these systems. Second, AI-based software programs are essentially black boxes, making it difficult or impossible to understand how and why they make decisions. As a result, biased outcomes may go unnoticed.

Let's look at automated face recognition tools used to determine someone's gender as an example. These tools' accuracy varies depending on skin type and gender. While they're generally accurate, they're not equally accurate for everyone. The error rate is 8–21% higher for women compared to men. The difference is even more pronounced when considering skin tone, with a 12–19% higher error rate for people with darker skin. The most striking difference is between light-skinned men and dark-skinned women: the tools correctly identify light-skinned men 100% of the time, but dark-skinned women only 72.9% of the time. This error likely occurs because the data used to train these systems mostly includes images of light-skinned men.

Because of these issues, researchers like Timnit Gebru argue that companies selling these AI tools should be required to perform specific tests to prove their products work fairly for all groups of people.

Watch Timnit Gebru talk about when algorithms fail

What is the Percentage of African Countries in the United Nations?

October 23rd

ANCHORING BIAS

Anchoring bias occurs when a specific reference point, or "anchor", influences our decision-making process. This anchor could be a number or any other kind of cue, even if it is completely unrelated to the decision at hand. Despite this, we often use the anchor as a starting point and adjust our decisions or judgments from there, without realizing it. As a result, our final estimates, decisions, or judgments can be significantly different from what they might have been without the influence of the anchor.

The term "anchoring bias" first appeared in a study by Amos Tversky and Daniel Kahneman in 1974, which demonstrated how strongly unrelated information can influence our decisions. They presented two striking examples to showcase this discovery.

In their first experiment, participants were asked to estimate the percentage of African countries in the United Nations. Before making their estimate, they were shown a 'wheel of fortune' that was spun to generate a random number between 0 and 100. They were first asked whether the percentage was higher or lower than this random number, and then asked to make their final estimate. Remarkably, the random number heavily influenced their estimation. For instance, when the wheel showed 10, the median estimate was 25%. Conversely, when the wheel showed 65, the median estimate rose to 45%. Despite the random number being completely irrelevant to the actual answer, this demonstrates how an arbitrary figure can anchor and influence decisions.

The other example focused on intuitive numerical estimation. High school students were asked to rapidly estimate the product of a sequence of numbers, either in ascending ($1\times2\times3\times4\times5\times6\times7\times8$) or descending ($8\times7\times6\times5\times4\times3\times2\times1$) order. The students made initial calculations and then extrapolated to arrive at a final estimate. Due to the order of the numbers, the estimates were significantly different. The median estimate for the ascending sequence was 512, while it was 2,250 for the descending sequence. (The correct answer is 40,320.) This demonstrates how their initial calculations skewed the estimates due to anchoring bias.

The Bias Behind Chornobyl's Meltdown?

October 24th

OSTRICH EFFECT OR NORMALCY BIAS

Normalcy bias, also known as "ostrich effect," makes us downplay warnings about dangers or ignore negative situations completely. We underestimate how likely it is that a disaster will happen and how it might affect us. We do that because we want to avoid an unpleasant emotional impact in the short term. The name comes from the popular (but false) belief that ostriches bury their heads in the sand when in danger.

On the fateful night of April 26, 1986, the Chernobyl nuclear power plant in Ukraine suffered a catastrophic explosion, marking it as the most severe nuclear disaster the world has ever witnessed. Subsequent investigations revealed that the primary cause of this disaster was the plant workers' disregard for established operating procedures. Viktor Bryukhanov, the power plant's director, was also held accountable for the incident. His failure to respond appropriately to the early warning signs serves as a prime example of the ostrich effect.

Viktor Bryukhanov's statements following the disaster lend credence to the theory that the ostrich effect was in action. Before the explosion, Bryukhanov had personally witnessed the damage to the reactor building. Despite this, he reported to Moscow that the reactor was still intact. In a later statement, Bryukhanov admitted: "That night, I walked around the plant's courtyard. I saw chunks of graphite under my feet. But I still couldn't accept that the reactor had been destroyed. The idea just didn't fit in my head. It was only later, when I saw the helicopter fly around."

The presence of graphite chunks under Bryukhanov's feet was clear proof of the tragedy because graphite was a core component of the reactor, indicating that the reactor's protective shell had been breached and a catastrophic failure had occurred. Despite this physical evidence, Bryukhanov was not able to grasp the magnitude of the tragedy and rapidly dismissed it.

Watch the trailer for the gripping series "Chernobyl."

Are You Secretly Stereotyping?

October 25th

STEREOTYPING

Stereotypes exist when we think that a category of people always has certain characteristics or behaviors. The brain has a natural tendency to put things into groups. By grouping into categories, we can process our environments more efficiently. It is a mental shortcut that saves time and mental energy. Because of that, we might assume that certain stereotypes apply to a certain member of a group even though we know nothing about that individual.

You may consider yourself aware of your thoughts. Perhaps you like to think that you never hold prejudices, are never racist, and always treat people with fairness, regardless of their personal background. If this is what you're striving for, that's great!

But there's a detail that might burst your bubble. Whether we like it or not, we're all likely to stereotype people. This means we unconsciously form opinions about others based on what we know about the groups they belong to. Researchers developed a tool to prove exactly that: the Implicit Associations Test. This test was designed to help people detect unconscious stereotypes and biases they hold about others.

Research findings have shown that people commonly associate "young" with "good" or "old" with "bad." Studies have also found evidence that people attribute specific associations to nationalities, ethnicities, and religious groups. For example, many people might associate the UK with being "tradition-loving" or "conservative." However, in a recent study published in Nature, researchers suggest that these stereotypes do not indicate an unconscious "cognitive monster" within fair-minded people but are learned associations arising from the normal working of the predictive brain in everyday life.

We all make these associations at some point in our lives, even if our moral principles immediately silence these thoughts. You can detect your own unconscious biases and stereotyping by taking the Implicit Association Test online.

Take the Implicit Association Test yourself

Infidelity or Illusion?

October 26th

CONFIRMATION BIAS

Confirmation bias is our tendency to look for, acknowledge, favor, and remember information in a way that supports what we already think or believe. This bias occurs when we ignore information that contradicts our ideas or interpret ambiguous facts as evidence supporting our existing beliefs. Situations that involve emotionally charged topics, strongly held beliefs, or things we really want to happen are most susceptible to this bias.

Most of us have all been so suspicious of someone's behavior that their tiniest, most meaningless gestures take on a special valence. Let's say that you suspect your partner of cheating on you. Once the idea sprouts in your mind, you can never be fully objective again about your partner's actions. Suddenly, the five minutes they're late for dinner could feel like the end of the world. A message notification on their phone can mean that someone else is competing for their attention. Could all these signs mean something? Or is your brain distorting their proportions to fit the dramatic reality you've created with your cheating suspicions?

Statistically, infidelity rates vary by age and relationship status. Around 20% of married individuals admit to cheating, with the likelihood peaking for men in their 50s and 60s (28%) and women in the same age group at 17%.

While statistically speaking, the probability of a cheating partner is always there, do not despair. Confirmation bias can do an excellent job of distorting our perception of reality. If you become too fixated on a certain belief (in the current example, your partner being unfaithful), all the subsequent information you'll take in about your partner's actions will be filtered through this one belief. When we're convinced of a fact, our brain goes hunting for evidence to reinforce it over and over again. This means that you don't merely perceive your partner's being late as what it is; you see it as evidence that you are right about them cheating on you.

Believing negative things about your partner without evidence can cause unwarranted pain and damage the relationship's foundation.

Is Social Media Stardom One Post Away or a Pipe Dream?

October 27th

SURVIVORSHIP BIAS

Survivorship bias is the mental short-cut we take when we focus on a certain subgroup that made it through a selection process—the survivors—and ignore the ones that didn't—the failures. Because we don't pay equal attention to both survivors and failures, we might mistakenly assume that a shared trait of the survivors caused their survival. This seduces us to mistake correlation for causation.

Being an influencer or content creator may seem like easy money. From the outside, it looks like all you need to do is post some pictures and share some stories, and your wealth is guaranteed. However, the only reason some of us may hold such views is because we only see the winners of the attention economy among content creators. Due to survivorship bias, our attention is most likely to go to the "survivors," while we fail to consider those who consistently try to reach the top but never succeed.

According to HubSpot's 2024 State of Consumer Trends report, 21% of consumers consider themselves content creators or influencers, jumping up to 45% for Gen Zers and Millennials. The creator economy is estimated to be worth $104 billion, which is equivalent to Ethiopia's GDP. The industry is made up of people who make their own online content as well as bloggers, curators, influencers, and videographers who sell their content. Surveys indicate a disproportionately top-heavy economy, with only a small percentage of creators earning bigger paychecks. The creator economy strongly favors those at the top, with 95% of the entire money going to only 5% of influencers.

As a result of survivorship bias, Generation Z (children born after 2001) frequently sees content creation as a viable career option. In fact, one in four American kids wants to become a professional content creator, likely because they see only the shining 5% at the top, neglecting the 95% who tried and failed.

Read more about the income disparity distribution in the creator economy

Astro-Logic: When Science Checked the Stars

October 28th

BARNUM EFFECT

The Barnum effect describes how people accept vague, general personality descriptions as uniquely applicable to themselves, even though these descriptions could apply to almost anyone. This psychological phenomenon helps explain why horoscopes and personality readings feel personally relevant despite their generic nature.

Are Capricorns really ambitious and melancholic? Are Cancers truly warm-hearted and mysterious? A comprehensive Danish-German study in 2006 challenged these astrological assumptions by analyzing the personality traits of over 15,000 individuals – and found absolutely no connection between birth months and character traits.

We often read our horoscopes with a sense of recognition, nodding along as they seem to capture our essence perfectly. Yet, as the researchers discovered, this perceived accuracy is more about psychology than astronomy. Their research included a diverse dataset: over 4,000 middle-aged people and 11,000 young people aged 15-24, examining everything from intelligence quotients to personality profiles.

Take a typical horoscope line: "you are sociable but selective about your friendships." The researchers point out that such statements work because everyone, regardless of their zodiac sign, has experienced being both outgoing and reserved at different times. Out of our vast collection of life experiences, our brain readily finds memories that match these descriptions, creating a compelling illusion of personal relevance.

The study revealed that people who believe in astrology were more likely to report that their personalities matched their zodiac signs. This demonstrates how the Barnum effect works in tandem with our beliefs. When we expect to find meaning in our zodiac sign, we interpret vague character descriptions as uniquely personal insights.

The stars may shine bright, but they don't dictate our personality traits. The next time you read a horoscope that feels remarkably accurate, remember: it's not the position of celestial bodies that makes it resonate, but rather our human tendency to see ourselves in general descriptions crafted to fit everyone.

Do You Overestimate Your Household Heroics?

October 29th

AVAILABILITY BIAS

The availability bias is our tendency to make decisions based on information that comes to mind quickly and easily. It's a mental shortcut that gives more weight to information that was learned recently or that is easy to remember, for example, because it is an emotionally loaded memory. Our brain wants to save mental energy. So, we often go with the first information that comes to mind instead of putting in more mental effort to dig deeper.

When it comes to taking credit for something, we are more likely to notice our contribution to a group task than other people's. This is why, in group projects, we feel that our efforts are more significant or that our contribution was better. At home, when splitting house chores, we often think we do more work than our partners. But if we ask them, our spouses seem to have the same opinion about themselves - they are the ones who always do more work.

Conduct your own experiment and ask each member of a household, "How much percent of the house chores do you do?" You will almost always obtain a total of greater than 100%.

In a study, pairs of husbands and wives were asked to rate the contributions they made to each activity in the house. The researchers found that most pairs overestimated their contributions, which meant that at least one of the spouses was overestimating their responsibility for daily chores. Out of 37 couples, 27 showed a degree of overestimation of effort, which can be explained by availability bias. Each person has more access in their memory to the chores they complete themselves and remembers them more vividly. On the other hand, they might not pay attention each time the other person takes the trash out or does something around the house.

Therefore, the next time we feel biased about our contributions to daily tasks, let's remember that availability bias makes it easier for us to notice and remember the things we do ourselves than those performed by others.

What Does the Media Contribute to Gender Stereotypes?

October 30th

GENDER BIAS

Gender bias refers to a widely held set of implicit biases that discriminate against one gender. These biases include stereotypes like men being more logical and women more emotional. When there are no gender indicators, people often default to assuming subjects are male. Gender bias also manifests in double standards used to judge behavior - for instance, when men are praised for their sexual activities while women are derogated.

The things we hear and read about men and women have an impact on how we perceive gender differences. One important aspect of gender bias that you might not have considered so far is the contexts used in the media to discuss women and men. A recent study analyzed how the media uses language differently when quoting men versus women.

The researchers behind this study used some clever techniques to analyze a massive amount of news articles - over 600,000 in total - from seven major Canadian news outlets. They used a tool that can automatically spot when people are quoted in news stories and figure out if they're men or women. They looked closely at the actual words used in articles that quote mostly women compared to those that quote mostly men. By doing this for two years' worth of news (from 2018 to 2020), they were able to spot some clear patterns in how men and women are represented differently across various news topics.

They found that news articles use different words and verb-object combinations when discussing women, and these are also quoted in different contexts than men's. For instance, women are frequently mentioned on topics related to lifestyle, healthcare, entertainment, and sexual assault. When cited as experts, women are mostly quoted on emotional and subjective matters, compared to men, who speak on topics like politics and business. Whenever they do appear in these topics, women will speak as citizens, not as experts. Women's position as caretakers and men's status as leaders and breadwinners are reinforced in the media. This happens through more frequent references to female sources in caregiving roles and male sources in political and economic responsibilities.

Do Happy Endings Outweigh Unpleasant Beginnings?

October 31st

PEAK–END RULE

The peak-end rule states that we tend to judge an experience based on the most intense moment as well as how the experience ended. The overall memory of the experience will be based on the average of the peak moment and the end. This bias happens because we remember events in snapshots rather than in their entirety. Furthermore, we remember things better when they are emotionally intense (the peak) or more recent (the end).

Picture this: you're about to have a colonoscopy, involving the insertion of a long, flexible tube into the rectum. Unpleasant, right? Researchers used this situation to uncover something remarkable about human memory.

During colonoscopies, patients rated their pain every minute. The study focused on two groups: Group A had shorter procedures ending with high pain, while Group B had longer procedures finishing with less discomfort. Surprisingly, Group B - despite longer procedures and more total discomfort - rated the experience as less unpleasant than Group A. Researchers then extended some procedures for patients in Group A by a few minutes, causing mild additional discomfort. Result? These patients had a better memory of the experience, despite more time in discomfort.

This reveals our brains don't simply "add up" all moments of an experience. We tend to remember the most intense part (the peak) and the ending. This explains why a mediocre vacation can be saved by an amazing final day, or a bad ending can taint a good experience. Patients with longer procedures and more tolerable endings perceived less overall pain, considered the procedure less invasive, and were about 50% more likely to return for follow-ups.

This peak-end bias means we evaluate experiences based on peak feelings and endings, not averages. If doctors can make procedures more pleasant at the end, patients may have better overall impressions and be more willing to return for check-ups - though making any medical procedure pleasant remains challenging.

Watch Daniel Kahneman's TED Talk about the riddle of experience vs. memory

∞
NOVEMBER

Feeling Sick? Should You Got for an Early Doctor's Appointment?

November 1st

DECISION FATIGUE

Decision fatigue is the mental exhaustion that comes from having to make a lot of complex decisions in a short amount of time. It is similar to using a muscle that becomes more fatigued the more we use it in a short period. This happens because our brain has a limited amount of mental energy and willpower to use for making decisions. This phenomenon can be caused by external factors such as stress and lack of sleep and can lead to difficulty concentrating, irritability, and impulsive behavior.

Decision fatigue can affect various aspects of our lives, including – perhaps surprisingly – healthcare and the type of medicine prescribed by physicians. One revealing study has found that clinicians tend to prescribe more antibiotics later in their shift when they become more tired. This is a direct consequence of decision fatigue, which occurs after repeated decision-making processes. Clinicians who see many patients during their shift are more likely to make effective decisions in the first few hours of work than towards the end of their shift.

The research study tested this idea on clinicians who prescribe antibiotics for acute respiratory infections. Although antibiotic prescription is a common practice, evidence shows that it is not highly effective when used excessively. Therefore, doctors are advised to avoid prescribing antibiotics when alternative treatment options exist. Well-rested clinicians are more likely to follow these guidelines and prescribe antibiotics only when necessary.

However, the more decisions clinicians make, the less they can resist prescribing antibiotics for respiratory infections. When clinicians are fatigued, their decision-making process is more likely to be influenced by patient demand, fear of complications, or the desire to conclude patient visits quickly. This can lead to unnecessary antibiotic prescriptions. Results from 23 different practices showed that antibiotic prescriptions increased throughout the day as clinicians became more fatigued. Doctors were 24% more likely to prescribe antibiotics in the last hours of their shift compared to the first ones.

For the best medical decisions, schedule your appointments with doctors earlier in their shifts when they are less fatigued.

Pain Relief or Mind Trick?

November 2nd

ILLUSIONS OF CAUSALITY

The illusion of causality occurs when we erroneously perceive a cause-and-effect relationship between two events. Assessing evidence requires cognitive effort, so our brain seeks mental shortcuts to expedite the process. This cognitive bias leads us to hastily infer a causal connection, even if there is none. This stems from our evolutionary need to comprehend the causes of events quickly in our surroundings for the sake of survival.

How can you tell if a treatment is working? While many rely on perceived health improvements, this perception can be misleading. The placebo effect, a prime example of the illusion of causality, demonstrates how your belief in a treatment's effectiveness can influence your perception of symptom improvement, creating a false sense of cause and effect.

Rory Sutherland, Vice Chairman of the renowned marketing firm Ogilvy, is an avid proponent of placebo effects and offers a compelling perspective. He suggests that Western societies struggle with accepting the placebo effect as a significant component of medicine. Yet research tells a different story: blue sleeping pills are perceived as more effective, and painkillers are believed to work better when they are red or priced higher.

However, this phenomenon isn't just theoretical; it has real-world implications. Take this example from Australia: Nurofen, a pain reliever manufacturer, capitalized on this effect by selling chemically identical versions of their medication but marketing them as being specifically for menstrual pain or back pain. These specialized painkillers were priced higher, likely leveraging the perception that higher-priced medications are more effective. The consumer rights council took the company to court to halt this practice, and they prevailed.

Due to the placebo effect, charging more for a drug that pretends to specifically treat back pain could potentially be more effective. However, the company was essentially charging a premium for an identical product. What do you think? Is it ethically sound or questionable?

Watch Rory Sutherland talk about why everything is a placebo

To Choose or Not to Choose: Are Defaults Draining Your Wallet?

November 3rd

DEFAULT EFFECT

When offered a choice that has a pre-selected default option, we tend to choose this default option. This is called the default effect. Defaults are the options that take effect if we do nothing. Our brains try to save as much mental energy as possible. Accepting the default option saves energy because we don't have to think about the pros and cons of each choice.

Our brains are wired to economize mental energy. This predisposition often leads us to choose the path of least resistance—accepting the default option. While this default effect can be beneficial, it's also a double-edged sword. On one hand, it spares us from expending time and cognitive resources on weighing the pros and cons of each available option. On the other hand, it can lead to potential drawbacks.

One such instance is the default option for bank overdrafts. This feature could be inadvertently used if account holders are not vigilant, resulting in them spending more money than is available and incurring substantial fees. Many banks had this option set as a default, and it has proven to be a lucrative revenue stream for them. In 2009 alone, banks generated $38.5 billion in fees from overdrawn accounts. Each instance of exceeding the debit card limit resulted in additional fees and interest. However, it's worth noting that most people would have preferred to forgo the overdraft option had they been given the choice, but the convenience of the default setting led them to accept it.

While some countries continue to have this default overdraft option, others, like the United States, have implemented regulations to protect bank customers. The US Federal Reserve now mandates that banks cannot automatically enroll customers in overdraft services. Instead, customers must explicitly opt-in if they want transactions to be approved when their account lacks sufficient funds. If customers don't opt-in, transactions will be declined when there's insufficient balance, protecting them from unexpected overdraft fees. This measure helps to mitigate the costly implications of the default effect in such scenarios.

Read about the Federal Reserve banning overdraft penalties

Is Patience Really a Virtue Or Just a Way to Get More Candy?

November 4th

HYPERBOLIC DISCOUNTING

Hyperbolic discounting is our tendency to favor more immediate payoffs in comparison to later payoffs. We do prefer the immediate reward, even when it is objectively less valuable. We all make decisions today that we would have preferred not to have made in the future due to hyperbolic discounting. Our brains are hardwired to do so because immediate reward meant a better chance of survival in evolutionary terms.

What drives us to reject instant gratification, like eating sweets, when waiting promises a larger reward? It turns out that multiple factors influence our ability to delay gratification.

To explore this phenomenon, researchers devised a clever experiment. Picture this: a child sits in a room with a marshmallow on the table. They're told if they can wait 15 minutes without eating it, they'll get two marshmallows instead. This is the famous Marshmallow experiment. Children were given a choice: eat one treat now or wait for two later. Some kids were offered toys or fun tasks to think about while waiting. Others weren't promised any reward at all.

The study results showed that children were more willing to wait the full 15 minutes when they were promised the reward they desired. In contrast, children who weren't promised a reward showed less willingness to wait and called for the experiment to end sooner. The availability of distractions significantly influenced their ability to wait. Those who were offered toys or fun tasks to think of were more likely to wait.

The Marshmallow experiment, although done on schoolchildren, is an excellent example of our innate tendency to favor immediate rewards when a longer-term reward is not guaranteed. People are willing to sacrifice present-moment gratification, but only when there is a bigger reward in the future. It also matters whether we have some strategies to divert our minds from the immediate reward; otherwise, saying no to the marshmallow in front of us becomes difficult.

Interestingly, follow-up studies linked this childhood ability to delay gratification with adult success, including higher test scores, healthier weight, and better educational outcomes.

Is the Earth Flat?

November 5th

ILLUSORY TRUTH EFFECT

The illusory truth effect causes us to believe information is true if we hear it repeatedly, even when it's not. This happens because repeatedly hearing the same information makes it familiar, and our brain processes familiar things more easily. This ease is due to the activation of well-established neural pathways, which require less effort to process than new or unfamiliar information. When our brains process information with less effort, we tend to interpret this ease as a sign of truth. Thus, if something is easier to understand, we are more likely to believe it's true.

The flat Earth theory, which has gained popularity recently, is a prime example of the illusory truth effect in action. This cognitive bias suggests that we are more likely to believe false information if we hear it often enough. In the age of social media, where misinformation spreads quickly, the flat Earth theory has found a new lease on life, despite overwhelming scientific evidence to the contrary.

According to Google Trends, there has been a significant increase in interest in flat Earth theories since 2015. This resurgence can be partially attributed to prominent figures like Mark K. Sargent and his movie "Flat Earth Clues." Also, a YouGov survey showed that up to 1 in 6 Americans are not sure if the world is round, and a survey of more than 2,000 Brazilian adults showed that 7% of people think the earth is flat.

One issue is the volume of content about the flat Earth theory. One study found that pro-flat Earth videos on YouTube significantly outnumbered debunking videos. The pro-flat Earth videos were also almost twice as long on average and more likely to include conspiracy ideation, science denial, and religious thought.

The illusory truth effect plays a crucial role in the spread of misinformation, like the flat Earth theory. As people encounter this information repeatedly, it becomes more familiar and easier to process. The more people speak, tweet, or make videos about the flat Earth theory, the more the message is repeated, and the more people come to believe it. The modern revival of flat Earth beliefs, despite overwhelming scientific evidence to the contrary, illustrates how repetition can lend credibility to false ideas.

The Billion-Dollar Streaming Dream?

November 6th

OVERCONFIDENCE EFFECT

We speak of the overconfidence effect when our subjective confidence in our judgments is higher than their objective accuracy. We can overestimate a variety of things, including our own performance or likelihood of success, our abilities in comparison to others, and the certainty of our answers or judgments.

Sometimes, the combination of deep expertise and abundant resources can lead to spectacular failures due to overconfidence. The story of Quibi, a short-form streaming platform, perfectly illustrates this phenomenon. Led by Jeffrey Katzenberg, a former Disney executive and DreamWorks co-founder, and Meg Whitman, former CEO of eBay and HP, Quibi launched in April 2020 with $1.75 billion in funding and the backing of major Hollywood studios.

The founders' impressive track records and deep industry knowledge led them to severely overestimate their likelihood of success – a classic manifestation of the overconfidence effect. They convinced investors to pour nearly two billion dollars into the venture before launch, secured deals with A-list celebrities, and boldly predicted 7.4 million subscribers in their first year.

When industry experts questioned whether users would pay for mobile-only content when platforms like YouTube and TikTok were free, the founders remained steadfast in their vision. Quibi's leadership was so convinced of their concept that they didn't even allow users to take screenshots or share clips on social media – features that had become fundamental to modern streaming success and were key drivers of TikTok's viral growth.

The platform shut down just six months after launch, having attracted only 500,000 subscribers – less than 7% of their projected goal. Quibi's premium short-form experiment ended in one of the fastest and most expensive failures in entertainment history.

This case demonstrates how even the most experienced leaders and seasoned investors can fall victim to the overconfidence effect, leading them to vastly overestimate the likelihood of success based on past achievements and expertise.

When Expectations Price Our Reality?

November 7th

ANCHORING BIAS

Anchoring bias occurs when a specific reference point, or "anchor", influences our decision-making process. This anchor could be a number or any other kind of cue, even if it is completely unrelated to the decision at hand. Despite this, we often use the anchor as a starting point and adjust our decisions or judgments from there, without realizing it. As a result, our final estimates, decisions, or judgments can be significantly different from what they might have been without the influence of the anchor.

In 2010, Apple was about to release its first iPad. Before the announcement, rumors suggested the device would cost around $999. Tech journalists debated whether consumers would pay that much for what was essentially a big iPhone, and the public largely accepted this price point given Apple's premium positioning.

During the keynote, Steve Jobs addressed these expectations: "When we set out to develop the iPad, we not only had very ambitious technical goals and user interface goals, but we had a very aggressive price goal because we want to put this in the hands of lots of people." He acknowledged the expected "under $1,000, which is code for $999," then announced: "I am thrilled to announce to you that the iPad pricing starts not at $999, but at $499." The audience erupted in applause.

This is a masterclass in anchoring bias. By allowing the $999 rumor to circulate for months, Apple had effectively anchored consumers to expect a much higher price. Had they never let this anchor set in, the $499 price tag might have seemed expensive for a device that couldn't even make phone calls. Instead, as Jobs pointed out, "a lot of people can afford an iPad" – a statement that felt true only because of the psychological relief from the higher anchor price.

Steve Jobs didn't just launch a tablet that day – he demonstrated how thoroughly modern marketing understands human psychology. The real genius wasn't just making $499 feel cheap – it was showing how easily our perception of value can be manipulated.

Watch Steve Jobs reveal the price for the iPad

Do Good Deeds Get You a Divine Upgrade?

November 8th

JUST WORLD HYPOTHESIS

The Just World Hypothesis is the belief that the world is just and fair, and that people get what they deserve. This means that if someone is experiencing bad things, it is because they have done something to deserve it and are punished. On the other hand, if someone is successful or happy, it is because they made good choices and are rewarded. This idea can be comforting because it gives us a sense of control over our lives and the belief that we can influence our own outcomes.

The Just World Hypothesis posits that people believe in a world where good deeds are rewarded and bad deeds are punished. This idea is reflected in the way the afterlife is depicted in various mythologies, such as Egyptian, Christian, Nordic, and Greek.

In Egyptian mythology, the Judgment of Osiris involves weighing the deceased's heart against the feather of Maat, symbolizing truth and justice. A lighter heart indicates a virtuous life, granting the soul eternal life in the afterlife. Ammit, a hybrid creature with the head of a crocodile, the body of a lion, and the hindquarters of a hippopotamus, will eat the soul if it has a heavier heart, which denotes sin and injustice. Christian mythology focuses on Heaven and Hell. Righteous individuals are rewarded with eternal life in heaven, while sinners who reject God's grace face eternal torment in hell. Nordic mythology presents Valhalla, where honorable fallen warriors are welcomed, and Helheim, a cold, gloomy realm for those who died of illness or old age. Greek mythology portrays Hades, where souls are judged and assigned their afterlife fate. Virtuous and heroic souls enjoy eternal happiness in Elysium, while wrongdoers are condemned to Tartarus. Neutral souls dwell in the Asphodel Meadows.

The prevalence of the Just World Hypothesis in afterlife narratives demonstrates its enduring significance across human societies. This idea has shaped moral frameworks since ancient times and continues to influence modern thinking. Even in today's secular societies, the popular notion that "what goes around comes around" - the belief that one's actions will eventually have consequences of a similar nature - reflects the persistent impact of this hypothesis on our worldview.

Beginning of ingroup bias

November 9th

INGROUP BIAS

Ingroup bias is when we like and support people who are part of our own group more than people who are not part of our group. These groups can be divided based on seemingly trivial observable traits. This is rooted in the intrinsic human need for a group identity, which provides a sense of belonging and purpose. Additionally, we all have a desire to feel good about ourselves, and one way to achieve that is to see our own group as being superior to others.

In our everyday lives, we often find ourselves favoring those who are part of our own group, whether they are family, friends, colleagues, or even supporters of our favorite sports team. This phenomenon is a fascinating aspect of human behavior and a universal trait that we all share.

One of the most compelling studies that demonstrates ingroup bias was conducted by researcher Henri Tajfel in 1970. His experiment became a classic example of what social psychologists call the "minimal group paradigm" - a methodology used to investigate the minimal conditions required for discrimination between groups. In Tajfel's experiment, groups of boys were asked to estimate the number of dots in clusters flashed on a screen. The researchers then divided the boys into groups based on their estimates. While these groups were entirely arbitrary and had no real-world significance, what followed was remarkable. When the boys were asked to distribute rewards between two anonymous individuals - one from their group (ingroup) and one from the other group (outgroup) - they consistently favored their own group members.

This behavior emerged even without any apparent conflict of interest or previous history of hostility. The boys demonstrated a clear preference for their own group members simply because they identified with that group, despite the group formation being based on an insignificant task.

Are You Giving Yourself Too Much Credit?

November 10th

SELF-SERVING BIAS

The self-serving bias is our tendency to take credit for good things that happen to us and blame other things or people for bad things that happen. We do that because we have the desire to feel good about ourselves. Being responsible for good things happening boosts our confidence and gives us a sense of control in our lives. When we blame external factors for bad things that happen to us, it can help us feel better about ourselves by protecting our ego.

We've all had that feeling at least once. You're playing a board or card game, and you win. After you win, you feel like you can't even comprehend your genius. On the other hand, when you lose, you may think that anyone but you is at fault. Whether the game mechanics are broken or other people cheated in some way, your skills seem impeccable. That is the self-serving bias, a tendency to attribute our success to ourselves and our failures to someone or something else.

This way, we feel better about ourselves and who we are. We overemphasize our abilities to influence outcomes and underestimate external effects. Conversely, when something bad happens, we attribute it to bad luck or external factors.

The self-serving bias is observed in different areas, particularly in sports but also in the workplace environment. In one study, wrestlers who won were more likely to attribute their success to their abilities. On the other hand, the wrestlers who lost did not see this link between their abilities and the outcome of the competition. In another study, people were more likely to attribute their hiring to their characteristics and blame external factors when they were fired.

While this bias may make us feel better about ourselves, it can be a major threat to self-growth. If you never evaluate your skills and never realize that success sometimes is a matter of luck, then you will find it very hard to motivate yourself to try to do things differently.

Are You Falling for the Rule of 100 in Retail Sales?

November 11th

FRAMING EFFECT

The framing effect occurs when we draw different conclusions from identical information based solely on how that information is presented. This can happen when something is framed either positively or negatively, or as a gain versus a loss - we naturally tend to avoid losses in such situations. Our judgment can also shift depending on which features of the information are highlighted, even though the underlying facts remain exactly the same.

What sounds more appealing to you: 10% off or a $120 discount? When we think about discounts, we often pay more attention to how the information is presented than to what it says. This is called the framing effect, a bias that makes us pay more attention to how certain information is presented than to the facts behind it.

Consider the following scenario: You want to buy a new Apple Mac that is currently on sale in stores. In one shop, they display the offer as "10% off all MacBooks." While browsing for other options, you find a different offer in a store that offers $120 off for the same MacBook. If you are like most people, you'll probably go with the second option. Even if, in theory, the discounted price is the same, saving $120 sounds better than just 10%. This is how the framing effect works. The same information can be laid out in different ways, which can lead to different outcomes or interpretations.

In retail, the scenario above is called "the rule of 100." This says that any discount for items with prices below $100 is more convincing when presented as a percentage. For example, a 10% discount on a $10 item is more appealing than a $1 discount. In contrast, goods over $100 have a different rule. An item worth $500 will look way more appealing when presented as $50 off rather than 10% off.

So, the next time a discount makes you want to buy something, stop and think about how the discount was framed.

Are We Misjudging Our Own Happiness?

November 12th

PRIMING EFFECT

The priming effect occurs when something we see or hear influences our thoughts or actions without us being aware of it. This can happen with words, pictures, or sounds we encounter. When our brain is primed, it becomes easier for us to think about, remember, and act on related information because the things we read, see, or hear activate connected information in the brain.

Think about these two questions: "On a scale from 1 to 10, how happy are you with your life?" and "How many dates have you had recently?" In a study, researchers asked people these questions, varying their order to test how one answer might influence the other. Sometimes they asked about happiness first, then dates. Other times, they reversed the order.

Here's what they found: When they asked about happiness first, there seemed to be no link between how happy people said they were and how many dates they had. But when they asked about dates first, suddenly there appeared to be a strong connection. People who had been on more dates rated themselves as much happier, but only if they were asked about dates before happiness! When asked about happiness first, even people who had lots of dates didn't report higher happiness levels.

What happened here? The number of dates strongly influenced people's happiness ratings, but only when they thought about dates first. This reveals something about how we think: our judgments are often influenced by information we've just considered, without us realizing it.

Simply thinking about their dating life right before evaluating overall happiness caused people to see a strong connection between the two, even though this connection didn't exist when the questions were asked in the other order. This clearly demonstrates the priming effect. The date question primed people's minds, making their dating life more influential in their happiness evaluation. It shows how our brains overemphasize recent information when making judgments, even if it's not directly related to the question. As a result, our views on complex issues like life satisfaction can be unconsciously swayed by whatever thoughts are fresh in our minds at the moment.

What Would You Do to Prevent a Possible Pandemic?

November 13th

HINDSIGHT BIAS

The hindsight bias is also called the "I-knew-it-all-along" effect. It describes the retrospective overestimation of predictability. In the present, it's hard to tell how something will turn out in the future, but is easy to understand how or why an event happened in retrospect. This bias happens because we mistakenly assume that we had the same understanding of an event before it happened as we do after it happened.

The 1976 swine flu outbreak in the United States prompted a nationwide vaccination campaign in response to the fear of a new pandemic. However, when the outbreak turned out to be less severe than anticipated, critics claimed that the vaccination program was unnecessary. This event serves as a prime example of hindsight bias.

In 1976, the Centers for Disease Control and Prevention (CDC) were asked to identify a new illness that was spreading. After testing the throat cultures of infected people, the CDC found evidence of the H1N1 virus, commonly known as swine flu. This strain was responsible for the 1918-19 flu pandemic, which killed millions of people. Scientists evaluated the possibility of a new H1N1 pandemic and presented the information to the U.S. Congress. As a result, President Gerald Ford asked Congress for funds to vaccinate everyone in the United States.

The vaccination campaign faced challenges, including a rare paralysis affecting one in every 100,000 people who got the swine flu vaccine, leading to the program's halt. Fortunately, the virus did not propagate, and a pandemic was prevented. Critics of the vaccination campaign claimed that it was unnecessary, given the less severe nature of the outbreak. However, this assertion is an example of hindsight bias, as it judges past decisions based on current knowledge. At the time, public health officials were confronted with the potential of a pandemic akin to the 1918-19 pandemic and made decisions based on the information at hand. As the saying goes, "There is no glory in prevention."

Genes, Circumstances, or Choices: What Is Steering Your Happiness?

November 14th

ILLUSION OF CONTROL

The illusion of control occurs when we believe we have more control over external events than we do. We frequently believe we have (or had) some control over events that are actually random. Researchers have found that people who feel in control will engage in healthier behaviors, feel less stress, and have better overall mental health. Therefore, this illusion makes us feel better about ourselves and the world around us, but it can also seduce us into relying on superstitions.

To what extent do we actually control our happiness? According to a 2005 research study, there are three main factors that determine long-term subjective happiness: 10% of life circumstances, 50% genetic set point, and 40% of intentional activity.

Each person has a genetically determined "happiness set point" that's difficult to change. Twin studies support this: identical twins (100% shared genes) show similar happiness levels even when raised apart, while fraternal twins (50% shared genes) exhibit much less similarity. This demonstrates a strong genetic influence on our happiness set point.

Life circumstances like where we live, our age, how much money we have accumulated have a small impact on happiness (about 10%) because we adapt quickly. We can control our happiness to a small degree by changing our circumstances, but a temporary boost or drop in happiness will likely fade over time due to adaptation.

Intentional activity refers to the things we do and think in our daily lives. This can influence well-being through behavior (e.g., exercise), cognitive activity (e.g., positive reframing), and voluntary activity (e.g., pursuing personal goals). We have significant control over this 40%, choosing how to spend our time and what thoughts to think.

While our genetic predisposition to happiness is largely fixed, our daily actions and choices significantly impact our well-being. The illusion of control plays a crucial role here. Feeling in control of our intentional activities, even if sometimes overestimated, boosts our happiness and motivation. This positive illusion encourages us to engage more fully in beneficial behaviors and thoughts, potentially leading to real improvements in our happiness.

Are You Stuck in a Sunk-Cost Romance?

November 15th

SUNK COST FALLACY

The sunk cost fallacy is when we make a decision based on how much we have already invested in something rather than on whether it is the best choice for us right now. When we feel like we have already invested a lot in something, we feel like we would be losing something if we were to let it go. Another reason that the sunk cost fallacy occurs is because we tend to focus on the past rather than the present when we make decisions.

Ever wondered why some relationships, which clearly seem to have run their course, still continue? We've all been there, or at least witnessed others who have. The more time, money, and effort we pour into a relationship, the harder it becomes to walk away—a classic example of the sunk cost fallacy. After all, who wants to see all that investment go to waste? Sometimes, putting in extra effort is necessary, perhaps when a relationship has been neglected. However, sometimes we're just holding on because we've invested so much already.

An intriguing study conducted in 2016 examined how the sunk-cost fallacy influences relationship decisions. In the first experiment, participants were presented with a scenario of an unhappy relationship and asked to choose: stay or leave? What's fascinating is that people were more likely to stay if they had invested money and effort, but not necessarily time. The second experiment revealed even more insights. When researchers focused on time investment and asked participants how much longer they would be willing to continue an unhappy relationship, they found that the more time people had already invested, the more additional time they were willing to commit—even when unhappy.

It's important to understand that investing substantial time, effort, and money into a relationship doesn't necessarily mean it's the best choice for our future. While the time we've already spent cannot be recovered, we can save our future time for healthier relationships.

Read a blog post of one of my favorite authors on this topic

How Do You Make Vegetables More Appealing to Children?

November 16th

IKEA EFFECT

The IKEA effect refers to our tendency to place a disproportionately high value on objects that we helped create, such as IKEA furniture. We do that regardless of the quality of the end product. This bias helps us to feel better about ourselves in two ways. First, we want to feel that our effort was well invested and that we did not waste our time but instead created something of value. Secondly, creating things makes us feel more competent.

If you happen to be raising children who are extremely fussy with food and would never eat their vegetables, here's something that might help you. The IKEA effect suggests that people tend to value things more when they have put some personal effort into them. This psychological principle is partly what makes IKEA so popular. As it turns out, people don't simply like an end product—they like to feel they contributed to it in some way.

Why not apply this same principle to your child who seems determined to hate vegetables? There is compelling research evidence showing that this could be a successful approach. In a longitudinal study conducted over a 10-month period, 924 parent-child pairs were instructed to cook together to test whether this increased children's liking of vegetables. At the end of the experiment, children's preference for and intake of vegetables increased simply because they were involved in the meal preparation process—a clear demonstration of the IKEA effect. While the same improvement wasn't observed in parents' preferences for vegetables, that wasn't the primary focus of the study.

Therefore, if you have tried everything to make vegetables more appealing to your little ones, consider taking advantage of the IKEA effect by involving them in meal preparation.

You Probably Don't Understand Your Dog

November 17th

ANTHROPOMORPHISM

Anthropomorphism is our natural tendency to attribute human traits, emotions, and intentions to non-humans, for example, animals, gods, natural forces, and the like. We do this because we naturally know more about human traits than non-human ones. Therefore, these come easier to mind, and that saves mental energy.

If you read the headlines in 1961, chances are you didn't miss the comical picture of Ham the chimpanzee, the first hominid to go to space. The image left few people without a reaction, as it displayed Ham posing with pride on his first journey into space. Just imagine a chimpanzee cramped into a tiny capsule, all buckled up to go to space. You can only think, "How much fun he must have had!"

In fact, what most people commented on about the picture was how happy and proud the chimpanzee looked when he accomplished such a significant milestone. Of course, it is hard not to attribute any emotion to Ham's happy face. But if you gave the picture a second thought, you would soon remember that perhaps he wasn't even aware of where he was. Perhaps he couldn't even care less about going to space. Upon closer inspection, this wasn't far from the truth. Ham's expression of excitement and pride, as commonly interpreted by commentators, was nothing but a manifestation of fear. In chimpanzees, facial expressions that resemble happiness in humans indicate a "fear grin." Yet, few of Ham the chimpanzee's fans were ready to spot that.

Our anthropomorphic tendencies, well embedded in our psyche, generalize human-like traits and emotional expressions to species that manifest very differently from us. This is because our brains do not suddenly question, "How does fear manifest in non-primates?" when seeing a picture of an animal with a grin. We just see a grin, and we think "happiness." This automatic interpretation stems from our brain's preference for familiar patterns and quick categorizations, leading us to engage in anthropomorphism by projecting our own emotional experiences onto others, even when those others are not human.

Watch a video of Ham's journey

Does Sugar Really Turn Kids into Tiny Tornadoes?

November 18th

ILLUSORY TRUTH EFFECT

The illusory truth effect causes us to believe information is true if we hear it repeatedly, even when it's not. This happens because repeatedly hearing the same information makes it familiar, and our brain processes familiar things more easily. This ease is due to the activation of well-established neural pathways, which require less effort to process than new or unfamiliar information. When our brains process information with less effort, we tend to interpret this ease as a sign of truth. Thus, if something is easier to understand, we are more likely to believe it's true.

We've heard it from our parents, seen it in movies, read it in parenting magazines, and shared it at countless birthday parties: The idea that sugar makes kids hyperactive. "Don't give them too much sugar, they'll go crazy!" The message is everywhere, repeated so often that questioning it feels almost strange.

Think about how this belief gets reinforced. Every parent has told another parent about it. Every teacher has warned about sugary snacks before nap time. Every lifestyle article about healthy eating mentions the dreaded "sugar rush." Each repetition makes the idea feel more true, more reliable, more obvious.

What's fascinating is that when scientists actually studied this connection - not just once, but in 23 different scientific studies - they all reached the same conclusion: there is absolutely no link between sugar consumption and hyperactivity in children. But here's the thing - this scientific finding feels harder to accept than the familiar story we've heard hundreds of times. The myth about sugar and hyperactivity just feels right because we've processed this information so many times before.

This perfectly showcases how the illusory truth effect works in our daily lives. We're not believing the sugar-hyperactivity link because we've carefully examined the evidence. We're believing it because we've heard it so often that our brains process it effortlessly, mistaking that ease for truth.

Is the "Woke" Movement a Groupthink Dynamic?

November 19th

GROUPTHINK

Groupthink is when our desire for harmony and conformity within a group leads to dysfunctional decision-making. Group members prioritize agreement over critical evaluation, resulting in a loss of individual creativity and thinking. This can lead to an inflated sense of confidence in the group's abilities, an undervaluation of opponents, group pressure, and potentially harmful actions towards outsiders.

The "woke" movement has emerged as a prominent force advocating for social justice, particularly in addressing issues like racism, sexism, and the recognition of diverse gender identities. However, left-leaning philosopher Slavoj Žižek offers a critical perspective on this phenomenon. He argues that the movement, while well-intentioned in its pursuit of social justice, may inadvertently perpetuate the very issues it seeks to resolve.

A key concern raised by Žižek is the movement's inclination towards establishing a moral high ground. This approach often manifests in the form of a rigid ethical stance on various social issues, such as proclaiming a definitive "correct" way to confront racism or gender inequality. This moral certitude not only stifles dissent but also fosters an environment where questioning the dominant narrative is viewed as morally reprehensible. A notable manifestation of this tendency is the phenomenon of "cancel culture," where individuals or groups are publicly shamed for dissenting opinions. This practice exemplifies how the movement exhibits groupthink by demonizing opposing viewpoints, prioritizing unanimous agreement over critical evaluation.

A 2022 survey found 84 percent of adults view speech suppression due to fear of retaliation as a serious concern. This highlights how the movement's rigid moral stances discourage open dialogue, with widespread fear of backlash stifling free expression. Žižek argues that this self-censorship undermines the movement's goal of inclusivity. By inhibiting the free exchange of ideas, the environment may paradoxically hinder the very understanding and inclusivity the movement aims to promote.

Read "Wokeness Is Here To Stay" by Slavoj Žižek

Are Teachers Misreading the Behavior of Struggling Students?

November 20th

HALO EFFECT

The halo effect is a type of cognitive bias in which our overall opinion of a person or brand affects how we feel about the specific qualities of that person or brand. If we have a good feeling about something as a whole, we are more likely to think that its individual parts are good as well. We do that because it saves cognitive effort to use our overall impressions as a shortcut to make judgments rather than evaluating each aspect of something separately.

Have you noticed how one impression can influence how you view everything else about a person? This is the halo effect - our initial judgment about a single trait affects how we perceive other characteristics.

A fascinating 2021 study revealed how this effect might be influencing teachers' perceptions of their students. The researchers followed first-grade classrooms to examine whether teachers' views of students' reading abilities were affecting how they judged these same students' behavior. To investigate this, they collected three key pieces of information: teachers' ratings of student behavior at the start of the year, teachers' assessments of reading skills mid-year, and both teacher ratings of behavior and objective reading tests they did with the students at year's end.

What they discovered was eye-opening. Teachers who thought a student was struggling with reading were also likely to report that the same student was misbehaving in class. But here's the interesting part: when researchers checked these students' actual reading abilities through standard tests, they found that most weren't acting out any more than their classmates. Put simply, the way teachers viewed a student's reading ability had a bigger influence on how they rated that student's behavior than how well the student could actually read.

This reveals a classic halo effect at work: teachers' early concerns about a student's reading abilities colored their later judgments about that student's classroom behavior. The study reminds us that even dedicated teachers can unconsciously let one perceived struggle influence their overall view of a student.

Where is the ice-free North Polar Sea?

November 21st

CONFIRMATION BIAS

Confirmation bias is our tendency to look for, acknowledge, favor, and remember information in a way that supports what we already think or believe. This bias occurs when we ignore information that contradicts our ideas or interpret ambiguous facts as evidence supporting our existing beliefs. Situations that involve emotionally charged topics, strongly held beliefs, or things we really want to happen are most susceptible to this bias.

The story of August Petermann, a 19th-century German cartographer who believed in and promoted the idea of an ice-free North Polar Sea, provides a striking example of confirmation bias.

Petermann was a celebrated cartographer of his time. His conviction in an ice-free passage to the North Pole led to numerous expeditions in search of this route. Petermann was convinced that, due to the influence of the Gulf Stream, the sea in that region would not completely freeze. He believed that even in winter, one would find an open, navigable sea up to the North Pole after penetrating the drift ice. He surrounded himself with other explorers and investors who supported his idea with money and resources. Even though there was plenty of evidence against the existence of such a passage, Petermann never stopped defending his theory. For example, when a German Arctic expedition encountered heavy pack ice east of Greenland, Petermann simply dismissed these findings by arguing that they had chosen the wrong route and that an ice-free passage must exist. Instead of adjusting his theory to match the new evidence, he reinterpreted the evidence to maintain his position. Despite numerous failed expeditions, he remained steadfast in his conviction. Petermann's reputation depended on proving his theory. Admitting he was wrong would have jeopardized his credibility.

The Jeannette expedition under the command of U.S. Navy Lieutenant George De Long was one tragic outcome of Petermann's confirmation bias. The ship became trapped in ice, and ultimately, the passengers saw their ship crushed. During their desperate attempt to get across the ice to Siberia, many crew members, including the commander De Long, died because of starvation, the cold, or because they drowned.

How to Make People Pay Taxes on Time?

November 22nd

BANDWAGON EFFECT

The bandwagon effect refers to the phenomenon in which a belief or behavior becomes more popular as more people adopt it. This can lead to a self-reinforcing cycle, as the increased popularity of the belief or behavior encourages more people to adopt it. The effect is caused by our desire to conform to social norms and our belief that the majority must be correct. It can also be caused by peer pressure and the fear of being left out or made fun of if we don't fit in.

How do you get people to comply with tax rules? You tell them that everyone is already doing it.

In 1995, the Minnesota Department of Revenue conducted an experiment called the Minnesota Income Tax Compliance Experiment. Nearly 50,000 households participated in this experiment. The department sent the following letter to 20,000 taxpayers, providing this information:

"According to a recent public opinion survey, many Minnesotans believe that other people routinely cheat on their taxes. This is not true, however. Audits by the Internal Revenue Service show that people who file tax returns report correctly and pay voluntarily 93 percent of the income taxes they owe. Most taxpayers file their returns accurately and on time."

The letter demonstrated that most people pay their taxes properly, making taxpayers more likely to comply since they believed this was the common behavior among their peers. If everyone pays their taxes correctly and on time, why would someone be the only person who doesn't? Not surprisingly, this letter was the most effective in increasing tax compliance. The experiment proved remarkably successful, estimating a total recoverable tax gap of $100-105 million, representing approximately 3% of Minnesota's $3.5 billion in state income taxes collected that fiscal year. The Minnesota tax authorities provided a clever example of how institutions can use bias as a kind of nudge to encourage a certain behavior, in this case, paying taxes.

Remember the Fyre Festival?

November 23rd

OSTRICH EFFECT OR NORMALCY BIAS

Normalcy bias, also known as "ostrich effect," makes us downplay warnings about dangers or ignore negative situations completely. We underestimate how likely it is that a disaster will happen and how it might affect us. We do that because we want to avoid an unpleasant emotional impact in the short term. The name comes from the popular (but false) belief that ostriches bury their heads in the sand when in danger.

The infamous Fyre Festival of April 2017 perfectly illustrates this phenomenon. Thousands of festivalgoers paid hefty sums for tickets to what was promoted as a high-end music event on a private island in the Bahamas. Instead, visitors encountered a disorganized, chaotic situation that left them stranded and dealing with deplorable conditions. The disaster was later documented in Netflix's "FYRE: The Greatest Party That Never Happened." The behavior of the festival's founder, Billy McFarland, became a textbook example of the ostrich effect.

The festival, which had promised luxury accommodations, gourmet cuisine, and a lineup of renowned musicians, left 5,000 people stranded in the Bahamas with nothing but inadequate tents, scarce food, and no musical performances. The ensuing chaos and outrage led to multiple lawsuits, and McFarland ultimately received a six-year prison sentence. He eventually pleaded guilty to scamming 80 investors who had funded the festival. After serving four years of his sentence, including two years in solitary confinement, McFarland was released in 2022.

In a post-release interview, McFarland admitted to deceiving investors who had collectively invested $26 million in the doomed Fyre Festival. He revealed that he had deliberately ignored staff warnings about the site's unpreparedness and the impossibility of executing such an event in just four months. McFarland confessed that he had been so fixated on moving quickly that he disregarded both the consequences of rushing and the numerous warnings from his team. His behavior perfectly exemplified the ostrich effect as he willfully ignored the obvious dangers and inevitable consequences of his actions.

Watch the trailer for FYRE

When Life Gives You Lemons:
Can Overconfidence Land You Behind Bars?

November 24th

DUNNING–KRUGER EFFECT

The Dunning–Kruger effect describes our tendency to overestimate our own abilities in areas that we are unskilled in or lack knowledge in. This happens when we know just enough to think we are great but not enough to tell the difference between good and bad. We just don't know yet what we could do better. The effect also applies to society as a whole. The most uninformed citizens are often also the most confident ones.

If you haven't encountered the intriguing story of McArthur Wheeler up to this point, now is your opportunity to witness a humorous and somewhat baffling illustration of the Dunning-Kruger effect in action.

In 1995, McArthur Wheeler, a self-proclaimed ingenious bank robber, daringly attempted to rob not one but two Pittsburgh banks in broad daylight. His face was slathered in nothing more than lemon juice as a disguise. Predictably, he was promptly arrested, a development that left Mr. Wheeler utterly dumbfounded. In his confusion, he blurted out, "But I wore the juice!" Regrettably for the ambitious criminal, his limited knowledge proved to be more hazardous than helpful. He possessed only fragments of information: lemon juice has the ability to make ink invisible, and thus, Wheeler naively concluded that applying it to his face would render him invisible as well. He had ample time to reconsider his flawed hypothesis during his subsequent 5-year incarceration.

The downfall of McArthur Wheeler can be attributed to his overconfidence in his knowledge. This misguided self-assurance led him to take swift, uninformed action without questioning the validity of his knowledge or conducting further research to support his assumptions.

This story shows us something important: when we're too sure of ourselves and our ideas, we can lose the ability to see where we might be wrong. Just like Wheeler couldn't see the obvious problems with his lemon juice plan, we sometimes can't spot the mistakes in our own thinking.

Read the Wikipedia article about McArthur Wheeler

Is Hypoxia Misleading Doctors in Infant Brain Damage Cases?

November 25th

ILLUSION OF VALIDITY

The illusion of validity is a cognitive bias where we overestimate our ability to understand and predict an outcome based on the information we have. When analyzing new information, we rely on things we already know, for example, stereotypes and prior beliefs. When we assume that what we know is valid enough to predict what will happen in different contexts, we make confident predictions that can turn out to be utterly inaccurate.

In 2017, a fascinating study shed light on a common misunderstanding in the medical field related to a specific type of brain damage in newborns. This condition is often labeled "hypoxic-ischemic encephalopathy" (brain damage or disease). To break it down, "hypoxia" means a lack of oxygen, "ischemia" refers to reduced blood flow, and "encephalopathy" means any disease or damage affecting the brain. Therefore, the term "hypoxic-ischemic encephalopathy" suggests that a lack of oxygen and blood flow is what causes brain damage.

However, this term is frequently used even when there's no clear evidence of either hypoxia (lack of oxygen) or ischemia (reduced blood flow). The problem stems from what psychologists call the "illusion of validity": when medical professionals see the term "hypoxic-ischemic," they automatically assume oxygen deprivation must be the cause, simply because it's in the name. This assumption can prevent them from considering other potential causes of brain damage.

While it's true that a lack of oxygen can cause brain abnormalities, the label "hypoxic-ischemic encephalopathy" oversimplifies a complex condition. According to the study, doctors often rely on this simplified diagnosis without having actual evidence of oxygen deprivation or reduced blood flow. This can lead to incorrect diagnoses and potentially overlook other important factors that might be causing the brain damage.

To avoid this diagnostic bias, the authors of the study suggest using a more general term, "encephalopathy of prematurity." This term doesn't point to a specific cause, making it a more accurate description of the condition. It acknowledges that brain damage in preterm infants can be due to a variety of factors, not just a lack of oxygen or reduced blood flow.

How do you spot a good witness?

November 26th

BINARY BIAS

Binary bias is our tendency to categorize things or people into two distinct categories, often based on their perceived characteristics or attributes. This can lead to oversimplification, stereotyping, and discrimination. We do that because it helps us make sense of the world around us quickly. From an evolutionary perspective, we need to quickly distinguish between potential allies and threats, categorizing people as friends or foes.

Our brains often sort things into simplistic "good" or "bad" boxes, lacking crucial nuance. This tendency becomes particularly dangerous in courtrooms, where the evaluation of witness testimony can determine someone's fate. Jurors frequently fall into the trap of binary thinking, especially when faced with expert witnesses.

The tragic case of Sally Clark illustrates how this bias can lead to devastating consequences. In 1999, Clark was charged with murdering her two infant sons after they died in separate incidents. Her defense argued that both deaths were cases of Sudden Infant Death Syndrome (SIDS), a diagnosis initially given for her first son's death. Professor Roy Meadow, a renowned pediatrician called by the prosecution, testified that the chance of two children from an affluent family dying of SIDS was 1 in 73 million – a statistic that profoundly influenced the jury.

Through diligent investigation, lawyer Marilyn Stowe discovered crucial microbiology evidence that had never been shared with the court. These results, found in hospital records, revealed that Sally's second son had died from a natural infection, not SIDS or murder.

The binary bias displayed by the jury was evident in their response to expert testimony. Because Professor Meadow was a distinguished medical professional, jurors placed him firmly in the "good witness" category and accepted his statistical claims without scrutiny. This oversimplified categorization prevented them from critically evaluating the validity of his testimony, which was later proven to be statistically flawed. The Court of Appeal ultimately overturned Clark's conviction, and emphasized that Meadow's dramatic statistical evidence had likely had a profound impact on the jury's decision-making.

53 Fever: What Went Wrong in Italy?

November 27th

GAMBLER'S FALLACY

The gambler's fallacy arises from the mistaken belief that past events can affect the probability of future outcomes that are actually independent of the past. It is often manifested in the belief that a certain outcome is more or less likely to occur due to its frequency in the past, despite the fact that the probability remains the same. This fallacy is often driven by a desire for pattern-finding and prediction, as well as a dislike of uncertainty.

In early 2005, a peculiar madness gripped Italy. The source wasn't a viral outbreak or a political crisis, but a simple lottery number: 53. The Italian State Lottery operates through city-based wheels, with Venice's wheel being at the heart of this story. Five numbers between 1 and 90 are selected. Players can bet any amount on a single number, with a payout of 11.23 times their stake – meaning a €100 bet on that single number would win €1,123 if successful. When 53 hadn't appeared on Venice's wheel for an unprecedented stretch of time, rather than seeing this as mere chance, people became convinced it was "due" to appear.

What followed was a textbook example of the gambler's fallacy in action. Bettors, convinced they could predict the unpredictable, began placing increasingly large wagers on 53. The logic seemed compelling: after such a long absence, surely the number had to appear soon. This collective belief spread across the country like wildfire, earning the name "53 fever." By the time the number finally appeared on February 9, 2005, after 182 consecutive no-shows, Italians had wagered an astonishing four billion euros on their conviction.

The aftermath was devastating. Thousands of people faced financial ruin, having bet their savings, taken out loans, or mortgaged their homes to place what they thought was a "sure bet." The psychological toll was equally severe, with reports of suicides linked to the gambling losses. What makes this tragedy particularly poignant is that each draw remained steadfastly independent – the probability of 53 appearing never changed, remaining at 1 in 90 for every single draw.

The "53 fever" serves as a sobering reminder of how our minds can deceive us when it comes to probability.

Did Your Vote Cloud Your Judgment? The Ballot Box's Sneaky Side Effect

November 28th

COGNITIVE DISSONANCE

Cognitive dissonance describes the mental discomfort we experience when there is a conflict between our beliefs, actions, or perceptions. This discomfort often arises when our actions contradict our beliefs or when we hold two opposing beliefs simultaneously. To alleviate this discomfort, we may adjust our beliefs, perceptions, or actions to create a more consistent internal state. Achieving this internal consistency is crucial, as it helps maintain our sense of identity and coherence.

You're more likely to continue buying products from a brand you've publicly praised to friends and family, even if you later discover some questionable business practices. According to cognitive dissonance theory, we would rather downplay or reject negative information about our endorsed brand than admit we were wrong, as this would lead to mental discomfort, and our minds want to avoid this at all costs.

This same psychological principle applies even more strongly to political decisions, where the stakes are often higher and more personal. A study found that people find it harder to change their opinion of a political candidate if they had voted for them. In comparison, those who did not express their vote (for reasons such as age ineligibility) were more malleable in their willingness to change their opinion of the candidate. Let's say that, at the time of the 2016 election, two people supported Donald Trump. One of them was only 17 and therefore unable to vote. The other person was 18 and expressed their political beliefs by voting. Studies show that, when presented with the same evidence that supporting Donald Trump was a bad (or good) decision, the person who voted was more likely to stick with their political preferences two years after the election than the person who did not vote.

This happens because the person who voted would not want to feel the mental discomfort of the conflict between their behavior (the vote) and the evidence. As a result, they prefer to refuse the evidence that they made a bad decision rather than change their beliefs. By doing this, they maintain consistency between their past behavior (voting) and their beliefs (Trump was the best choice of candidate).

Why Do We Hate New Songs, Then Sing Them in the Shower?

November 29th

MERE EXPOSURE EFFECT

The mere exposure effect says the more we are exposed to something, the more we like it. Familiarity breeds liking. When asked to make a choice, we tend to prefer what is familiar, even if this is not the optimal choice. One reason for this behavior is that evolution has taught us to be careful around new things. Everything unfamiliar could be potentially dangerous. When we see something over and over again without any bad results, we assume it is safe.

According to the mere exposure effect, we are more likely to prefer things we're frequently exposed to. Through repeated exposure, we become familiar with them. Our brain translates familiarity into likeability. Just think about fashion trends – when chunky sneakers first appeared, many people found them hideous. Yet after seeing them everywhere for months, these same critics often ended up buying a pair. The mere exposure effect makes us use familiarity to form preferences, even when our initial reaction was negative.

This same pattern plays out with music all the time. Perhaps this happened to you with a new song you totally disliked when hearing it for the first time. After you heard it for a while, you found yourself going from thinking, "This is so bad," to humming it in the shower. But don't worry; this is not a sign of your degrading taste in music.

A good example of how mere exposure changes our preferences comes from the American teen romantic comedy "Easy A." In one scene, the main character, played by Emma Stone, gets a birthday card. The card comes from a person that is important to Emma and plays the song "Pocketful of Sunshine" by Natasha Bedingfield when it is opened. Her first reaction is strong disgust: "Ugh, the worst song ever," she concludes while closing the card. But the song stays in her mind as she opens and closes the card throughout the day. Over the next few hours, she finds herself in her room wholeheartedly singing the same song she deeply hated a few hours ago. It's not that she starts to embrace it — but repeated exposure to it makes the song seem more entertaining.

View the scene from the movie "Easy A."

Did you ever hear of the "New Coke"?

November 30th

OUTCOME BIAS

We are subject to outcome bias when we judge a decision by its outcome. This is biased because we should rather base our judgment on the quality of the decision at the time it was made, given what was known at that time. We never have all the information we need, and every result has random and unpredictable parts. Bad outcomes are not always a sign of bad decision-making.

Did you ever try the "New Coke" from Coca-Cola? If you were born after 1985, your chances are close to zero because that New Coke was a huge commercial failure. The story of New Coke remains a classic example of outcome bias.

On April 23, 1985, Coca-Cola announced a change in the formula for their flagship product, Coca-Cola, in an attempt to re-energize the brand and the cola category in the United States, This decision marked the first formula change in 99 years and led to a massive consumer backlash, ultimately resulting in the return of the original formula, now called Coca-Cola Classic, just a few months later.

At that time, Coca-Cola was slowly losing its lead over its main competitor, Pepsi, and cola sales were not growing much. To combat this, Coca-Cola decided to change the formula of its iconic drink. The new formula was based on taste tests involving nearly 200,000 consumers. However, the change did not go as planned. Customers hated the new taste. The reintroduction of the original Coca-Cola formula as Coca-Cola Classic on July 11, 1985, marked the end of the New Coke experiment. The return of the classic formula garnered widespread media coverage and applause from consumers.

The New Coke story serves as a reminder of how outcome bias leads us to focus only on the outcome when making judgments. While the commercial failure of New Coke is undeniable, it is essential to acknowledge the rationale behind the decision and the market research that went into it. The New Coke experiment ended up reviving the Coca-Cola brand eventually, though in a different way than was planned initially.

∞
DECEMBER

Are You Letting Netflix Make Your Watching Decisions?

December 1st

DEFAULT EFFECT

When offered a choice that has a pre-selected default option, we tend to choose this default option. This is called the default effect. Defaults are the options that take effect if we do nothing. Our brains try to save as much mental energy as possible. Accepting the default option saves energy because we don't have to think about the pros and cons of each choice.

Have you ever found yourself still watching Netflix late into the night, even though you intended to watch just one episode? A University of Chicago study reveals how Netflix's autoplay feature, enabled by default, profoundly shapes our viewing habits. The research found that while most users had concerns about watching longer than planned, only 4 out of 20 participants had taken the step to turn off autoplay in their settings.

The power of this default lies in its design. When an episode ends, Netflix automatically starts the next one after a brief 5-second countdown. This small window of decision-making time, combined with our natural tendency to follow the path of least resistance, creates what researchers call "temporal inertia." As one study participant noted, "If the next episode is playing, it's probably because I was lazy to pick up my remote and do something." Most participants reported regularly watching beyond their intended stopping point simply because the next episode started playing.

What makes this default particularly effective is that it removes natural "stopping cues" - those moments of pause that would typically prompt us to reflect on whether to continue watching. While half of the study participants expressed appreciation for autoplay's convenience, the same number criticized how it made it easier to watch more than they originally wanted. Some weren't even aware they could change this setting until researchers mentioned it. Did you know that you can change that setting?

But remember, defaults are just pre-selected choices, not mandates. Next time you open Netflix, consider whether you want to let the platform make these decisions for you, or if it's worth the small effort to take control of your viewing habits.

Maybe It's Time to Stop Running Away from Numbers and Stats?

December 2nd

BASE RATE FALLACY

We fall prey to the base rate fallacy when we ignore general information in favor of information that is specific to a certain case, even if the general information is more important. We ignore the statistical base rate. This happens because we tend to think that information about an individual is more important than information about a group. This bias can make us perpetuate stereotypes and overgeneralize.

Our minds often prioritize specific, vivid details over cold, hard statistics, a sneaky mental shortcut known as the base-rate fallacy. This cognitive bias pushes us to sideline general information that should shape our decisions, leading us to inaccurate conclusions.

Here's a classic example: Imagine a city where 85% of the cabs are blue and 15% are green. One night, a hit-and-run occurs, and a witness claims the cab was green. The court tests the witness's ability to distinguish between blue and green cabs under similar nighttime conditions. The results show they're 80% accurate at identifying colors in these conditions, meaning they make mistakes 20% of the time. What are the actual odds that the cab involved was indeed green?

Many people immediately conclude there's an 80% chance the witness is correct, based on their accuracy rate. However, this overlooks a crucial factor: the city's overwhelming proportion of blue cabs. When we calculate properly, considering both the witness's accuracy and the actual distribution of cab colors, the probability of the cab being green is only 41%. Here's why: Out of every 100 cabs, the witness will correctly identify 12 of the 15 green cabs as green (80% accuracy), but they'll also mistakenly identify 17 of the 85 blue cabs as green (20% error rate). So when the witness says "green," they're actually correct in only 12 out of 29 cases (because 12/(12+17) ≈ 41%).

Read a detailed explanation of the solution to the taxi problem

This fallacy frequently affects our real-life decisions. Whether we're investing in stocks based on recent trends or dismissing broad health statistics in favor of personal anecdotes, the base-rate fallacy can lead us to flawed conclusions by causing us to overlook crucial background information.

Would You Have Believed the News of an Invasion from Mars in 1938?

December 3rd
BELIEF BIAS

Belief bias distorts our evaluation of the logical strength of an argument because we judge it by the believability of the conclusion. In other words, when we believe the conclusion, we are inclined to believe that the method used to get the results must also be correct. Belief bias happens when we rely too much on what we remember and not enough on evaluating new information. Belief bias is more likely to happen when we really care about something.

"The War of the Worlds" was a Halloween episode of the radio series "The Mercury Theatre on the Air," both directed and narrated by Orson Welles. It was an adaptation of H.G. Wells' novel of the same name, performed and broadcast live on October 30, 1938. The show depicted an invasion of Earth by Martians, beginning with strange explosions on Mars, followed by alien spaceships landing in New Jersey, and culminating in Martians attacking people with heat rays and poison gas.

The episode was presented in a groundbreaking "breaking news" style, which significantly enhanced its authenticity. The Mercury Theatre on the Air's lack of commercial interruptions further reinforced the broadcast's credibility. Many listeners who tuned in believed they were hearing actual news coverage of a Martian invasion. This reaction was particularly strong among those who already believed in the possibility of extraterrestrial life or were anxious about the growing threat of war with Nazi Germany. These preexisting beliefs made them more susceptible to accepting the broadcast's content as truth without critically examining the evidence – a perfect example of belief bias in action.

In the aftermath of the broadcast, the media expressed widespread outrage. Critics condemned the news-bulletin format as misleading, leading to a backlash against the broadcasters and calls for intervention from the Federal Communications Commission. While Welles apologized at a hastily called news conference the following morning, no punitive action was ultimately taken against the production team.

Listen to the original radio broadcast of "War of the Worlds"

Do We Forgive Celebs Based on Fame or Fundamental Attribution Error?

December 4th

FUNDAMENTAL ATTRIBUTION ERROR

The fundamental attribution error refers to our tendency to assume that a person's behavior is a perfect reflection of their personality. We overestimate explanations that are due to the internal characteristics of a person and underestimate situational or environmental explanations. We do that simply because it saves mental energy to explain someone's behavior by attributing it to their personality rather than considering all possible situational and environmental factors.

If you followed the famous trial between Johnny Depp and Amber Heard, you probably noticed an increase in social media sympathy for the former. Public support appeared to weigh far more heavily in favor of Depp than Heard. At some point during the scandal, #IStandWithAmberHeard had reached about 8.2 million views, while #JusticeForJohnnyDepp earned about 15 billion views.

The striking difference between these numbers might be explained by how we relate to celebrities and our tendency toward fundamental attribution error. While this error typically leads us to believe that a person's behavior reflects their personality rather than their circumstances, new research has shown something surprising: we react differently when the person involved is a celebrity we admire.

The study found that when people don't like a public figure, the fundamental attribution error prevails, and their bad behavior is blamed on their personalities. However, we're more likely to forgive celebrities we like for major mistakes or transgressions, explaining their bad behavior in terms of context and external factors. This is the complete opposite of how the fundamental attribution error typically works.

If you're someone hugely famous like Johnny Depp, people tend to attribute your mistakes to situational circumstances. But if you're someone who has fallen from public grace, your mistakes are more likely to be seen as an extension of your bad character or flawed personality.

Read about the Depp v Heard trial on social media

Can you see the wagon in the Big Dipper?

December 5th

CLUSTERING ILLUSION

The clustering illusion is our tendency to give meaning to random patterns we perceive. We see these patterns because we see them in data sets that are very large or very small. For small data sets, it could be a winning-streak or a so-called "hot-hand" in sports. We think there is a pattern, but actually it is just coincidence. For very large datasets, random patterns will inevitably occur because of the sheer size.

When we look up at the starry night sky, we can see loads of star constellations. In 1922, the International Astronomical Union created a list of 88 official constellations. Star patterns that don't appear on this list are referred to as asterisms. An asterism is a recognizable pattern of stars that serves as a useful guide for astronomers and stargazers alike.

Forty-eight of these 88 "formal" constellations originated from the ancient Greek star configurations documented by the astronomer Ptolemy in the 2nd century. Each one is named after characters from Greek mythology, such as the legendary hero Perseus and his wife, the stunning princess Andromeda. All these constellations are fantastic examples of the clustering illusion. Take, for example, the Big Dipper. This iconic constellation is supposed to resemble a wagon. Or look at Pisces, the constellation that's supposed to represent two fish swimming in the great cosmic sea. What you actually might see is a bunch of stars that look like someone playing a cosmic game of connect-the-dots.

These star patterns are perfect demonstrations of how our minds create meaningful shapes from random arrangements. Just as we might see faces in clouds or patterns in sports statistics, we've projected our stories and shapes onto the random scattering of stars above us. The constellations we know today are simply our ancestors' clustering illusion at work.

Tricky Trio: How Do Trio-Options Trick Your Wallet?

December 6th

DECOY EFFECT

The decoy effect describes how, when deciding between two options, adding a third, less appealing option (the decoy) can change how we feel about the two options we were originally considering. Decoys are much worse than one option, but only partially inferior to the second option. The decoy is there to nudge you towards one specific target option. Decoys work because they serve us as reference points that help us (unconsciously) justify our choices.

Ever wondered why subscription plans often include a peculiar middle option that no one seems to choose? It's a strategic sales technique based on behavioral science. Let's take the example of The Economist's subscription plan. This newspaper offers three types of subscriptions, all at different prices: a web subscription for $59, a print subscription for $125, and a web and print subscription for $125. Wait, what?

The price for the first subscription seems reasonable ($59). Then, a second option is introduced: a print subscription for $125. However, the third option covers both of them for the price of the second one. While the second option might seem useless, its role is to create a drastic asymmetry between the first and third options. The decoy, in this case, the print subscription for $125, offers less value than the third one, in which magazine readers can have access to both print and Internet subscriptions for the same price. When asked what option they would go for, students made the following choices: 16% for the first option, 0% for the second one, and 84% for the third one.

When the decoy (the second one) was taken out, the preferences changed: 68% chose the first option and 32% the third one. Therefore, the decoy seems to be there only to show you what a great deal you can get if you go for the more expensive option. If you originally wanted to go for the cheapest subscription, you may now have second thoughts. Since there are people who pay $125 for the print subscription only, why can't you have the best of both worlds for the same price?

Watch a TED Talk by Dan Ariely about this topic

Can Our Emotions Outweigh Cold, Hard Data?

December 7th

AFFECT HEURISTIC

The affect heuristic is our tendency to make decisions based on our emotions. If we feel good about something, we might think it's a good choice. On the other hand, if we feel bad about something, we might think it's a bad choice. This can save us time and energy when making decisions, but it can also lead to choices that are not ideal. It is thought to be a result of our evolution as a species, as quick decisions led to an increased chance of survival.

Emotions often sway our decisions, even when statistical data is available. This was demonstrated in a fascinating study.

Participants were psychiatrists and forensic psychologists that evaluated the risk of a mental health inpatient committing violence after discharge. They were split into two groups and given mathematically identical information in different formats. The first group received relative frequency data: "20 out of every 100 patients similar to Mr. Jones are estimated to commit violence." The second group received the same statistical information as a probability: "Mr. Jones has a 20% chance of violence." While these statements are mathematically equivalent—both indicating the same one-in-five risk—they triggered very different emotional responses.

The results were striking: 41% of the first group opposed discharging the patient, compared to 21% of the second group. This disparity stems from how each data format affects our emotions differently. The relative frequency format—"20 out of 100"—creates vivid mental images of twenty specific individuals committing violent acts, triggering a stronger emotional response of fear. In contrast, the probability format—"20% chance"—presents the risk as an abstract number attached to a single individual. This more abstract presentation feels less personal and immediate, generating a weaker emotional response.

This study demonstrates how the affect heuristic influences professional judgment: even when presented with identical statistical information, the format that evoked stronger emotions led to more cautious decisions. While these gut reactions can help us make quick decisions, they may not always lead to the most rational choices.

Is Your Stomach Growling at Your Moral Compass?

December 8th

EGO-DEPLETION

Ego depletion refers to the limited capacity of our mental willpower and self-control, which can be exhausted through demanding activities like decision-making, emotional restraint, or resisting temptations. When this psychological resource is depleted, our ability to maintain behavioral control diminishes. This mental fatigue can be triggered by stress, physical exhaustion, or insufficient sleep.

Our moral judgments, it turns out, are deeply influenced by our physiological states, particularly hunger. Like a muscle that fatigues with use, our willpower draws from a limited pool of mental resources—a phenomenon known as ego depletion. When these resources are depleted through factors like hunger, fatigue, or stress, our capacity for careful decision-making and self-control diminishes significantly.

A compelling 2020 study revealed that hunger's impact on our moral judgments goes beyond what we might expect. The researchers found that hungry participants were more likely to consider harmful actions morally acceptable, even when these actions served no greater purpose. This wasn't just about being more sympathetic to someone stealing food—hunger actually made people more tolerant of various moral violations across different contexts.

This makes evolutionary sense: when our basic survival needs aren't met, our brain may prioritize immediate responses over careful moral deliberation. The impact of hunger on moral judgment extends beyond laboratory settings into real-world scenarios. For example, studies of judicial decisions have shown that judges' rulings can vary depending on the time since their last meal, highlighting how physiological states can influence even highly trained professionals making crucial decisions.

These findings reveal that what we deem moral or immoral isn't solely influenced by our personal values or higher cognitive functions. Our basic physiological states, through the mechanism of ego depletion, can directly influence what types of harm we find acceptable. After all, who has time to carefully analyze moral actions when baseline hunger needs are not met?

Are Tarot Cards an Insightful Guidance or Just a Barnum Bluff?

December 9th

FORER EFFECT OR BARNUM EFFECT

The Forer effect, also known as the Barnum effect, describes the observation that people will give high accuracy ratings to personality descriptions that are supposedly tailored specifically for them. However, in reality, these descriptions are vague and general enough to apply to many people. This effect can help explain why some beliefs and practices, like astrology, palm reading, graphology, and some types of personality tests, are so popular.

Tarot cards have surged in popularity, serving as tools for introspection and self-discovery. While their origins can be traced to Renaissance Italy in the 15th century, they've managed to retain their allure to this day. A standard tarot deck consists of 78 cards, split into the major arcana (22 cards) and the minor arcana (56 cards). The major arcana cards symbolize significant life themes, while the minor arcana cards reflect more everyday aspects of life.

According to research in the field of psychological studies, there are two principal approaches to interpreting tarot cards. The first, the paranormal approach, proposes that the cards mirror an individual's innermost processes, opportunities, hidden motives, and potentials rather than foretelling a predetermined future.

However, the second approach, the nonparanormal one, attributes the effectiveness of tarot readings to cognitive biases. This perspective spotlights the Barnum effect as a key psychological explanation. In tarot readings, the Barnum effect leads us to perceive general card interpretations as remarkably specific to our personal lives, even though these interpretations could apply to almost anyone.

"You have been disappointed in the past" and "Your life will change radically in 3 years" are statements that describe the universal experience of any human being. But are they relevant to you? Of course they are, which is why the Barnum effect will delude you into thinking that these kinds of spiritual readings are worth trusting. You can experiment with them, but remain aware of your brain's vulnerability to this bias.

Watch James Randis debunking psychic fraud

Who is the Hero in Our Own Story?

December 10th

SELF-SERVING BIAS

The self-serving bias is our tendency to take credit for good things that happen to us and blame other things or people for bad things that happen. We do that because we have the desire to feel good about ourselves. Being responsible for good things happening boosts our confidence and gives us a sense of control in our lives. When we blame external factors for bad things that happen to us, it can help us feel better about ourselves by protecting our ego.

In the Star Wars saga, the cocky space pilot Han Solo is a master of self-serving explanations. When he outsmarts Imperial ships in a dogfight, he boasts "That's how it's done!" After cleverly hiding from the Empire by attaching his ship to the back of their destroyer, he boasts "Not bad, not bad at all." His greatest achievement, making the Kessel Run in less than twelve parsecs, becomes his favorite story to tell – proof of his extraordinary piloting skills.

But watch how quickly his tune changes when things go wrong. During the escape from Cloud City, the Millennium Falcon's hyperdrive fails repeatedly. Instead of considering his maintenance choices, Han blames the ship: "It's not my fault!" When they're caught in the Death Star's tractor beam, he blames the overwhelming power of the Empire. Even when he fails to spot Imperial ships hiding in Cloud City, he deflects responsibility by blaming Lando's betrayal rather than his own lack of caution. Each failure has a convenient external cause, while every success is attributed to his incredible abilities.

This mental gymnastics routine helps us maintain a positive self-image while protecting us from harsh realities. It's a clever psychological safety net we've developed. By taking credit for successes while deflecting blame for failures, we build confidence while protecting our ego. Just like Han Solo, we're all starring in our own movie where we're the capable hero, and external circumstances are the villains holding us back. The self-serving bias lets us feel in control when things go well, while preserving our self-esteem when they don't.

True growth though only comes when we learn, like Han eventually did, to take responsibility for both our successes and our failures.

Do you know about Jim Jones and the People's Temple?

December 11th

AUTHORITY BIAS

Authority bias is our tendency to attribute greater accuracy and credibility to the opinions of people in positions of power, regardless of the content of their statements. This makes people give more weight to the opinions of those in power, which makes it more likely that they will follow orders. There is an evolutionary benefit to authority bias. It helped people stick together and stay alive as a group.

The cult People's Temple, led by Jim Jones, is a prime example of authority bias gone very wrong.

Jim Jones established the People's Temple as a religious organization in the 1950s. The cult gained popularity in the United States, eventually moving its headquarters to San Francisco and then to Jonestown, Guyana, in South America. The People's Temple cult blended elements of Christianity, socialism, and Jones' personal beliefs. Its core tenets revolved around racial equality, social justice, and communal living. Members were encouraged to sever ties with their families and turn over their assets to the cult to further its goals. Jones claimed he was the reincarnation of Jesus Christ and convinced followers he possessed divine healing powers, often staging elaborate fake healing ceremonies to "cure" planted actors of various ailments.

Through a combination of isolation, sleep deprivation, and constant propaganda, Jones gradually convinced his followers that powerful forces were conspiring against them. He held regular "White Nights" - emergency drills where members practiced mass suicide - while broadcasting fabricated news about external threats, including claims that the U.S. government was planning to torture and kill cult members.

The People's Temple is widely known for the 1978 mass suicide of over 900 members in Jonestown, under Jones' command. This is also the most striking example of authority bias in the People's Temple cult. Jones convinced his followers that they were under threat and that the only solution was to commit "revolutionary suicide." Despite the drastic nature of this decision, the majority of cult members complied, as they had been conditioned to trust and follow Jones' orders.

Will Your Future Self Thank You for Today's Choices?

December 12th

END-OF-HISTORY ILLUSION

The end-of-history illusion refers to our tendency to underestimate the extent of personal changes that will occur in the future. While we acknowledge that our personalities, values, and tastes have evolved over time, we often believe that they will remain relatively stable going forward. This misconception persists regardless of age. The illusion arises because we find it hard to imagine personal changes and thus assume that such changes are unlikely to occur.

Dan Gilbert is recognized for his studies on happiness, decision-making, and behavioral psychology. Gilbert's concept of the "end of history illusion," developed with two colleagues, is one of his most profound contributions to the field of psychology.

The "end of history illusion" suggests that people tend to underestimate how much they will change in the future. Even when aware of significant changes they've experienced in the past, most people assume that the most substantial changes to their lives and personalities are behind them.

In a study of over 6,000 participants aged 18 to 68, researchers divided subjects into two groups. One group compared their current values and preferences to those they had 10 years ago, while the other group described their current preferences and predicted what they would be in 10 years. The researchers then compared the predicted changes against the actual reported changes. Across all age groups, people consistently underestimated future changes compared to the changes their older counterparts had actually experienced.

For example, 28-year-olds predicted their 38-year-old selves would have the same food preferences, but 38-year-olds reported their tastes had changed significantly from a decade earlier. While the rate of change decreased with age, all participants underestimated their capacity for change. This "end of history illusion" leads us to incorrectly believe that most of our personal development is complete. We tend to see our current selves as the finished product, overlooking our continuing potential for change.

Watch this TED Talk of Dan Gilbert about the psychology of your future self

How Many Animals Did Moses Bring on His Ark?

December 13th

MOSES ILLUSION

The Moses Illusion (also known as the Moses Effect) refers to a cognitive phenomenon where people fail to detect distortions in familiar information, particularly when answering questions containing false presuppositions. This demonstrates how we sometimes process information superficially, especially with familiar knowledge. Rather than carefully analyzing every detail, our brains take shortcuts and focus on the overall meaning or gist of the question.

Before you read any further, answer this question: How many animals of each kind did Moses bring on his ark? The Moses Illusion gets its name from this exact question. When asked this question, approximately 50% of people confidently answer "two" rather than pointing out the error. Think about it again: if you're familiar with the biblical story, you know that it was Noah, not Moses, who built the ark. However, our minds typically see a biblical context and assume "Moses" fits naturally within it, without checking the specific details.

This occurs because our brains excel at focusing on certain environmental features while overlooking others. We search for patterns and coherence in the world around us rather than perfect accuracy. While this ability helps us navigate our environments, it can lead to systematic errors like the one demonstrated above.

The Moses Illusion demonstrates how our minds operate using two distinct systems: fast thinking and slow thinking. Fast thinking is automatic and intuitive – like recognizing a friend's face or understanding simple sentences. Slow thinking is more deliberate and analytical – the kind we use for solving complex problems. When we encounter the Moses question, our fast thinking quickly processes the familiar biblical context without scrutiny, while our slow thinking remains dormant unless deliberately activated.

Our "fast thinking" system excels at quick decisions and intuitive conclusions, but it's our reflective, "slow thinking" system that carefully evaluates whether these conclusions are correct. This explains why we can know the correct information (that Noah built the ark) yet still fall for the Moses Illusion when we're not being deliberate in our analysis.

Are We More Generous to Like-Minded People?

December 14th

INGROUP BIAS

Ingroup bias is when we like and support people who are part of our own group more than people who are not part of our group. These groups can be divided based on seemingly trivial observable traits. This is rooted in the intrinsic human need for a group identity, which provides a sense of belonging and purpose. Additionally, we all have a desire to feel good about ourselves, and one way to achieve that is to see our own group as being superior to others.

We all show preferential treatment to members of our groups. For example, we tend to view people who support our preferred political candidates more favorably than those who don't. We form invisible bonds with those who share our political views while often dismissing those who hold different beliefs.

A study used the "dictator game" to examine how generous Democrats were toward supporters of Obama or Clinton in 2008. In this game, one participant, the dictator, divides a sum of money between themselves and another participant however they choose, with the other participant having no say in the decision. The participants first indicated their preferred candidate (Obama or Clinton) and were then told whether their partner agreed or disagreed with their choice.

The researchers conducted this test at three key moments in 2008: in June right after Clinton's concession speech, in early August before the Democratic National Convention (DNC), and in late August after the DNC ended. The DNC is a major party gathering where Democrats officially choose their presidential nominee and unite behind them.

The results revealed that in the first two tests, men demonstrated significant ingroup bias, giving substantially more money to partners who supported the same candidate. However, this bias decreased after the DNC, when Clinton supporters shifted their allegiance to Barack Obama following Clinton's defeat. This shift demonstrates that while we initially prefer people who support the same candidate, we're capable of adjusting our preferences to maintain our broader group identity.

Watch this video to understand the dictator game theory

Was Fox News too Busy on January 6?

December 15th

COGNITIVE DISSONANCE

Cognitive dissonance describes the mental discomfort we experience when there is a conflict between our beliefs, actions, or perceptions. This discomfort often arises when our actions contradict our beliefs or when we hold two opposing beliefs simultaneously. To alleviate this discomfort, we may adjust our beliefs, perceptions, or actions to create a more consistent internal state. Achieving this internal consistency is crucial, as it helps maintain our sense of identity and coherence.

In early 2021, the United States Capitol witnessed an unprecedented breach, leading to the establishment of the January 6 hearings. These hearings aimed to thoroughly investigate the events of that day, when a violent mob stormed the Capitol in an attempt to overturn the 2020 presidential election results. Thus, the hearings represented a pivotal moment in U.S. political history.

Fox News' decision not to air the January 6 hearings illustrates cognitive dissonance at work within media practices. The hearings presented information that could create significant psychological discomfort for viewers who held beliefs about the legitimacy of the election protests. By choosing not to broadcast these significant political proceedings, Fox News acted to protect its audience from the mental tension that could arise from confronting evidence that contradicted their existing worldview.

This avoidance strategy became even more apparent through Fox News' deliberate counter-programming during the hearings. Instead of facing potentially uncomfortable truths, Fox viewers were presented with Tucker Carlson's alternative narrative - a classic example of how cognitive dissonance can lead to the active rejection of threatening information in favor of more comfortable explanations. By offering content that aligned with viewers' existing beliefs, the network provided a psychological shelter that helped its audience avoid the discomfort of reconciling contradictory information about January 6th.

This approach demonstrates how media outlets can shield their audiences from cognitive dissonance by creating alternative narratives.

A Drop of Delusion

December 16th

GROUPTHINK

Groupthink is when our desire for harmony and conformity within a group leads to dysfunctional decision-making. Group members prioritize agreement over critical evaluation, resulting in a loss of individual creativity and thinking. This can lead to an inflated sense of confidence in the group's abilities, an undervaluation of opponents, group pressure, and potentially harmful actions towards outsiders.

The story of the company Theranos exemplifies groupthink in action. Founded by Elizabeth Holmes, it promised to revolutionize healthcare with single-drop blood testing technology. It attracted $700 million in investments and reached a $10 billion valuation by 2014.

However, the operations of Theranos soon became a textbook example of groupthink's most damaging effects. The company's leadership ignored critical flaws in their blood testing technology and silenced whistleblowers who bravely voiced their concerns. This created a toxic environment where dissent was systematically suppressed and whistleblowers faced legal intimidation and professional isolation, signaling that any challenge to the company's narrative was unacceptable.

Central to Theranos's culture was the ethos Holmes cultivated, which prioritized unwavering belief in the company's mission above the stark reality of its technological shortcomings. Holmes created an environment that marginalized doubters, suggesting they had no place in the company. This approach coerced employees into misplaced loyalty.

Holmes and her team crafted an "us versus them" narrative, portraying Theranos as a misunderstood pioneer fighting against a skeptical world. This narrative fostered a culture of defiance against external criticism and vilified dissent, embedding a mindset where opposing views were demonized.

By 2018, the company had burned through nearly all investor capital, and the truth about its dysfunctional technology became public. In January 2022, Holmes was found guilty of defrauding investors and is now serving an 11-year prison sentence.

Watch the trailer for the documentary about Theranos

A Tale of Two Infections

December 17th

COGNITIVE DISSONANCE

Cognitive dissonance describes the mental discomfort we experience when there is a conflict between our beliefs, actions, or perceptions. This discomfort often arises when our actions contradict our beliefs or when we hold two opposing beliefs simultaneously. To alleviate this discomfort, we may adjust our beliefs, perceptions, or actions to create a more consistent internal state. Achieving this internal consistency is crucial, as it helps maintain our sense of identity and coherence.

The contrasting reactions of Donald Trump and Chris Christie after both tested positive for COVID-19 are a great example of how we deal differently with the reduction of mental discomfort.

As the pandemic raged in 2020, Trump and Christie both repeatedly downplayed the severity of the virus and mocked mask-wearing. Experiencing COVID-19 personally confronted both Trump and Christie with the virus's true severity, creating a direct conflict with their previous public understatements. This created a classic scenario for cognitive dissonance.

Rather than acknowledging his previous dismissive stance was misguided, Trump doubled down, calling his diagnosis "a blessing from God" that exposed him to experimental antibody treatments. By framing his sickness as fortuitous, Trump avoided admitting he was wrong, protecting his ego from the mental discomfort stemming from cognitive dissonance.

Christie, on the other hand, exhibited a starkly different response after spending a week in intensive care with COVID-19. The former New Jersey governor acknowledged he had been "mistaken" about feeling safe without a mask at White House events. By adjusting his stance to align with his first-hand experience of the virus's severity, Christie reduced his mental discomfort. His admission demonstrated a rare willingness to update beliefs in the face of contradictory evidence.

The divergent reactions spotlight how human beings can employ myriad strategies, some more psychologically comfortable than others, to mitigate cognitive dissonance. While rationalizing away contradictions protects our ego, it can reinforce flawed beliefs.

Blinded by the Light?

December 18th

HALO EFFECT

The halo effect is a type of cognitive bias in which our overall opinion of a person or brand affects how we feel about the specific qualities of that person or brand. If we have a good feeling about something as a whole, we are more likely to think that its individual parts are good as well. We do that because it saves cognitive effort to use our overall impressions as a shortcut to make judgments rather than evaluating each aspect of something separately.

In 1920, psychologist Edward L. Thorndike published a groundbreaking study that exposed a concerning tendency in how we evaluate others and introduced the concept of the halo effect.

In his research, he examined workplace evaluations where supervisors rated employees on distinct qualities like intelligence, industriousness, and technical skill. Thorndike discovered that the ratings the evaluators were giving weren't truly independent assessments. Supervisors who thought highly of an employee tended to give them uniformly high scores in all categories, even when evaluating unrelated skills.

Furthermore, Thorndike found this effect among U.S. Army officers evaluating their subordinates. Although the rating system explicitly instructed them to assess qualities like intelligence, leadership, and character separately, the scores still exhibited an eerie uniformity, with high ratings in one area radiating a "halo" over the others.

The halo effect didn't just manifest in judging personalities; it crept into evaluations of highly specialized skills. Thorndike was baffled that officers' assessments of a pilot's overall capability strongly influenced their scoring of the pilot's technical flying proficiency, which requires a distinct aptitude.

The inescapable pattern led Thorndike to a disquieting conclusion: even the most well-intentioned, capable evaluators cannot seem to separate their assessment of someone's distinct qualities from the glowing—or tarnished—aura of their general perception. As he bluntly stated, we are "unable to treat an individual as a compound of separate qualities."

The Founding Father of Self-Serving Bias

December 19th

SELF-SERVING BIAS

The self-serving bias is our tendency to take credit for good things that happen to us and blame other things or people for bad things that happen. We do that because we have the desire to feel good about ourselves. Being responsible for good things happening boosts our confidence and gives us a sense of control in our lives. When we blame external factors for bad things that happen to us, it can help us feel better about ourselves by protecting our ego.

Have you ever noticed how easy it is to take credit for your successes but blame outside factors for your failures? This common tendency is called the self-serving bias.

For example, imagine a student who gets an A on a test and thinks, "I studied really hard and I'm great at this subject!" But when the same student gets a D on another test, they might say, "The teacher made the questions too tricky" or "I was having a bad day." This is the self-serving bias in action.

Fritz Heider, born in early 1900s Austria, was one of the first psychologists to study this fascinating aspect of human behavior. During his time, Austria was a hub of new psychological thinking, particularly influenced by the Gestalt school of psychology. The Gestalt approach wasn't a physical school, but rather a group of thinkers who believed that our minds naturally organize information into complete patterns rather than separate pieces.

Heider's work was groundbreaking because he showed that people naturally try to maintain a balanced psychological state. He explained that the self-serving bias isn't just about protecting our ego – it's a fundamental part of how our minds work to maintain healthy self-esteem and mental well-being. His research laid the foundation for attribution theory, which explores how people explain the causes of different events in their lives.

Through his pioneering research, Heider opened the door for future psychologists to better understand how people make sense of their social world, including the ways we perceive ourselves and interpret our interactions with others.

You're Always Smarter in Hindsight

December 20th

HINDSIGHT BIAS

The hindsight bias is also called the "I-knew-it-all-along" effect. It describes the retrospective overestimation of predictability. In the present, it's hard to tell how something will turn out in the future, but is easy to understand how or why an event happened in retrospect. This bias happens because we mistakenly assume that we had the same understanding of an event before it happened as we do after it happened.

In 1975, Baruch Fischhoff introduced the concept of hindsight bias through a study examining predictions about President Nixon's international trips. Participants estimated the chances of events like meeting Chinese Communist Party leader Mao or visiting Lenin's tomb before Nixon's return, with predictions made between two weeks and six months in advance.

The key aspect of the study was the follow-up conducted after the completion of Nixon's trips. Participants were asked to recall their original predictions and to state which of the events they believed had actually occurred. This follow-up phase revealed a clear demonstration of hindsight bias.

The findings were compelling. Participants consistently recalled giving higher probabilities to events that actually occurred and lower probabilities to those that didn't. When events were unlikely, participants initially overestimated their probability. However, after knowing the outcomes, they remembered their predictions as being even less likely than they had initially predicted. For example, before Nixon's trips, a participant might have guessed there was a 50% chance Nixon would meet Chairman Mao. After learning that Nixon did meet Mao in 1972, this person might remember their guess as being 80%. Conversely, if they initially thought there was a 30% chance of an event that didn't happen, later they might remember guessing only a 10% chance.

Fischhoff's study showed how knowledge of actual outcomes can significantly alter an individual's memory of their predictions, leading them to overestimate their foresight.

Building a Cozy Confirmation Bunker With Your News Feed

December 21st

CONFIRMATION BIAS

Confirmation bias is our tendency to look for, acknowledge, favor, and remember information in a way that supports what we already think or believe. This bias occurs when we ignore information that contradicts our ideas or interpret ambiguous facts as evidence supporting our existing beliefs. Situations that involve emotionally charged topics, strongly held beliefs, or things we really want to happen are most susceptible to this bias.

In today's fractured media landscape, it's becoming increasingly difficult to separate fact from opinion. This has created a vicious circle fueled by confirmation bias across the media ecosystem.

Opportunistic media companies have latched onto this bias, realizing there is a market for opinionated "news" that panders to an audience's preconceived notions. By providing a steady stream of narratives and cherry-picked facts that validate their viewers' beliefs, they attract loyal followings hooked on nursing their confirmation bias.

For example, a conservative viewer who gravitates to a right-leaning outlet will be served a diet of commentary that reinforces negative viewpoints about liberals, perceived threats to their values, and affirmation of conservative policies. Contradictory evidence that clashes with this narrative often gets ignored or branded as unfounded liberal propaganda.

The reverse happens on the left, with progressive audiences receiving a steady stream of reasons to feel morally superior and disdainful of conservative ideology. Both audiences become entrenched in their partisan camps, surrounding themselves with self-reinforcing rhetoric that hardens their existing beliefs.

This feedback loop is tremendously profitable for media outlets, ensuring high engagement among their audience bases. However, it is disastrous for society's ability to engage in reasoned discourse. All sides become increasingly alienated from differing perspectives and less capable of evaluating new information objectively.

Look at the AllSides Media Bias Chart

How Can Two Auction Houses Play Ping-Pong With Your Brain?

December 22nd

ANCHORING BIAS

Anchoring bias occurs when a specific reference point, or "anchor", influences our decision-making process. This anchor could be a number or any other kind of cue, even if it is completely unrelated to the decision at hand. Despite this, we often use the anchor as a starting point and adjust our decisions or judgments from there, without realizing it. As a result, our final estimates, decisions, or judgments can be significantly different from what they might have been without the influence of the anchor.

A fascinating natural experiment in New York City reveals just how powerful the anchoring effect is. Twice a year, the world's two largest auction houses, Sotheby's and Christie's, hold their major art auctions in the same week. They take turns going first - one leads in spring, the other in fall. This simple rotation has revealed something remarkable about how our minds work: when the auction house with more expensive paintings goes first, it changes how everyone values art for the entire week.

The effect is so powerful that researchers can measure it precisely. During weeks when the house with pricier paintings leads, the overall sales prices are 21% higher than when the house with less valuable pieces goes first. Think about that - the exact same painting might sell for a dramatically different price based simply on which auction happened first that week.

What makes this even more fascinating is that this effect isn't just about amateur buyers getting carried away. Even professional art dealers and investors, who study market values for a living, can't escape this psychological trap. When an auction week opens with more expensive pieces, everyone's mental math about what constitutes a "reasonable" price gets quietly adjusted upward.

While most of us will never bid at a high-end art auction, this discovery about how our minds process value offers a window into how we make all sorts of decisions. Any time we encounter a number - whether it's a price, a statistic, or a measurement - it can become an anchor that influences our subsequent judgments in ways we don't even realize.

Why Do Americans Keep Pressing Non-Functional Elevator Buttons?

December 23rd

ILLUSION OF CONTROL

The illusion of control occurs when we believe we have more control over external events than we do. We frequently believe we have (or had) some control over events that are actually random. Researchers have found that people who feel in control will engage in healthier behaviors, feel less stress, and have better overall mental health. Therefore, this illusion makes us feel better about ourselves and the world around us, but it can also seduce us into relying on superstitions.

Have you ever frantically pressed an elevator's "close door" button, convinced that your repeated pressing would make the doors shut faster? You're not alone. In most modern elevators in the United States, particularly those built after the 1990s, these buttons are actually non-functional – mere placeholders installed to give passengers a sense of control. The reason behind this lies in the Americans with Disabilities Act of 1990, which mandated that elevator doors must remain open long enough for people with disabilities to safely enter and exit. This effectively rendered the "close door" buttons useless in public elevators across America. Interestingly, in many other countries, from Japan to Germany, these buttons remain fully functional, creating a unique American phenomenon where elevator manufacturers discovered that people feel more comfortable and report higher satisfaction when they believe they can influence the elevator's operation, even if that control is just an illusion.

In New York City, studies suggest that up to 80% of "close door" buttons are disconnected, yet millions of people press them daily. This perfectly illustrates how we cling to the illusion of control in our daily lives. The buttons aren't entirely useless though – they do work for firefighters and maintenance workers with special keys. But for the general public, they're simply psychological placebos, making our daily commute feel a little more within our control. As Harvard University psychology professor Ellen Langer noted in an interview with The Times, "Perceived control is very important - it diminishes stress and promotes well-being." Sometimes, the comfort of perceived control is more valuable than actual control itself.

Would You Flip the Switch in Milgram's Experiment?

December 24th

AUTHORITY BIAS

Authority bias is our tendency to attribute greater accuracy and credibility to the opinions of people in positions of power, regardless of the content of their statements. This makes people give more weight to the opinions of those in power, which makes it more likely that they will follow orders. There is an evolutionary benefit to authority bias. It helped people stick together and stay alive as a group.

Stanley Milgram, a psychologist, conducted experiments in the early 1960s to study how people obey authority. His goal was to understand how ordinary people could be influenced into committing atrocities, like those committed by Germans during World War II. 40 men from different backgrounds participated. The subjects were "teachers" instructed to give electric shocks (ranging from 15 to a potentially lethal 450 volts) to a learner whenever they made mistakes. The learner was actually an actor, and the shocks were harmless.

Milgram found that 65% of participants continued giving electric shocks up to the maximum 450 volts – a level that could have caused severe injury or death in real life – even though the learner screamed in pain and begged them to stop. The experiment showed that ordinary people were likely to follow orders from an authority figure, even to the extent of potentially fatal harm to another person. Participants obeyed because they perceived the experimenter as a legitimate authority. Milgram's theory suggests that people will obey authority when they believe it will take responsibility for the consequences. In the experiment, participants allowed the experimenter to direct their actions and shift responsibility. The experimenter's lab coat and formal setting contributed to their obedience. This shows that uniforms and symbols of authority can increase perceived legitimacy. If placed in a similar situation, would you follow orders or resist and follow your moral compass?

Watch the original Milgram experiment from 1963

Holy Hunch or Heavenly Humbug: Can We Trust Pastoral Prophecies?

December 25th

FORER EFFECT OR BARNUM EFFECT

The Forer effect, also known as the Barnum effect, describes the observation that people will give high accuracy ratings to personality descriptions that are supposedly tailored specifically for them. However, in reality, these descriptions are vague and general enough to apply to many people. This effect can help explain why some beliefs and practices, like astrology, palm reading, graphology, and some types of personality tests, are so popular.

Charismatic Christianity, a subset of Christianity, boasts around half a billion followers worldwide. This movement places significant emphasis on the Holy Spirit's activity and spiritual gifts. The idea of prophecy, or foretelling the future, as a divine gift from God, is a key component of many charismatic Christians' faith. Individuals believed to possess this gift are regarded as spiritually advanced and capable of direct communication with God. Particularly in times of stress or uncertainty, individuals often seek out prophecies in search of answers to their pressing concerns. However, critics suggest that these prophecies often reflect a psychological phenomenon known as the Barnum effect rather than divine insight.

Stephen Graham, a critic of the Christian movement's practices, described the vagueness, evasiveness, and broad applicability of many prophecies he encountered during a workshop. Recalling prophets' statements such as "God wants to take you to a new level of intimacy with him. God will give you the gift of wisdom," or "God has transformed something in your life into something beautiful. I had a vision of you in a field, dancing." Graham observed that these broadly applicable prophecies can seem uncannily accurate to those who receive them.

Such prophecies often articulate what people desire or need to hear, making them highly appealing to believers. The perceived accuracy and personal relevance of these prophecies can, therefore, serve to reinforce individuals' faith and commitment to the movement.

Read this article about Christian prophets becoming more prominent

Can a Little Knowledge Be More Dangerous Than None?

December 26th

DUNNING–KRUGER EFFECT

The Dunning–Kruger effect describes our tendency to overestimate our own abilities in areas that we are unskilled in or lack knowledge in. This happens when we know just enough to think we are great, but not enough to tell the difference between good and bad. We just don't know yet what we could do better. The effect also applies to society as a whole. The most uninformed citizens are often also the most confident ones.

In 1930s Soviet Russia, a man who never finished high school decided he understood genetics better than the world's leading scientists. That man was Joseph Stalin, and his misplaced confidence would lead to the deaths of countless scientists and the collapse of Soviet agriculture. This historical disaster perfectly illustrates how dangerous it can be when someone knows just enough to feel like an expert, but not enough to realize they're wrong.

Enter Trofim Lysenko, an agronomist who claimed plants could be "trained" to grow in any conditions and that acquired characteristics could be inherited - ideas that contradicted established genetic science. Despite the global scientific consensus against these theories, Stalin enthusiastically embraced them. Why? They aligned perfectly with his political ideology, promising that organisms, like society, could be reshaped through "education." Stalin's overconfidence in his scientific judgment led him to reject traditional genetics as "bourgeois science." Real geneticists who opposed Lysenko's theories were persecuted or executed, including renowned scientist Nikolai Vavilov, who died in prison for daring to defend actual genetic science.

The human cost of this scientific hubris was staggering. Following Lysenko's methods, Soviet grain yields fell to 35% of their previous levels between 1940 and 1954. The failed agricultural policies contributed to severe famines, with Ukraine alone losing an estimated 5 million people to starvation. Even after Stalin's death, Lysenko's influence persisted until 1964, leaving Soviet biological science isolated from global advances in genetics and molecular biology for over three decades.

Remember Stalin's story when you feel like an expert after a quick Google search.

Q-pid's Errant Arrow

December 27th

GROUPTHINK

Groupthink is when our desire for harmony and conformity within a group leads to dysfunctional decision-making. Group members prioritize agreement over critical evaluation, resulting in a loss of individual creativity and thinking. This can lead to an inflated sense of confidence in the group's abilities, an undervaluation of opponents, group pressure, and potentially harmful actions towards outsiders.

The QAnon conspiracy movement provides a disturbing case study of the groupthink bias taking hold. The movement began in October 2017 on a 4chan board, an anonymous messaging forum, where a user "Q" claimed to be a high-level government insider sharing classified information. QAnon's central claim was that former President Trump was fighting a satanic, cannibalistic cabal of pedophiles running a global child sex trafficking ring. The beginning can be traced back to the 2016 "Pizzagate" conspiracy theory, which falsely claimed emails from Hillary Clinton's campaign contained coded messages about a non-existent child sex trafficking ring at a D.C. pizza restaurant. This rumor inspired a man to show up and fire a rifle inside the restaurant.

Despite the bizarre nature of Q's information "drops," they quickly amassed a dedicated following of believers known as "anons." Q's unsubstantiated claims and cryptic posted "clues" allowed followers to engage in rampant speculation, believing they were piecing together a secret truth. This "gamified" conspiracy theory rapidly spread across internet fringes like 4chan and dedicated QAnon message boards. Q's predictions that mass arrests of the pedophile cabal were imminent, including predictions of Hillary Clinton's supposed imprisonment at Guantanamo, stoked fervor when they failed to materialize.

Rather than scrutinizing the obvious implausibility of the assertions from an unverified source, devoted QAnon followers displayed classic symptoms of groupthink. They exhibited a strong illusion of invulnerability, convinced they alone possessed special knowledge that made them superior to "sleeping" non-believers. When predictions failed, followers engaged in collective rationalization, creating elaborate explanations to maintain their beliefs.

Control Over Your Life is Just One Book Away

December 28th

ILLUSION OF CONTROL

The illusion of control occurs when we believe we have more control over external events than we do. We frequently believe we have (or had) some control over events that are actually random. Researchers have found that people who feel in control will engage in healthier behaviors, feel less stress, and have better overall mental health. Therefore, this illusion makes us feel better about ourselves and the world around us, but it can also seduce us into relying on superstitions.

The self-help industry, with its vast reach and profound influence on millions, offers a prime example of the illusion of control. This multi-billion-dollar market, filled with an array of books, seminars, coaching, and online courses, promises personal transformation and happiness. The market was expected to be worth 41.2 billion dollars in 2023. Yet, beneath the surface, it inadvertently perpetuates the belief that we have more control over our lives and mental states than we actually do.

The allure of self-help lies in its promise that, through certain techniques or knowledge, one can achieve an ideal state of being. It suggests that happiness, success, and personal fulfillment are just a book or seminar away. This notion feeds into the human desire for control over one's life and circumstances. However, many aspects of our lives are subject to forces outside of our immediate control, such as our socioeconomic status, our genetic makeup, and unforeseen circumstances.

Ironically, the most fundamental step towards genuine self-improvement—acceptance of oneself as adequate—contradicts the premise that one needs external self-help solutions to be "fixed." This paradox underscores the inherent contradiction in seeking control over one's self-improvement from external sources. While meaningful personal change is both possible and achievable, true growth often comes from accepting the limits of our control and working within them, rather than chasing the illusion of total control over our personal development.

Watch this video on why the self-help industry is lying

Stories That Are More Believable Than the Evidence

December 29th

ILLUSORY TRUTH EFFECT

The illusory truth effect causes us to believe information is true if we hear it repeatedly, even when it's not. This happens because repeatedly hearing the same information makes it familiar, and our brain processes familiar things more easily. This ease is due to the activation of well-established neural pathways, which require less effort to process than new or unfamiliar information. When our brains process information with less effort, we tend to interpret this ease as a sign of truth. Thus, if something is easier to understand, we are more likely to believe it's true.

The illusory truth effect has played a significant role in the proliferation of urban legends like the Loch Ness Monster or Bigfoot.

The Loch Ness Monster found its fame in the 20th century, particularly after 1933, when a surge in reported sightings and the publication of the now-infamous "Surgeon's Photograph" cemented "Nessie" in public consciousness. This photograph, later revealed to be a hoax, depicted a creature with a long neck protruding from the water, resembling a plesiosaur - an ancient marine reptile that lived alongside dinosaurs. Loch Ness itself, a massive freshwater lake in Scotland, has been extensively studied with sonar and underwater cameras. No evidence of a large unknown creature has ever been found. For decades, the "Surgeon's Photograph" was considered the best evidence of Nessie's existence, prompting numerous expeditions to Loch Ness.

Bigfoot, also known as Sasquatch, captured the American public's attention in the mid-20th century, with a significant spike in interest following the 1967 release of the Patterson-Gimlin film. This short motion picture claimed to show a female Bigfoot walking through a clearing in Northern California. The footage's grainy and ambiguous nature only fueled speculation and debate, leading to an explosion of Bigfoot hunting expeditions, books, and films. However, numerous analyses suggest the film was a hoax.

Modern audiences view the Loch Ness Monster and Bigfoot as entertaining myths rather than real mysteries. But during their peaks, these stories transcended their origins as mere legends, becoming embedded in cultural lore largely due to the illusory truth effect.

How to Not Apply Psychological Principles

December 30th

DEFAULT EFFECT

When offered a choice that has a pre-selected default option, we tend to choose this default option. This is called the default effect. Defaults are the options that take effect if we do nothing. Our brains try to save as much mental energy as possible. Accepting the default option saves energy because we don't have to think about the pros and cons of each choice.

Facebook's Beacon disaster of 2007 illustrates a company exploiting the default effect, with significant repercussions. Beacon, the name for an innovative advertising feature, aimed to enhance engagement on the platform by sharing details of our online activities with friends.

For instance, if you purchased a book from a participating site, that information could be shared on your Facebook profile to recommend it to friends. However, the feature automatically shared users' activities without their explicit consent, unless they opted out.

The backlash was immediate and intense. Users and privacy advocates accused Facebook of infringing on personal privacy. Since Beacon's default setting shared information automatically, many users were unaware of their participation, fueling the controversy. The outcry from users and privacy advocates culminated in a petition with 69,000 signatures, calling for an end to these intrusive practices.

In response to the uproar, Facebook's founder, Mark Zuckerberg, issued an apology to the site's 57 million users. He acknowledged that Facebook had made mistakes in both the development and deployment of Beacon. Facebook changed Beacon to require an opt-in from users, shifting away from automatic enrollment.

Facebook's "move fast and break things" ethos severely miscalculated the trade-off between innovation and user privacy here. This incident underscores the misuse of psychological insights regarding the default effect, serving as a cautionary tale on how not to apply psychological principles to technological innovations.

How Does Wanting to Be Right Make Us Wrong?

December 31st

CONFIRMATION BIAS

Confirmation bias is our tendency to look for, acknowledge, favor, and remember information in a way that supports what we already think or believe. This bias occurs when we ignore information that contradicts our ideas or interpret ambiguous facts as evidence supporting our existing beliefs. Situations that involve emotionally charged topics, strongly held beliefs, or things we really want to happen are most susceptible to this bias.

In 1912, a British fossil hunter announced a discovery that would perfectly confirm what the scientific establishment desperately wanted to believe. Charles Dawson unveiled Piltdown Man - supposedly the "missing link" between apes and humans, conveniently found in England. The scientific community, eager to prove that human evolution had centered in Europe rather than Africa, embraced this finding with remarkable enthusiasm and astonishingly little scrutiny.

For 40 years, Piltdown Man stood as "proof" of British evolutionary superiority. Even when contradictory fossils were discovered in Africa, many scientists twisted themselves into intellectual knots trying to make these new findings fit with Piltdown rather than question their prized discovery. The skull was eventually exposed as an elaborate hoax in 1953 - a modern human cranium combined with an orangutan's jaw, artificially aged using chemicals. The teeth had been deliberately filed down to match the wear pattern they expected to see.

The price of this collective confirmation bias was steep: four decades of evolutionary research was built on a fabrication, legitimate African fossils were marginalized or misinterpreted, and the true story of human evolution was delayed by decades. The British Museum, the Geological Society of London, and many other prestigious institutions had seen exactly what they wanted to see - ignoring obvious signs of forgery that modern scientists find almost embarrassingly clear.

Remember Piltdown Man when you find yourself collecting only the evidence that supports what you already believe.

BIBLIOGRAPHY

JANUARY 1ST - *Are You Insuring Against Reality or Disaster Hype?*
Michel-Kerjan, E., de Forges, S. L., & Kunreuther, H. (2011). Policy tenure under the U.S. national flood insurance program (NFIP). Risk Analysis, 32(4), 644–658. https://doi.org/10.1111/j.1539-6924.2011.01671.x

JANUARY 2ND - *Astro-Not: Are Horoscopes Really Written in the Stars?*
Fichten, C. S. (1983). Popular horoscopes and the "Barnum effect." The Journal of Psychology Interdisciplinary and Applied, 114(1), 123–134. https://doi.org/10.1080/00223980.1983.9915405

JANUARY 3RD - *Why Can't Top Execs Admit Their Mistakes?*
Woollacott, E. (2018, July 18). Lessons from history's worst CEOs. The CEO Magazine. Retrieved September 3, 2022, from https://www.theceomagazine.com/business/management-leadership/lessons-from-historys-worst-ceos/

Lee, T. B. (2015, October 29). Carly Fiorina's controversial record as CEO, explained. Vox. Retrieved September 3, 2022, from https://www.vox.com/2015/9/17/9346877/carly-fiorina-hewlett-packard

JANUARY 4TH - *Beauty and the Bias: Do Attractive People Win in Court?*
Castellow, W. A., Wuensch, K. L., & Moore, C. H. (1990). Effects of physical attractiveness of the plaintiff and defendant in sexual harassment judgements. Journal of Social Behavior and Personality, 5(6), 547–562. https://doi.org/10887248/effects_of_physical_attractiveness_of_the_plaintiff_and_defendant_in_sexual_harassment_judgments.pdf

JANUARY 5TH - *Surcharge or discount?*
Robbennolt, J. K. (2017, October 1). Differential pricing for credit cards: Surcharge or discount? Monitor on Psychology, 48(9). https://www.apa.org/monitor/2017/10/jn

Thaler, R. H. (2016). Misbehaving: The making of behaviroal economics. National Geographic Books.

JANUARY 6TH - *Can We Really Predict a Crisis or Are We Just Blinded by Hindsight?*
Chen, J. (2022, August 17). Hindsight bias. Investopedia. Retrieved August 20, 2022, from https://www.investopedia.com/terms/h/hindsight-bias.asp

JANUARY 7TH - *What is your favorite animal from a Disney movie?*
Yeung, K. Y. M. G. (2020). Anthropomorphic animal characters in Disney animated films: The representations and impositions of human nature. EdUHK Research Repository. https://repository.eduhk.hk/en/publications/anthropomorphic-animal-characters-in-disney-animated-films-the-re

JANUARY 9TH - *Frozen in FOMO?*
Ice Bucket Challenge. (2024). In Wikipedia. Retrieved March 27, 2024, from https://en.wikipedia.org/wiki/Ice_Bucket_Challenge

JANUARY 10TH - *Can Superstition and Finger Snaps Sway the Odds?*
Henslin, J. M. (1967). Craps and magic. American Journal of Sociology, 73(3), 316–330. https://www.jstor.org/stable/2776031

JANUARY 11TH - *How to Make a Rolls Royce Look Like a Bargain?*
GDS Summits. (2018, October 31). The psychology of digital marketing. Rory Sutherland, Ogilvy. [Video]. YouTube. https://youtu.be/hhQRH49Y54k

JANUARY 12TH - *Is Karma a Bitch?*
Hamsaka. (2014, August). The "just world hypothesis" and karma. Newbuddhist. Retrieved September 3, 2022, from https://newbuddhist.com/discussion/21689/the-just-world-hypothesis-and-karma

JANUARY 13TH - *Why Did Some 9/11 Survivors Hit Ctrl+Alt+Del Before Escaping?*
Ripley, A. (2005, April 25). How to Get Out Alive. Time. https://content.time.com/time/printout/0,8816,1053663,00.html

JANUARY 14TH - *Is Emily in Paris' Ignorance a Classic Case of Dunning-Kruger?*
Friendly Space Ninja. (2021, February 4). Emily in Paris: Romanticizing Ignorance [Video]. YouTube. Retrieved March 26, 2024, from https://www.youtube.com/watch?v=cTLIIik_o2k

Henley, J. (2021, November 29). "Plenty to feel insulted about": French critics round on Emily in Paris. The Guardian. https://www.theguardian.com/world/2020/oct/06/plenty-to-feel-insulted-about-french-critics-round-on-emily-in-paris

JANUARY 15TH - *How to Win the Lottery*
Langer, E. J. (1975). The illusion of control. Journal of Personality and Social Psychology, 32(2), 311–328. https://doi.org/10.1037/0022-3514.32.2.311x

JANUARY 16TH - *When Should You Really Quit a Dull Movie?*
Strough, J., Mehta, C. M., McFall, J. P., & Schuller, K. L. (2008). Are older adults less subject to the Sunk-Cost fallacy than younger adults? Are Older Adults Less Subject to the Sunk-Cost Fallacy Than Younger Adults?, 19(7), 650–652. https://doi.org/10.1111/j.1467-9280.2008.02138.x

JANUARY 17TH - *DIY: A Billion-Dollar Question of Self-Worth and Identity?*
Ariely, D., Mochon, D., & Norton, M. I. (2011). The "IKEA effect": when labor leads to love. (Working Paper No. 11 091) Harvard Business School. https://www.hbs.edu/ris/Publication%20Files/11-091.pdf

JANUARY 18TH - *Do you feel like a forensic expert after watching CSI?*
Robbers, M. L. P. (2008). Blinded by science. Criminal Justice Policy Review, 19(1), 84–102. https://doi.org/10.1177/0887403407305982

JANUARY 19TH - *Are We Trading Lifelong Bliss for a Quick Fix of Happiness?*
Bellows, A. (2016, May). Hyperbolic Discounting. Damn Interesting. Retrieved August 21, 2022, from https://www.damninteresting.com/retired/hyperbolic-discounting/

JANUARY 20TH - *How Can Repetition Breed Belief?*
The illusory truth effect: Why we believe fake news, conspiracy theories and propaganda. (n.d.). Farnam Street. Retrieved September 3, 2022, from https://fs.blog/illusory-truth-effect/

Newton, C. (2019, February 25). The trauma Floor. The secret lives of Facebook moderators in America. The Verge. Retrieved March 26, 2024, from https://www.theverge.com/2019/2/25/18229714/cognizant-facebook-content-moderator-interviews-trauma-working-conditions-arizona

JANUARY 21ST - *Outsmarting Yourself: Does Expertise Make You More Susceptible to Scams?*
Frick, B. (2011, April 7). Why we fall for scams. Kiplinger. Retrieved August 29, 2022, from https://www.kiplinger.com/article/investing/t031-c000-s002-why-we-fall-for-scams.html

Lea, S. E. G., Fischer, P., & Evans, K. M. (2009). The psychology of scams: Provoking and committing errors of judgement. University of Exeter School of Psychology. https://ore.exeter.ac.uk/repository/handle/10871/20958

JANUARY 22ND - *Discrimi-nation: Is Our In-Group Bias Fueling Unfair Judgment?*
Cadsby, C. Bram & Du, Ninghua & Song, Fei, (2016). In-group favoritism and moral decision-making, Journal of Economic Behavior & Organization, Elsevier, vol. 128(C), pages 59-71. https://ideas.repec.org/a/eee/jeborg/v128y2016icp59-71.html

Kaufman, S. B. (2019, June 19). In-Group Favoritism Is Difficult to Change, Even When the Social Groups Are Meaningless. Scientific American. Retrieved March 26, 2024, from https://www.scientificamerican.com/blog/beautiful-minds/in-group-favoritism-is-difficult-to-change-even-when-the-social-groups-are-meaningless/

JANUARY 23RD - *Why Are We Still Waiting for Hose-Cleaning Homes?*

Patoway, K. (2010, November 13). Miracles you'll see in the next fifty years: An article from 1950. Amusing Planet. Retrieved March 26, 2024, from https://www.amusingplanet.com/2010/11/miracles-youll-see-in-next-fifty-years.html

JANUARY 24TH - *Can We Escape the Web of Our Own Opinions?*

How filter bubbles distort reality: Everything you need to know. (n.d.). Farnam Street. Retrieved August 27, 2022, from https://fs.blog/filter-bubbles/

Epstein, R., & Robertson, R. E. (2015). The search engine manipulation effect (SEME) and its possible impact on the outcomes of elections. Psychological and Cognitive Science, 112(33), E4512–E4521. https://doi.org/10.1073/pnas.1419828112

JANUARY 25TH - *Ending on a High Note: Are We Biased by Our Last Impressions?*

Kane, L. (2018, December 30). The Peak–End rule: How impressions become memories. Nielsen Norman Group. Retrieved September 1, 2022, from https://www.nngroup.com/articles/peak-end-rule/

Kahneman, D., Fredrickson, B. L., Schreiber, C. A., & Redelmeier, D. A. (1993). When More Pain Is Preferred to Less: Adding a Better End. Psychological Science, 4(6), 401–405. https://doi.org/10.1111/j.1467-9280.1993.tb00589.x

JANUARY 27TH - *50 Shades of Grey Matter: Can Nuanced Thinking Bridge Divides?*

Grant, A. (2021). Think again: The power of knowing what you don't know. Vinking.

Fisher, M., & Keil, F. C. (2018). The Binary Bias: A Systematic Distortion in the Integration of Information. Psychological Science, 29(11), 1846–1858. https://doi.org/10.1177/0956797618792256

JANUARY 28TH - *Monte Carlo Missteps: Can Losing Big Teach Us a Winning Lesson?*

Inglis-Arkell, E. (2014, August 1). The night the gambler's fallacy lost people millions. Gizmodo. Retrieved August 25, 2022, from https://gizmodo.com/the-night-the-gamblers-fallacy-lost-people-millions-1496890660

Fortune, E. E., & Goodie, A. S. (2012). Cognitive distortions as a component and treatment focus of pathological gambling: A review. Psychology of Addictive Behaviors, 26(2), 298–310. https://doi.org/10.1037/a0026422

JANUARY 29TH - *It is never your fault, is it?*

The Associated Press. (2001, August 31). Ford chief says Firestone rejected '99 suspicions of tire problem. The New York Times. https://www.nytimes.com/2001/08/31/business/ford-chief-says-firestone-rejected-99-suspicions-of-tire-problem.html

JANUARY 30TH - *Was It Really Predictable?*

Carli, L. L., & Leonard, J. B. (1989). The effect of hindsight on victim derogation. Journal of Social and Clinical Psychology, 8(3), 331–343. https://doi.org/10.1521/jscp.1989.8.3.331

JANUARY 31ST - *Can We Balance Compassion and Self-Preservation?*

Lueders, A., Prentice, M., & Jonas, E. (2019). Refugees in the media: Exploring a vicious cycle of frustrated psychological needs, selective exposure, and hostile intergroup attitudes. European Journal of Social Psychology, 49(7), 1471–1479. https://doi.org/10.1002/ejsp.2580

Heap, C. (2019, April 7). Cognitive dissonance: How we dismiss the refugee crisis. Swhelper. Retrieved August 24, 2022, from https://swhelper.org/2015/09/28/cognitive-dissonance-dismiss-refugee-crisis/

FEBRUARY 1ST - *Are Vitamins Really Helping?*

Warren, M. (2019, March 20). How to combat the "Illusion of causality" that contributes to so many healthy people taking multivitamin pills they don't need. The British Psychological Society. Retrieved September 3, 2022, from https://www.bps.org.uk/research-digest/how-combat-illusion-causality-contributes-so-many-healthy-people-taking

MacFarlane, D., Hurlstone, M. J., & Ecker, U. K. H. (2018). Reducing demand for ineffective health remedies: overcoming the illusion of causality. Psychology & Health, 33(12), 1472–1489. https://doi.org/10.1080/08870446.2018.1508685

Solan, M. (2022, April 01). Don't waste time (or money) on dietary supplements. Harvard Medical School. Retrieved April 18, 2024, from https://www.health.harvard.edu/staying-healthy/dont-waste-time-or-money-on-dietary-supplements

FEBRUARY 3RD - *What's the Real Struggle with Stuttering?*

Zeigler-Hill, V., Besser, A., & Besser, Y. (2021). The negative consequences of stuttering for perceptions of leadership ability. Journal of Individual Differences, 42(3), 116–123. https://doi.org/10.1027/1614-0001/a000336

CNN. (2020, February 6). Biden shares vulnerable story on how he overcame stuttering. [Video]. YouTube. https://youtu.be/iWn1CkIU_rc

FEBRUARY 4TH - *Is Your GPS a Roadmap to Disaster or Trusty Co-Pilot?*

Hanson, B. (2012, March 19). GPS leads japanese tourists to drive into australian bay. Huffpost. Retrieved September 3, 2022, from https://www.huffingtonpost.co.uk/entry/gps-tourists-australia_n_1363823

Phillips, D. (2015, October 15). How directions on the Waze app led to death in Brazil's favelas. The Washington Post. https://www.washingtonpost.com/news/worldviews/wp/2015/10/05/how-directions-on-the-waze-app-led-to-death-in-brazils-favelas/

FEBRUARY 5TH - *Survival of the Fittest Frame: How Does Perspective Impact Decisions?*

O'Connor, A. M. (1989). Effects of framing and level of probability on patients' preferences for cancer chemotherapy. Journal of Clinical Epidemiology, 42(2), 119–126. https://doi.org/10.1016/0895-4356(89)90085-1

FEBRUARY 6TH - *Workplace favouritism is annoying - and irrational*

Waters, S. (2021, October 4). The cognitive biases caused by the availability heuristic. Better Up. Retrieved August 24, 2022, from https://www.betterup.com/blog/the-availability-heuristic

FEBRUARY 7TH - *To Sell Or Not To Sell?*

Kahneman, D., Knetsch, J. L., & Thaler, R. H. (1991). Anomalies: The endowment effect, loss aversion, and status quo bias. Journal of Economic Perspectives, 5(1), 139–206. https://doi.org/10.1257/jep.5.1.193

FEBRUARY 8TH - *What Would it Take for a Philosopher to Skip Their Bubble Bath?*

Jones, N. F. (2001). Pliny the Younger's Vesuvius "Letters" (6.16 and 6.20). The Classical World, 95(1), 31–48. https://doi.org/10.2307/4352621

FEBRUARY 9TH - *Are Police Officers Snoozing on Equality? The Sleep-Bias Connection*

James, L. (2017). The stability of implicit racial bias in police officers. Police Quarterly, 21(1), 30–52. https://doi.org/10.1177/1098611117732974

FEBRUARY 10TH - *Can You Drop Out and Win Like Steve Jobs and Bill Gates?*

Hess, A. J. (2017, May 10). 10 ultra-successful millionaire and billionaire college dropouts. CNBC. https://www.cnbc.com/2017/05/10/10-ultra-successful-millionaire-and-billionaire-college-dropouts.html

FEBRUARY 11TH - *Mirror, Mirror on the Wall: Are We Building Robots Too Human After All?*

Bruni, D., Perconti, P., & Plebe, A. (2018). Anti-anthropomorphism and its limits. Frontiers in Psychology, 9, Article 2205. https://doi.org/10.3389/fpsyg.2018.02205

Sandini, G., & Sciutti, A. (2018). Humane robots—from robots with a humanoid body to robots with an anthropomorphic mind. ACM Transactions on Human-Robot Interaction, 7(1), 1–4. https://doi.org/10.1145/3208954

The Economist. (2022, November 10). Humanoid robots are getting close to reality. The Economist. https://www.economist.com/science-and-technology/2022/11/07/humanoid-robots-are-getting-close-to-reality

FEBRUARY 12TH - *Do You Know How Disastrous the Bay of Pigs Invasion Was?*

The Bay of Pigs. (n.d.). John F. Kennedy Presidential Library and Museum. https://www.jfklibrary.org/learn/about-jfk/jfk-in-history/the-bay-of-pigs

Kornbluh, P. (1998). Bay of Pigs declassified: The Secret CIA Report on the Invasion of Cuba. The New Press

FEBRUARY 13TH - *A One-Way Ticket with the Bandwagon to Bubble Trouble?*
The Investopedia Team. (2022, June 3). Bandwagon effect. Investopedia. Retrieved August 25, 2022, from https://www.investopedia.com/terms/b/bandwagon-effect.asp

FEBRUARY 15TH - *Coincidence or Conspiracy? Why Do We Suddenly See Things Everywhere?*
Staff, P. S. (2017, June 14). There's a Name for That: The Baader-Meinhof Phenomenon. Pacific Standard. Retrieved September 3, 2022, from https://psmag.com/social-justice/theres-a-name-for-that-the-baader-meinhof-phenomenon-59670

FEBRUARY 17TH - *Are We Biased Towards Zero-Risk, Even When It's Not the Best Option?*
Baron, J., Gowda, R., & Kunreuther, H. (1993). Attitudes toward managing hazardous waste: What should be cleaned up and who should pay for it? Risk Analysis, 13, 183-192. https://www.sas.upenn.edu/~baron/papers.htm/gowda.html

FEBRUARY 18TH - *Is the Fear of Loss Ruining Your Investments?*
Why do we tend to hold on to losing investments? (n.d.). The Decision Lab. Retrieved August 21, 2022, from https://thedecisionlab.com/biases/disposition-effect

Shefrin, H., & Statman, M. (1985). The disposition to sell winners too early and ride losers too long: Theory and evidence. The Journal of Finance, 40(3), 777–790. https://doi.org/10.2307/2327802

Barberis, N., & Xiong, W. (2009). What drives the disposition effect? An analysis of a Long-Standing Preference-Based explanation. The Journal of Finance, 64(2), 751–784. https://doi.org/10.1111/j.1540-6261.2009.01448.x

FEBRUARY 19TH - *Can We Outsmart Lady Luck? The Mind's Gamble with Control*
Cowley, E., Briley, D. A., & Farrell, C. (2015). How do gamblers maintain an illusion of control? Journal of Business Research, 68(10), 2181–2188. https://doi.org/10.1016/j.jbusres.2015.03.018

FEBRUARY 21ST - *Can Believers Bounce Back from Galactic Ghosting?*
Festinger, L., Riecken, H. W., & Schachter, S. (2009). When prophecy fails. Martino Fine Books.

FEBRUARY 23RD - *Banking on the Wrong Numbers?*
Ceravolo, M. G., Farina, V., Fattobene, L., Leonelli, L., & Raggetti, G. (2022). Anchoring effect in visual information processing during financial decisions: An eye-tracking study. Journal of Neuroscience, Psychology, and Economics, 15(1), 19–30. https://doi.org/10.1037/npe0000153

FEBRUARY 25TH - *What's More Deadly: Fireworks or Asthma?*
Slovic, P., Fischhoff, B., & Liechtenstein, S. (1976). Cognitive Processes and Societal Risk Taking. In Decision Making and Change in Human Affairs. Theory and Decision Library, Vol. 16, pp. 7–36. Springer, Dordrecht. https://doi.org/10.1007/978-94-010-1276-8_2

Gilbert, D. (2005). Why we make bad decisions [Video]. TED Conferences. https://www.ted.com/talks/dan_gilbert_why_we_make_bad_decisions?language=en

FEBRUARY 26TH - *Is Your Partner Really Slacking, or Are You Just Biased?*
Talks at Google. (2015, November 5). Dating & Relationships | Dan Ariely | Talks at Google [Video]. YouTube. https://www.youtube.com/watch?v=RS8R2TKrYi0

FEBRUARY 27TH - *Are We Seeing Predictions or Just Connecting Dots?*
Dsouza, M. (n.d.). Outcome bias – do not make decisions based on results. Productive Club. Retrieved August 30, 2022, from https://productiveclub.com/outcome-bias/#3_Nostradamus_Predictions

FEBRUARY 28TH - *Can Familiarity Breed Liking for Words We Do Not Understand?*
Zajonc, R. B., & Rajecki, D. W. (2013). Exposure and affect: A field experiment. Psychonomic Science, 17, 216–217. https://doi.org/10.3758/BF03329178

Monahan, J. L., Murphy, S. T., & Zajonc, R. B. (2000). Subliminal mere exposure: Specific, general, and diffuse effects. American Psychological Society, 11(6), 462–466. https://annenberg.usc.edu/sites/default/files/2015/04/29/Subliminal%20Mere%20Exposure%20Sheila%20Murphy.pdf

FEBRUARY 29TH - *How Does Gender Affect How We Judge Leaders' Mistakes?*

American Psychological Asociation. (2019, October 24). Women CEOs judged more harshly than men for corporate ethical failures: Female leaders receive less negativity for general business failures, study says. ScienceDaily. Retrieved September 3, 2022, from https://www.sciencedaily.com/releases/2019/10/191024093604.htm

MARCH 1ST - *Can You Judge the Quality of a Decision Separately from the Outcome?*

Baron, J., & Hershey, J. C. (1988). Outcome bias in decision evaluation. Journal of Personality and Social Psychology, 54(4), 569–579. https://www.sas.upenn.edu/~baron/papers/outcomebias.pdf

MARCH 2ND - *Are Celebrities Truly as Perfect as They Seem?*

Coane, J. (2013, February 6). Are Celebrities Really THAT Perfect? How the Halo Effect Impacts the Way We View and Treat Others. Cogblog. Retrieved August 24, 2022, from https://web.colby.edu/cogblog/2020/11/20/are-celebrities-really-that-perfect-how-the-Halo Effect-impacts-the-way-we-view-and-treat-others/

MARCH 3RD - *How Did the Normalcy Bias Contribute to the Catastrophe of Katrina?*

Singletary, M. (2019, September 5). Why do some people refuse to evacuate during a hurricane? For the same reasons people don't listen to warnings they should save money. The Washington Post. Retrieved September 3, 2022, from https://www.washingtonpost.com/business/2019/09/05/why-do-some-people-refuse-evacuate-during-hurricane-same-reasons-people-dont-listen-warnings-they-should-save/

World Vision. (2023, November 20). Hurricane Katrina: Facts, FAQs, and how to help. https://www.worldvision.org/disaster-relief-news-stories/2005-hurricane-katrina-facts

MARCH 4TH - *Too Many Pills to Swallow: Do More Choices Lead to Worse Decisions?*

Redelmeier, D. A., & Shafir, E. (1995). Medical decision making in situations that offer multiple alternatives. JAMA, 273(4), 302–305. https://pubmed.ncbi.nlm.nih.gov/7815657/

Ariely, D. (2008). Predictably Irrational. HarperCollins.

MARCH 5TH - *Can Your Voting Booth Location Influence Your Vote?*

Berger, J., Meredith, M., & Wheeler, S. C. (2008). Contextual priming: Where people vote affects how they vote. Proceedings of the National Academy of Sciences of the United States of America, 105(26), 8846-8849. https://doi.org/10.1073/pnas.0711988105

MARCH 6TH - *What Price Do We Pay for Free Games?*

Bycer, J. (2020, August 13). How Free-to-Play Games Trap Players by Design. Medium. https://medium.com/super-jump/how-free-to-play-games-trap-players-by-design-43ae161bc227

Diablo Immortal. (2022, June 2). Metacritic. https://www.metacritic.com/game/pc/diablo-immortal

Stewart, S. (2022, November 4). Diablo Immortal has reportedly made over $300 million. Game Rant. Retrieved March 26, 2024, from https://gamerant.com/diablo-immortal-made-300-million-dollars/

MARCH 7TH - *Won't somebody please think of the children?*

Crane, E. (2023, March 17). Florida ban on gender transitioning for minors now in effect. New York Post. https://nypost.com/2023/03/17/florida-ban-on-gender-transitioning-for-kisd-now-in-effect/

Respaut, R., & Terhune, C. (2022, October 6). Putting numbers on the rise in children seeking gender care. Reuters Investigates. https://www.reuters.com/investigates/special-report/usa-transyouth-data/

MARCH 8TH - *Are We Assembling Our Own Overwork Nightmare?*

Moss, S. A., Wilson, S. G., & Davis, J. M. (2016). Which cognitive biases can exacerbate our workload? The Australasian Journal of Organisational Psychology, 9. https://doi.org/10.1017/orp.2016.1

MARCH 9TH - *Overpaying for Underperformance?*

Bitwell, M. (2011). Paying more to get less: The effects of external hiring versus internal mobility. Administrative Science Quarterly, 56(3), 369–407. https://doi.org/10.1177/0001839211433562

Knowledge at Wharton Staff. (2012, March 28). Why external hires get paid more, and perform worse, than internal staff. Knowledge at Wharton. Retrieved August 29, 2022, from https://knowledge.wharton.upenn.edu/article/why-external-hires-get-paid-more-and-perform-worse-than-internal-staff/

MARCH 10TH - *Who decides what you see on Instagram or Facebook?*

Eslami, M., Rickman, A., Vaccaro, K., Aleyasen, A., Vuong, A., Karahalios, K., Hamilton, K., & Sandvig, C. (2015, April). "I always assumed that I wasn't really that close to [her]": Reasoning about invisible algorithms in news feeds. CHI '15, 153–162. https://doi.org/10.1145/2702123.2702556

Bechmann, A., & Nielbo, K. L. (2018). Are we exposed to the same "News" in the news feed? Digital Journalism, 6(8), 990–1002. https://doi.org/10.1080/21670811.2018.1510741

Büchi, M., Fosch-Villaronga, E., Lutz, C., Tamò-Larrieux, A., & Velidi, S. (2023). Making sense of algorithmic profiling: user perceptions on Facebook. Information, Communication & Society, 26(4), 809–825. https://doi.org/10.1080/1369118X.2021.1989011

MARCH 11TH - *False Balance: When Does Encouraging Debate Go Too Far?*

Boykoff, M. T., & Boykoff, J. M. (2004). Balance as bias: Global warming and the US prestige press☆.Global Environmental Change, 14(2), 125–136. https://doi.org/10.1016/j.gloenvcha.2003.10.001

Grimes, D. R. (2019). A dangerous balancing act. EMBO Reports, 20(8). https://doi.org/10.15252/embr.201948706

MARCH 12TH - *Riding the Rails to Recruitment: Get the German Army Back on Track?*

Schumacher, E. (2019, August 16). German soldiers to get free train travel. DW.COM. Retrieved September 3, 2022, from https://www.dw.com/en/german-soldiers-to-get-free-train-travel/a-50057011

MARCH 14TH - *Is the Supernatural Real or Are We Just Houdini-ed by Our Beliefs?*

Held, L. (2019, March 19). Psychic mediums are the new wellness coaches. The New York Times. Retrieved August 30, 2022, from https://www.nytimes.com/2019/03/19/style/wellness-mediums.html

Ballard, J. (2019, October 21). Many Americans believe ghosts and demons exist. YouGov. https://today.yougov.com/topics/society/articles-reports/2019/10/21/paranormal-beliefs-ghosts-demons-poll

Industry Market Research, Reports, and Statistics. (2021, April 9). IBISWorld. https://www.ibisworld.com/united-states/market-research-reports/psychic-services-industry/

MARCH 15TH - *Fear Factor: Are We Hardwired to Overreact to Disasters?*

Breckenridge, J., Zimbardo, P. G., & Sweeton, J. L. (2010). After years of media coverage, can one more video report trigger heuristic judgments? A national study of american terrorism risk perceptions. Behavioral Sciences of Terrorism and Political Aggression, 2(3), 163–178. https://doi.org/10.1080/19434471003768826

Sunstein, C. R. (2004). Precautions against what - the availability heuristic and Cross-Cultural risk perception. Law & Economics Working Papers, 220. https://doi.org/10.2139/ssrn.578303

Herre, B., Samborska, V., Ritchie, H., Hasell, J., Mathieu, E., & Roser, M. (2024, February 12). Terrorism. Our World in Data. https://ourworldindata.org/terrorism

MARCH 16TH - *Did you think Amanda Knox was guilty?*

Pisa, N. (2012, April 12). Amanda Knox "is a diabolical she-devil" | London Evening Standard. Evening Standard. https://www.standard.co.uk/hp/front/amanda-knox-is-a-diabolical-shedevil-6447176.html

MARCH 17TH - *Driven to Stay in School: Can Losing Licenses Curb Dropouts?*

Loewenstein, G., & Thaler, R. H. (1989). Anomalies: Intertemporal Choice. The Journal of Economic Perspectives, 3(4), 181–193. https://www.jstor.org/stable/1942718

MARCH 18TH - *Can AI Really Think, or Are We Just Projecting Our Own Intelligence?*

Tiku, N. (2022, June 11). The Google engineer who thinks the company's AI has come to life. The Washington Post. Retrieved September 3, 2022, from https://www.washingtonpost.com/technology/2022/06/11/google-ai-lamda-blake-lemoine/

The Economist. (2022, September 2). Artificial neural networks are making strides towards consciousness, according to Blaise Agüera y arcas. Retrieved September 3, 2022, from https://www.economist.com/by-invitation/2022/06/09/artificial-neural-networks-are-making-strides-towards-consciousness-according-to-blaise-aguera-y-arcas

MARCH 19TH - *Pandemic Panacea or Placebo?*

Why do we believe misinformation more easily when it's repeated many times? (n.d.). The Decision Lab. Retrieved August 30, 2022, from https://thedecisionlab.com/biases/illusory-truth-effect#section-8

Schwartz, I. S., Boulware, D. R., & Lee, T. C. (2022). Hydroxychloroquine for COVID19: The curtains close on a comedy of errors. The Lancet Regional Health - Americas, 11, 100268. https://doi.org/10.1016/j.lana.2022.100268

MARCH 20TH - *What led to the Challenger disaster?*

Berkes, H. (2016, March 22). Challenger engineer who warned of shuttle disaster dies. NPR. https://www.npr.org/sections/thetwo-way/2016/03/21/470870426/challenger-engineer-who-warned-of-shuttle-disaster-dies

Berkes, H. (2012, Frebruary 6). Remembering Roger Boisjoly: He tried to stop Shuttle Challenger launch. New Hampshire Public Radio. https://www.nhpr.org/national/2012-02-06/remembering-roger-boisjoly-he-tried-to-stop-shuttle-challenger-launch#stream/0

MARCH 21ST - *Was Napoleon the Emperor of Excuses?*

MilitaryHistoryNow.com. (2019, November 19). Napoleon on Waterloo – What did Bonaparte actually say about his most famous defeat? Retrieved March 27, 2024, from https://militaryhistorynow.com/2019/11/19/napoleon-on-waterloo-what-did-historys-greatest-conqueror-say-about-his-most-famous-defeat/

MARCH 22ND - *Are Women Dodging the Bullet on Dating Apps?*

The darkest side of online dating. (2021, June 23). BBC. Retrieved August 30, 2022, from https://www.bbc.com/worklife/article/20210623-the-darkest-side-of-online-dating

Distribution of Tinder monthly active users in the united states as of march 2021, by gender. (2021). [Dataset]. Statista. https://www.statista.com/statistics/975925/us-tinder-user-ratio-gender/

Anderson, M., Vogels, E. A., & Turner, E. (2020, February 6). The Virtues and Downsides of Online Dating. Pew Research Center: Internet, Science & Tech. https://www.pewresearch.org/Internet/2020/02/06/the-virtues-and-downsides-of-online-dating/

MARCH 23RD - *A Draft Disaster That Stemmed from Overconfidence?*

Reports, S. (1999, April 18). Saints' draft gives Ditka chills. Chicago Tribune. Retrieved March 26, 2024, from https://www.chicagotribune.com/1999/04/18/saints-draft-gives-ditka-chills/

OwnersBox Fantasy. (2022, April 26). The Ricky Williams 1999 NFL draft was INSANE! [Video]. YouTube. Retrieved March 26, 2024, from https://www.youtube.com/watch?v=meBYmSW2aV4

MARCH 24TH - *Should We Gargle with Doubt Over Time-Honored Medical Treatments?*

Rikkers, L. F. (2002). The bandwagon effect. Journal of Gastrointestinal Surgery, 6, 787–794. https://doi.org/10.1016/S1091-255X(02)00054-9

Why do we support opinions as they become more popular? (n.d.). The Decision Lab. Retrieved September 1, 2022, from https://thedecisionlab.com/biases/bandwagon-effect#section-8

MARCH 25TH - *How Two Brothers' Rivalry Shaped a Town's Identity*

Schwär, H. (2018, November 8). Puma and Adidas' rivalry has divided a small German town for 70 years — here's what it looks like now. Business Insider. https://www.businessinsider.com/how-puma-and-adidas-rivalry-divided-their-founding-town-for-70-years-2018-10

MARCH 26TH - *Memory Makeover: Did You Really Predict That?*

Gilbertson, L. J., Dietrich, D., Olson, M., & Guenther, R. K. (1994). A study of hindsight bias: The rodney king case in retrospect. Psychological Reports, 74(2), 383–386. https://doi.org/10.2466/pr0.1994.74.2.383

MARCH 27TH - *Heads or Tails: Do You Really Have a Handle on Chance?*
Burger, J. M. (1986). Desire for control and the illusion of control: The effects of familiarity and sequence of outcomes. Journal of Research in Personality, 20(1), 66–76. https://doi.org/10.1016/0092-6566(86)90110-8

Langer, E. J., & Roth, J. (1975). Heads I win, tails it's chance: The illusion of control as a function of the sequence of outcomes in a purely chance task. Journal of Personality and Social Psychology, 32(6), 951–955. https://doi.org/10.1037/0022-3514.32.6.951

MARCH 29TH - *Would Lady Luck Have Spared You from the Vietnam Draft?*
Vietnam War draft lottery - Would your number have been called? (n.d.). USA Today. https://www.usatoday.com/vietnam-war/draft-picker/

MARCH 30TH - *Are We Happier When We're Stuck with Our Decisions?*
Gilbert, D. T., & Ebert, J. E. J. (2002). Decisions and revisions: The affective forecasting of changeable outcomes. Journal of Personality and Social Psychology, 82(4), 503–514. https://doi.org/10.1037/0022-3514.82.4.503

MARCH 31ST - *Graded for Your (Un)lucky Genes?*
Talamas, S. N., Mavor, K. I., & Perrett, D. I. (2016). Blinded by beauty: Attractiveness bias and accurate perceptions of academic performance. PLoS ONE, 11(2), Article e0148284. https://doi.org/10.1371/journal.pone.0148284

Bonefeld, M., & Dickhäuser, O. (2018). (Biased) grading of students' performance: students' names, performance level, and implicit attitudes. Frontiers in Psychology, 9. https://doi.org/10.3389/fpsyg.2018.00481

APRIL 1ST - *Did you hear of the Torrey Canyon oil spill?*
Bell, B., & Cacciottolo, M. (2017, March 17). Torrey canyon oil spill: The day the sea turned black. BBC News. Retrieved August 21, 2022, from https://www.bbc.com/news/uk-england-39223308

APRIL 2ND - *How to not stick to what we know*
Montier, J. (2006). Behaving badly. Social Science Research Network. https://doi.org/10.2139/ssrn.890563

APRIL 3RD - *How Assertive Are You Really?*
Gleason, C. (2021, November 3). Availability heuristic and decision making. Simply Psychology. Retrieved September 1, 2022, from https://www.simplypsychology.org/availability-heuristic.html

APRIL 4TH - *How Can User Experience Design Be Peak-End Rule Friendly?*
Kane, L. (2018, December 30). The Peak–End rule: How impressions become memories. Nielsen Norman Group. Retrieved September 1, 2022, from https://www.nngroup.com/articles/peak-end-rule/

APRIL 5TH - *How Can Poverty Cloud Your Decision-Making Skills?*
Mani, A., Mullainathan, S., Shafir, E., & Zhao, J. (2013). Poverty impedes cognitive function. Science, 341(6149), 976–980. https://doi.org/10.1126/science.1238041

Yglesias, M. (2013, September 3). Bad decisions don't make you Poor. Being poor makes for bad Decisions. Slate Magazine. Retrieved September 3, 2022, from https://slate.com/business/2013/09/poverty-and-cognitive-impairment-study-shows-money-troubles-make-decision-making-difficult.html

Thompson, D. (2013, November 2). Your brain on poverty: Why poor people seem to make bad decisions. The Atlantic. Retrieved September 3, 2022, from https://www.theatlantic.com/business/archive/2013/11/your-brain-on-poverty-why-poor-people-seem-to-make-bad-decisions/281780/#main-content

APRIL 6TH - *Is Your Expertise Foolproof Against Anchors?*
Northcraft, G. B., & Neale, M. A. (1987). Experts, amateurs, and real estate: An anchoring-and-adjustment perspective on property pricing decisions. Organizational Behavior and Human Decision Processes, 39(1), 84–97. https://doi.org/10.1016/0749-5978(87)90046-X

APRIL 7TH - *Do We Secretly Believe Victims Had It Coming?*
Why do we believe that we get what we deserve? (n.d.). The Decision Lab. Retrieved August 25, 2022, from https://thedecisionlab.com/biases/just-world-hypothesis

APRIL 8TH - *Framing the Debate: Are We Pro-Choice, Pro-Life, or Pro-Compromise?*

Riley, B. (2022, January 29). Letters to the editor: Both sides of the abortion issue. Mansfield News Journal. Retrieved August 29, 2022, from https://www.mansfieldnewsjournal.com/story/news/2022/01/29/letters-editor-pro-choice-vs-pro-life/6608918001/

Piper, K. (2022, May 19). Pro-Life and Pro-Choice: What does it mean? Https://Www.Focusonthefamily.Com/pro-Life/Abortion/Pro-Life-pro-Choice/. Retrieved August 29, 2022, from https://www.focusonthefamily.com/pro-life/abortion/pro-life-pro-choice/

APRIL 9TH - *Did a Mummy's Curse Doom the Titanic?*

Dessem, M. (2018, October 14). One month after the Titanic sank, The Washington Post suggested a mummy's curse was to blame. Slate Magazine. Retrieved March 26, 2024, from https://slate.com/culture/2018/10/mummy-curse-titanic-sinking-washington-post-article.html

APRIL 10TH - *Are You a Slave to Your Self-Image?*

Stielstra, G. (2018, December 18). Commitment & consistency. Lirio. Retrieved August 30, 2022, from https://lirio.com/blog/commitment-consistency-lirio-bias-brief/

APRIL 11TH - *Are We Suffering from the 'Someone Like You' Syndrome?*

Dan Gilbert. What is Happiness? (2007, June 12). [Video]. Big Think. https://bigthink.com/videos/what-is-happiness/

APRIL 12TH - *Did you try Crystal Pepsi?*

VCRchivist. (2009, August 20). Crystal Pepsi Launch Ad - 1-minute Version - 1993 [Video]. YouTube. Retrieved March 27, 2024, from https://www.youtube.com/watch?v=KPvyq_KmX-hc

Kelly, D. (2018, September 12). Why Crystal Pepsi was a flop. Mashed. Retrieved March 27, 2024, from https://www.mashed.com/111261/crystal-pepsi-flop/

Saturday Night Live. (2017, November 16). Crystal Gravy - SNL [Video]. YouTube. Retrieved March 27, 2024, from https://www.youtube.com/watch?v=g0sjRG34DlA

APRIL 13TH - *Did You Use Auto-Save in Microsoft Word?*

Spool, J. (2011, September 14). Do users change their settings?. Archive of UIE/Brainsparks. Retrieved March 26, 2024, from https://archive.uie.com/brainsparks/2011/09/14/do-users-change-their-settings/

APRIL 14TH - *Did We Miss the Apocalypse?*

National Geographic. (2011, December 20). End of world in 2012? Maya "Doomsday" Calendar explained. Retrieved March 26, 2024, from https://www.nationalgeographic.com/science/article/111220-end-of-world-2012-maya-calendar-explained-ancient-science

APRIL 15TH - *How could you be motivated to do your cancer screening?*

Stoffel, S.T., Yang, J., Vlaev, I., von Wagner, C. (2019) Testing the decoy effect to increase interest in colorectal cancer screening. PLoS ONE 14(3): e0213668. https://doi.org/10.1371/journal.pone.0213668

Data & Progress. (2022, August 26). National Colorectal Cancer Roundtable. https://nccrt.org/data-progress/

APRIL 16TH - *Can a Bad CEO Teach Us Good Leadership Lessons?*

Woollacott, E. (2018, July 18). Lessons from history's worst CEOs. The CEO Magazine. Retrieved September 3, 2022, from https://www.theceomagazine.com/business/management-leadership/lessons-from-historys-worst-ceos/

APRIL 17TH - *Who Was Captain Hindsight?*

Elgot, J. (2021, March 23). Boris Johnson admits regrets over handling of first Covid wave. The Guardian. Retrieved March 26, 2024, from https://www.theguardian.com/world/2021/mar/23/boris-johnson-admits-regrets-handling-first-covid-wave

APRIL 18TH - *Trusting Your Gut with Finances?*

Miller, A. (2019, August 16). Social cognition and how to spot a fraudster. Process.St. Retrieved August 30, 2022, from https://www.process.st/social-cognition/

April 19th - *Too Tired for Salad? How Ego Depletion Affects Our Choices*
Ariely, D. (2012, August 15). Understanding ego depletion. Dan Ariely. Retrieved August 27, 2022, from https://danariely.com/tag/eating/

April 20th - *Why Was the Barnum Effect Named After the Master of Hoaxes?*
Gracey, M. (Director). (2017). The Greatest Showman. 20th Century Studios. https://www.imdb.com/title/tt1485796/

Meehl, P. E. (1956). Wanted—A Good Cookbook. American Psychologist, 11(39), 263–272. https://meehl.umn.edu/sites/meehl.umn.edu/files/files/039cookbook.pdf

April 21st - *Does Mother Earth Have a Mind of Her Own?*
Baerlocher, F. J. (1990). The Gaia hypothesis: A fruitful fallacy? Experientia, 46(3), 232–238. https://doi.org/10.1007/bf01951752

April 22nd - *Do You Remeber the Satanic Panic?*
Yuhas, A. (2021, March 31). It's time to revisit the satanic panic. The New York Times. Retrieved March 27, 2024, from https://www.nytimes.com/2021/03/31/us/satanic-panic.html

April 23rd - *Why Did Liberty, Equality, and Fraternity Turn Into a Bloody Feast?*
Mark, H. W., & Demachy, P. (2022, November 1). Reign of terror. World History Encyclopedia. https://www.worldhistory.org/Reign_of_Terror/

April 24th - *Can You Outsmart the Market's Herd Mentality?*
Treanor, J. (2017, November 29). The 2010 "flash crash": how it unfolded. The Guardian. https://www.theguardian.com/business/2015/apr/22/2010-flash-crash-new-york-stock-exchange-unfolded

April 25th - *Can confirmation bias explain the Salem Witch Trails?*
Wallenfeldt, J. (2023, December 3). Salem witch trials. Encyclopedia Britannica. https://www.britannica.com/event/Salem-witch-trials

April 26th - *Why Does Cupid's Arrow Attract More When We're in Relationships?*
Burch, R. L., Moran, J. B., & Wade, T. J. (2021). The reproductive priming effect revisited: Mate poaching, mate copying, or both? Evolutionary Behavioral Sciences, 15(3), 251–264. https://doi.org/10.1037/ebs0000232

April 27th - *Would You Buy a Ticket Twice?*
Kahneman, D., & Tversky, A. (1982). The Psychology of Preferences. Scientific American, 246(1), 160–173. https://doi.org/10.1038/scientificamerican0182-160

Arkes, H. R., & Ayton, P. (1999). The sunk cost and Concorde effects: Are humans less rational than lower animals? Psychological Bulletin, 125(5), 591–600. https://doi.org/10.1037/0033-2909.125.5.591

April 28th - *Iceland's Icarus: Flying Too Close to the Sun of Self-Belief?*
Grant, A. (2021). Think again: The power of knowing what you don't know. Vinking.

Spruk, Rok (2010): Iceland's Economic and Financial Crisis: Causes, Consequences and Implications. EEI Policy Paper, Vol. 1, No. 2010. https://mpra.ub.uni-muenchen.de/29972/1/MPRA_paper_29972.pdf

April 29th - *Change of Heart: Are We Ever Done Changing?*
Quoidbachdaniel, J. T., Gilbert, T., & Wilson, T. D. (2013). The end of history illusion. Science, 339(6115), 96–98. https://doi.org/10.1126/science.1229294

April 30th - *Eco-Friendly or Ego-Friendly?*
Cho, S., & Kim, Y. (2012). Corporate social responsibility (CSR) as a halo effect in issue management: Public response to negative news about pro-social local private companies. Asian Journal of Communication, 22(4), 1–14. https://doi.org/10.1080/01292986.2012.681666

May 1st - *Can Trusting Tech in Medicine be a Deadly Dose of Misjudgment?*
Fabio, A. (2015, October 26). Killed by a machine: the Therac-25. Hackaday. Retrieved March 26, 2024, from https://hackaday.com/2015/10/26/killed-by-a-machine-the-therac-25/

MAY 2ND - *When Should Homeopathy Take a Backseat?*

Freckelton, I. (2012). Death by homeopathy: Issues for civil, criminal and coronial law and for health service policy. Journal of Law and Medicine, 19(3), 454–478. https://pubmed.ncbi.nlm.nih.gov/22558899/

Reporter, G. S. (2017, November 26). Homeopathy couple jailed over daughter's death. The Guardian. https://www.theguardian.com/world/2009/sep/28/homeopathy-baby-death-couple-jailed

MAY 3RD - *Possession Obsession: Are We Overvaluing What's Ours?*

Kahneman, D., Knetsch, J. L., & Thaler, R. H. (1990). Experimental Tests of the Endowment Effect and the Coase Theorem. Journal of Political Economy, 98(6), 1325–1348. https://www.jstor.org/stable/2937761

MAY 4TH - *Head in the Sand: Do Investors Ignore Bad News?*

Karlsson, N., Seppi, D. J., & Loewenstein, G. (2005). The "ostrich effect": Selective attention to information about investments. SSRN. https://doi.org/10.2139/ssrn.772125

MAY 5TH - *Mirror, Mirror on the Wall: Does Our Group Shape Our Self-View After All?*

Sachs, N. M., Veysey, B. M., & Rivera, L. M. (2021). Implicit social cognitive processes underlying victim self and identity: Evidence with College-Aged adults. Journal of Interpersonal Violence, 36(3–4), 1256–1282. https://doi.org/10.1177/0886260517741625

Cox, W. T. L., Abramson, L. Y., Devine, P. G., & Hollon, S. D. (2012). Stereotypes, prejudice, and depression: The integrated perspective. Perspectives on Psychological Science, 7(5), 427–449. https://doi.org/10.1177/1745691612455204

Correll, S. J. (2001). Gender and the career choice process: The role of biased Self-Assessments. American Journal of Sociology, 106(6). https://doi.org/10.1086/321299

Correll, S. J. (2004). Constraints into preferences: Gender, status, and emerging career aspirations. American Sociological Review, 69(1), 93–113. https://doi.org/10.1177/000312240406900106

MAY 6TH - *More effort, more love?*

Dholakia, U. (2015, September 24). Why are so many indian arranged marriages successful? Psychology Today. Retrieved August 27, 2022, from https://www.psychologytoday.com/us/blog/the-science-behind-behavior/201511/why-are-so-many-indian-arranged-marriages-successful

Norton, M. I., Mochon, D., & Ariely, D. (2011). The "IKEA effect": When labor leads to love (Working Paper No. 11–091). Harvard Business Schoolhttps://www.hbs.edu/ris/Publication%20Files/11-091.pdf

Madathil, J., & Benshoff, J. M. (2008). Importance of Marital Characteristics and Marital Satisfaction: A Comparison of Asian Indians in Arranged Marriages and Americans in Marriages of Choice. The Family Journal, 16(3), 222–230. https://doi.org/10.1177/1066480708317504

MAY 8TH - *All In with the House Money?*

Thaler, R. H., & Johnson, E. J. (1990). Gambling with the House Money and Trying to Break Even: The Effects of Prior Outcomes on Risky Choice. Management Science, 36(6), 643–660. https://doi.org/10.1287/mnsc.36.6.643

MAY 9TH - *Are Referendums Failing to Capture the Full Story?*

Nurse, A., & Sykes, O. (2019). It's more complicated than that!: Unpacking 'Left Behind Britain' and some other spatial tropes following the UK's 2016 EU referendum. Local Economy, 34(6), 589–606. https://doi.org/10.1177/0269094219881356

MAY 10TH - *Cheat Now, Rationalize Later: Are We Fooling Ourselves into Morality?*

Stanley, M. L., Stone, A. R., & Marsh, E. J. (2021). Cheaters claim they knew the answers all along. Psychonomic Bulletin & Review, 28, 341–350. https://doi.org/10.3758/s13423-020-01812-w

Oltermann, P. (2021, May 23). German politicians suffer higher degree of embarrassment from plagiarism than from sex scandals. The Guardian. https://www.theguardian.com/world/2021/may/22/german-politicians-suffer-higher-degree-of-embarrassment-from-plagiarism-than-from-sex-scandals

MAY 11TH - *Do Trending Topics Dictate Political Decisions?*

Vis, B. (2019). Heuristics and political elites' judgment and Decision-Making. Political Studies Review, 17(1), 41–52. https://doi.org/10.1177/1478929917750311

MAY 12TH - *What Are the Secret Ingredients in the Recipe for Success?*

Blaine, B., & Crocker, J. (1993). Self-Esteem and Self-Serving biases in reactions to positive and negative events: An integrative review. In R. F. Baumeister (Ed.), Self-Esteem (pp. 55–85). Springer New York, NY. https://doi.org/10.1007/978-1-4684-8956-9_4

Strutner, S. (2020, March 17). 13 Entrepreneurs on Whether Luck or Skill Grew Their Startup. Netsuite. https://www.netsuite.com/portal/resource/articles/small-business/luck-in-business.shtml

MAY 13TH - *Fortune Favors the Bold: Do Entrepreneurs Make Their Own Luck?*

Kahneman, D. (2011). Thinking fast and slow. Farrar, Straus and Giroux.

Huddleston, T., Jr. (2021, December 1). Elon Musk has worried about SpaceX bankruptcy before. CNBC. https://www.cnbc.com/2021/11/30/elon-musk-warning-not-first-time-spacex-has-risked-bankruptcy.html

MAY 14TH - *Why do you make terrible life choices?*

Mani, L. (n.d.). Hyperbolic discounting: Why you make terrible life choices. Nir and Far. Retrieved September 1, 2022, from https://www.nirandfar.com/hyperbolic-discounting-why-you-make-terrible-life-choices/

MAY 15TH - *Are We Falling Prey to the Illusory Truth Effect of Diet Trends?*

Wells, I. (2019, September 22). Celery juice: The big problem with a viral instagram "cure." BBC. Retrieved August 30, 2022, from https://www.bbc.com/news/blogs-trending-49763144

MAY 16TH - *Mirror, Mirror on the Car: Are We Really the Best Drivers of Them All?*

Campbell, A. J. (2020, July 20). Most drivers are better than average. Adam Campbell. Retrieved August 27, 2022, from https://www.adam-campbell.com/post/most-drivers-are-better-than-average/

Roy, M. M., & Liersch, M. J. (2014). I am a better driver than you think: Examining Self-Enhancement for driving ability. Journal of Applied Social Psychology, 2013(43), 1648–1659. https://papers.ssrn.com/sol3/papers.cfm?abstract_id=2463245

MAY 17TH - *From Touchdowns to Lockdowns: How Far Will You Go for Your Team?*

Wann, D. L., & Grieve, F. G. (2005). Biased evaluations of In-Group and Out-Group spectator behavior at sporting events: the importance of team identification and threats to social identity. The Journal of Social Psychology, 145(5), 531–546. https://doi.org/10.3200/socp.145.5.531-546

Herbert, W. (2011, March 31). Yankees-Red Sox rivalry elicits extreme fanfare. Association for Psychological Science - APS. Retrieved March 26, 2024, from https://www.psychologicalscience.org/observer/yankees-red-sox-rivalry-elicits-extreme-fanfare

MAY 18TH - *How Can Seeking Confirmation Lead to Deception?*

Frick, B. (2011, April 7). Why we fall for scams. Kiplinger. Retrieved August 29, 2022, from https://www.kiplinger.com/article/investing/t031-c000-s002-why-we-fall-for-scams.html

Partridge, M. (2019, August 13). Great frauds in history: Marc Dreier. MoneyWeek. Retrieved March 26, 2024, from https://moneyweek.com/512729/great-frauds-in-history-marc-dreier

MAY 19TH - *Can Purchase Limits Make Us Soup-er Spenders?*

Wansink, B., Kent, R. J., & Hoch, S. J. (1998). An anchoring and adjustment model of purchase quantity decisions. Journal of Marketing Research, 35(1), 71–81. https://doi.org/10.2307/3151931

May 20th - Is Karma Really a B*tch?

Kaplan, H. (2012). Belief in a just world, religiosity and victim blaming. Archive for the Psychology of Religion, 34(3), 397–409. https://doi.org/10.1163/15736121-12341246

MAY 21ST - *Can Basketball Players Really Get on a 'Hot Streak'?*

Rabin, M., & Vayanos, D. (2009). The gambler's and Hot-Hand fallacies: Theory and applications. Review of Economic Studies, 77, 730–778. https://doi.org/10.1111/j.1467-937X.2009.00582.x

Gilovich, T., Vayone, R., & Tversky, A. (1985). The hot hand in basketball: On the misperception of random sequences. Cognitive Psychology, 17(3), 295–314. https://doi.org/10.1016/0010-0285(85)90010-6

MAY 22ND - *Bullet holes, aircrafts, and survivorship*

Boyd, R. (2020). Redressing Survivorship Bias Giving voice to the voiceless. Education Today. Uwa. https://www.academia.edu/43984480/Redressing_Survivorship_Bias_Giving_voice_to_the_voiceless

MAY 23RD - *Big Brother or Brain Trick?*

Simpson, J. (2017, August 25). Finding brand success in the digital world. Forbes. Retrieved September 3, 2022, from https://www.forbes.com/sites/forbesagencycouncil/2017/08/25/finding-brand-success-in-the-digital-world/

MAY 25TH - *Is Performance-Support Bias Fueling the Gender Pay Gap?*

Fanning, J. (2012). Performance-Support bias and the gender pay gap among stockbrokers. Gender & Society, 26(3), 488–518. https://doi.org/10.1177/0891243212438546

Greenfield, G., Levine, B., & Gaertner, S. (2016). When women thrive, businesses thrive: Pay equity [PDF]. Mercer. Retrieved 12.05.2024 from https://www.oliverwyman.com/content/dam/oliver-wyman/global/en/2016/june/WiFS/WiFS_2016_PAYEQUITY_Pages.pdf

MAY 27TH - *Did you know about the Children's Crusades?*

Cartwright, M., & Art, M. M. O. (2018, September 4). Children's crusade. World History Encyclopedia. https://www.worldhistory.org/Children's_Crusade/

Kings and Generals. (2021, February 7). Children's Crusade: Real story of the tragic event [Video]. YouTube. https://www.youtube.com/watch?v=9RfHz2gVcUo

MAY 28TH - *Do you know the most handsome killer in history?*

Michaud, S. G., & Aynesworth, H. (1999). The only living witness. Authorlink.

Rule, A. (2001). The stranger beside me. Signet Book.

MAY 29TH - *Are We Trading Our Opinions for Acceptance?*

Asch, S. E. (1956). Studies of independence and conformity: I. A minority of one against a unanimous majority. https://doi.org/10.1037/h0093718

Berns, G. S., Chappelow, J., Zink, C. F., Pagnoni, G., Martin-Skurski, M. E., & Richards, J. (2005). Neurobiological correlates of social conformity and independence during mental rotation. Biological Psychiatry, 58(3), 245–253. https://doi.org/10.1016/j.biopsych.2005.04.012

MAY 30TH - *How Much Does Yesterday's Kiss or Clash Tint Your Love Goggles?*

Scharfe, E., & Bartholomew, K. (1998). Do you remember?: Recollections of adult attachment patterns. Personal Relationships, 5(2), 219–234. https://doi.org/10.1111/j.1475-6811.1998.tb00169.x

Gottman, J. M., & Levenson, R. W. (1992). Marital processes predictive of later dissolution: Behavior, physiology, and health. Journal of Personality and Social Psychology, 63(2), 221–233. https://doi.org/10.1037/0022-3514.63.2.221

MAY 31ST - *Why Do We Flee from Checkups Like Ostriches on the Run?*

Persoskie, A., Ferrer, R. A., & Klein, W. M. P. (2013). Association of cancer worry and perceived risk with doctor avoidance: An analysis of information avoidance in a nationally representative US sample. Journal of Behavioral Medicine, 37, 977–987. https://doi.org/10.1007/s10865-013-9537-2

JUNE 1ST - *Serving Up Overconfidence: Do Men Think They Can Score on Serena?*

Recko, A. (2022, April 25). The Dunning-Kruger effect: You (Probably) don't know what you don't know. https://web.colby.edu/cogblog/2022/04/25/the-dunning-kruger-effect-you-probably-dont-know-what-you-dont-know/

YouGov. (2019, July 12). Could you win a point off Serena Williams? Plus, avoiding hen/stag parties, and being naked results. YouGov | What the World Thinks. Retrieved March 26, 2024, from https://yougov.co.uk/opi/surveys/results?utm_source=twitter&utm_medium=daily_questions&utm_campaign=question_1#/survey/344ce84b-a48d-11e9-8e40-79d1f09423a3/question/4d73bd62-a48f-11e9-aee6-6742cfe83f15/gender

JUNE 2ND - *Does a Happy Ending Excuse Questionable Actions?*
Gino, F., Moore, D. A., & Bazerman, M. H. (2008). No harm, no foul: The outcome bias in ethical judgments. Workin Paper Summaries, HBS Working Paper No. 08–080. https://hbswk.hbs.edu/item/no-harm-no-foul-the-outcome-bias-in-ethical-judgments

JUNE 3RD - *Got Guts? How Default Laws Impact Organ Donation Rates*
Citation for Figure 4:

Notes: Figure 4. Effective organ donation consent rates of different countries. From "Do Defaults Save Lives?" by E. J. Johnson and D. Goldstein, 2001, Science, 302 (5649). Reprinted with permission from AAAS.

Citation for critic:

Collins, J. (2015, February 11). Charts that don't seem quite right - organ donation edition. Jason Collins Blog. Retrieved August 27, 2022, from https://www.jasoncollins.blog/charts-that-dont-seem-quite-right-organ-donation-edition/

Notes: Figure 4. Effective organ donation consent rates of different countries. From "Do Defaults Save Lives?" by E. J. Johnson and D. Goldstein, 2001, Science, 302 (5649). Reprinted with permission from AAAS.

JUNE 5TH - *Do Numbers Hold the Key to so Many Secrets?*
The Daily Show. (2022, August). Michael Jackson is still alive and Osama Bin Laden's real name is "Tim." Get a load of Gematria. @jordanklepper. Instagram. https://www.instagram.com/p/ChH-KVSFJ02/

JUNE 7TH - *What Are the Reasons for Your Success?*
The Diary Of A CEO. (2022, September 27). The number one reason this generation is struggling: Scott Galloway | E190 [Video]. YouTube. Retrieved March 27, 2024, from https://www.youtube.com/watch?v=vHpZEMesriU

JUNE 8TH - *Framing the War on Drugs: A Sobering Look at Fear Tactics?*
Dufton, E. (2012, March 26). The war on drugs: How president nixon tied addiction to crime. The Atlantic. Retrieved August 30, 2022, from https://www.theatlantic.com/health/archive/2012/03/the-war-on-drugs-how-president-nixon-tied-addiction-to-crime/254319/

JUNE 9TH - *Why Do Misfortunes Seem Obvious Only in the Rearview Mirror?*
Giroux, M. E., Coburn, P. I., Harley, E. M., Connolly, D. A., & Bernstein, D. M. (2016). Hindsight bias and law. Zeitschrift Für Psychologie, 224(3), 190–203. https://doi.org/10.1027/2151-2604/a000253

JUNE 10TH - *Familiarity breeds liking*
Zajonc, R. B. (1968). Attitudinal effects of mere exposure. Journal of Personality and Social Psychology, 9(2, Pt.2), 1–27. https://doi.org/10.1037/h0025848

JUNE 11TH - *Can We Manifest Our Dreams and Control Our Destiny? ?*
Yarritu, I., Matute, H., & Vadillo, M. A. (2014). Illusion of control. Experimental Psychology, 61(1), 38–47. https://doi.org/10.1027/1618-3169/a000225

Gollwitzer, P. M. (1990). Action phases and mind-sets. Handbook of motivation and cognition: Foundations of social behavior, 2(53-92), 2.

McGurk, S. (2022, March 20). Making dreams come true: Inside the new age world of manifesting. The Guardian. Retrieved 11.11.2024, from https://www.theguardian.com/lifeandstyle/2022/mar/20/making-dreams-come-true-inside-the-new-age-world-of-manifesting

JUNE 13TH - *How Can Tweaking Feedback Order Make Feedback More Pleasant?*
Hoogerheide, V., Vink, M., Finn, B., Raes, A., & Paas, F. (2017). How to bring the news . . . peak-end effects in children's affective responses to peer assessments of their social behavior. Cognition & Emotion, 32(5), 1114–1121. https://doi.org/10.1080/02699931.2017.1362355

JUNE 14TH - *Feeling cold changes how you perceive people*
Williams, L. E., & Bargh, J. A. (2008). Experiencing physical warmth promotes interpersonal warmth. Science, 322(5901), 606–607. https://doi.org/10.1126/science.1162548

JUNE 15TH - *Did Trump's Loss Lingo Win Him the White House?*

Chupka, K. (2016, June 14). Donald Trump may be exploiting a psychological bias to win votes. Yahoo! Finance. Retrieved August 27, 2022, from https://finance.yahoo.com/news/trump-clinton-2016-loss-aversion-201827730.html?guccounter=1

JUNE 16TH - *Hungry for Justice: Can Meal Breaks Impact Parole Decisions?*

Bryant, B. (2011, April 11). Judges are more lenient after taking a break, study finds. The Guardian. Retrieved August 27, 2022, from https://www.theguardian.com/law/2011/apr/11/judges-lenient-break

Danziger, S., Levav, J., & Avnaim-Pesso, L. (2011). Extraneous factors in judicial decisions. Proceedings of the National Academy of Sciences of the United States of America, 108(17), 6889–6892. https://doi.org/10.1073/pnas.1018033108

JUNE 18TH - *Ever Heard of the 1954 Windshield Pitting Epidemic?*

Weeks, L. (2015, May 28). The Windshield-Pitting Mystery of 1954. NPR. https://www.npr.org/sections/npr-history-dept/2015/05/28/410085713/the-windshield-pitting-mystery-of-1954

JUNE 19TH - *Is the IKEA Effect the Secret Ingredient to Loving Healthy Food?*

Dohle, S., Rall, S., & Siegrist, M. (2016). Does self-prepared food taste better? Effects of food preparation on liking. Health Psychology, 35(5), 500–508. https://doi.org/10.1037/hea0000315

JUNE 20TH - *Can Fund Managers Really Predict the Market?*

Carhart, M. M. (2012). On persistence in mutual fund performance. The Journal of Finance, 52(1), 57–82. https://doi.org/10.1111/j.1540-6261.1997.tb03808.x

Elton, E. J., Gruber, M. J., Das, S., & Hlavka, M. (2015). Efficiency with costly information: A reinterpretation of evidence from managed portfolios. The Review of Financial Studies, 6(1), 1–22. https://doi.org/10.1093/rfs/6.1.1

Magnusson, J. (2018). Expert Illusion - Evaluating Persistence in Mutual Fund Performance [Bachelor's essay, Departments of Economics, Lund University]. lund university libraries. https://lup.lub.lu.se/student-papers/search/publication/8943324

JUNE 21ST - *Is the Spotlight Effect Serving Up Unnecessary Anxiety?*

Why do we feel like we stand out more than we really do? (n.d.). The Decision Lab. Retrieved August 25, 2022, from https://thedecisionlab.com/biases/spotlight-effect#section-8

JUNE 22ND - *Is There a Middle Ground in the US Gun Control Debate?*

Black, T. (2022, May 25). Bloomberg - Are you a robot? Bloomberg. https://www.bloomberg.com/news/articles/2022-05-25/how-many-guns-in-the-us-buying-spree-bolsters-lead-as-most-armed-country

JUNE 23RD - *Is Cognitive Dissonance Driving Your Purchases?*

Gleeson, P. (2019, March 1). What is cognitive dissonance in marketing? Small Business Chron. Retrieved August 24, 2022, from https://smallbusiness.chron.com/differences-between-persuasive-misleading-advertisements-17727.html

JUNE 25TH - *Is it Attraction or an Arousal Mix-Up?*

Dutton, D. G., & Aron, A. P. (1974). Some evidence for heightened sexual attraction under conditions of high anxiety. Journal of Personality and Social Psychology, 30(4), 510–517. https://doi.org/10.1037/h0037031

Schachter, S., & Singer, J. E. (1962). Cognitive, social, and physiological determinants of emotional state. Psychological Review, 69, 379–399. https://doi.org/10.1037/h0046234

JUNE 26TH - *Do Pretty Faces Make Products and Services Shine?*

Ozanne, M., Liu, S.Q. & Mattila, A.S. (2019), Are attractive reviewers more persuasive? Examining the role of physical attractiveness in online reviews. Journal of Consumer Marketing, Vol. 36 No. 6, pp. 728-739. https://doi.org/10.1108/JCM-02-2017-2096

JUNE 28TH - *Do We Really Like It, or Is It Just Familiarity?*

Bornstein, R. F., & D'Agostino, P. R. (1992). Stimulus recognition and the mere exposure effect. Journal of Personality and Social Psychology, 63(4), 545–552. https://doi.org/10.1037/0022-3514.63.4.545

Zajonc, R. B. (2001). Mere exposure: A gateway to the subliminal. Current Directions in Psychological, 10(6), 224–228. https://doi.org/10.1111/1467-8721.00154

JUNE 29TH - *People don't mind their own business, but I do*

Epley, N., & Dunning, D. (2000). Feeling "holier than thou": Are self-serving assessments produced by errors in self- or social prediction? Journal of Personality and Social Psychology, 79(6), 861–875. https://doi.org/10.1037/0022-3514.79.6.861

JUNE 30TH - *'My teddy bear is upset!'*

Gjersoe, N. L., Hall, E. L., & Hood, B. (2015). Children attribute mental lives to toys when they are emotionally attached to them. Cognitive Development, 34, 28–38. https://doi.org/10.1016/j.cogdev.2014.12.002

Saleh, N. (2015, December 22). Which toys do children anthropomorphize? Psychology Today. Retrieved September 1, 2022, from https://www.psychologytoday.com/us/blog/the-red-light-district/201512/which-toys-do-children-anthropomorphize

JULY 1ST - *Understanding the Human Face of Atrocity*

Browning, C. R. (2001). Ordinary men: Reserve Police Battalion 101 and the Final Solution in Poland. Penguin Group(CA).

JULY 2ND - *How Can Price Anchors Bake Sales Success?*

Belludi, N. (2015, November 17). Clever marketing exploits the anchoring bias. Right Attitudes. Retrieved August 24, 2022, from https://www.rightattitudes.com/2015/11/17/clever-marketing-anchoring-bias/

JULY 3RD - *Do We Really Reap What We Sow?*

Why do we believe that we get what we deserve? (n.d.-b). The Decision Lab. Retrieved September 3, 2022, from https://thedecisionlab.com/biases/just-world-hypothesis#section-8

JULY 4TH - *Can You Bank on a CEO's Self-Serving Bias?*

Waida, M. (2021, September 27). Understanding Self-Serving bias in the workplace | wrike. Wrike. Retrieved September 3, 2022, from https://www.wrike.com/blog/understanding-self-serving-bias-at-work/#What-does-self-serving-bias-mean

Corkery, M. (2016, September 8). Wells Fargo fined $185 million for fraudulently opening accounts. The New York Times. https://www.nytimes.com/2016/09/09/business/dealbook/wells-fargo-fined-for-years-of-harm-to-customers.html

JULY 5TH - *Can Cognitive Biases Convict the Innocent?*

Cutler, Brian L. (Ed). (2012). Conviction of the innocent: Lessons from psychological research , (pp. 303-323). Washington, DC, US: American Psychological Association, xiv, 370 pp.

Dragicevic, N. (2020, February 27). Tunnel vision can significantly influence police investigations, say experts. CBC. Retrieved September 4, 2022, from https://www.cbc.ca/documentaries/the-oland-murder/tunnel-vision-can-significantly-influence-police-investigations-say-experts-1.5476025

Death of Richard Oland. (2022, March 22). In Wikipedia. https://en.wikipedia.org/wiki/Death_of_Richard_Oland

JULY 6TH - *Is the Crypto Craze Just a Bandwagon Gone Bad?*

Banks, D. A. (2022, December 15). Crypto was meant to solve financial corruption. The FTX scandal shows it's got worse. The Guardian. https://www.theguardian.com/commentisfree/2022/dec/15/crypto-financial-and-corruption-making-it-worse-ftx

JULY 7TH - *Why Can We Easily Get Into a Car but Fear Taking Flight?*

National Safety Council. (n.d.-a). Odds of dying. Injury Facts. Retrieved August 27, 2022, from https://injuryfacts.nsc.org/

JULY 8TH - *Can You Trust Your Memory?*

Blank, H., Fischer, V., & Erdfelder, E. (2003). Hindsight bias in political elections. Memory, 11(4–5), 491–504. https://doi.org/10.1080/09658210244000513

Synodinos, N. E. (1986). Hindsight distortion: "I knew-it-all along and I was sure about it." Journal of Applied Social Psychology, 16(2), 107–117. https://doi.org/10.1111/j.1559-1816.1986.tb02282.x

JULY 10TH - *Can You Band-aid Ignorance? The Dunning-Krugger Effect Strikes a Chord*
Kimmel, J. [Jimmy Kimmel Live]. (2014, March 14). Lie witness news - SXSW edition [Video]. YouTube. https://www.youtube.com/watch?v=frjaQ17yAww

JULY 12TH - *Did the Illusory Truth Effect Rig Many Minds in 2020?*
Murray, M. (2022, September 27). Poll: 61% of Republicans still believe Biden didn't win Fair and Square in 2020. NBC News. Retrieved March 26, 2024, from https://www.nbcnews.com/meet-the-press/meetthepressblog/poll-61-republicans-still-believe-biden-didnt-win-fair-square-2020-rcna49630

JULY 14TH - *Why is it always "us" versus "them"?*
Muzafer Sherif, O. J., Harvey, B., White, J., Hood, W. R., & Sherif, C. W. (1988). Intergroup Conflict and Cooperation: The Robbers Cave Experiment. Wesleyan University Press.

JULY 15TH - *Is Your Loan Approval a Victim of the Gambler's Fallacy?*
Chen, D., Moskowitz, T. J., Shue, K., Decision-making under the Gambler's Fallacy: Evidence from Asylum Judges, Loan Officers and Baseball Umpires, NBER Working Papers Series, Working Paper 22026, (2016). DOI: https://doi.org/10.3386/w22026.

Fortune, E. E., & Goodie, A. S. (2012). Cognitive distortions as a component and treatment focus of pathological gambling: A review. Psychology of Addictive Behaviors, 26(2), 298–310. https://doi.org/10.1037/a0026422

JULY 16TH - *Are We Kicking Logic Aside in Football Penalty Shootouts?*
Kausel, E. E., & Ventura, S. (2019). Outcome bias in subjective ratings of performance: Evidence from the (football) field. Journal of Economic Psychology, 75(Part B). https://doi.org/10.1016/j.joep.2018.12.006

JULY 17TH - *Depressed or Realist?*
Martin, D. J., Abramson, L. Y., & Alloy, L. B. (1984). Illusion of control for self and others in depressed and nondepressed college students. Journal of Personality and Social Psychology, 46(1), 125–136. https://doi.org/10.1037/0022-3514.46.1.125

Alloy, L. B., & Abramson, L. Y. (1982). Learned helplessness, depression, and the illusion of control. Journal of Personality and Social Psychology, 42(6), 1114–1126. https://doi.org/10.1037/0022-3514.42.6.1114

Golin, S., Terrell, F., & Johnson, B. (1977). Depression and the illusion of control. Journal of Abnormal Psychology, 86(4), 440–442. https://doi.org/10.1037/0021-843X.86.4.440

JULY 19TH - *Are You Saving for Your Golden Years?*
Cribb, J., & Emmerson, C. (2020). What happens to workplace pension saving when employers are obliged to enrol employees automatically? International Tax and Public Finance, 27, 664–693. https://doi.org/10.1007/s10797-019-09565-6

JULY 20TH - *Who's the Real Loser?*
BigBeachFilms. (2010, November 4). Little Miss Sunshine - Official trailer [HD] [Video]. YouTube. Retrieved March 27, 2024, from https://www.youtube.com/watch?v=wvwVkllXT80

JULY 21ST - *Can We Really Trust Personality Tests for Hiring the Right Fit?*
Stagner, R. (1958). The gullibility of personnel managers. Personnel Psychology, 11, 347–352. https://doi.org/10.1111/j.1744-6570.1958.tb00022.x

Chamorro-Premuzic, T. (2015, July 6). Ace the Assessment. Harvard Business Review. https://hbr.org/2015/07/ace-the-assessment

JULY 22ND - *I did not like that toy anyway*
Festinger, L. (1962). Cognitive Dissonance. Scientific American, 207(4), 93–106. http://www.jstor.org/stable/24936719

JULY 23RD - *How funny are you?*
Kruger, J., & Dunning, D. (1999). Unskilled and unaware of it: How difficulties in recognizing one's own incompetence lead to inflated self-assessments. Journal of Personality and Social Psychology, 77(6), 1121–1134. https://doi.org/10.1037/0022-3514.77.6.1121

JULY 24TH - *From Passion to Payment: Are We Selling Out Our Favorite Activities?*
Lepper, M. R., Greene, D., & Nisbett, R. E. (1973). Undermining children's intrinsic interest with extrinsic reward: A test of the "overjustification" hypothesis. Journal of Personality and Social Psychology, 28(1), 129–137. https://doi.org/10.1037/h0035519

JULY 25TH - *Who Will You Become in a Decade?*
Quoidbach, J., Gilbert, D. T., & Wilson, T. D. (2013). The end of history illusion. Science, 339(6115), 96–98. https://doi.org/10.1126/science.1229294

JULY 26TH - *Are you afraid of sharks?*
Harrison, K., & Cantor, J. (1999). Tales from the Screen: Enduring Fright Reactions to Scary Media. Media Psychology, 1(2), 97–116. https://doi.org/10.1207/s1532785xmep0102_1

Evans, C. (2022, July 15). What makes people so afraid of sharks? "Jaws," some scientists say. CBS News. Retrieved March 27, 2024, from https://www.cbsnews.com/news/what-makes-people-so-afraid-of-sharks-jaws-scientists/

Diaz, A. (2022, July 15). "Jaws" made people irrationally afraid of sharks, scientists declare. New York Post. Retrieved March 27, 2024, from https://nypost.com/2022/07/15/jaws-made-people-so-afraid-of-sharks-scientists-say/

JULY 27TH - *Are 'Healthier' Fast Food Choices Just a Calorie-Loaded Illusion?*
Chandon, P., & Wansink, B. (2007). The biasing health halos of Fast-Food restaurant health claims: Lower calorie estimates and higher Side-Dish consumption intentions. Journal of Consumer Research, 34(3), 301–314. https://doi.org/10.1086/519499

De Vogli, R., Kouvonen, A., & Gimeno, D. (2011). 'Globesization': Ecological evidence on the relationship between fast food outlets and obesity among 26 advanced economies. Critical Public Health, 21(4), 395-402. https://doi.org/10.1080/09581596.2011.619964

JULY 28TH - *Does Disconfirmatory Info Break Bias or Cement Convictions?*
Lord, C. G., Ross, L., & Lepper, M. R. (1979). Biased assimilation and attitude polarization: The effects of prior theories on subsequently considered evidence. Journal of Personality and Social Psychology, 37(11), 2098–2109. https://doi.org/10.1037/0022-3514.37.11.2098

JULY 29TH - *What prevents us from owning traffic mistakes?*
Roh, M., & Song, M. (2020). The impact of Self-Serving bias on the adoption of autonomous vehicles: The moderating role of defensive driving ability and car accident experience. SSRN. https://doi.org/10.2139/ssrn.3657426

Kay, G. (2022, September 15). Elon Musk believes self-driving cars are the future, but most Americans are wary, new survey shows. Business Insider. https://www.businessinsider.com/americans-feel-unsafe-around-self-driving-cars-survey-2022-9?international=true&r=US&IR=T

JULY 30TH - *Are Algorithms Amplifying Our Social Biases?*
Gebru, T. [Databricks]. (2019, April 25). Understanding the limitations of AI: When algorithms fail | timnit gebru (google brain) [Video]. YouTube. https://www.youtube.com/watch?v=aKf6pB4p06E

JULY 31ST - *Did Someone See 9/11 Coming?*
Commission on Terrorist Attacks upon the United States. (2004). The 9/11 Commission report: Final Report of the National Commission on Terrorist Attacks Upon the United States. Government Printing Office. https://www.govinfo.gov/content/pkg/GPO-911REPORT/pdf/GPO-911REPORT.pdf

AUGUST 1ST - *Is Our Primate Brain Making Us Irrationally Attached?*
Why do we value items more if they belong to us? (n.d.). The Decision Lab. Retrieved September 1, 2022, from https://thedecisionlab.com/biases/endowment-effect#section-8

Lakshminaryanan, V., Chen, M. K., & Santos, L. R. (2008). Endowment effect in capuchin monkeys. Philosophical Transactions of the Royal Society B, 363(1511), 3837–3844. https://doi.org/10.1098/rstb.2008.0149

AUGUST 2ND - *Is Your Culture Making You a Lone Dollar Ranger?*
Kahneman, D. (2011). Thinking fast and slow. Farrar, Straus and Giroux.

Vohs, K. D., Mead, N. L., & Goode, M. R. (2006). The Psychological Consequences of Money. Science, 314(5802), 1154–1156. https://doi.org/10.1126/science.1132491

AUGUST 3RD - *Ponzi or Not Ponzi: How Ignorance Fueled a Financial Fiasco?*

Agrafiotis, D. (2015, December 5). Effect of cognitive biases on decision making and crisis management. LinkedIn. Retrieved August 29, 2022, from https://www.linkedin.com/pulse/effect-cognitive-biases-decision-making-crisis-dimitris-agrafiotis/

AUGUST 4TH - *Can Objects Be Your New BFF?*

Peaked Interest. (2019, January 25). Castaway : The Volleyball That Caused a Thousand Tears [Video]. YouTube. https://www.youtube.com/watch?v=k5HToaL0-sY

AUGUST 5TH - *Would You Tell President Nixon He Was Mistaken?*

Bernstein, C., & Woodward, B. (1973, June 3). Dean alleges Nixon knew of cover-up plan. Washington Post. https://www.washingtonpost.com/wp-srv/national/longterm/watergate/articles/060373-1.htm

Yager, J. (2009, January 6). Journalist recalls the honor of being on Nixon's Enemies List. The Hill. https://thehill.com/capital-living/17776-journalist-recalls-the-honor-of-being-on-nixons-enemies-list/

AUGUST 6TH - *Can You Trust the Buzz?*

Bessi, A., & Ferrara, E. (2017). Social bots distort the 2016 US presidential election online discussion. First Monday, 21(11). https://ssrn.com/abstract=2982233

Kupferschmidt, K. (2017, September 13). Social media 'bots' tried to influence the U.S. election. Germany may be next. Science. Retrieved September 4, 2022, from https://www.science.org/content/article/social-media-bots-tried-influence-us-election-germany-may-be-next

Guglielmi, G. (2020, October 28). The next-generation bots interfering with the US election. Nature. Retrieved September 4, 2022, from https://www.nature.com/articles/d41586-020-03034-5

AUGUST 7TH - *Was the Maginot Line a Costly Monument to Misjudgment?*

HISTORY. (2022, October 4). Maginot Line: Definition & World War II - HISTORY. Retrieved March 26, 2024, from https://www.history.com/topics/world-war-ii/maginot-line

AUGUST 8TH - *From Apu to Yunioshi: Do TV and Film Characters Reinforce Prejudices?*

HIS204W, Eastern Kentucky University eCampus. (2017, January 9). Gone with the wind: Sugarcoating slavery? [Video]. YouTube. Retrieved March 27, 2024, from https://www.youtube.com/watch?v=oRq7nsI33bc

Peter Griffin. (2019, November 9). Breakfast at Mr. Yunioshi's [Video]. YouTube. Retrieved March 27, 2024, from https://www.youtube.com/watch?v=Hb3gdUrIC4Q

AUGUST 9TH - *How Did Shreddies Turn a 45-Degree Twist into a Marketing Masterpiece?*

Alex Dunsdon. (2012, February 23). Diamond shreddies: the single best case for how advertising intangible value [Video]. YouTube. https://www.youtube.com/watch?v=B8McutvNwtI

Lloyd, J. (2008, September 17). More diamonds from Shreddies. Marketing Magazine. http://marketingmag.ca/brands/more-diamonds-from-shreddies-17677/

AUGUST 10TH - *Are You Really a Wine Connoisseur?*

Aqueveque, C. (2018). Ignorant experts and erudite novices: Exploring the Dunning-Kruger effect in wine consumers. Food Quality and Preference, 65, 181–184. https://doi.org/10.1016/j.foodqual.2017.12.007

AUGUST 11TH - *Why Do We Get More Satisfaction from Work Than Leisure Activities?*

White, M. P., & Dolan, P. (2009). Accounting for the richness of daily activities. Psychological Science, 20(8), 1000–1008. https://doi.org/10.1111/j.1467-9280.2009.02392.x

AUGUST 12TH - *A Side Hustle Gone Wrong?*

Thinking Digital Conference. (2017, February 23). Rory Sutherland - Behavioural Economics, Humans and Advertising [Video]. YouTube. https://www.youtube.com/watch?v=zUe-JoS3cTu8

AUGUST 13TH - *Are Judges Rolling the Dice on Criminal Sentencing?*

Englich, B., Mussweiler, T., & Strack, F. (2006b). Playing dice with criminal sentences: The influence of irrelevant anchors on experts' judicial decision making. Personality and Social Psychology Bulletin, 32(2), 188–200. https://doi.org/10.1177/0146167205282152

AUGUST 14TH - *The media's focus on the negative makes us unnecessarily pessimistic*

Ray Kurzweil: Singularity, superintelligence, and immortality | Lex Fridman Podcast #321. (2022, September 17). [Video]. YouTube. https://www.youtube.com/watch?v=ykY69lSpDdo&t=2772s

Rosling, H., Rosling Rönnlund, A., & Rosling, O. (2020). Factfulness: Ten reasons we're wrong about the world and why things are better than you think. Flatiron Books.

AUGUST 15TH - *Fortune Favors the... Ideologue?*

Ülkümen, G., Bogard, J., Fox, C. R., & Krijnen, J. M. (2022). Lay theories of financial well-being predict political and policy message preferences. Journal of Personality and Social Psychology, 122(2), 310–336. https://doi.org/10.1037/pspp0000392

AUGUST 16TH - *Are We Melting the Middle Ground in Climate Change Conversations?*

Petersen, A. M., Vincent, E. M., & Westerling, A. L. (2019). Discrepancy in scientific authority and media visibility of climate change scientists and contrarians. Nature Communications, 10(3502). https://doi.org/10.1038/s41467-019-09959-4

Mildenberger, M., & Tingley, D. (2019). Beliefs about Climate Beliefs: The Importance of Second-Order Opinions for Climate Politics. British Journal of Political Science, 49(4), 1279–1307. https://doi.org/10.1017/S0007123417000321

Marlon, J., Neyens, L., Jefferson, M., Howe, P., Mildenberger, M., Leiserowitz, A.(2022) Yale Climate Opinion Maps 2021. Yale Program on Climate Change Communication. https://climatecommunication.yale.edu/visualizations-data/ycom-us/

AUGUST 17TH - *Survival of the Foodiest: Are We Blind to Fallen Culinary Ventures?*

Tedx Talks. (2015, February 3). Missing what's missing: How survivorship bias skews our perception | David McRaney | TEDxJackson [Video]. YouTube. https://www.youtube.com/watch?v=NtUCxKsK4xg

Parsa, H. G., Gregory, A., & Terry, M. (n.d.). Why do restaurants fail? Part III: An analysis of macro and micro factors [Daniels College of Business]. https://daniels.du.edu/assets/research-hg-parsa-part-3-2015.pdf

AUGUST 18TH - *How Could the Swedish Police Miss the Elk in the Room?*

Maidment, J. (2009, November 28). Sweden: Woman "murdered" by Elk, not husband. The Telegraph. https://www.telegraph.co.uk/news/newstopics/howaboutthat/6678397/Sweden-woman-murdered-by-elk-not-husband.html

AUGUST 19TH - *Do Doctors Have Diagnosis Déjà Vus?*

Purohit, K. (2019). The Baader-Meinhof phenomenon in radiology. Academic Radiology, 26(6). https://doi.org/10.1016/j.acra.2019.01.025

AUGUST 20TH - *Familiarity Breeds Sobriety: Can Pop Culture Save Lives?*

Kunkle, F. (2017, April 26). This Harvard professor used TV sitcoms to fight drunk driving. Can he do the same for distracted driving? Washington Post. https://www.washingtonpost.com/news/tripping/wp/2017/04/26/this-harvard-professor-used-tv-sitcoms-to-fight-drunk-driving-can-he-do-the-same-for-distracted-driving/

Harvard University. (2011, October 13). Designated drivers [Video]. YouTube. Retrieved March 26, 2024, from https://www.youtube.com/watch?v=mWcM2nSUYLY

AUGUST 21ST - *Is Your Work Review Unfairly Biased?*

Mackenzie, L. N., Wehner, J., & Correll, S. J. (2019, January 11). Why most performance evaluations are biased, and how to fix them. Havard Business Review. Retrieved August 25, 2022, from https://hbr.org/2019/01/why-most-performance-evaluations-are-biased-and-how-to-fix-them

AUGUST 22ND - *How to Make People Feel Flattered After Donating Blood?*

Basu, T. (2015, July 1). Now blood donors can get a text when they save lives. Time. https://time.com/3943272/blood-donation-sweden-text/

Nine marketing examples that tap into cognitive biases. (n.d.). Marketing Examples. Retrieved November 11, 2022, from https://marketingexamples.com/creative/cognitive-biases

AUGUST 23RD - *Why Do Golf Skills Drive CEO Salaries? A Hole-in-One Misconception*

Why do we think some things are related when they aren't? (n.d.). The Decision Lab. Retrieved August 25, 2022, from https://thedecisionlab.com/biases/illusory-correlation#section-9

Hogarth, R. M., & Kolev, G. I. (2009). Illusory correlation in the remuneration of chief executive officers: It pays to play golf, and well. SSRN. https://doi.org/10.2139/ssrn.1374239

AUGUST 26TH - *Fashion Faux-pas or Brainpower Boost?*
Bloem, C. (2018, February 28). Successful people like barack obama and mark zuckerberg wear the same thing every day — And it's not a coincidence. Insider. Retrieved September 1, 2022, from https://www.businessinsider.com/successful-people-like-barack-obama-wear-the-same-thing-every-day-2018-2

AUGUST 27TH - *Can Herbs Sniff Out the Black Death?*
The Black Death. (2017). Retrieved March 27, 2024, from https://hosted.lib.uiowa.edu/histmed/plague/

AUGUST 28TH - *Keep Calm and Go Swimming, Mayor Vaughn?*
Jrider24. (2009, July 4). Jaws Mayor Fourth of July [Video]. YouTube. Retrieved March 27, 2024, from https://www.youtube.com/watch?v=NB8m0CI4Kfg

AUGUST 29TH - *Why Can't We Face the Change in Climate Change*
Akpan, N. (2019, January 7). How your brain stops you from taking climate change seriously. PBS NewsHour. Retrieved August 24, 2022, from https://www.pbs.org/newshour/science/how-your-brain-stops-you-from-taking-climate-change-seriously

AUGUST 31ST - *Lunacy or Just Loony: Are We Really Swayed by Lunar Cycles?*
Rotton, J., & Kelly, I. W. (1985). Much ado about the full moon: A meta-analysis of lunar-lunacy research. Psychological Bulletin, 97(2), 286–306. https://doi.org/10.1037/0033-2909.97.2.286

SEPTEMBER 1ST - *Was It German Accuracy?*
Gilovich, T. (1991). How we know what isn't so. The Free Press.

SEPTEMBER 2ND - *Feeling Lucky? The Lottery Reality Check*
Gilbert, D. (2005). Why we make bad decisions [Video]. TED Conferences. https://www.ted.com/talks/dan_gilbert_why_we_make_bad_decisions?language=en

Quoteresearch, A. (2017, October 21). A Lottery Is a Taxation Upon All the Fools in Creation – Quote Investigator. https://quoteinvestigator.com/2017/10/21/lottery/

Garrett, T. A. (2001). An International Comparison and Analysis of Lotteries and the Distribution of Lottery Expenditures. International Review of Applied Economics, 15(2), 213–227. https://doi.org/10.1080/02692170151137096

Allingham, T. (2022, February 10). 14 things more likely than winning the lottery. Save the Student. https://www.savethestudent.org/save-money/things-more-likely-than-winning-lottery.html

SEPTEMBER 3RD - *Can a Third Wheel Swing an Election? The Decoy Effect in Action*
Slaughter, J. E., Sinar, E. F., & Highhouse, S. (1999). Decoy effects and attribute-level inferences. Journal of Applied Psychology, 84(5), 823–828. https://doi.org/10.1037/0021-9010.84.5.823

O'Curry, Y. P. S., & Pitts, R. (1995). The attraction effect and political choice in two elections. Journal of Consumer Psychology, 4(1), 85–101. https://doi.org/10.1207/s15327663jcp0401_04

Hedgcock, W., Rao, A. R., & Chen, H. (2009). Could Ralph Nader's entrance and exit have helped al gore? The impact of decoy dynamics on consumer choice. Journal of Marketing Research, 46(3), 330–343. https://www.jstor.org/stable/20618895

SEPTEMBER 4TH - *Medicine that is Too Good to Be True?*
Chalmers, I., & Matthews, R. (2006). What are the implications of optimism bias in clinical research? The Lancet, 367(9509), 449–450. https://doi.org/10.1016/S0140-6736(06)68153-1

Why do we overestimate the probability of success? (n.d.). The Decision Lab. Retrieved September 3, 2022, from https://thedecisionlab.com/biases/optimism-bias#section-8

SEPTEMBER 5TH - *Free love and fishing—what could go wrong?*
Chancellor, J. D. (2000). Life in the family: An Oral History of the Children of God. Syracuse University Press.

Grunge. (2021, August 19). The truth about the Children of God Cult [Video]. YouTube. https://www.youtube.com/watch?v=6SA097FBw1o

SEPTEMBER 6TH - *What Game of Thrones Character Are You?*
Nasir, S. (2020, June 18). The barnum effect and application in marketing. Medium. Retrieved September 1, 2022, from https://medium.com/@sohaibnasir/the-barnum-effect-and-application-in-marketing-8e66c1316788

SEPTEMBER 7TH - *How Can We Outsmart Our Impulsive Brains for a Comfy Retirement?*
Thaler, R., & Benartzi, S. (2004). Save More TomorrowTM: Using Behavioral Economics to Increase Employee Saving. Journal of Political Economy, 112(S1), S164–S187. https://doi.org/10.1086/380085

SEPTEMBER 8TH - *Will Robots and AI Deserve Social Responsibility?*
Horstmann, A. C., & Krämer, N. C. (2022). The fundamental attribution error in Human-Robot interaction: An experimental investigation on attributing responsibility to a social robot for its Pre-Programmed behavior. International Journal of Social Robotics, 14, 1137–1153. https://doi.org/10.1007/s12369-021-00856-9

SEPTEMBER 9TH - *Deja Vu and True? How Familiarity Breeds Believability*
Hasher, L., Golstein, D., & Toppino, T. (1977). Frequency and the conference of referential validity. Journal of Verbal Learning and Verbal Behavior, 16(1), 107–112. https://doi.org/10.1016/S0022-5371(77)80012-1

Polage, D. C. (2012). Making up history: False memories of fake news stories. Europe's Journal of Psychology, 8(2), 245–250. https://doi.org/10.5964/ejop.v8i2.456

Fazio, L. K., Payne, B. K., Brashier, N. M., & Marsh, E. J. (2015). Knowledge does not protect against illusory truth. Journal of Experimental Psychology: General, 144(5), 993–1002. https://doi.org/10.1037/xge0000098.supp

SEPTEMBER 10TH - *Did you know about the speedo-wearing spiritual guru?*
Rotten Tomatoes Indie. (2016, May 2). Holy Hell Official Trailer 1 (2016) - Documentary HD [Video]. YouTube. https://www.youtube.com/watch?v=2f2BG43JW0o

Wang, E. (2016, May 27). This is what it's like to spend almost half your life in a cult. Esquire. https://www.esquire.com/entertainment/interviews/a45261/holy-hell-buddhafield-documentary-will-allen-interview/

SEPTEMBER 11TH - *Does Your Birthplace Predict Your Saving Behaviour?*
Bommier, A., & le Grand, F. (2018). Risk aversion and precautionary savings in dynamic settings. Management Science, 65(3), 1386–1397. https://doi.org/10.1287/mnsc.2017.2959

Hermansson, C. (2015). Relationships between bank customers' risk attitudes and their balance sheets. (CEFIN Working Paper No. 2015:12). KTH Royal Institute of Technology. https://www.diva-portal.org/smash/get/diva2:899738/FULLTEXT01.pdf

SEPTEMBER 12TH - *Saving Lives or Losing Them?*
Montier, J. (2006). Behaving badly. Social Science Research Network. https://doi.org/10.2139/ssrn.890563

SEPTEMBER 13TH - *Why Do We Cling to Beliefs Despite Contradictory Evidence?*
Newport, F. (2003, June 16). Americans still think iraq had weapons of mass destruction before war. Gallup. Retrieved August 30, 2022, from https://news.gallup.com/poll/8623/americans-still-think-iraq-had-weapons-mass-destruction-before-war.aspx

SEPTEMBER 14TH - *When Does Confidence Become a Risky Business?*
CFI Team. (2022, January 25). Overconfidence bias: The false assumption that someone is better than others. Corporate Finance Institute. Retrieved August 30, 2022, from https://corporatefinanceinstitute.com/resources/knowledge/trading-investing/overconfidence-bias/

Montier, J. (2006). Behaving badly. Social Science Research Network. https://doi.org/10.2139/ssrn.890563

SEPTEMBER 15TH - *Would You Trade Land for a Tulip?*
Ross, D., Cretu, E., & Lemieux, V. L. (2021). NFTs: Tulip Mania or Digital Renaissance? 2021 IEEE International Conference on Big Data (Big Data). https://doi.org/10.1109/bigdata52589.2021.9671707

Hayes, A. (2022, November 22). Tulipmania: About the Dutch tulip bulb market bubble. Investopedia. https://www.investopedia.com/terms/d/dutch_tulip_bulb_market_bubble.asp

SEPTEMBER 16TH - *Can You Spot the Difference?*

Michel, C., Rossion, B., Han, J., Chung, C.-S., & Caldara, R. (2006). Holistic processing is finely tuned for faces of one's own race. Psychological Science, 17(7), 608–615. https://doi.org/10.1111/j.1467-9280.2006.01752.x

Wong, H. K., Estudillo, A. J., Stephen, I. D., & Keeble, D. (2021). The other-race effect and holistic processing across racial groups. Scientific Reports, 11(1). https://doi.org/10.1038/s41598-021-87933-1

SEPTEMBER 17TH - *Doc, Are You a Pro or Just a Show?*

Davis, D. A., Mazmanian, P. E., Fordis, M., Van Harrison, R. T. K. E., Thorpe, K. E., & Perrier, L. (2006). Accuracy of physician self-assessment compared with observed measures of competence: a systematic review. Jama, 296(9), 1094-1102.

Campbell-Meiklejohn, D., Simonsen, A., Frith, C. D., & Daw, N. D. (2016). Independent Neural Computation of Value from Other People's Confidence. The Journal of Neuroscience, 37(3), 673–684. https://doi.org/10.1523/jneurosci.4490-15.2016

SEPTEMBER 18TH - *Is the Gambler's Fallacy Tipping the Scales of Justice?*

Chen, D. L., Moskowitz, T. J., & Shue, K. (2016). Decision making under the gambler's fallacy: Evidence from asylum judges, loan officers, and baseball umpires. The Quarterly Journal of Economics, 131(3), 1181–1242. https://doi.org/10.1093/qje/qjw017

SEPTEMBER 19TH - *Who's to Blame?*

Ross, H., Smith, J., Spielmacher, C., & Recchia, H. (2004). Shading the Truth: Self-Serving Biases in Children's Reports of Sibling Conflicts. Merrill-Palmer Quarterly, 50(1), 61–85. https://www.jstor.org/stable/23096117

SEPTEMBER 20TH - *Could a Presidential Shortcut Have Prevented 9/11?*

Kahneman, D. (2011). Thinking fast and slow. Farrar, Straus and Giroux.

SEPTEMBER 21ST - *Rule of Thumb or More Like Rule Nnumb?*

Wason, P. C. (1960). On the Failure to Eliminate Hypotheses in a Conceptual Task. Quarterly Journal of Experimental Psychology, 12(3), 129–140. https://doi.org/10.1080/17470216008416717

SEPTEMBER 22ND - *Can looking smart boost a political career?*

Torodov, A., Mandisodza, A. N., Goren, A., & Hall, C. C. (2005). Inferences of competence from faces predict election outcomes. Science, 308(5728), 1623–1626. https://doi.org/10.1126/science.1110589

SEPTEMBER 23RD - *Yanny or Laurel?*

Becker, R., & Lopatto, E. (2018, May 15). Yanny or laurel? The science behind the audio version of the dress. The Verge. Retrieved September 1, 2022, from https://www.theverge.com/2018/5/15/17358136/yanny-laurel-the-dress-audio-illusion-frequency-sound-perception

Cherry, K. (2021, June 18). Priming and the psychology of memory. Verywell Mind. Retrieved September 1, 2022, from https://www.verywellmind.com/priming-and-the-psychology-of-memory-4173092

Matazat. (2011, October 21) BillBill Bill Bill Bill Bale Pale Pail Mayo. [Video]. YouTube. https://youtu.be/KiuO_Z2_AD4

Matazat. (2011, October 21). Do you hear "Yanny" or "Laurel"? (solution to the problem proven with science) [Video]. YouTube. https://youtu.be/yDiXQl7grPQ

SEPTEMBER 24TH - *Will you bury your head in the sand until the sand is too hot?*

IPCC. (2023, June 16). FAQ 2: How will nature and the benefits it provides to people be affected by higher levels of warming? IPCC https://www.ipcc.ch/report/ar6/wg2/about/frequently-asked-questions/keyfaq2/

SEPTEMBER 25TH - *Is The Price Right?*

Dustin Johnson. (2012, December 19). The price is right Stupid perfect bid [Video]. YouTube. Retrieved March 27, 2024, from https://www.youtube.com/watch?v=8lAJZMF830s

SEPTEMBER 26TH - *Do Different Cultures Have Different Views on Financial Responsibility?*

Haerpfer, C., Inglehart, R., Moreno, A., Welzel, C., Kizilova, K., Diez-Medrano J., M. Lagos, P. Norris, E. Ponarin & B. Puranen (eds.). 2022. World Values Survey: Round Seven - Country-Pooled Datafile Version 5.0. Madrid, Spain & Vienna, Austria: JD Systems Institute & WVSA Secretariat. doi:10.14281/18241.20

SEPTEMBER 27TH - *Billions Down the Drain: When Should You Abandon a Costly Project?*

Ronayne, D., Sgroi, D., & Tuckwell, A. (2021, July 15). How susceptible are you to the sunk cost fallacy? Harvard Business Review. Retrieved August 19, 2022, from https://hbr.org/2021/07/how-susceptible-are-you-to-the-sunk-cost-fallacy

The Decision Lab. (n.d.-a). Why are we likely to continue with an investment even if it would be rational to give it up? Retrieved August 21, 2022, from https://thedecisionlab.com/biases/the-sunk-cost-fallacy

Farnsworth, C. H. (1971, March 4). Concorde's cost now at $2-billion. The New York Times. Retrieved August 27, 2022, from https://www.nytimes.com/1971/03/04/archives/concordes-cost-now-at-2billion-airline-project-is-under-new-attack.html#:~:text=PARIS%2C%20March%203%E2%80%94%20Costs%20of,the%20supersonic%20airliner%20in%201962.

SEPTEMBER 28TH - *Cracking the Cake Code: Are We Hardwired to Love Handmade Treats?*

Norton, M. I., Mochon, D., & Ariely, D. (2011). The "IKEA effect": When labor leads to love (Working Paper No. 11–091). Harvard Business School https://www.hbs.edu/ris/Publication%20Files/11-091.pdf

Park, M. Y. (2013, September 26). A history of the cake mix, the invention that redefined "Baking." Bon Appétit. https://bonappetit.com/entertaining-style/pop-culture/article/cake-mix-history

Grillo, C. (2021, May 14). The history of boxed cake mix. Cook's Illustrated. https://www.americastestkitchen.com/cooksillustrated/articles/3334-the-history-of-boxed-cake-mix

SEPTEMBER 29TH - *Is Your Crystal Ball Deceiving You?*

Kahneman, D. (2011, October 19). Don't Blink! The Hazards of Confidence. The New York Times Magazine. Retrieved March 26, 2024, from https://www.nytimes.com/2011/10/23/magazine/dont-blink-the-hazards-of-confidence.html

SEPTEMBER 30TH - *Are You a Winner or a Loser?*

Josh Busfield aka bitterphase. (2022, January 15). Little Miss Sunshine - "Winners" - Greg Kinnear [Video]. YouTube. Retrieved March 27, 2024, from https://www.youtube.com/watch?v=TcebHelScM4

OCTOBER 1ST - *How to Control a Lifeline Beyond the Grave?*

Amah, M., & Uanikhehi, I. (2018, November 27). Celebrating Death in style: Ghana's fantasy coffins. CNN. Retrieved March 26, 2024, from https://edition.cnn.com/2017/12/29/africa/ghana-fantasy-coffin/index.html

OCTOBER 2ND - *Politics and Math: A Divisive Formula for Logic?*

Van Bavel, J. J., & Pereira, A. (2018). The Partisan Brain: An Identity-Based Model of Political belief. Trends in Cognitive Sciences, 22(3), 213–224. https://doi.org/10.1016/j.tics.2018.01.004

OCTOBER 3RD - *How Many Innocents Served Time for a Crime They Didn't Commit?*

Glover, S., & Lait, M. (2005, May 2). Special Report: The evidence seemed overwhelming against Bruce Lisker but was justice served? Los Angeles Times. Retrieved September 3, 2022, from https://www.latimes.com/local/la-me-lisker22may22-b-story.html

National Registry of Exonerations. (2020, April 15). Bruce Lisker. The National Registry of Exonerations. Retrieved September 3, 2022, from https://www.law.umich.edu/special/exoneration/Pages/casedetail.aspx?caseid=3386

OCTOBER 4TH - *Is Exposure to Gay TV Characters the Remote Control for Tolerance?*

Borden, J. (2017, September 15). 'Will & grace' reduced homophobia, but can it still have an impact today? The Washington Post. Retrieved August 30, 2022, from https://www.washingtonpost.com/entertainment/will-and-grace-reduced-homophobia-but-can-it-still-have-an-impact-today/2017/09/14/0e6b0994-9704-11e7-82e4-f1076f6d6152_story.html

OCTOBER 6TH - *Are Money-Back Guarantees the Ultimate Sales Hack?*

Why do we seek certainty in risky situations? (n.d.). The Decision Lab. Retrieved August 30, 2022, from https://thedecisionlab.com/biases/zero-risk-bias#section-8

Akçay, Y., Boyacı, T., & Zhang, D. (2012). Selling with Money- Back Guarantees: The Impact on Prices, Quantities, and Retail Profitability. Production and Operations Management, 22(4), 777–791. https://doi.org/10.1111/j.1937-5956.2012.01394.x

OCTOBER 7TH - *Pay Now or Pay Later: What Motivaes More?*

Fryer Jr., R. G., Levitt, S. D., List, J., & Sadoff, S. (2012). Enhancing the efficacy of teacher incentives through loss aversion: A field experiment. National Bureau of Economic Research, Workin Paper No. 18273. https://doi.org/10.3386/w18273

Vedantam, S. (2012, September 18). Do scores go up when teachers return bonuses? NPR. Org. Retrieved September 3, 2022, from https://www.npr.org/2012/09/19/161370443/do-scores-go-up-when-teachers-return-bonuses?t=1656248247992

OCTOBER 8TH - *Are You Really the Center of Attention?*

Gilovich, T., Savitsky, K., & Medvec, V. H. (2000). The spotlight effect in social judgment: An egocentric bias in estimates of the salience of one's own actions and appearance. Journal of Personality and Social Psychology, 78(2), 211–222. https://doi.org/10.1037//0022-3514.78.2.211

OCTOBER 9TH - *Are Sporty Getaways the Secret to Boosting Birth Rates?*

Robinson, J. (2016, June 6). Denmark sees baby boom. . . nine months after running a campaign urging people to have more sex. Daily Mail. Retrieved August 22, 2022, from https://www.dailymail.co.uk/news/article-3627629/Denmark-sees-baby-boom-nine-months-running-campaign-urging-people-sex.html

White, G. L., Fishbein, S., & Rutsein, J. (1981). Passionate love and the misattribution of arousal. Journal of Personality and Social Psychology, 41(1), 56–62. https://doi.org/10.1037/0022-3514.41.1.56

Data Commons. (2021). Dänemark [Dataset]. https://datacommons.org/place/country/DNK?utm_medium=explore&mprop=fertilityRate&popt=Person&cpv=gender%2CFemale&hl=de

OCTOBER 10TH - *Feeling Down or Just Well-Informed? The Curious Case of Depression Ads*

Sootae, A. (2008). Antidepressant Direct-to-Consumer advertising and social perception of the prevalence of depression: Application of the availability heuristic. Health Communication, 26(6), 499–505. https://doi.org/10.1080/10410230802342127

OCTOBER 11TH - *Can You Afford That?*

Soman, D. (2004). Framing, Loss Aversion, and Mental Accounting. In Blackwell Handbook of Judgment and Decision Making. Wiley-Blackwell. http://www.communicationcache.com/uploads/1/0/8/8/10887248/blackwell_handbook_of_judgement__decision_maling_-_2004.pdf#page=391

OCTOBER 12TH - *Do You Underrate Your Emotional Resilience?*

Gilbert, D. T., Pinel, E. C., Wilson, T. D., Blumberg, S. J., & Wheatley, T. P. (1998). Immune neglect: A source of durability bias in affective forecasting. Journal of Personality and Social Psychology, 75(3), 617–638. https://doi.org/10.1037/0022-3514.75.3.617

OCTOBER 13TH - *Why Do We Save Species That Are Simiar To Us?*

Urquiza-Haas, E. G., & Kotrschal, K. (2015). The mind behind anthropomorphic thinking: Attribution of mental states to other species. Animal Behaviour, 109, 167–176. https://doi.org/10.1016/j.anbehav.2015.08.011

OCTOBER 15TH - *Who's to Blame: Teachers, Students, or Self-Serving Bias?*

McAllister, H. A. (1996). Self-serving bias in the classroom: Who shows it? Who knows it? Journal of Educational Psychology, 88(1), 123–131. https://doi.org/10.1037/0022-0663.88.1.123

OCTOBER 16TH - *Are You a True Fan or Just Riding the Bandwagon Wave?*
Bias: Bandwagon effect. (2022, August 30). Taft College. Retrieved September 1, 2022, from https://lib.taftcollege.edu/c.php?g=861448&p=6299112

OCTOBER 17TH - *X-Ray Vision: Are We All Expert Radiologists in Retrospect?*
Johnson, E., & Eyal, N. (n.d.). Hindsight bias: Why you make terrible life choices. Nir and Far. Retrieved August 25, 2022, from https://www.nirandfar.com/hindsight-bias/

Berlin, L. (2000). Hindsight bias. American Journal of Roentgenology, 175(3), 597–601. https://doi.org/10.2214/ajr.175.3.1750497

OCTOBER 18TH - *Is Your Driving Confidence Steering You Toward Danger?*
Svenson, O. (1981). Are we all less risky and more skillful than our fellow drivers? Acta Psychologica, 47, 143–148. https://doi.org/10.1016/0001-6918(81)90005-6

Road Traffic Injuries and Deaths - A global problem. (2023, January 10). Centers for Disease Control and Prevention. https://www.cdc.gov/injury/features/global-road-safety/index.html

OCTOBER 19TH - *Did Outcome Bias Pull the Plug on Dell's Reputation?*
Rosenzweig, P. (2007). Misunderstanding the Nature of Company Performance: The Halo Effect and other Business Delusions. California Management Review, 49(4), 6–20. https://doi.org/10.2307/41166403

OCTOBER 21ST - *Health Halo: Do Organic Labels Feed Your Brain More Than Your Body?*
Schouteten, J. J., Gellynck, X., & Slabbinck, H. (2019). Influence of organic labels on consumer's flavor perception and emotional profiling: Comparison between a central location test and home-use-test. Food Research International, 116, 1000–1009. https://doi.org/10.1016/j.foodres.2018.09.038

OCTOBER 22ND - *Are AI Face Recognition Tools Discriminating by Design?*
Gebru, T. [Databricks]. (2019, April 25). Understanding the limitations of AI: When algorithms fail | timnit gebru (google brain) [Video]. YouTube. https://www.youtube.com/watch?v=aKf6pB4p06E

OCTOBER 23RD - *What is the percentage of African countries in the United Nations?*
Tversky, A., & Kahneman, D. (1974). Judgment under Uncertainty: Heuristics and Biases. Science, 185(4157), 1124–1131. https://doi.org/10.1126/science.185.4157.1124

OCTOBER 24TH - *The Bias Behind Chornobyl's Meltdown?*
Dobbs, M. (1992, April 27). Chernobyl's "shameless lies." Washington Post. https://www.washingtonpost.com/archive/politics/1992/04/27/chernobyls-shameless-lies/96230408-084a-48dd-9236-e3e61cbe41da/

Volianska, H. (2021, October 22). Victor Bryukhanov Former Director of Chernobyl Nuclear Plant Died. Chernobyl X. https://chernobylx.com/victor-bryukhanov-former-director-of-chernobyl-nuclear-plant-died/

OCTOBER 25TH - *Are You Secretly Stereotyping?*
Hinton, P. (2017). Implicit stereotypes and the predictive brain: Cognition and culture in "Biased" person perception. Palgrave Communications, 3(17086). https://doi.org/10.1057/palcomms.2017.86

Project Implicit. (n.d.). Understanding and interpreting IAT results. Retrieved March 26, 2024, from https://implicit.harvard.edu/implicit/user/demo.ireland/ire.static/takeatest.html

OCTOBER 27TH - *Is Social Media Stardom One Post Away or a Pipe Dream?*
Geyser, W. (2024, January 30). 20 Creator economy statistics that will blow you away in 2023. Influencer Marketing Hub. Retrieved March 26, 2024, from https://influencermarketinghub.com/creator-economy-stats/

Mileva, G. (2022, May 4). The disparity between revenue distribution in the creator economy. Influencer Marketing Hub. https://influencermarketinghub.com/income-disparity-creator-economy/

OCTOBER 28TH -*Astro-Logic: When Science Checked the Stars*
Hartmann, P., Reuter, M., & Nyborg, H. (2006). The relationship between date of birth and individual differences in personality and general intelligence: A large-scale study. Personality and Individual Differences, 40(7), 1349-1362. https://doi.org/10.1016/j.paid.2005.11.017

OCTOBER 29TH - *Do You Overestimate Your Household Heroics?*
Ross, M., & Sicoly, F. (1979). Egocentric biases in availability and attribution. Journal of Personality and Social Psychology, 37(3), 322–336. https://doi.org/10.1037/0022-3514.37.3.322

OCTOBER 30TH - *What Does the Media Contribute to Gender Stereotypes?*
Rao, P., & Taboada, M. (2021). Gender bias in the news: A scalable topic modelling and visualization framework. Frontiers in Artificial Intelligence. https://doi.org/10.3389/frai.2021.664737

OCTOBER 31ST - *Do Happy Endings Outweigh Unpleasant Beginnings?*
Redelmeier, D. A., Katz, J., & Kahneman, D. (2003). Memories of colonoscopy: a randomized trial. Pain, 104(1), 187–194. https://doi.org/10.1016/S0304-3959(03)00003-4

Kahneman, K. (2010). The riddle of experience vs. memory

[Video]. TED Conferences. https://www.ted.com/talks/daniel_kahneman_the_riddle_of_experience_vs_memory?language=de

NOVEMBER 1ST - *Feeling Sick? Should You Got for an Early Doctor's Appointment?*
Linder J.A., Doctor J.N., Friedberg M.W., et al. (2014) Time of Day and the Decision to Prescribe Antibiotics. JAMA Intern Med, 174(12), 2029–2031. doi:10.1001/jamainternmed.2014.5225

NOVEMBER 2ND - *Pain Relief or Mind Trick?*
Blanco, F., Moreno-Fernández, M. M., & Matute, H. (2020). Are the symptoms really remitting? How the subjective interpretation of outcomes can produce an illusion of causality. Judgment and Decision Making, 15(4), 572–585. https://journal.sjdm.org/19/191104/jdm191104.pdf

The Weekend University, & Sutherland, R. (2020, May 31). Placebos and Behaviour Change – Rory Sutherland [Video]. YouTube. Retrieved March 26, 2024, from https://www.youtube.com/watch?v=B2Bafx7xyRw

Australian Competition and Consumer Commission. (2015, December 13). Court finds Nurofen made misleading Specific Pain claims.https://www.accc.gov.au/media-release/court-finds-nurofen-made-misleading-specific-pain-claims

NOVEMBER 3RD - *To Choose or Not to Choose: Are Defaults Draining Your Wallet?*
Jaipuria, T. (2018, May 14). The power of defaults - tanay jaipuria. Medium. Retrieved September 3, 2022, from https://medium.com/@tanayj/the-power-of-defaults-976bc8b015b7

Mui, Y. Q. (2009, November 13). Fed takes aim at overdraft penalties. Washington Post. Retrieved March 26, 2024, from https://www.washingtonpost.com/wp-dyn/content/article/2009/11/12/AR2009111208541.html

NOVEMBER 4TH - *Is Patience Really a Virtue Or Just a Way to Get More Candy?*
Mischel, W., & Ebbesen, E. B. (1970). Attention in delay of gratification. Journal of Personality and Social Psychology, 16(2), 329–337. https://doi.org/10.1037/h0029815

NOVEMBER 5TH - *Is the Earth Flat?*
Picheta, R. (2019, November 18). The Flat-Earth conspiracy is spreading around the globe. Does it hide a darker core? CNN. Retrieved March 26, 2024, from https://edition.cnn.com/2019/11/16/us/flat-earth-conference-conspiracy-theories-scli-intl/index.html

Google. (n.d.). [Google Trends on Flat Earth] Retrieved March 26, 2024, from https://www.projectimplicit.net/

Mohammed, S. N. (2019). Conspiracy theories and Flat-Earth videos on YouTube. The Journal of Social Media in society, 8(2). https://thejsms.org/index.php/JSMS/article/view/527

NOVEMBER 6TH - *The Billion-Dollar Streaming Dream?*
Alexander, J. (2020, October 23). Inside Quibi's rapid collapse. The Verge. Retrieved November 13, 2024, from https://www.theverge.com/21559189/quibi-final-days-streaming-platform-coronavirus

NOVEMBER 7TH - *When Do Expectations Price Our Reality?*
Lifes Codes. (2018, January 28). Steve Jobs introducing iPad: The anchoring effect in action [Video]. YouTube. https://www.youtube.com/watch?v=XjuF-2w0wno

NOVEMBER 9TH - *Beginning of ingroup bias*
Tajfel, H. (1970) Experiments in Intergroup Discrimination. Scientific American, 223(5):96-102. PMID: 5482577.

NOVEMBER 10TH - *Are You Giving Yourself Too Much Credit?*
De Michele, P. E., Gansneder, B., & Solomon, G. B. (1998). Success and failure attributions of wrestlers: Further evidence of the self-serving bias. Journal of Sport Behavior, 21(3), 242–255.

Walther, J. B., & Bazarova, N. N. (2007). Misattribution in virtual groups: The effects of member distribution on Self-Serving bias and partner blame. Human Communication Research, 33(1), 1–26. https://doi.org/10.1111/j.1468-2958.2007.00286.x

NOVEMBER 12TH - *Are We Misjudging Our Own Happiness?*
Strack, F., Martin, L. L., & Schwarz, N. (1988). Priming and communication: Social determinants of information use in judgments of life satisfaction. European Journal of Social Psychology, 18(5), 429–442. https://doi.org/10.1002/ejsp.2420180505

NOVEMBER 14TH - *Genes, Circumstances, or Choices: What Is Steering Your Happiness?*
Cummins, R. A., & Nistico, H. (2002). Maintaining life satisfaction: The role of positive cognitive bias. Journal of Happiness Studies, 3, 37–69. https://doi.org/10.1023/A:1015678915305

Lyubomirsky, S., Sheldon, K. M., & Schkade, D. (2005). Pursuing Happiness: The Architecture of Sustainable Change. Review of General Psychology, 9(2), 111–131. https://doi.org/10.1037/1089-2680.9.2.111

NOVEMBER 15TH - *Are You Stuck in a Sunk-Cost Romance?*
Rego, S., Arantes, J., & Magalhães, P. (2016). Is there a Sunk Cost Effect in Committed Relationships? Current Psychology, 37(3), 508–519. https://doi.org/10.1007/s12144-016-9529-9

NOVEMBER 16TH - *How do you make vegetables more appealing to children?*
Radtke, T., Liszewska, N., Horodyska, K., Boberska, M., Schenkel, K., & Luszczynska, A. (2019). Cooking together: The IKEA effect on family vegetable intake. British Journal of Health Psychology, 24(4), 896–912. https://doi.org/10.1111/bjhp.12385

NOVEMBER 17TH - *You don't understand your dog (like you probably think you do)*
Dacey, M. (2016). Anthropomorphism as Cognitive Bias. PhilSchi Archive

NOVEMBER 18TH - *Does Sugar Really Turn Kids into Tiny Tornadoes?*
Wolraich, M. L., Wilson, D. B., & White, J. W. (1995). The effect of sugar on behavior or cognition in children: a meta-analysis. Jama, 274(20), 1617-1621.

NOVEMBER 19TH - *Is the "woke" movement a groupthink dynamic?*
Žižek, S. (2023, February 22). Wokeness is here to stay. Compact. https://www.compactmag.com/article/wokeness-is-here-to-stay/

The Learning Network. (2021, April 21). What's going on in this graph? | Free speech. The New York Times. https://www.nytimes.com/2022/04/21/learning/whats-going-on-in-this-graph-april-27-2022.html

NOVEMBER 20TH - *Are Teachers Misreading the Behavior of Struggling Students?*
Elies, A., Schabmann, A., & Schmidt, B. M. (2021). Associations between teacher-rated behavioral problems and reading difficulties? Interactions over time and halo effects. Journal of Research in Special Educational Needs, 21(4), 368–380. https://doi.org/10.1111/1471-3802.12536

NOVEMBER 21ST - *Where is the ice-free North Polar Sea?*
Tammiksaar, E., Sukhova, N. G., & Stone, I. R. (1999). Hypothesis versus Fact: August Petermann and Polar Research. Arctic, 52(3), 237–243. http://www.jstor.org/stable/40511776

NOVEMBER 22ND - *How to Make People Pay Taxes on Time?*
Coleman, S. (1996). The Minnesota income tax compliance experiment: State tax results. Minnesota Department of Revenue. https://mpra.ub.uni-muenchen.de/4827/

NOVEMBER 23RD - *Remember the Fyre Festival?*
Smith, H., & Oliveira, A. (2022, November 29). Billy McFarland reveals he IGNORED warnings from staff to cancel elaborate Fyre Festival. Mail Online. Retrieved March 27, 2024, from

https://www.dailymail.co.uk/news/article-11479437/Fyre-Festivals-Billy-McFarland-says-lying-investors-f-d-scam.html

NOVEMBER 25TH - *Is Hypoxia Misleading Doctors in Infant Brain Damage Cases?*
Gilles, F. H., Gressèns, P., Dammann, O., & Leviton, A. (2017). Hypoxia–ischemia is not an antecedent of most preterm brain damage: the illusion of validity. Developmental Medicine & Child Neurology, 60(2), 120–125. https://doi.org/10.1111/dmcn.13483

NOVEMBER 26TH - *How do you spot a good witness?*
Understand the binary bias. (2018, November 5). Lexology. Retrieved September 3, 2022, from https://www.lexology.com/library/detail.aspx?g=0c6529ec-d495-49e0-bf27-a12b9e90d-7de

Iles, A. (2023, March 6). 4 famous expert witness cases. Expert Court Reports. https://www.expertcourtreports.co.uk/blog/four-famous-expert-witness-cases/

NOVEMBER 27TH - *53 Fever: What Went Wrong in Italy?*
Robson, D. (2020, February 17). The simple maths error that can lead to bankruptcy. BBC Worklife. Retrieved November 14, 2024, from https://www.bbc.com/worklife/article/20200217-the-simple-maths-error-that-can-lead-to-bankruptcy

NOVEMBER 28TH - *Did Your Vote Cloud Your Judgment? The Ballot Box's Sneaky Side Effect*
Mullainathan, S., & Mullainathan, E. (2009). Sticking with your vote: Cognitive dissonance and political attitudes. American Economic Journal: Applied Economics, 1(1), 86–111. https://doi.org/10.1257/app.1.1.86

Beasley, R. K., & Joslyn, M. R. (2001). Cognitive dissonance and Post-Decision attitude change in six presidential elections. Political Psychology, 22(3), 521–540. https://www.jstor.org/stable/3792425

NOVEMBER 29TH - *Why Do We Hate New Songs, Then Sing Them in the Shower?*
Professor Ross. (2021, June 6). Easy A - Mere Exposure Effect. [Video]. YouTube. https://youtu.be/Ktd6NBVFL6c

hyllos. (2010, December 4). HIMYM - I'm gonna be (500 miles). [Video]. YouTube. https://youtu.be/738OEa5NZ9A

NOVEMBER 30TH - *Did you ever hear of the "New Coke"?*
New Coke: the most memorable marketing blunder ever? (n.d.-b). The Coca-Cola Company. Retrieved March 27, 2024, from https://www.coca-colacompany.com/about-us/history/new-coke-the-most-memorable-marketing-blunder-ever

DECEMBER 1ST - *Are You Letting Netflix Make Your Watching Decisions?*
Schaffner, B., Stefanescu, A., Campili, O., & Chetty, M. (2023). Don't Let Netflix Drive the Bus: User's Sense of Agency Over Time and Content Choice on Netflix. Proceedings of the ACM on human-computer interaction, 7(CSCW1), 1-32.

DECEMBER 2ND - *Maybe it's time to stop running away from numbers and stats?*
Bar-Hillel, M. (1980). The base-rate fallacy in probability judgments. Acta Psychologica, 44(3), 211–233. https://doi.org/10.1016/0001-6918(80)90046-3

Why do we rely on specific information over statistics? (n.d.-c). The Decision Lab. Retrieved August 30, 2022, from https://thedecisionlab.com/biases/base-rate-fallacy#section-8

DECEMBER 4TH - *Do We Forgive Celebs Based on Fame or Fundamental Attribution Error?*
Hu, M., Young, J., Liang, J., & Guo, Y. (2018). An investigation into audiences' reactions to transgressions by liked and disliked media figures. Psychology of Popular Media Culture, 7(4), 484–498. https://doi.org/10.1037/ppm0000146

DECEMBER 6TH - *Tricky Trio: How Do Trio-Options Trick Your Wallet?*
Sridharan, M. (2017, September 19). Decoy effect and irrational behaviour. Think Insights. Retrieved August 19, 2022, from https://thinkinsights.net/strategy/decoy-effect/

TED. (2009, May 19). TED Talk: Dan Ariely - Are we in control of our decisions? [Video]. YouTube. https://www.youtube.com/watch?v=9X68dm92HVI

Manimaran, H. (2021). The effect and influence of the decoy price on consumer preferences. International Journal of Social Science and Economic Research, 06(07), 2349–2355. https://doi.org/10.46609/IJSSER.2021.v06i07.020

DECEMBER 7TH - *Can Our Emotions Outweigh Cold, Hard Data?*

Why do we rely on our current emotions when making quick decisions? (n.d.). The Decision Lab. Retrieved August 30, 2022, from https://thedecisionlab.com/biases/affect-heuristic#section-8

Slovic, P., Monahan, J., & MacGregor, D. G. (2000). Violence risk assessment and risk communication: The effects of using actual cases, providing instruction, and employing probability versus frequency formats. Law And Human Behavior, 24(3), 271–296. https://doi.org/10.1023/a:1005595519944

DECEMBER 8TH - *Is Your Stomach Growling at Your Moral Compass?*

Brown H, Proulx MJ and Stanton Fraser D (2020) Hunger Bias or Gut Instinct? Responses to Judgments of Harm Depending on Visceral State Versus Intuitive Decision-Making. Frontiers in Psychology. 11:2261. doi: 10.3389/fpsyg.2020.02261

DECEMBER 9TH - *Are Tarot Cards an Insightful Guidance or Just a Barnum Bluff?*

Ivtzan, I. (2007). Tarot cards: a literature review and evaluation of psychic versus psychological explanations. The Journal of Parapsychology, 71, 139+. https://link.gale.com/apps/doc/A185487253/AONE?u=anon~ce8b8013&sid=googleScholar&xid=d049fe92

DECEMBER 11TH - *Do you know about Jim Jones and the People's Temple?*

ABC News. (2018, September 28). Jonestown Part 1: Who was the Peoples Temple leader Jim Jones? [Video]. YouTube. https://www.youtube.com/watch?v=_0B1sMfxWYw

DECEMBER 12TH - *Will Your Future Self Thank You for Today's Choices?*

Harris, H., & Busseri, M. A. (2019). Is there an 'End of history illusion' for life satisfaction? Evidence from a three-wave longitudinal study. Journal of Research in Personality, 83. https://doi.org/10.1016/j.jrp.2019.103869

DECEMBER 13TH - *How Many Animals Did Moses Bring on His Ark?*

Erickson, T. D., & Mattson, M. E. (1981). From words to meaning: A semantic illusion. Journal of Verbal Learning and Verbal Behavior, 20(5), 540–551. https://doi.org/10.1016/S0022-5371(81)90165-1

DECEMBER 14TH - *Are We More Generous to Like-Minded People?*

Why do we treat our in-group better than we do our out-group? (n.d.). The Decision Lab. Retrieved September 3, 2022, from https://thedecisionlab.com/biases/in-group-bias

Rand, D. G., Pfeiffer, T., Dreber, A., Sheketoff, R. W., Wernerfelt, N., & Benkler, Y. (2009). Dynamic remodeling of in-group bias during the 2008 presidential election. Proceedings of the National Academy of Sciences of the United States of America, 106(15), 6187–6191. https://doi.org/10.1073/pnas.0811552106

DECEMBER 15TH - *Was Fox News too busy for a date with democracy on January 6?*

McCarthy, B. (2022, June 10). As America watched Jan. 6 hearing, Fox viewers heard Tucker Carlson's alternate reality. Politifact. https://www.politifact.com/article/2022/jun/10/america-watched-jan-6-hearing-fox-viewers-heard-tu/

Stalder, D. R. (2022, June 10). Confirmation bias during the January 6 hearings. Psychology Today. https://www.psychologytoday.com/intl/blog/bias-fundamentals/202206/confirmation-bias-during-the-january-6-hearings

DECEMBER 16TH - *A drop of delusion*

Carreyrou, J. (2016, November 18). Theranos whistleblower shook the company—and his family. The Wall Street Journal. https://www.wsj.com/articles/theranos-whistleblower-shook-the-companyand-his-family-1479335963

Torres, M. (2022, November 18). 4 Ways Elizabeth Holmes manipulated her Theranos employees. HuffPost. https://www.huffpost.com/entry/elizabeth-holmes-office-employees_l_5c92abe3e4b01b140d351b6f

DECEMBER 18TH - *Blinded by the light?*

Thorndike, E.L. (1920). A constant error in psychological ratings. Journal of Applied Psychology, 4(1), 25–29. https://doi.org/10.1037/h0071663

DECEMBER 19TH - *The founding father of self-serving bias*
Heider, F. (1982). The Psychology of Interpersonal Relations. Psychology Press.

DECEMBER 20TH - *You're always smarter in hindsight*
Fischhoff, B. (2003). Hindsight ≠ foresight: the effect of outcome knowledge on judgment under uncertainty. Quality & Safety in Health Care, 12(4), 304–311. https://doi.org/10.1136/qhc.12.4.304

DECEMBER 21ST - *Building a cozy confirmation bunker with your news feed*
Ajkusi. (2020, November 24). The Rise of Opinionated News Sources: How Confirmation Bias is Affecting How We Vote. CogBlog. https://web.colby.edu/cogblog/2020/11/24/the-rise-of-opinionated-news-sources-how-confirmation-bias-is-affecting-how-we-vote/

DECEMBER 22ND - *How Can Two Auction Houses Play Ping-Pong With Your Brain?*
Hong, H., Kremer, I., Kubik, J. D., Mei, J., & Moses, M. (2015). Ordering, revenue and anchoring in art auctions. The RAND Journal of Economics, 46(1), 186-216. https://doi.org/10.1111/1756-2171.12081

DECEMBER 23RD - *Why Do Americans Keep Pressing Non-Functional Elevator Buttons?*
CBS Boston. (2016, October 31). 'Door Close' buttons on most elevators don't actually work. Retrieved November 15, 2024, from https://www.cbsnews.com/boston/news/door-close-elevator-button-dont-work-placebo/

DECEMBER 24TH - *Would You Flip the Switch in Milgram's Experiment?*
Mcleod, S., PhD. (2023, November 14). Stanley Milgram Shock Experiment: Summary, Results, & Ethics. Simply Psychology. Retrieved March 27, 2024, from https://www.simplypsychology.org/milgram.html

PsychHubUK. (2014, September 24). Milgram Experiment 1963 [Video]. YouTube. Retrieved March 27, 2024, from https://www.youtube.com/watch?v=Kzd6Ew3TraA

DECEMBER 25TH -*Holy Hunch or Heavenly Humbug: Can We Trust Pastoral Prophecies?*
Graham, S. (2015, September 14). Charismatic prophecy: Christian astrology? Stephenjgraham. Retrieved August 25, 2022, from https://stephenjgraham.wordpress.com/2015/09/14/charismatic-prophecy-christian-astrology/

Graham, R. (2021, February 11). Christian prophets are on the rise. What happens when they're wrong? The New York Times. https://www.nytimes.com/2021/02/11/us/christian-prophets-predictions.html

DECEMBER 26TH - *Can a Little Knowledge Be More Dangerous Than None?*
Reznik, S., & Fet, V. (2019). The destructive role of Trofim Lysenko in Russian science. European Journal of Human Genetics, 27(9), 1324-1325.

DECEMBER 28TH - *Control over your life is just one book away*
Manson, M. (2024, February 12). 5 Problems with the Self-Help industry. Mark Manson. https://markmanson.net/self-help

John, J. (2024, January 9). Global Self-Improvement market size reach $81.6 billion by 2032. Custom Market Insights. https://www.custommarketinsights.com/press-releases/self-improvement-market-size/

DECEMBER 30TH - *How to not apply psychological principles*
Clark, A. (2007, December 6). Facebook apologises for mistakes over advertising. The Guardian. https://www.theguardian.com/technology/2007/dec/06/facebook.socialnetworking

DECEMBER 31ST - *How Does Wanting to Be Right Make Us Wrong?*
Oakley, K. P., & Weiner, J. S. (1955). Piltdown man. American Scientist, 43(4), 573-583.

ABOUT THE AUTHOR

I'm a digital marketing professional living in Berlin, Germany, with a deep-seated fascination for how our minds work, particularly when it comes to cognitive biases. My journey into the complex world of psychology started in my twenties. Despite reading almost every book I could find on cognitive biases, I often struggled to remember all these biases, how they work and apply this knowledge in real-life situations. This gap between theory and practice spurred me to devise a method to not only better remember these biases but also comprehend their application in everyday situations.

"Daily Dose of Psychology" is my attempt to bridge this gap. It has taken me three years to bring this project to life. I authored the book on biases that I had always wished to read. My aim is to render the subject approachable and to raise awareness of these biases because I believe it is immensely beneficial to understand how both you and those around you tick. This knowledge fosters inner peace and cultivates greater empathy for both oneself and others by creating a more forgiving perspective, grounded in the understanding that we all share the same biases.

As a first-time author, I approach this topic with humility and a genuine desire to share my passion with you. I'm not a seasoned psychologist or a career author; I'm someone deeply intrigued by the quirks of human behavior and how understanding them can enrich our lives.

Printed in Poland
by Amazon Fulfillment
Poland Sp. z o.o., Wrocław